Soviet Choreographers in the 1920s

Soviet Choreographers in the 1920s

Elizabeth Souritz

Translated from the Russian by Lynn Visson

Edited, with additional translation, by Sally Banes

Duke University Press, *Durham and London*

1990

This book was originally published as *Khoreograficheskoe
iskusstvo dvadtsatykh godov* (Iskusstvo, 1979).
Publication of this book was supported by grants
from the Mericos Foundation, the Benenson
Funding Corporation, the Josiah Charles Trent
Memorial Foundation, and the National
Endowment for the Humanities, a federal agency
which supports the study of such fields as
history, philosophy, literature, and languages.
© 1990 Duke University Press
All rights reserved
Printed in the United States of America
on acid-free paper ∞
Library of Congress Cataloging-in-Publication Data
appear on the last page of this book

■ Contents

The aim of this study is to discuss the work of the choreographers of the lyric theaters in Moscow and Leningrad/Petrograd* during the 1920s, the formative years of Soviet ballet. I began to collect material when Soviet scholars were able for the first time (in however limited a way) to discuss the arts of this period with historical accuracy. Previously, either nothing at all had been written, or what did exist treated the period negatively. I do not deal here with choreographic productions in studios and music halls. Nor is the art of the performers examined in detail; it is discussed only in relation to the analysis of new ballets. The book ends in 1927, when *The Ice Maiden* was staged in Leningrad and *The Red Poppy* in Moscow. Three choreographers occupy a central role here: Alexander Gorsky and Kasian Goleizovsky in Moscow and Fedor Lopukhov in Leningrad. A separate chapter is devoted to each of them. Two additional chapters cover the work of various other choreographers who contributed to the creation of Soviet ballet.

Many early productions, especially those by Gorsky and Goleizovsky, have been ignored in the theater literature. Therefore I have considered it essential to supply detailed descriptions of the productions (using archival materials whenever possible as well as press reviews, photographs, sketches, and the reminiscences of performers) before making evaluations.

Scholars' opinions about several of the ballets of the 1920s have at various times been totally contradictory. An objective assessment can be made only after defining the place of these ballets in the complex process of the development of Russian choreography. First of all, it is necessary

*The city known before 1914 as St. Petersburg was called Petrograd from 1914 to 1924 and since 1924 has been known as Leningrad. In the text the city is referred to by whatever name it had at the time in question. (Ed.)

to note the degree of continuity between the artistic traditions of the first Soviet choreographers and their predecessors—both the "academic" choreographers of the nineteenth century and the reformers of the early twentieth century. It is also important to show the link between the Soviet choreographers' works and contemporary art and life. Judgments had to be made as to which works had fundamental significance for the future and which were haphazard attempts or mistakes that developed no further.

After we have reconstructed an accurate picture of the past, it is possible to do justice to those artists who, during the years when the foundations of Soviet ballet were being laid, persistently sought new content and new forms and discovered new paths.

Since the beginning of *glasnost,* many changes have taken place in the Soviet Union, one of the most important being a new view of the past. Bit by bit, the whitewashing of our society, culture, and art is being rubbed away. Since the writing of this book, I have set about intensively collecting previously inaccessible material and am finding a rich and complex picture of theatrical dance in the twenties.

A number of memoirs appeared in the 1970s, including those of Fedor Lopukhov, Yuri Faier, Mikhail Mikhailov, and Asaf Messerer. Scholars have also begun to show interest in the ballet theater of the twenties; we have Galina Dobrovolskaya's book *Fedor Lopukhov* and articles on individual artists and productions. I am much indebted to colleagues working on related topics who shared their unpublished works with me (some of which have since been published): Margarita Yusim, who wrote a monograph on Goleizovsky; Natalia Chernova, who researched the art of the performers of the period; and Natalia Sheremetyevskaya, who studied dance on the popular stage. Those choreographers who were part of the creative process of the twenties were of great assistance: Fedor Lopukhov patiently and carefully answered my letters; I was lucky enough to talk with Kasian Goleizovsky on several occasions, and I am also grateful to Vera Vasilieva for access to the choreographer's archives. Much useful information on the ballet in Moscow was obtained from Anastasia Abramova, Elena Adamovich, Liubov Bank, Alexander Bryndin, Irina Charnotskaya, Vasily Chudinov, Yuri Faier, Elena Ilyushchenko, Margarita Kandaurova, Serafima Kholfina, Natalia Klimenkova, Antonina

Kudriavtseva, Anna Ratser, Maria Reisen, Ivan Smoltsov, Vera Svetin-skaya, and Irina Vronskaya. I was able to get some ideas of the Petrograd/Leningrad productions from Piotr Gusev and Elizaveta Gerdt. The memoirs of my late husband, Vladimir Varkovitsky, were the basis for my description of *The Ice Maiden*.

This book was written under the auspices of the Institute of the History of Art. I would like to thank my colleagues in the department of the History of the Theater of the Peoples of the USSR for valuable comments made in discussions of the manuscript. I am also grateful for the help of scholars Vera Krasovskaya, David Zolotnitsky, Vera Vasina-Grossman, and Anna Nekhendsi. I particularly appreciate the interest taken in this work by the late ballet historians Yuri Slonimsky, Arseny Ilyin, Yuri Bakhrushin, and Olga Martynova and for the assistance I received in gathering materials and illustrations from colleagues at the A. A. Bakhrushin State Central Theatrical Museum, the Museum of the State Academic Bolshoi Theater, the Central State Archives of Literature and Art, the Leningrad Theatrical Museum, the bibliographic divisions of the Central Research Library of the All-Union Theatrical Society, and the State Central Theatrical Library.

For their help and work on the English translation, thanks go to Sally Banes, Selma Jeanne Cohen, Al Pischl, and Lynn Visson.

—E. S.

Editor's Note: In the translation and romanization I have opted for clarity and familiarity over consistency. I am grateful for the help and advice of Joan Acocella, Daniel Banes, Noël Carroll, Selma Jeanne Cohen, Joanne Ferguson, Lynn Garafola, Mel Gordon, Edward Lee, Barbara Palfy, Wendy Perron, Al Pischl, and Tobi Tobias.

—S. B.

Introduction
and Context
to Soviet Ballet
in the
1920s

Few moments in history have held forth such promise, while beset by such awesome problems, as the early years of the Soviet Union in the 1920s. A massive population, an entire civilization, was moving—and being moved—into the twentieth century. The old regime was being dismantled; a new society was being constructed. Turbulence, change, and utopian optimism marked every facet of the culture, and the arts played an emblematic role in the October Revolution, seizing a vital moment when political and aesthetic revolt seemed to fuse in an unprecedented surge forward. In film and theater, striking new forms were invented to generate an art of the future; painters made posters to galvanize the new society and designs to vibrantly house and clothe it; poets channeled their creative energies into political speech-making; composers celebrated the sounds of modernization. Dance, too, sought to shed its aristocratic skin and to expand its horizons in order to become a people's art.

As the privations, instability, and isolation of World War I and the civil war years gave way to renewed contact with the West and the internal consolidation of the NEP period (the New Economic Policy, 1921–27), the fledgling Bolshevik government, preoccupied at first with winning and preserving power both militarily and in terms of mass support, found itself facing the even more enormous task of organizing and rebuilding all aspects of life in the new state from its very foundations. In practical terms, because of the realities of the new Soviet state's situation—embryonic, fragile, inchoate and chaotic, heterogeneous and incomplete—the Bolsheviks had to muster scarce resources for a risky, unpredictable experiment on a gigantic scale, with shaky support. But their political theory gave them, if not a seamless plan, ideas about the relationships between various aspects of culture that suggested programs of change. According to their Marxist-Leninist understanding of human society, the most basic and pressing issues of economics, politics, and history were integrally linked with what might seem to others marginal arenas of art and culture. For the Bolsheviks, life was a whole cloth—on more than an individual basis. Thus the quality of that tightly woven social fabric was affected not only by hunger, cold, homelessness, unemployment, and illiteracy, by who owned and tilled land and who ate the food the farmers produced, by who owned the factories and who wielded power in the country (and in the world), but also by the press and the media, by education, by political understanding, by organization, by song, by dance, by literature, and by secular rituals of all kinds. The twenties were a decade in which the questions surrounding all these issues, which in theory might be neatly resolved, were worked through with difficulty, as well as with imagination, in all the complex ramifications of practice.

The Arts and the Avant-Garde
After October

To provide a context for understanding the role and development of the ballet during the early years of the Soviet Union in the 1920s I will discuss in this essay the institutional and aesthetic transformations in the various arts during the period covered by Souritz in this book, that is, the Civil War and NEP years, 1917–27. This was the time of the greatest freedom and innovation in the arts, the formative years of the country and the culture, when debates and experiments were deemed not only possible, but important. After 1928, with the first five-year plan and the consolidation of arts institutions, stylistic freedom gradually narrowed, until the 1934 Congress of the Union of Soviet writers proclaimed Socialist Realism the only official style. I will also outline the place of ballet in the Soviet dance world of the twenties and analyze the significance of those experiments today.

To us in the West, especially in the United States, the integral and morally significant role of the arts in Soviet culture may be difficult to comprehend fully. Yet in order to see the often astounding art of the Soviet twenties in context, as it became a paradigm and an inspiration for the rest of the world, one must understand it as a link in a longer cultural chain in which Slavic and Western attitudes peculiarly interlaced. Russian art was rooted in a tenacious folk tradition, rich in social satire as well as religious art and lore; from the cosmopolitan imperial "hothouse" came the imported European traditions of a court system of patronage that brilliantly exploited art's symbolic and expressive powers for political ends. These two streams of Russian art, diametrically opposed in terms of class origins and interests, converged in a view of art as didactic and constituent to human society. It was Diaghilev and the *Mir Iskusstva* (World of Art) movement that introduced to Russia the newer European Romantic notion of *l'art pour art*. Yet ironically, it was the modernist, aestheticist legacy ultimately stemming from the *Mir Iskusstva* that originally informed many of the styles of the Russian revolutionary avant-garde, even though it was the legacy of realist, socially conscious art (against which *Mir Iskusstva* had railed in its day) that dictated its function. (Diaghilev himself worked in Western Europe exclusively by then, though some of his circle still contributed to postrevolutionary Russian culture, for example, Benois and Merezhkovsky.) After the twenties, as we know, it was the latter tendency that prevailed in both style and function. The Marxist theory, which many construed to view art as an activity central, not marginal, to human society—as a necessity, not a luxury—thus dovetailed with an indigenous Russian view that cut across classes. The Bolshevik encouragement of the arts came from this theoretical basis, but also from the need to fulfill certain practical tasks in the realm of education, agitation, propaganda, and publicity.

While the arts were vital to the Russian revolution, one can imagine alternative scenarios to the historical fact that it was the avant-garde that first served and celebrated October. This triumph of the avant-garde was in part due to the (not surprising) allegiance of older, more academic artists to the Whites; it was the young, rebellious, modernist artists— Cubists, Cubo-Futurists, Constructivists, Imagists, Suprematists—who were attracted to the Reds, some because they sympathized with their specific political principles, some because the new regime generally symbolized radical change, some because the new government had jobs to allot. It was partly a theoretical alliance; both groups, while they may not have always shared a political program, were inimical to the bourgeoisie. It was also partly a practical partnership, for each side had much to offer: labor, imagination, skill, and enthusiasm on the one side and unparalleled artistic opportunities in terms of scale, institutional resources, and distribution on the other. But it was not simply that. Camilla Gray aptly describes the revolutionary fervor of the vanguard artists:

> The intuitive need of these artists to be active builders, first indicated in Tatlin's constructions in "real materials and real space," was now to be given an opportunity to be expressed. . . . It is difficult to believe that they were almost literally starving—with the chaos in the countryside leading to monstrous difficulties in transportation, living conditions were reduced to the most primitive. They rode lightheaded on the surge of release and the sense of a new-born purpose to their existence; an intoxication drove them on to the most heroic feats: all was forgotten and dismissed but the great challenge which they saw before them of changing the world in which they lived. Surely it is the first time in history that it has been given to so young a group of artists to realize their vision in practical terms on such a scale.[1]

When, shortly after the Bolsheviks took power, they invited 120 established artists in painting, literature, and theater to join them at a meeting to discuss the role of art in the new government, only five accepted: the painter and sculptor Natan Altman, the poets Alexander Blok and Rurik Ivnev, the writer, painter, and performer Vladimir Mayakovsky, and the theater director Vsevolod Meyerhold. It was the young, unestablished artists who flocked to the revolution. Mayakovsky exclaimed in 1918 in a spirit that synthesized utopian, Futurist aspirations and proletarian vigor, "We do not need a dead mausoleum of art where dead works are worshipped, but a living factory of the human spirit—in the streets, in the tramways, in the factories, workshops and workers' homes."[2]

Certainly the appointment of Anatoly Lunacharsky as the first Soviet Commissar of Education, to whose department the arts were assigned (for exactly the reasons discussed above), was another factor in the dominance of the avant-garde. A sophisticated critic and dramatist (his plays ranged from early Promethean visionary epics to historical dramas, for example, *Oliver Cromwell*), Lunacharsky had met many of the Russian avant-garde artists in various Western European capitals before 1917. He encouraged innovation in art as a metaphor for political change, appointed artists to run state arts institutions, defended the "leftist" artists against the more conservative taste of Lenin and other party leaders (he also defended traditional art from the attacks of the leftists), and advocated relative freedom of expression and pluralism of styles.[3] And while other Soviet officials did not necessarily share Lunacharsky's enthusiasm for advanced art, they at first tolerated its participation in the revolution, for it at least signaled political support by the intelligentsia. For Lunacharsky and the artistic left, it did much more than that: it provided new models for an uncharted future.

As history has shown, the union of the avant-garde artists with the revolution was problematic and short-lived for all sorts of reasons. A revolution in the arts, while analogous to a political revolution, does not necessarily share the same values, goals, and methods. The Russian avant-garde, in dance as in the other arts, had begun long before 1917, though one could argue that the abortive revolution of 1905 and even the seeds of the early avant-garde in the late nineteenth century reflected the general malaise and foreshadowed the sweeping upheavals that would culminate in the October Revolution. But we sometimes tend to forget this and to see a simpler, more monolithic image of the revolutionary avant-garde Russian arts in the early twentieth century—one that yokes the vanguard arts to October—than befits the situation. Of course, that poster-like image *is* partly true: the early Soviet government did indeed both inspire and commission advanced art. But the artistic program of the revolution was more successful in some arts than in others—film and theater, for instance, rather than literature. And it was not always successful in ways that suited the political leaders. Furthermore, in some cases an avant-garde that had been in motion before the revolution contributed to a new, vibrant Soviet political art, and in some it sprang out of present needs, but in other cases artists tried to work in a clearing free of political demands, and in still others the best and most innovative simply left the country for a variety of reasons, not always political. The road to revolutionary art was not always a clear-cut, smooth, or even innovative one, and its twists and turns, while they may seem odd or aberrant in retrospect, should not really surprise us. In dance, for instance, we can see that in rather short order choreographers seem to careen dizzyingly from a refined Symbolist aestheticism to a flat poster propaganda style to naturalistic stagings of classic European literature to cabaret Expressionism to folk-style nationalism. Perhaps Russia would have been inundated by these "isms," as Western Europe was, even without a socialist revolution. Perhaps not all of the avant-garde's experiments were successful on either political or aesthetic grounds. But other artists were motivated to find new forms and new content precisely because of the revolution. Undeniably October catalyzed and mobilized a need for the new; it also sparked debate about the value of the old.

Institutions, Groups, Policies

Both old and new art found—or at least sought—new audiences in the masses, for egalitarian reasons as well as because it was art's function to propagandize and to celebrate the revolution. The government had to concern itself not only with developing methods for mass distribution of art, but also with questions of supervising political content, organizing artists, and socializing means of production in art as in other realms. Not only forms, but also institutions were transformed. In looking at the various activities of Lunacharsky's division, *Narkompros* (the People's Commissariat of Enlightenment [or Education]), it is important to keep in mind that the government, while resolutely framing specific programs concerning arts institutions in keeping with its political theories as well as its political needs, did not always have the power to enforce its policies or the resources to carry out its projects. It is worth looking at the separate arts to see not only the range of enterprise, but also the ways in which they were embarked on similar, often parallel, at times interdisciplinary projects.

The leftist visual artists took over the established museums; opened a series of galleries devoted to abstract art; devised new curricula for free art schools combining fine and practical arts; staged mass pageants with casts of thousands and spectators numbering up to 100,000; produced innovative typography, book, and poster designs; worked in the theater; painted murals on agitprop trains, ships, and trams; built monuments to revolutionary heroes; and sent exhibitions of Soviet art and design abroad. In 1918 *Narkompros* established a Department of Fine Arts (IZO), which was responsible for centralizing the activities of arts organizations. David Shterenberg, who was Lunacharsky's close friend, was its director. Its board included Natan Altman, Osip Brik, Vasily Kandinsky, Nikolai Punin, Olga Rosanova, and Vladimir Tatlin. (Gray points out that both rightist and leftist artists were invited to join IZO, but only the left cooperated.)

However, *Narkompros* had a rival of sorts in *Proletkult*, the Organization of the Representatives of Proletarian Art, which had been created by the prerevolutionary Marxist theorist Alexander Bogdanov. *Proletkult* was an autonomous group, in keeping with Bogdanov's idea that art and culture are separate from party politics. The group was rooted in Bogdanov's idea, dating from at least 1906, of "god-building"—constructing a proletarian religion of labor—and after 1917 it became more active in calling for a new proletarian art, independent of the prerevolutionary heritage, in the union of art and industry. Although Lunacharsky, who had long been involved with Bogdanov, actually supported *Proletkult*, permitted it to sponsor independent exhibitions, studios (in literature as well as the fine arts), publishing, and performances, and even appointed its members to posts within *Narkompros*, Lenin opposed an autonomous organization for proletarian culture, and Trotsky opposed it on both theoretical and aesthetic grounds. *Proletkult*, in its turn, protested the state centralization of artistic organizations. Lenin eventually made *Proletkult* subordinate to *Narkompros* and finally abolished it in 1923, but the organization's principles continued to flourish. With the introduction of a freer marketplace in the NEP years, many of the leftist artists, no longer patronized by the state (and certainly not by the new Soviet bourgeoisie), and increasingly attracted to Constructivism and production art, joined *Proletkult* and worked in industry. After 1928, when NEP gave way to stringent collectivization, the principles of proletarian culture were advanced by the party, but the vestiges of *Proletkult* and other proletarian arts organizations were dissolved, thus giving the party a monopoly on artistic organization.

Like the painters, sculptors, architects, and designers, dancers looked at the materials of their art in new ways, seeking abstraction and functional composition; like the artists, they turned to folk style and industrial imagery for both vivacity and stark design. They, too, sought to teach their art through countless studios and to use art in the service of agitprop.

In literature, partly because of its ambivalence toward the intelligentsia, the government adopted a relatively laissez-faire attitude toward the various groups of poets and writers that formed both before and after the revolution. While *Proletkult* organized literature studios to train working-class poets, and RAPP (Russian Association of Proletarian Writers) was formed as the official party organization to represent writers, in 1925 a state declaration pronounced a policy of pluralism (RAPP's power grew stronger after 1928). The Symbolist aesthetic of the prewar poets continued, alongside the vigorously propagandizing Cubo-Futurists (Mayakovsky and his circle, which in 1923 organized *Lef*, or Left Front of Art), the Constructivists, Imagists, Acmeists, the individualist Serapion Brotherhood, and antimodernist proletarian groups such as the Smithy and the Cosmists.

At first the government did not censor books (though it did newspapers). Immediately after 1917 private publishing houses continued to operate, but a severe wartime paper shortage and the difficulties of transportation, and hence distribution, essentially crippled them. As with other areas of culture, *Narkompros* set up a department to deal specifically with publishing (with uneven success), and in 1918 undertook the mass publication of Russian classics. In 1919 *Gosizdat* (the acronym for the State Publishing House), the major centralized outlet for book production, was established, after some debate, as a section of *Narkompros*. Although *Gosizdat* gradually took on more control as it absorbed the national book registry in 1920, it did not have a monopoly. There were other state-supported publishers, including *Vsemirnaia literatura*, run by Maxim Gorky (it was eventually absorbed by *Gosizdat*), and other small publishers. With the advent of the New Economic Policy, state, private, and cooperative firms coexisted, although *Gosizdat* officially monitored manuscripts (it censored relatively sparingly) and ran a central distribution network (with poor results). There were joint publishing ventures with European firms. With the first five-year plan of 1928 centralization of institutions and proletarian style were stressed, and by 1932, by government decree, all literary groups were dissolved and a single organization, the Union of Soviet Writers, was formed which adopted Socialist Realism as the authorized state style at its first congress in 1934, setting the official standards for all the other arts.

Once again, we can see the parallels with the dance world, which saw a diversity of styles. Symbolism—the older avant-garde—was at first influential, while simultaneously newer forms were sought and the classics were "nationalized" for posterity and accessibility.

The theatrical department (TEO) of *Narkompros* coordinated the country's theatrical life, which the March revolution had already partly freed by abolishing censorship and setting up democratic theater administrations and performers' unions. After the October Revolution, unions, factories, and schools were given free tickets to professional performances, agitprop troupes were mobilized to travel around the country, and amateur activity was organized not only in workers', peasants', and soldiers' drama groups, but also in the various outdoor mass spectacles. As during the Paris Commune of 1871, the famine and cold of the war years, though daunting, almost seemed to catalyze more theatrical life rather than stifling it. Visitors and natives alike commented on the extraordinary vitality and persistence of music and theater performances, on the enthusiasm of the new, mass audiences and the revolutionary zeal of the performers. The Formalist critic Viktor Shklovsky recalls of the civil war years:

> In this terrifying world made of frost, stale herrings, rags, typhoid fever, arrests, bread lines and armed soldiers, one first night followed the other, and every evening theaters were jammed. Toward the middle of a show the huge unheated houses were warmed up by the breath of the audience. Lights would flicker and often go out, there was little current and no coal. Isadora Duncan danced by the light of torches brought on the stage while thousands of voices, hoarse from the cold, sang "Bravely forward, keep your step, comrades" in the dark house. In operas, members of orchestras played with their fur coats on and fur caps over their ears, and steam came from brass instruments as if they were locomotive pipes or smokestacks. And dancers in tights and tulle skirts danced in polar draughts.[4]

During 1918–22 there were more than 3,000 theatrical organizations in Russia. In 1921–22 alone, there were forty theatrical magazines in the two principal cities. Shklovsky writes, "There is a theater attached to almost every organization. We even have a school of instructors in theater work with a section for preparing prompters attached to the Baltic Fleet. . . . I would not be astonished if the Murmansk Railroad or the Central Nail Factory were to begin training actors, and not just for themselves, but for others as well."[5] By 1926 there were more than 20,000 peasants' drama groups in the Union. TEO published drama classics, lists of plays for local professional and amateur theaters, state studios, schools, and theaters, collected materials on theater history, and organized a theater encyclopedia. As in dance, the concern for the education of future generations found expression in a strong children's theater movement.

Although the theaters were nationalized according to state decree in 1917, in fact it was the "academic" theaters that were both subsidized and regulated (though at first very liberally) by the government, while the less-established theaters were neither funded nor restricted. By 1923 the state theaters constituted only 33 percent of the existing theaters. The distinction between academic, or state, and private theaters was not based on scale; Tairov's Kamerny Theater as well as the Bolshoi were considered academic theaters. The academic theaters were run by boards of directors with representatives from the *Narkompros* and from the theater collectives themselves (artists and staff alike).

Olga Kameneva (Trotsky's sister) became the first director of TEO; Meyerhold, originally her assistant as the head of TEO's Petrograd branch, replaced her in 1920 and despite party criticisms of his productions (he was eventually dismissed from the TEO post, with the introduction of NEP in 1921) continued his own theatrical experiments with biomechanics and with Constructivist sets throughout the twenties. Some theater directors were less enthusiastic about state centralization and the revolutionary role of theater than Meyerhold, but nevertheless a lively theatrical scene ensued, especially among the avant-garde; Alexander Tairov, Evgeny Vakhtangov, Nikolai Evreinov, and a host of other directors worked both in formal theaters and on the vaudeville and cabaret stage. The more traditional Moscow Art Theater, though plagued by difficulties, continued to operate and also spawned several studios.

In theater, as in the other arts, the *Proletkult* movement organized studios to train proletarian actors, set up theaters, and devised mass performances (though most of the notorious outdoor spectacles, such as Evreinov's *The Storming of the Winter Palace*, were directed by non-*Proletkult* artists). Again, as in the other arts, one irony was that those who were involved in *Proletkult* were not necessarily proletarians. The relationship between Meyerhold, as director of TEO, and *Proletkult* was a complex one that serves as a paradigm for the symbiotic relationship between the avant-garde and popular aspirations in the theater at the time. On the one hand, Meyerhold found *Proletkult* neither truly proletarian nor truly amateur, and on the other, the organization moved more and more toward his avant-garde use of circus and music hall techniques in a search for a new popular culture. Sergei Eisenstein, who had worked with Meyerhold, elaborated his theory of "attractions," involving, among other techniques, the use of film montage and vaudeville compartmentalization in two productions he directed for the *Proletkult* First Proletarian Theater—*The Mexican*, which featured a boxing match between socialism and capitalism, and *The Wise Man* (1923), which included tightrope walking and film projections.

Eisenstein, of course, was shortly to become one of the extraordinary figures, with Dziga Vertov, Vsevolod Pudovkin, Lev Kuleshov, and Alexander Dovzhenko, in the meteoric rise of the infant Russian film industry. On the eve of the revolution, both foreign and domestic films were shown in the country, but the international film industry was itself quite young. The history of film art, a distinctively twentieth-century phenomenon, is inextricably linked to the Russian revolution. Here was one art form that had no traditions to either overcome or preserve; international film art as we know it was partly born from the experiments of the Russian revolutionary filmmakers of the 1920s. The All-Russian Photo-Movie Department (VKFO) of *Narkompros* was established in 1919, but, because of the expensive resources required by the film medium, including film stock, projection equipment, and sufficient electricity to show the films, it was not until the NEP years that the Soviet film industry branched out far beyond the distribution of agitprop newsreels. With the introduction of NEP, commercial movie theaters reopened, showing primarily foreign films at first. Here, as in the other arts, a remarkable heterogeneity reigned, and it was here that enormous profits were made both by the state and by private entrepreneurs. Lenin himself recommended the ideal programming, which would include both entertainment and political instruction, and which would use imports as a way to stimulate the indigenous film industry. In 1922 VFKO was replaced by a more independent branch of *Narkompros*, the Central State Photographic and Cinematic Enterprise (*Goskino*), which oversaw film imports, the organization of Soviet film studios, and held a monopoly on rentals. And again, the links to Western Europe, especially Germany, were salutary. Most important, the Russian audiences were fascinated by Hollywood, and Russian directors inspired by it.

Already in the early 1920s, not only newsreels and *agitki,* or semific-tional newsreels, were produced—Vertov's *Kino-Pravda* began in 1922—but also such feature films as *Aelita,* a science-fiction fantasy directed by Yakov Protazanov and designed by Exter, and Kuleshov's comedy *The Extraordinary Adventures of Mr. West in the Land of the Bolsheviks.* In the late twenties some 500 films were made and the viewing public averaged two and a half million. Eisenstein's signal works, like Meyerhold's and Mayakovsky's great milestones in art serving revolutionary ends, began in 1924 with *Strike.*

In the realm of music during 1917 and 1918, theaters, stores, instru-ment factories, warehouses, and publishers, the Moscow and Petrograd conservatories, libraries and archives, and private music schools and choirs were nationalized and placed under the musical section of *Narkom-pros,* MUZO, which also established the first state orchestras and choirs and organized chamber music concerts in workers' clubs, factories, and schools. Here too the aesthetic was a varied one; it ranged from that of the more staid members of the older generation, such as Glazunov and Vasilenko, to that of the more progressive Miaskovsky (the teacher of Khachaturian), Prokofiev, Asafiev (a critic and scholar as well as a composer), and, somewhat later, Shostakovich. The visionary Scriabin, who had died in 1915, was second only to Beethoven and Tchaikovsky in frequency of performance in the early years of the century (by the mid-twenties, his music would be considered too mystical and erotic). During the NEP years, as in literature, pluralism flourished and relations with Western Europe, especially Germany, were revived. An experimen-tal collective orchestra without a conductor was formed. In addition to concert music and the more conservative operatic theater, a lively popu-lar music scene, including jazz, thrived, but at the same time the return of a paying public and marketplace relations with artists put a strain on budgets and government subsidies. Throughout the twenties, composers and musicians formed ranks on various sides of aesthetic debates; the largest group was the modernist Association of Contemporary Musicians (ACM), whose journal reflected current trends in music with articles by foreigners, such as Darius Milhaud, as well as by Russians. The Russian Association of Proletarian Musicians (RAPM) was formed in 1923 but was outnumbered by ACM; a faction of RAPM active in composing agit-music formed the Association of Revolutionary Composers and Music Workers

(ORKIMD) in 1925; there were also various proponents of the traditional Russian heritage. After 1928, like RAPP, RAPM, battling what it considered the decadence of NEP-man aesthetics—including modernism, jazz, and classical music—grew in power, but in 1932 it was disbanded along with other proletarian organizations in all the arts. The experiences of the opera houses—for instance, the debate between Lunacharsky and Lenin on the importance of preserving the Bolshoi Theater, in Lenin's opinion, "a piece of pure landlord culture"—are discussed by Souritz in the present volume.

We see in all the arts of the Soviet twenties the same paradoxes and trends that affected the dance: an urge toward modernism, especially in terms of the abstraction of form, an emphasis on essential medium, and a fascination with machine aesthetics; a conflicting urge toward "proletarian" art that would be accessible to the masses, but that, in retrospect, fit with modernism in turning toward folk and popular styles; an old-new genre of agitprop; a determination to preserve, indeed, to distribute the classics, as well as programmatically to stimulate new work; a dissemination not only of arts products, but also of the experience of the arts throughout the population, via amateur groups and studio courses; a new focus on children's art; and cross-pollination between Europe, the United States, and Russia.

Soviet Dance in the 1920s

The changes in artists' styles paralleled, reflected, and at times directly shaped the vicissitudes of these volatile institutions as the Bolshevik government experimented and modified its policies and theories in the arts. In a larger sense, changing styles reflected the new society's fitful vector into the twentieth century, as the artists gradually forged bold new forms out of elements from the old world with the tools of the present. They moved from the decorative aestheticism of nineteenth-century Symbolism to the brash vibrancy of Futurism, the stark polarities of melodrama, the eccentric comedy of the grotesque, and the streamlined purity of Constructivism. Like their contemporaries in Europe, the avant-garde artists in Russia were inspired by folk and popular arts, but the Soviet political program gave this inclination a special import. The clown image that threads through so much of late nineteenth- and early twentieth-century arts exemplifies this great shift. Meyerhold's use of the clown is a case in point. From the Symbolist icon of Pierrot—the lovesick, sensitive, melancholy figure emblematic of the suffering artist, eternally trapped in a triangle of fatal eroticism (he had been utterly transformed by the French from his origins as a ribald commedia del l'arte character)—so often invoked by innumerable poets, playwrights, painters, and choreographers bridging the turn of the century, there evolved a brazen, earthy buffoon—a trickster inspired by the subversive vernacular roots of commedia and the Russian *skomorokhi*, whose raucous persona, in keeping with the stridency of modern life and the momentum of revolutionary society, was built of an electrifying physical dynamism. In dance, Lopukhov especially explored the potential of this new icon.

The dance world did not undergo the institutional reorganizations in quite the same way as the other arts, since its studios and theaters fell under either the music or theater sections of various government departments. But, especially in the NEP years, it saw the same feverish proliferation. Professional and amateur groups multiplied, doing dances of every style and description, from folk and social dancing to modern dance and ballet to gymnastics and machine dances. Isadora Duncan, invited by the government in 1921 to start a school, served as an inspiration, but so did the various practitioners of Middle European *ausdruckstanz*, from Mary Wigman to Rudolf von Laban, Dalcroze eurhythmics, and such artistic gymnastics groups as the Czechoslovakian Sokol League. Since avant-garde theater itself was moving more toward dance, with its emphasis on the physical and on music hall techniques, at times it was hard—and pointless—to firmly separate the arts.

In the present volume Elizabeth Souritz focuses on one particular aspect of Soviet choreography in the 1920s—the changes within the ballet institution, that is, the state lyric theaters. Although her main purpose is to excavate the choreography itself, and especially the work of three key figures (Alexander Gorsky, Kasian Goleizovsky, and Fedor Lopukhov), in the course of reading about the ballets, we also learn a great deal about the dance and theater life on the periphery, about who was included and who excluded from the mainstream and why, about the aesthetic and political debates that brought some of the projects to fruition and buried others, and about the ways in which the period served as a kind of linchpin in the history of ballet. We see here a microcosm of both the larger

Soviet dance world of the 1920s and of the larger picture of state cultural institutions, as we follow the fluctuations in style and policy in the Bolshoi Theater in Moscow and the former Maryinsky Theater in Petrograd (later, Leningrad). That these are the dance institutions and styles to survive from the twenties could not have been predicted at the time; hence, the significance of Souritz's study, which shows how an art that seemed doomed to wither with the passing of the old regime managed to adapt and accommodate itself to the new era. These were not only the germinal years of the Soviet ballet, but in some measure of the American ballet as well, for George Balanchine figures in this story, as does Mikhail Mordkin (out of whose company the American Ballet Theatre was formed), and others who have shaped our own academic dance.

Souritz documents the legacy inherited by the postrevolutionary ballet, not only the oeuvre of Petipa, but also older ballets from the Romantic era and the more recent reforms and innovations by Gorsky, Michel Fokine, and Boris Romanov. The striking variety of work immediately following the revolution emerges, as Romanov moves from eccentricism to Classicism, as the Symbolist figures of Pierrot and of Solveig from Grieg's *Peer Gynt* obsess a number of choreographers, and as a new generation, including Goleizovsky, Lopukhov, Balanchine, Mordkin, Novikov, and Riabtsev, comes of age, often finding alternative venues, for example, Mordkin's work in the circus and Goleizovsky's in cabarets. Gorsky, a transitional figure between the "old" reformers and the younger generation, seems a paradigm, embodied in a single person, of the aesthetic battles taking place on the political front in his attempts to incorporate modernist and populist trends in his work—more to stay in step with the times than out of deep political convictions—and in his struggles with the more conservative dancers in the Bolshoi Theater, his revivals of the masterworks of the classical repertory, and his experiments with symphonic choreography and with revolutionary ballets.

The Muscovite Goleizovsky is a different kind of exemplar; he, like his fellow artists committed to the avant-garde, followed a personal quest that led from Symbolism through Constructivism to a telegraphic poster art style. We have learned in recent years of Goleizovsky's influence on Balanchine's early work, in particular his laconic, erotic style of flowing and knotted composition. Goleizovsky staked out a leftist position not only in regard to political content in the work, but also in terms of radically changing ballet technique. His use of minimal costumes and Constructivist decors that changed the surface of the stage transformed both the movement itself and the way the spectator perceived the dance design. His streamlined, modernist groupings drew on social dancing and on the variety stage, where he also worked.

With the success of *The Red Poppy* (1927) in Moscow, a model for Soviet ballet was discovered and consolidated. A melodrama cum detective story set in China, which at that time was exploding into revolution (the Chinese revolution was the topic of other contemporary works, notably Meyerhold's production of Tretyakov's *Roar, China!* in 1926), the ballet made use of folk style in the famous scene of the sailor's dance to the popular song "Yablochko," but also exploited various plot turns to present the "decadent" jazz dancing of the international bourgeoisie and, in an opium dream, a sparkling fairytale scene reminiscent of nineteenth-century ballet spectacle.

The Red Poppy had its premiere in Moscow the same year that Lopukhov presented in Leningrad his *The Ice Maiden*, a culmination of his experiments during the decade. Lopukhov explored the relationships between dance and music (the apotheosis of this work was his dance symphony), created agitprop on the ballet stage, reconstructed the classics, plumbed folklore (especially the buffoon play) to make political commentary, and ultimately reshaped the classical vocabulary with a new, modernist vision of Solveig in the acrobatic brilliance of *The Ice Maiden*.

In this book Souritz limns a portrait of the early Soviet ballet that, while less publicized and perhaps less overtly successful than the avant-garde in the other arts, shared many of its problems as well as aspirations —from radical experimentation to populist accessibility—and many of its stylistic features, including an anti-realist and anti-spectacular bent that, to an American reader, seems ultimately to have reached its acme not in Russia but in the American ballet aesthetic as formed by Balanchine, for the emphasis on formal elements explored in the early Soviet ballet could not continue under Socialist Realism. Balanchine's exploration of the relations between dance and symphonic music, his analytic attention to human form in the dance image, and his attraction to jazz, all of which began in Petrograd, developed in the West under Diaghilev, and flourished in New York for fifty years, are strongly connected to his origins in the Soviet ballet of the twenties.

Souritz's book is a critical contribution to dance literature not only for the light it sheds on the history of early Soviet ballet, on the beginnings of American ballet in its Russian cradle, and on the cross-fertilization of various strains of early European and American modern dance with ballet, but also for its currency and relevance to us in the United States. Once again, though in a quite different context, the future of ballet seems uncertain, and artists look simultaneously to the avant-garde and to popular and folk forms, to athletics and acrobatics, for revitalization. Once again the question of attracting mass audiences, as opposed to carrying out relatively inaccessible laboratory artwork, confronts our (post)modernists. Choreographers move between the ballet stage and avant-garde venues, between theater and cabaret. Our most advanced choreography has, like the early Soviets, pared dance theater down to essentials, explored abstraction, repudiated psychologizing, theorized about the role of music and of gesture systems, multiplied dramatic personae, moved into the clubs and cabarets, and borrowed from popular culture. Some American choreographers over the past twenty-five years, like their colleagues in painting and sculpture, have been inspired directly by early Soviet art, but it has been primarily the visual art, film, and performance of that period, rather than dance per se (about which very little information has been available), that has influenced them. But even more striking are the less consciously motivated parallels. The language changes, while the fundamental questions remain the same.

—Sally Banes

Notes to Introduction

1 Camilla Gray, *The Russian Experiment in Art: 1863–1922* (New York: Harry Abrams, 1971), pp. 220–221.

2 Gray, p. 219.

3 In "Svoboda i revoliutsiia," *Pechat i revoliutsiia*, no. 1 (1921), p. 8, Lunacharsky, while acknowledging the need for some censorship by the Soviet government to protect its political position, repudiated "the person who says 'Down with all those prejudices about the freedom of expression. . . . Censorship is not a terrible component of our time of transition, but a regular part of socialist life.'" Quoted in Peter Kenez, *The Birth of the Propaganda State: Soviet Methods of Mass Mobilization 1917–1929* (Cambridge and New York: Cambridge University Press, 1985), pp. 245–246.

4 Viktor Shklovsky, *Khod Konia* (Moscow and Berlin: Gelikon, 1923). Quoted in Marc Slonim, *Russian Theater from the Empire to the Soviets* (New York: Collier Books, 1961), p. 261.

5 Shklovsky, *Khod Konia*, p. 51, quoted in Nikolai A. Gorchakov, *The Theater in Soviet Russia* (New York: Columbia University Press, 1957), p. 121.

Selected Bibliography for Introduction

Art in Revolution: Soviet Art and Design Since 1917. Exhibition catalog. London: Arts Council / Hayward Gallery, 1971.

Barron, Stephanie, and Maurice Tuchman. *The Avant-Garde in Russia, 1910–1930: New Perspectives.* Exhibition catalog. Los Angeles: Los Angeles County Museum of Art, 1980.

Billington, James. *The Icon and the Axe.* New York: Alfred A. Knopf, 1966.

Bowlt, John E. *Russian Art of the Avant-Garde: Theory and Criticism, 1902–1934.* New York: Viking, 1976.

Brown, Edward J. *Mayakovsky: A Poet in the Revolution.* Princeton, N.J.: Princeton University Press, 1973.

———. *Russian Literature Since the Revolution.* Cambridge, Mass., and London: Harvard University Press, 1982.

Carroll, Noël. "For God and Country." *Artforum* 11 (January 1973): 56–60.

Carter, Huntly. *The New Theater and Cinema of Soviet Russia.* London: Chapman and Dodd, 1924.

Fülop-Miller, René. *The Mind and Face of Bolshevism.* Trans. F. S. Flint and D. F. Tait. New York: Alfred A. Knopf, 1928.

Gorchakov, Nikolai A. *The Theater in Soviet Russia.* New York: Columbia University Press, 1957.

Gray, Camilla. *The Russian Experiment in Art: 1863–1922.* New York: Harry Abrams, 1971.

Kenez, Peter. *The Birth of the Propaganda State: Soviet Methods of Mass Mobilization, 1917–1929.* Cambridge and New York: Cambridge University Press, 1985.

Krebs, Stanley Dale. *Soviet Composers and the Development of Soviet Music.* Unpublished Ph.D. dissertation, University of Washington, 1963.

L'équipe "Théâtre Moderne" du Groupe de recherches théâtrales et musicologiques du Centre national de la recherche scientifique. *Le Théâtre d'Agit-Prop de 1917 à 1932.* Ed. Denis Bablet. 2 volumes. Lausanne: La Cité—L'Age d'Homme, 1977. Théâtre Années Vingt series.

Leyda, Jay. *Kino: A History of the Russian and Soviet Film.* New York: Collier Books, 1960.

Lodder, Christina. *Russian Constructivism.* New Haven, Conn., and London: Yale University Press, 1983.

Maguire, Robert A. *Red Virgin Soil: Soviet Literature in the 1920's.* Princeton, N.J.: Princeton University Press, 1968.

Michelson, Annette, ed. *Kino-Eye: The Writings of Dziga Vertov.* Trans. Kevin O'Brien. Berkeley: University of California Press, 1984.

October. Winter 1978. Special issue on Soviet revolutionary culture.

Rudnitsky, Konstantin. *Meyerhold the Director.* Trans. George Petrov. Ed. Sydney Schultze. Introduction by Ellendea Proffer. Ann Arbor, Mich.: Ardis, 1981.

Sayler, Oliver. *The Russian Theatre under the Revolution.* Boston: Little, Brown, 1920.

Schechter, Joel. *Durov's Pig: Clowns, Politics, and Theatre.* New York: Theater Communications Group, 1985.

Schwarz, Boris. *Music and Musical Life in Soviet Russia, 1917–1981.* Bloomington: Indiana University Press, 1983.

Segel, Harold B. *Twentieth-Century Russian Drama.* New York: Columbia University Press, 1979.

Slonim, Marc. *Russian Theater from the Empire to the Soviets.* New York: Collier Books, 1961.

Starr, S. Frederick. *Red and Hot: The Fate of Jazz in the Soviet Union, 1917–1980.* New York and Oxford: Oxford University Press, 1983.

The Drama Review. Fall 1971 (T-52), March 1973 (T-57), March 1975 (T-65).

Trotsky, Leon. *Literature and Revolution.* New York: Russell and Russell, 1957.

Williams, Robert C. *Artists in Revolution: Portraits of the Russian Avant Garde, 1905–1925.* Bloomington: Indiana University Press, 1977.

On the eve of the October Revolution in 1917 the Russian ballet theater was quite rich. The Soviet ballet inherited a varied repertory that
included works created over a span of more than a hundred years.

The oldest ballet, dating from 1789, was Jean Dauberval's *La Fille
mal gardée*. This ingenuous French comedy was seen on the Russian
stage from the beginning of the nineteenth century and, despite various
changes, kept its basic virtues—dynamism and a vibrant tone, a logical
development of action (mostly through pantomime), and a clear delinea-
tion of character.

Giselle was almost constantly on the stage in Russia from 1842 onward,
and here the concept of Romanticism found its fullest expression. It was
in Russia, in Petipa's version, that *Giselle*'s choreography took on a new
perfection of movement, and the message of the ballet became more profound and in some respects changed its meaning. Other ballets of the
Romantic era were also preserved, such as Joseph Mazilier's *Le Corsaire*
(reworked by Perrot and then Petipa) and *Esmeralda*, which Jules Perrot staged in Petersburg at the end of the 1840s. The characters in these
dance-dramas were picturesque and unusual: the fearless pirate Conrad
and the Oriental slave girls, the Gypsy Esmeralda and the hunchback
Quasimodo. Events shifted rapidly, recounted through dance pantomime
and emotionally tinged movements.

The name of Arthur Saint-Léon, the master of dance *féeries*, was also
featured on ballet programs. Of the ballets that he staged in Russia in the
1860s, *The Little Humpbacked Horse*, considerably enriched in later revivals by Marius Petipa, Lev Ivanov, and Alexander Gorsky, was a lasting
work. The choreographic masterpieces of the various authors stood out
in this work in the kaleidoscopic glimpses of national and classical dances:
the "Frescoes" variations, the solo dance "The Nightingale," and Liszt's
Second Rhapsody. The buffoonery of the comic scenes was also strik-

ing. Also, *Coppélia*, first staged in Paris by Saint-Léon, was presented in Petersburg and Moscow.

The productions of Marius Ivanovich Petipa accounted for the lion's share of the nineteenth-century repertory. About twenty ballets bearing his signature—original or restaged works—were kept on the Petrograd stage, and some were presented in Moscow as well.

The great master worked for over half a century. His first productions were staged at the end of the era of Romanticism, and his last ballet was realized in 1903. By the end of the nineteenth century a style had been created that was the culmination of Petipa's many years of creative work: the style of the academic full-length ballet. Decorative spectacles in several acts, rich in special effects, were constructed according to strict aesthetic norms. Rules were worked out that defined both the overall composition of the ballet and the structure of individual dance forms.

The subjects of Petipa's ballets, whether they were fairytale or exotic, were quite traditional and had their roots in the Romantic theater. The plots were banal, and the same events were repeated in one ballet after another. External action was laid out through pantomime, replete with conventional gestures. Dramatic action was stereotyped. The construction of each act, the sequence of the dances—solo, group, ensemble—all followed an identical order. The triumphant coda and apotheosis of the last act was an indispensable element.

But within the borders of this canon—whose limitations were bound to make themselves felt sooner or later—the major expressive device of ballet—the dance itself—was undergoing intensive development. Petipa's ballets were distinguished by a selectivity and refinement of dance forms. Dance was separated from pantomime and became abstract; it lost its connection to everyday movement. Classical dance was distinguished from character dance, and a thorough process of cultivating the specific elements of classical ballet began. Pointe technique developed and changed radically: Instead of fleeting volatile rises there appeared springs onto pointe that demanded stability, strength, and endurance. Dancers mastered all kinds of turns—*tours*, pirouettes, *fouettés*—and heightened their speed and number.

The aspiration to virtuosity so characteristic of Petipa's era marks an important, inevitable stage in the development of the dance. Without it the further improvement and enrichment of the language of dance would have been impossible, and consequently there would have been no solution to the complex problems the art of the ballet was very soon to face. But changes were not only due to the growth of technique. Stable, crystallized, structural elements lay at the base of meaningful dance compositions. The use of the devices of repetition, contrast, and variation allowed for the elaboration of dance motifs and the juxtaposition of movement themes.

Petipa was an incomparable master of the language of classical dance, and he daily increased its vocabulary. He was also a master of the art of orchestrating dance movement. His best works are models not only of extraordinary professional competence, but also of rich significance.

Toward the end of the nineteenth century the dance element in ballet took on a new dimension: Thanks to its ability to communicate feelings and thoughts removed from concrete associations, it rose to the level of a symbolic language of art and became an independent means of expression appropriate for the creation of complex images. The path of ballet moved from decorative dances (of which there were many in the gala productions of Petipa) toward compositions in which dance movements revealed man's spiritual world in abstract terms. In this respect it resembled symphonic music. It is not coincidental that the greatest triumphs were achieved when dance found support in equivalent music, in the ballets of symphonic composers.

Comparatively early works by Petipa were also among the nineteenth-century productions that were kept in the repertory right up to the October Revolution. One was *La Fille du Pharaon* (1862), a work rich in the variety of its ornamental dances. The divertissements showed the choreographer's rare imagination in composing new steps.

Of particular importance was the dance-drama *La Bayadère* (1877), where the development of the main character was strikingly shown. The culmination of the performance was the death dance of Nikiya as she held a basket of flowers in which a snake had been hidden. *La Bayadère* also contained an outstanding example of pure lyrical dance—"The Kingdom of the Shades" in the last act—the original dance motif of the serenely swaying procession of veiled dancers as shades developed and changed. Contrasting themes emerged in the lively variations of the soloists and in the virtuosic dance of the ballerina. The whole was a superbly "orchestrated" choreographic ensemble foreshadowing the appearance of the great symphonic scenes in the ballets composed by Peter Tchaikovsky and Alexander Glazunov.

Petipa's encounter with symphonic composers took place in the 1890s. In the course of a single decade three ballets to music by Tchaikovsky, as well as Glazunov's *Raymonda* and two of his one-act ballets, appeared on the Petersburg stage. All except for *Les Saisons* were included in the repertory of the Maryinsky Theater on the eve of the revolution.

Tchaikovsky's move into ballet was the result of historical necessity. The course of the development of theatrical dancing brought it into a rapprochement with symphonic music. *Swan Lake*, which at first was not understood (hence the failure of the 1877 Moscow version) and *The Sleeping Beauty* (1890) answered vital needs of the ballet theater.

The ballets to music by Tchaikovsky and Glazunov were composed in compliance with the rules of the nineteenth-century full-length ballet raised to its highest level. Petipa's best production, *The Sleeping Beauty* (though it remained in form a *ballet-féerie*), thanks to Tchaikovsky achieved a depth of content that ballets by second-rate composers did not possess. The fairytale plot gave Tchaikovsky material for poetic abstraction, for reflection on the struggle between good and evil. The large music-dance episodes that make up the center of each act reveal the persistent, basic theme of the ballet—the triumph of love, light, and life.

The Sleeping Beauty ran continuously in Petersburg and Moscow and underwent fewer changes than other Petipa ballets; only the scenery and costumes were altered. In this production the "Petipa style" found its ideal expression. It was distinguished by its classical clarity. Serene, fluent, majestically unfolding action, a skillful combination of dance and pantomime episodes, a sequence of dancing planned down to the smallest detail—all of this once more reaffirmed the unshakeability of Petipa's canons. Yet already, in *Raymonda*, composed eight years later (1898), sober serenity had reached a certain stasis. Here were marvelous choreographic discoveries, above all in the area of combining classical and character dance (the "Pas classique hongrois" of the last act), but the ballet's monumental pomposity and excessive ornamentation were tiresome. Created on the threshold between two centuries, the ballet belonged to the past, and this affected its fate. Despite its extraordinary music *Raymonda* was performed more rarely and reworked more often. Petipa's staging of Glazunov's one-act ballets appeared infrequently in the repertory.

Lev Ivanovich Ivanov was Petipa's co-author for *The Nutcracker* (1892) and *Swan Lake* (1895). *The Nutcracker*, the "symphony about childhood," as Boris Asafiev called it, required an approach to the music that surpassed the capabilities of the ballet theater in those years. Only some of the divertissements and the "Waltz of the Snowflakes" were successful. In this lyric scene and later in the dances of the swans, Lev Ivanov did not violate the established principles of academic ballet. But the tone was different, elegiac. Petipa's confident, declarative statements gave way to more disquieting intonations; outlines lost their former clarity and colors were muted. This tendency testified to a need for introspection as well as to a certain unconscious dissatisfaction. His art was akin to such manifestations of turn-of-the-century Russian culture as Chekhov's plays, Levitan's paintings, and the flowering of lyric poetry.

Lev Ivanov's ballets were few. He did not have time to create much; not everything he created was of value, and not all has been preserved. The repertory of the Petrograd company on the eve of the October Revolution included *The Nutcracker*, Liszt's Second Rhapsody in *The Little Humpbacked Horse*, the elegant comedy *The Magic Flute* (music by Drigo), and, of course, *Swan Lake*, which featured both Petipa's brilliant staging of the dances at the ball and Ivanov's swan scenes.

Along with the model full-length ballets, Soviet theater inherited the choreographic traditions of the beginning of the century. The artists who replaced Marius Petipa and Lev Ivanov were critical of the work of their teachers. In the eyes of the next generation the achievements of these much-renowned masters were diminished by the outdated form of their productions: These naive fairytales with gala processions and marches belonged to the past. At that time it did not seem possible to investigate the contradictions of the aesthetics of academic ballet and to recognize its achievement in terms of pure dance. Nineteenth-century ballet was perceived as a unified complex of expressive means. Therefore it was totally rejected by those younger artists who embarked on the path of reform. They baptized nineteenth-century ballet the "old" ballet and set about creating their own "new" ballet.

Two choreographers were the initiators of these reforms. The first,

Alexander Alexeyevich Gorsky, a student at the Petersburg School, worked in Moscow all his life and in 1900 began his experiments in the Bolshoi Theater. The second, Mikhail Mikhailovich Fokine, turned to choreography five years later.

Fokine staged a few ballets in the Maryinsky Theater but even more productions during Diaghilev's Ballets Russes seasons—guest appearances abroad by dancers from the Imperial Theaters—and also for foreign theaters. Hence by no means all of Fokine's creative work became the property of the Russian theater.

The Fokine productions *Le Pavillon d'Armide*, *Chopiniana (Les Sylphides)*, *Une Nuit d'Égypte (Cléopâtre)*, *Le Carnaval*, and *Jota Aragonesa* became permanent fixtures in the repertory. The ballets *Eros* and, more rarely, *Islamey* were performed. His choreographic compositions were also preserved in operas: "Polovetsian Dances" from *Prince Igor* and the dances in *Ruslan and Ludmila* and *Orpheus*. Of the concert numbers, *The Dying Swan* was performed.

Such characteristic works of Fokine as *Schéhérazade*, *The Firebird*, and *Le Spectre de la Rose* were not presented in Russia. *Petrushka* was shown only in the 1920s in Petrograd and Moscow. Though fewer in number than the old works, this group of Fokine's productions did attest to the changes that had taken place in the Russian ballet at the beginning of the century. The extent of their impact on choreographers of the next generation, including those who were to build the Soviet ballet, is extremely significant, and Fokine's early ballets occupied a primary position.

Le Pavillon d'Armide (1907) owed its existence to Alexandre Benois, author of the scenario with which the composer, Nikolai Tcherepnin, worked, and it was Benois who was responsible for the scenery and costumes. This was a programmatic production for Benois. He wanted to construct a ballet based on the principles of the World of Art movement. The naive clumsiness of old productions had to give way to a visual spectacle of a totally different order. All kinds of theatrical devices were used to re-create a style from the past, that of Benois's beloved Versailles, with its artificially shaped trees, fountains and statues, mirrors and decorated interiors, powdered wigs, fans and feathers. But despite all of the innovations in artistic staging in terms of music, drama, and dance, *Le Pavillon d'Armide* was only a cautious first step away from the "old" ballet and toward the "new."

In *Chopiniana* (second version 1908) the music brought to life images of the airy winged dancers of the Romantic era. Dressed in long white tutus, with little wings on their backs and wreaths on their heads, they glided about the stage, now alone, now arranged in groups, as in old prints. A pensive youth with long locks in a black velvet tunic pursued one of the sylphs.

Having done away with the rigid immobility of academic forms, Fokine wanted to restore the former airy, poetic quality and the charm of the unspoken to classical dance on pointe. Here, to a greater extent than in *Le Pavillon d'Armide*, dance itself was the means for expressing the style of an era. And beyond that, in *Chopiniana* stylization was a means for the choreographer to express his own twentieth-century ideas. This was not a picture from a museum but a melancholy image imbued with radiant sadness. The return to the Romantic motif of the Sylphide incarnating a dream was born of an awareness of the imperfection of the world. At that time, when, in the words of Benois, "all of Russian reality was besmirched and trampled in dirt"[1] there was an attraction to fantastic beauty. Although the dream turned out to be unattainable, Fokine called it "a winged hope."

The Dying Swan (1907) reaffirmed the same idea. The brief dance, lasting two minutes, was built on traditional movements: pas de bourrée, attitude, bends, and arm movements both smooth and agitated. The image of the swan itself was not new, for it was widely used in Russian art and in ballet was known through *Swan Lake*. Yet Fokine's miniature was perceived and is still perceived as fully independent, perhaps the most inspired of all his creations. His contemporaries correctly saw in it a symbol of resistance to death, of striving toward life.

Le Carnaval (1910) was typical of the "new" ballet. Fokine brought onto the ballet stage the characters of the commedia del l'arte, which had been persistently revived by the Russian theater during those years. Everything was based on halftones and subtle hints: A gesture, a glance, a sly smile, a tilt of the head, a lace frill peeping out from under a crinoline, the very combination of the colors—black and white, various shades of light blue and green—were all no less significant than the dance steps. Never in the "old" ballet had dance, music, costumes, and decor been used to create such impressionistically shifting images to convey such vague, subtle moods. The very content of *Le Carnaval* was completely different from that of the simple Petipa-Drigo *Harlequinade*, staged ten years earlier. The theme of masks and the masquerade was treated by Fokine on a broad plane, as a symbol of reality, of the eternal fluctuations of all earthly things. In this respect he was close to modern poetry, in particular to Alexander Blok, who also turned to images of the Italian commedia del l'arte to express the state of ambivalence and confusion that had taken hold of people.

Une Nuit d'Égypte is a ballet strongly influenced by ancient art, by the impressions of enigmatic wall inscriptions and murals, decorated sarcophagi and strange hieroglyphs, from which Fokine created his own choreographic, fantastic world. Three years earlier Gorsky, reworking Petipa's *La Fille du Pharaon*, used poses in profile and removed the tutus of some of the characters. Stylistically new dances were, however, introduced into an old context. Following a similar pattern, Fokine achieved stylistic unity in his production. He created compositions unfurled, as it were, on a flat plane, using unusual angular movements, with the dancers dressed in sandals and straight, narrow dresses.

Une Nuit d'Égypte, to the music of Anton Arensky, remained in the repertory of the Maryinsky Theater in the form in which Fokine staged it in 1908. In the new version (*Cléopâtre*), created a year later for Paris, the plot was changed, music of various composers was interpolated, and the scenery was designed by Léon Bakst. In the Paris production Fokine's intention was fully realized. Now the youth Amoûn, enchanted by Cleopatra's beauty, paid with his life for the queen's caresses. One of the themes of the period was projected onto a stylized "Egyptian" background: Love and death were shown not in opposition but identified with one another, as in the work of the Symbolist poets.

This theme was an integral part of all of the Oriental ballets of Fokine, of which *Islamey* (1912) was included in the repertory of the Maryinsky Theater. Having replaced *Schéhérazade*, whose production in Russia had been forbidden by Rimsky-Korsakov's widow, *Islamey* displayed the same kind of passionate Eastern dances and swift development of dramatic action: An orgy of love turned into an orgy of murder. The production revealed one of the most essential aspects of Fokine's creative work. However, a different, more long-range side of his work was that which developed out of the "Polovetsian Dances" from Borodin's opera *Prince Igor*.

Rapacious figures in motley clothing decorated with metal ornaments, ragged caps, and multicolored skullcaps crowned with feathers whirled about the stage. The dancers at times crouched toward the ground in a creeping run and at times soared into the air. Lightning turns were replaced by frenzied, bristling movements.

The "Polovetsian Dances" became a graphic expression of the wild warriors' passionate outburst and assertion of will. This was a completely new concept of an ensemble dance in which the corps played the leading roles and the soloists, who were included in the dance, were subordinate to it. It was also an entirely new image; in the fiery spontaneity of the dance, in the bright bacchanalian violence lay that elemental force, a rebellion, that foreshadowed an approaching storm.

The motifs in the "Polovetsian Dances" were used by Fokine in the dances of the Cossacks in *Stenka Razin* (1915). However, there was nothing new here compared to his innovations six years earlier. The production had a short life on the stage and is of interest primarily because on the eve of revolution the choreographer turned to depicting popular revolt. But in the history of Soviet theater the experience of the "Polovetsian Dances" was to be recalled many times, up to the middle of the 1930s, when heroic mass ballet dances appeared on our stage.

The ballets most commonly featured in the repertory shortly before the October Revolution were *Eros*, to the music of Tchaikovsky's *Serenade in C Major for String Orchestra* (1915),* which was not one of Fokine's greatest contributions, and *Jota Aragonesa*, to music by Glinka (1916).

While living for several months in Spain Fokine studied various kinds of Spanish dances: rural and urban dances, gypsy dances, and those "classical" dances which are taught in special schools. He discovered whole layers of dance that had been untouched by choreographers. These were primarily peasant dances which were distinguished from the dances of the city taverns not only by the nature of their movements but also by their spirit. In *Jota Aragonesa* Fokine broke with the cliché of the frenzied fake Spanish style and rejected vulgar cabaret mannerisms. For him, the important thing was the charm of authenticity, sincerity, and integrity,

---

*George Balanchine later used this music for his first ballet choreographed in the United States, *Serenade* (1934). (Ed.)

the qualities he saw in the people themselves. The dances were like a witty improvisation. But these were not ethnographic motifs passively transferred to the stage. While Glinka expressed folk melodies symphonically, Fokine added to the movements of Spanish dance a finished quality that brought them closer to professional classical dance. Thus *Jota Aragonesa* marked a new stage in ballet's mastery of dance folklore.

Among Fokine's productions that did not find their way to the imperial stage were the ballets to the music of Igor Stravinsky, *The Firebird* (1910) and *Petrushka* (1911). The first projects for restructuring the repertory after the revolution definitely included *Petrushka*. Asafiev and Benois were ardent supporters of reviving this ballet, and they were right to insist that Fokine's best production should finally become the property of his own native theater.

Petrushka is one of the most representative ballets of the era. Particularly striking is the interest in city folklore that united poets, painters, and artists. In *Petrushka* emerge themes which were of concern to many of Fokine's contemporaries: the theme of the clown ironically recreating the world and that of the tender poetic soul, mocked and misunderstood.

Petrushka is Fokine's greatest achievement. Here the choreographer's principles are carried out most consistently. The content of the one-act ballet is revealed through the unity of expressive means. The music was composed for a scenario specially written by Benois. The sets, costumes, and properties are not a neutral background but form an image closely fused with the musical image. Canonic forms are absent from the dance, and no one speaks in the language of the abstract classics. Dance movements proper are joined with pantomime, forming various alloys. Each feature is in keeping with the historical era and the style of the production, and fits into the gallery of the extraordinarily picturesque, strongly shaped portraits, both crowd and solo.

Work on remounting *Petrushka* began in Petrograd in 1918, but a series of difficulties, of which perhaps the major one was Fokine's departure abroad, delayed the production. A decision was made not to wait for the return of the choreographer, and the task of reviving the ballet fell to Leonid Leontiev. The premiere took place in 1920. A year later *Petrushka* was also staged in Moscow (under Vladimir Riabtsev), and thus it turned out to be the only work by Fokine in the repertory of the Bolshoi Theater. No one undertook a reconstruction of the original version of *The*

Firebird. For this reason, Fedor Lopukhov thought it better to stage his own production of the ballet in Petrograd (1921).

The Petrograd repertory at the beginning of the revolution reflected the tastes and ideas of several choreographers. In Moscow the picture was different. Alexander Gorsky had been artistic director, sole producer, and one of the main teachers of the Moscow ballet from the beginning of the century. To a great extent he defined the artistic principles of the development of ballet in Moscow and the performance style of the Moscow school. Not only was he responsible for all new productions, he also staged his own versions of the classical repertory.

By 1917 many of Gorsky's early productions were no longer in the repertory. Nevertheless, they played their role in forming the aesthetic tastes of the Moscow troupe. One such ballet which was not kept was *Gudule's Daughter*, one of Gorsky's favorite works, created in 1902 in collaboration with the composer Anton Simon and the artist Konstantin Korovin. This was a "mimodrama" in several scenes that, as fully as possible, depicted the convolutions of Victor Hugo's novel *Notre-Dame de Paris*. From 1914 on, after a fire in the set warehouses, *Salammbô* (1910, music by Andrei Arends), the most monumental and spectacular of all Gorsky's choreodramas, was no longer part of the repertory. Occasionally *Études*, the elegiac suite of dances choreographed to music by Anton Rubinstein, Edvard Grieg, Frédéric Chopin, and Ernest Guiraud, or the *Dances of the Nations* was shown in the divertissements added to short ballets. "The Spirit of Belgium," a section of *Dances of the Nations*, was sometimes performed by Ekaterina Geltser under a new title, *The March of Freedom*. The ballet *Eunice and Petronius* was performed only a few times.

Only one work remained solidly within the repertory—*Love is Quick!* Created in 1913 to the music of Edvard Grieg's *Symphonic Dances*, the ballet reflected the dream of the purifying healing force of untouched nature, simple labor, and innocent love that rose in the troubled prewar years. Gorsky composed a lyric scene with comic overtones: a meeting between a shipwrecked fisherman and a shepherdess, love, an engagement, a village festival. He was determined to create a sense of authenticity in the events happening on the stage, in the stern Norwegian countryside (by the artist Korovin), the expanses of the ocean, the piled-up cliffs. People in this world are rough, unpolished as stones, clumsy, and slow, and their love is just as guileless and sincere, somewhat comic but touching. Here the accepted ballet canons were broken: The dancers' feet were turned in, they walked bowlegged, their arms stuck out. The unified tone of the ballet made it stylish and convincing.

For the most part the repertory preserved those ballets from the classical heritage that had been reworked by Gorsky before the revolution. He staged *La Fille mal gardée* at least seven times, *Swan Lake* and *Giselle* five times, and revised *Raymonda*, *Le Corsaire*, *La Bayadère*, and *The Little Humpbacked Horse*. He ordered new sets and costumes from Korovin and modernized the mise-en-scène and choreography of the ballets. Gorsky based his approach to the problem of reconstructing the classics on his own program of action and his own ideas about reforming the ballet.

To the abstract canons of the old productions Gorsky opposed new principles of realistic action and verisimilitude. He pierced the performance with a clear line of action, dramatized the dance, saturated the ensemble scenes with playful moments, and introduced details from everyday life, sometimes even specifically ethnographic details. By no means every ballet of the past fit into this kind of revision. Many works based on other aesthetic principles could not be squeezed into such a new schema without being destroyed. Therefore, in different cases the alterations led to different results. Gorsky added new integrity and meaning to Petipa's *Don Quixote*, which had previously been rather eclectic and amorphous, and in so doing made it more viable. In 1900 he restaged the entire ballet, breaking its symmetry of construction, and created constant movement in the corps, with Korovin's assistance decorating the stage in bright colors. The dynamic, stormy rhythm and the easy, lighthearted gaiety of *Don Quixote* as we know it today are due in great part to Gorsky. This mischievous ballet, sparkling with laughter, in which the young make fools of the old, the poor lead the rich by the nose, and everything ends with a happy wedding, was certainly attractive to the Soviet audience. And the virtuosic dances that permeate the work could not fail to make a strong impression.

One of the most frequently performed ballets in the repertory was *The Little Humpbacked Horse*. The ballet, by Saint-Léon, ran on the Russian stage from the 1860s on and was revised several times; in the course of these revisions something was lost, but something was also added. Gorsky staged the ballet in 1901 and again in 1914. At first he strengthened the character dancing in the individual roles and added to the ensemble scenes—at the bazaar and in the square of the Khan's city —a colorful quality and a vibrant authenticity. Later he began to introduce new dances already close to the "new" ballet along stylistic lines: The woman's dance with a bow, filled with wild passion, for Sofia Fedorova, and the pas de trois of the ocean and the pearls, where classical technique was combined with Duncanesque movements. As a result, *The Little Humpbacked Horse* became even more colorful than before. But since this color and eclecticism had always been a feature of this ballet, the innovations did no harm. New dances and comic themes were added, brilliantly performed by Moscow mimes Vladimir Riabtsev, Ivan Sidorov, and others.

In reworking Petipa's and Arseny Koreshchenko's *The Magic Mirror* in 1905, Gorsky tried to bring the action closer to Pushkin's "Fairytale about the Dead Princess and the Seven Knights," but it was impossible to reconcile the development of the plot with the music, written for divertissements. Nevertheless, thanks to the variety of the dances and the achievements of Alexander Golovine's designs, the ballet remained in the repertory until the mid-1920s.

Gorsky pursued the same goal—strengthening the original action—in his reworking of *Raymonda* (1908), which, in the words of Alexandre Benois, featured an "external liveliness, the illusion of life." [2] The folk element was stressed and an effort was made to "democratize" the ballet. In the "Pas classique hongrois," Gorsky was bolder in his use of "character" positions than was the case in the Petersburg version. The waltz of the courtiers congratulating Raymonda in the first act was transformed into a peasant dance with ribbons. Abderâme was treated not as a Saracen knight, but as a wandering Oriental merchant. The costumes were changed: where tutus were used, they were longer, and still more often use was made of dresses that fell below the knee, cut in a style close to that of the costumes of the period. In the "Pas classique hongrois," the traditional male tunics were replaced by embroidered leather dolman jackets, encircled by wide belts. Particular attention was paid to the color of the costumes. Gorsky's interpretation of the music was impressionistic. Under the influence of the then-fashionable theories of the interrelationship between color and sound, he gave each dance a particular tonality of color. Even the names changed: One of the dances of the Oriental suite was called "En bleu," another "En fleurs de grenadier," and in the third act "Rose d'Hongrie" and "En fleurs de pavot" appeared.

In addition to *Raymonda* Gorsky had reworked such masterpieces as *Giselle* and *Swan Lake*.[3] With each year, the original dances of Petipa and Ivanov had less and less place in the productions. These ballets entered the repertory of the Soviet Bolshoi Theater in a considerably changed form.

The new version of *Le Corsaire* (1912) was one of Gorsky's most popular productions and was kept during the Soviet period. The Petersburg variant was the work of Petipa, but that in turn had been a reworking of an earlier staging by Perrot. Gorsky wanted to add unity to the ballet, and to a considerable extent he was able to do this through the general artistic dynamics of the production.

The public liked the romantic exoticism of the ballet, in which episodes of pirate and harem life and of the slave market were crowned with the famous storm scene and the sinking of the felucca, both created by the famous stage machinist Karl Waltz. In the old production Petipa had artlessly led out onto the stage the corsaires and Oriental merchants, together with ballerinas in tutus. Gorsky and Korovin tried to reduce everything to a common denominator. They dressed the Greek Medora in a chiton, and they added an Oriental flavor to the inserted classical pas "Le jardin animé." It seemed as though the eclecticism for which the old ballet had been rightfully reproached had finally been eliminated, but in fact the unity of expressive means in Gorsky's version was only an illusion. The uncomfortable combination of old and new choreography, the execution of purely classical dances left over from Petipa's staging in new costumes—all of this led to a confusion of styles.

The last production prepared by Gorsky before the October Revolution (the premiere was on March 19, 1917) was *La Bayadère*. Korovin designed the sets, which were at times extravagantly bright and at times muted and pale, with magical mother-of-pearl hues. The costumes, adorned with pearls and gold, were not an exact imitation of Indian clothing, but rather a resurrection of the fantastic images in the paintings and sculptures of ancient temples. Having partially eliminated the old music by Léon Minkus, Arends introduced many new numbers, such as those by Alexandre Luigini, Henri Vieuxtemps, and Ernest Guiraud. Gorsky rechoreographed most of the dances. In the ensemble dances outside the temple, he imitated the dancing figures of ancient bas-reliefs and reproduced the poses of bronze statues. The influence of Indian art, which the choreographer had studied with considerable care, also made itself felt in the patterns of the dance and in the circular movements in the variations. This created the effect of Eastern ornamentation and floweriness that harmonized with the decor of the production. But the choreographer failed in the scene "The Kingdom of the Shades," where, having kept the old music and basic design of the dance, he dressed the dead bayadères in national costumes instead of the conventional tutus. "The Kingdom of the Shades" was conceived and staged on different aesthetic principles which radically conflicted with Gorsky's common sense.

Starting in 1911 the Petersburg theaters saw a new choreographer, Boris Georgievich Romanov, a soloist in character and mime roles at the Maryinsky Theater. His first productions at the Liteiny Theater and his opera productions at the Maryinsky Theater bore the stamp of Fokine's influence. However, a different sensibility soon made itself felt. Romanov's experience as an actor made him search for greater depth and intensity of character. The difference in outlook was clear. Fokine valued beauty. While recognizing its fatal power, he still believed in its purifying force. Romanov's views were more contrary: Inclined to reappraise values, he readily held up to ridicule what was generally accepted and at the same time felt an attraction to all that was ominous, gloomy, and morbid. What in Fokine's work would have been a romantic scene took on for him the features of a farce or *guignol*.

Boris Romanov owed many of his ideas to the Stray Dog,[*] that hearth of artistic bohemia that united rebels and "strays" who rejected official art. Here the piano improvisations of Ilya Satz and the verses of Mikhail Kuzmin, Romanov's colleagues in the theaters of miniatures, were heard. Here Romanov himself staged and performed dances "with a touch of an orgiastic bouquet, slightly immoral and a tiny bit pornographic."[4] Here the Satyriconian[†] Piotr Potemkin recounted to him the plot of Hans Ewers's "Tomato Sauce" over a glass of cognac. The story, which was

[*]An artists' cabaret. (Ed.)

[†]The authors of *Satyricon*, a satirical magazine published in St. Petersburg 1908–14. (Ed.)

included in the anthology *Horrors*, served as the basis for the ballet *Andalusiana*.[5] Here Romanov also met with Vsevolod Meyerhold, who played Pierrot in Romanov's pantomime ballet *Pierrot and the Masks* in February 1914 at a carnival in the Aeroclub. It is possible that Meyerhold influenced the choreographer's use of the theme based on a comedy of masks.[*]

Romanov displayed his "mischievous" side for the first time in his autumn 1912 production of *The Goatlegged*, with music by Ilya Satz, in the Liteiny Theater. Fokine's bacchanalia, the frenzy of the satyrs of the ballet *Daphnis and Chloe*, which had been staged a few months earlier, served him as a model. But it was as if the familiar motifs had been shifted to another level. Romanov did not resort to antiquity to show the spontaneity of feeling; the half-goats/half-humans of Satz and Romanov openly displayed their animal nature. In the comic sounds of the music the clatter of hoofs and bleating could be heard, and on the stage actors in goatskins with horns on their heads jumped about, butting each other and striking up amorous games. The Sabbat of the goatlegged bordered on satire.

In 1913–14 Romanov worked in Diaghilev's troupe abroad and staged Florent Schmitt's ballet *The Tragedy of Salomé* and the dances in Stravinsky's opera *The Nightingale*. In February 1915 the ballet *The Gardener-Prince* was put on in the Petrograd Theater of Musical Drama. Revising Valerian Svetlov's scenario and considerably cutting Alexei Davidov's music, Romanov added a sense of the grotesque to a naive children's ballet. The capricious princess expressed herself with gestures in "rococo" style, and the princess's girlfriends, in panniers, white wigs, and black stockings, moved about with awkward angular gestures, affectedly holding out their elbows. André Levinson wrote that classical dance was "used for the sake of caricature," and that "the simple-hearted smile of the fairytale has been reduced to a grimace.[6]

In the same year, Romanov staged two one-act ballets: *What Happened to the Ballerina, the Chinese, and the Jumpers*, to the music of Vladimir Rebikov, and *Andalusiana* to the music of Georges Bizet for Alphonse

---

[*] And Meyerhold, who in his own work was at that time fascinated by carnival and commedia del l'arte figures, had earlier played Pierrot in Fokine's *Carnaval*, first presented in 1910 at another Satyricon evening. (Ed.)

Daudet's drama *L'Arlésienne*. The first ballet was not a great success. It was a puppet farce in which Chinese dolls with mechanically nodding heads and quickly turning clowns moved about on the background of the painter Alexei Radakov's colorful screens. But the familiar images of *Coppélia*, *Die Puppenfee*, and *Nutcracker* were tinged with irony in this ballet.

Andalusiana was Romanov's most significant prerevolutionary work. It was retained in Russia after 1917 as well and was included in the repertory of Romanov's troupes that travelled abroad. The décor of *Andalusiana* showed a tavern, a cellar with vaulted, barred windows and cracked walls. In crimson semidarkness a bloody drama of rivalry, jealousy, and death played itself out. Incited by the coquettishness of the "cruel beauty," two rivals grappled in a hopeless duel; bound together, they continued to exchange dagger blows until both fell dead. The crowd, drunk with blood, poured out its feelings in a frenzied dance with ever-increasing tempi.

A breaking point of emotions leading to an outburst, a nightmare in which the comic and the horrendous absurdly mix—this is the atmosphere into which Romanov carried the action of Boris Asafiev's pantomime *The Dream of Pierrot*, presented in January 1917. At first entitled *Pierrot and the Masks*, this short ballet had been staged by Romanov three years earlier in the then customary manner of the stylized commedia del l'arte. The new version was both more fantastic and more tragic. The choreographer intensified its dark coloring. In the first scene Pierrot returns from a carnival. Drunk, he falls asleep, and the second scene shows his dream: Pierrot sees "certain mysterious masks, and his Columbine in Harlequin's voluptuous embraces." It seems to him that in his despair he is hanging from the chandelier hook: "His body dangles helplessly, turning on a thick rope."[7]

Romanov's prerevolutionary experiments took him further and further away from the academic ballet. Akim Volynsky, a partisan of the classics, vigorously opposed Romanov's attempts. He repudiated him as a dancer, berated him for taking liberties with the Spanish dances of old ballets, rejected his Expressionist productions with their element of the grotesque, and was horrified by his "barbaric" violation of the rules. The critic continually pointed out the lack of a clear design and harmonic rigor in the young choreographer's productions and termed this a lack of style.

Meanwhile, a new style was born. Romanov's "anticlassicism" was a principled position. A taut, convulsive quality opposed the earlier clarity and balance; a deliberate roughness, a breaking and distortion of line stood in contrast to a rounded, soft perfection of form. The critics accused Romanov of breaking every norm of taste and tact, of "orgiastics" and "sadism," of pandering to the taste of barroom bohemia.

Perhaps in Romanov's productions there actually was an element of *épatage*, but these extremes were not there merely for the sake of mischief. They represented the very essence of his quest. Yuri Beliaev sensed this when he wrote of Romanov's staging and performance of *Andalusiana*: "His dance is filled with a kind of Khlystian zeal.* He barely refrains from shouting and from hysterics. But his pale, expressive face is filled with passion, and the convulsive gestures and his whole frenzied, tumbling figure seem to cry out 'Oh, Spirit! Oh, God!' "[8]

Romanov's ballets reflected the tragic perception of the world by many artists during this era of crisis. Monstrous, inharmonious images thrust themselves into art. The device of the grotesque, uniting farce and drama, became a means for expressing the contradictions of the time.

By the 1920s the works by the reformers at the beginning of the century (Fokine and Gorsky) were accepted even by artists of the "old" school. And Fokine himself no longer criticized the "old" ballet with his former vehemence and even began to introduce into his works devices that he had formerly rejected as obsolete. However, having won recognition, the "new" ballet—the ballet of Fokine and Gorsky—stopped developing further. The next generation of choreographers tried to break this impasse. The experiments of Vaslav Nijinsky took place abroad, but the ballets of Romanov began to win a place for themselves on the Russian stage. Also, on the eve of the revolution the name of the choreographer Kasian Goleizovsky began to be heard; at that time he was only known on the variety stage.

This was the legacy handed down to revolutionary art by the old ballet theater. All the best had to be preserved for the future. This had to be the basis for the growth of the new Soviet ballet.

In the years just preceding the October Revolution the repertory of the

*The Khlysty, or "flagellants," were a group of seventeenth-century Russian ecstatic sectarians who believed in the imminence of the millennium. Calling themselves "God's people," they proclaimed one of their number God himself and another the new Christ. They chanted, performed ritual dances, and whipped themselves. (Ed.)

ballet was renewed only slightly. Gorsky was right when he said "Right now we are seeing a pause in progress."[9] The paths for further choreographic development were also unclear. Many felt this and wrote of the deterioration of the repertory and yet were unable to find a way out, for this lay beyond the realm of purely artistic problems.

The war brought additional financial and organizational complications to the theaters: Less and less money was allotted to them and many planned productions had to be put off; the companies were reduced in size. Dissatisfaction grew in the inner workings of the opera theaters as well. But the conservatism and apolitical nature of the artists of the imperial stage and their lack of unanimity made themselves felt. Each group —opera, chorus, orchestra, and ballet—pursued its own interests. The opera performers insisted that ballet played an auxiliary role in the theater, while the ballet dancers demanded equality. This resulted in a lack of agreement on actions to be taken. Thus, during the performance on February 21, 1917, in the Maryinsky Theater, the chorus, demanding a salary increase, refused to sing; the soloists onstage whispered indistinctly, and the audience became upset. However, the dancers undermined the strike. "N. A. Malko stopped the orchestra, and the curtain came down, but before it had dropped was raised again. The orchestra again began to play, the dancers appeared . . . and the opera continued."[10]

During the first days of the February revolution performances were still given in the lyric theaters. The ballet La Source was performed on February 26 in the Maryinsky Theater; on the next day performances were discontinued. The news that the autocracy had been overthrown spread through Moscow on February 28. That was the day of the last performance at the "Imperial" Bolshoi Theater—Evgeny Onegin.

On March 1 all of theatrical Moscow came to a meeting in the building of the Nikitsky Theater. The slogan "freedom of art and autonomy for the theaters" was proposed. Notes appeared on the weekly schedule of the Bolshoi Theater for March 1 and 2 that were quite characteristic of the high-minded moods of the time: "No rehearsals took place as a result of the revolution. Bloodless revolution. Performance cancelled."[11] In both theaters there were no performances until March 12, the end of the seventh week of Lent.

An internal reorganization of the theaters was begun. In Petrograd on March 5, at a general meeting of the Maryinsky company, the first item of business was the election of a commission to review the internal organizational structure. Representatives of the ballet were Lidia Stepanova, Alexander Alexeyev, Boris Romanov, Pavel Petrov, Alexander Monakhov, and Alexander Chekrygin.[12] Later, other elected bodies were formed, commissions and committees whose structure changed frequently. At one time Tamara Karsavina was the chair of a committee; Romanov took an active part in the work; Fokine headed the repertory commission. But administrative power still remained in the hands of the director of the ballet, the untalented Nikolai Sergeyev, whose dictatorial ways had a long time ago earned him the dislike of the troupe.* In Moscow on March 10 Vasily Tikhomirov was elected head of the Bolshoi ballet company. Gorsky, Riabtsev, and Vladimir Kuznetsov also worked on the committee.

The Maryinsky Theater resumed performances on March 12. Before the beginning of the opera *A May Night* the chorus sang Tcherepnin's new "Do not weep over corpses" and then "Ei, ukhnem," ("Song of the Volga Boatmen"); Ivan Ershov read his poem "Freedom." "Eternal Memory" was performed in memory of those who had fallen, and the performance ended with "The Marseillaise."[13]

The Bolshoi Theater opened on March 13 with a ceremonial performance, for which Gorsky staged the allegorical *tableau vivant Liberated Russia* (text by Konstantin Balmont, music by Alexander Grechaninov). Around Russia, played by Alexandra Yablochkina, who stood dressed in a sarafan with a sheaf in her hands, were grouped famous historical figures of the past: writers (Pushkin, Gogol, Shevchenko), composers (Mussorgsky, Rimsky-Korsakov), revolutionaries (Lieutenant Schmidt, the Petrashevtsy, Sofia Perovskaya), and representatives of the nationalities that populate Russia.

Six days later, on March 19, the premiere of the first ballet produced after the February revolution took place in Moscow: a new version of *La Bayadère* by Gorsky. In the company, which was shaken up over the political events, every possible clash arose. Many opposed Gorsky's

---

*The discrepancy between Sergeyev's reputation in the West, where he is revered for having brought the Stepanov notations of the great ballet classics out of Russia and for staging them in their authentic versions (thus enriching the European repertory immeasurably), and in Russia, where he was despised, is striking. (Ed.)

innovations. As a result of the debate over his *Bayadère*, some of Gorsky's former supporters abandoned him. The split within the ballet troupe deepened.

Gorsky was always distant from politics. This had already become apparent during the revolution of 1905, when the balletmaster saw the excitement in the company only as a threat to his artistic plans. In the first months after the February revolution, also, he stayed in the background. At meetings (which in those days were held constantly and on any excuse) he did not make speeches, he did not organize sessions devoted to warrior-heroes or political prisoners, he did not get subscriptions for the so-called "Freedom Loan."* Despite all this, the future of the ballet, the course of its development under the new conditions, was of constant concern to Gorsky. He could not fail to think about those areas toward which the performer should direct his powers to justify the expectations of the mass audience which, eager for art, began to filter into the theaters after the February revolution and became their master after October.

In those days people were deeply interested in the problem of the "popular theater." In May 1917 Gorsky spoke about this subject with the Petrograd critic Alexander Pleshcheyev. To the question of whether he thought it conceivable that ballet could be popular theater, Gorsky answered "Not only is it conceivable, but also one's hope, because, of course, then ballet will be preserved." He rejected the necessity of creating a special repertory "for the people" and maintained that "the people will understand the general artistic repertory; they are not only interested in Russian fairytales." Summarizing Gorsky's statements, Pleshcheyev wrote:

> The art of choreography, which in our country was considered . . . an art for the elite of society, turned out to be radiant and clear for the people, which understands, values, and reacts to it. As long as model state theaters exist, the ballet will be preserved. . . . All theaters with an artistic repertory are popular theaters. Discussion as to what is useful for the people, what they will understand and what is incomprehensible—these are crafty arguments of the old regime.

---

*In May 1917 the government declared a Freedom Loan Day to raise money for the war debt. Among other activities, subscription drives were held at the theaters, and artists performed on stands built for the occasion. (Ed.)

. . . People will understand and will respond to everything that is artistic. . . . Popular theaters, if we must use this term, are theaters that are accessible in terms of price. . . . And there is no need to create artificially popular theaters.[14]

The 1916–17 season of the Maryinsky Theater ended on May 7. No new productions were presented; there were ballet performances honoring the victims of the revolution. The dancers' attention was devoted to administrative, financial, and management questions. Karsavina recalls that for the most part in those days she had to deal with questions of promotions.[15] Most theater people had a weak grasp of politics; welcoming the revolution enthusiastically, they considered that the overthrow of the autocracy had solved all problems and eliminated all contradictions. An eyewitness to the events, Maryinsky dancer Nikolai Soliannikov, described the mood of the troupe: "One could say 'revolution,' 'freedom,' and even sing 'Dubinushka' unrestrainedly. Therefore, the artists did not plunge into the substance of the revolution and of all those 'freedoms.' " [16]

Meanwhile, it was quickly becoming clear that after the February revolution not much had changed in the former Imperial Theaters. The tendency toward the restoration of the "Imperial" system of theater management and toward the destruction of the theaters' promised autonomy was becoming increasingly obvious; on April 28 this brought on a strike in the Bolshoi Theater. Before the beginning of the opera *Prince Igor* the entire company as well as the production and technical personnel came out onto the stage and announced to the audience that the performance was cancelled. Representatives of the theater expressed their disappointment in the press as well. Their dreams of restructuring the company, reorganizing the studios, and forming a mobile troupe that would tour the country still remained dreams.[17] The audience also changed little, since the cost of tickets remained the same. In Moscow, the last ballet performance of the season, *La Fille mal gardée* with Geltser, took place on May 6 in a half-empty hall, and the newspapers pointed out that the reason for this was the high price of tickets.

In Petrograd a struggle was going on within the ballet company between the supporters of Fokine, who hoped that thanks to the revolution he would head the troupe, and the choreographer's opponents. Taking advantage of the fact that Fokine had fallen ill and had remained in Kislovodsk until after the beginning of the season, his foes published a note on "ballet deserters" in the *Petrogradskaya gazeta*.[18] Karsavina wrote a defense of Fokine, but the opposition was still strong, for after the events of February the administrators—above all, Sergeyev—continued to be people who had long been in conflict with Fokine. Among the artists and critics there were also quite a few people who did not accept Fokine's innovations. The place of Samuil Andrianov, who had died at the beginning of September, on the theater committee was filled by Yosif Kschessinsky, who even before the revolution had severely criticized Fokine in the press.

The October Revolution broke out. The Maryinsky Theater gave its last performance on October 27; then the Bolshoi Theater also closed. The artists, bewildered by the events that had taken place, met in the theater and signed resolutions expressing indignation at such "means of political struggle" as the firing on the Moscow Kremlin, the seizure of the Maly Theater by the Red Guard, and the appointment of Commissars for the Theaters. The artists of the Bolshoi Theater wrote:

> Aware that we are part of a great democracy, and grieving deeply over the spilled blood of our brothers, we protest against the violent vandalism that has not even spared the ancient holy of holies of the Russian people, the temples and monuments of art and culture. The State Moscow Bolshoi Theater, as an autonomous artistic institution, does not recognize the right of interference in its internal and artistic life by any authorities whatever who have not been elected by the theater and are not on its staff.[19]

It took several efforts by the representatives of the People's Commissariat—Anatoly Lunacharsky and Elena Malinovskaya—to set up contacts with the theaters. In part they were aided by direct dealings with the artists, bypassing those offices that served as a center of organized sabotage. Lunacharsky's letters calling on theater people not to yield to counter-revolutionary agitation and to find a common language with the new master of the country—the working people—are well-known.

In Moscow Elena Malinovskaya led meetings with the artists. Here this whole process took place somewhat faster than in Petrograd. The Bolshoi Theater began working normally on November 21, 1917 (old style). In the Maryinsky Theater, after a temporary restoration of order, disturbances again broke out at the end of November. The process of breaking down the entire managerial bureaucratic apparatus was taking place, and this led to a splintering of the company. Refusing to recognize the authority of the newly-created Commissariat of Education (*Narkompros*), under whose jurisdiction the theaters henceforth would be, some of the artists refused to perform. This sabotage continued until January 1918. Moreover, the opera, the orchestra, and the chorus showed the firmest resistance. A pitched battle went on in their very midst, and this time the struggle was in fact political. Part of the opera company was opposed to resuming performances, but a group of supporters of the new regime also emerged: The conductor Nikolai Malko; Meyerhold, who at the time was directing at the Maryinsky Theater; and a number of singers. The ballet observed a certain neutrality, and in January 1918, while the opera and chorus were again on strike, dance performances were going on fairly regularly.

On January 25, 1918, the first "popular performance" took place—the opera *Ruslan and Ludmila*. The press noted that "for the first time within the walls of the Maryinsky Theater an audience composed of representatives of the people was assembled. . . . The first step on the way to the democratization . . . of the theater has been taken."[20] Fokine's dances for the opera, which had been shown for the first time shortly before, on November 27, 1917, were very successful. This was the last ballet staged by the choreographer in his homeland.

During the first months after the resumption of performances the ballet was in great demand by the audience. This is shown by a refutation by the Department of State Theaters sent to the newspaper *Novye vedomosti* on March 30, 1918: "The afore-mentioned reduction does not correspond to the truth, for the ballet performances are sold out."[21]

Even the openly malevolent comments of the regular reviewer for the newspaper *Vechernie ogni*, Konstantin Ostrozhsky, reveal the changes in the audiences at the ballet. He squeamishly describes the atmosphere at the performances in the Maryinsky Theater. "The boxes remind one of Jewish carriages on a day at the bazaar. The gallery blackens, like a half-eaten piece of watermelon thickly covered with flies." But despite all his contempt for the new audience, "accustomed to balalaika songs from a coach house and a record player in a tearoom,"[22] the critic involuntarily drew a picture of people sincerely attracted to an art they had never seen before: "The non-subscription public, which packed the theater to overflowing, applauded and howled with such violence that all the old theater rats scurried off in horror to the snuggest little holes."[23]

For many this was something unexpected. Pleshcheyev, the senior St. Petersburg ballet critic, frankly admitted in March 1918: "This season I considered as a question of 'to be or not to be?' for the ballet. The question of whether the ballet would survive on the state stage or would be wiped out as an amusement and caprice of its elect admirers, was in the air of the theater. The new audience, the masses who flocked to the ballet after its liberation from the subscribers, took a definite stand: It valued the ballet and chose it as an accessible art. . . . The popular audience is sensitive, responsive, and perceptive."[24]

Despite the difficulties caused by the civil war and accompanying hardships, during the first years after the October Revolution performances in the lyric theaters continued uninterrupted. They even increased: Instead of forty or fifty ballet performances, in 1919–20 there were sixty or even seventy. This required enormous efforts on the part of the entire ballet company. In winter there was insufficient fuel, and the stage was so cold that steam poured out of the dancers' mouths. There were no ballet shoes, and the ballerinas, accustomed to changing slippers after each act, danced up to fourteen performances in a single pair. Everyone was undernourished, and many fell ill. And though "this continued for several years, . . . at eight o'clock the curtain never failed to rise in a single academic theater."[25]

The victory over the White Guard and foreign armies was won at the cost of enormous sacrifices. The transition to peacetime life also was accomplished under conditions of the most severe crisis. The solution for the country turned out to be the introduction in spring 1921 of the New Economic Policy (NEP).*

This very quickly made itself felt in the theaters. The state subsidies to the Bolshoi and the former Maryinsky Theaters were sharply cut back. In June 1921 the directors of the Bolshoi Theater wrote to Lunacharsky regarding the right of the collective to state assistance:

The management of the Bolshoi Theater, tirelessly fighting against the destructive spirit of bureaucracy, an unfortunate legacy of the

---

*The New Economic Policy (NEP) allowed limited capitalism, including freedom of trade, overtime and piece work, the encouragement of foreign business, and a reinstatement of private property. (Ed.)

past of this former Imperial Theater, has striven to carefully preserve and increase its precious resources in order to protect its best artistic traditions. . . . In the Russian ballet, which rightfully enjoys worldwide fame, a place of honor belongs to the ballet of the Bolshoi Theater. The management of the theater has been concerned that this ballet, to which a new audience has shown great attention and interest, remain on an appropriately high level . . .[26]

In summer 1921 a financial crisis broke out (money was no longer paid out to all the institutions) and the theaters found themselves in serious trouble. A strike caused by nonpayment of salaries and difficult material conditions broke out in the Bolshoi Theater just before the season began. As a result, the presidium of the Moscow State Council of Trade Unions (MGSPS) categorically insisted on closing the theater. It was difficult for Lunacharsky to settle the conflict; his arguments with the MGSPS are elucidated in detail in *Izvestia* during November 1921.

At that time the country was only just learning how to run the economy—precisely the task which Lenin put in the forefront of his speech to the Ninth All-Russian Congress of Soviets in December 1921. A restructuring of the entire state and economic machinery was taking place; there was even a special column in the newspapers called "Review of Soviet Institutions." The work of the opera and ballet theaters was also discussed in this connection.

On December 9, 1921, a public debate took place in the Central Theatrical Division regarding the lyric theaters, at which the director of the Bolshoi Theater, Malinovskaya, told in detail the difficulties the theater had endured and would continue to endure, and the goals that stood before her: "To preserve as much as possible the quality of the treasures we still have . . . to heighten the intensity of our work, to bring the repertory closer to the audience that should fill the theaters, and to make those theaters considerably more accessible."[27]

Speaking at that time at a discussion in the Polytechnical Museum, Lunacharsky posed the question of wise and foolish economy. The Bolshoi Theater "costs one million two hundred thousand rubles. After all, that is twenty thousand in gold. One can figure out how many paltry teachers' salaries that adds up to. But if you took that point of view, then you would have to close every single museum—every cultural institution." He cited the following figures: The Bolshoi Theater had created a deficit fifteen times less than the Tsarist theater and at the same time the price of tickets had decreased fivefold. "If you said to some Teliakovsky,* 'Can things be run so as to decrease the entrance price five times and at the same time decrease the deficit fifteen times?'—he would laugh. Yet we have done 'the impossible.'"[28] Moreover, closing the theater meant paying compensation to those who were fired, and also costs of guarding the building and heating to protect the property from plunder and decay; consequently, the money saved would have been wiped out. Passionately upholding the inexpediency of closing the Bolshoi Theater, at the beginning of January 1922 Lunacharsky pushed, with some difficulty, a proposal for preserving this theater through the Soviet People's Commissariat. From January to March 1922 the decision was revoked on Lenin's demand and then was discussed anew, until finally on March 13, 1922, the *Politburo* issued a final decree: "To satisfy the request of VTSIK (All-Union Central Executive Committee)" considering the closing of the Bolshoi Theater "economically inexpedient."[29]

Interesting figures, which to a great extent confirm Lunacharsky's statement regarding the degree to which expenses for state theaters had decreased during the Soviet period, were published in the *Ezhenedelnik petrogradskikh gosudarstvennykh akademicheskikh teatrov (Weekly of the Petrograd State Academic Theaters)*, no. 8, 1922: During 1913–16 the yearly deficit was 1,087,610 gold rubles, and from 1918–22 it was 119,435 gold rubles—the deficit decreased more than ninefold. Lunacharsky specifically called Lenin's attention to these figures. On November 8, 1922, he wrote to Lenin: "I earnestly ask you to take at least a glance at the enclosed book, which is a report of five years' work by the Petrograd State Theaters. Also enclosed are materials describing the unusually broad way these theaters have served the proletariat."[30]

In the fall of 1922 the question of the Bolshoi and the former Maryinsky theaters was once again discussed by the Party Central Committee. On October 26 the *Politburo* adopted a resolution regarding cutbacks of state subsidies to the *Proletkult* and state theaters. On November 16 the *Politburo* confirmed the "draft of a mandate to Comrade Kolegayev." It was necessary to "implement the decree reducing the subsidies to state theaters by 350 million a year, giving Comrade Kolegayev by a special

---

*Teliakovsky was the former director of the Imperial Theaters. (Ed.)

mandate of the Presidium of VTSIK the right to undertake those measures he deems necessary for carrying out this task, even including the closing of the Bolshoi and Maryinsky Theaters and the reorganization of the management of those theaters, with the goal of cutting back on expenditures and increasing income, attracting private capital, etc."[31]

Anxious, Lunacharsky again appealed to Lenin for support.[32] Nevertheless, Kolegayev, who had received the full right to undertake any measures—"even including the closing of the theaters"—chose that very course; on November 17, 1922, the artists of the Bolshoi Theater, who had shown up for work, read an announcement posted in the wings that made clear that, starting the first of December, they could consider themselves released from their jobs in the theater. A delegation of performers succeeded in being received by Mikhail Kalinin.*[33] On November 22 the same news came to Petrograd. The manager of the Petrograd State Theaters, I. V. Exkusovich, "communicated the sad news that subsidies to the academic theaters were cut back by the center from 28 million rubles in 1922 to 17 million rubles, which raised the question of closing the former Maryinsky Theater."[34] Vladimir Nemirovich-Danchenko† came out in defense of the Bolshoi Theater. On November 22 he sent a letter to Malinovskaya, the director of the Bolshoi, in which he wrote that closing the Bolshoi would be an irreparable misfortune "which could irrevocably destroy one of the most outstanding, richest institutions of Russian culture."[35]

This question was finally resolved in December 1922 when the management of the theaters made a statement that it "took on itself the commitment to continue administering activities of the academic theaters, given cutbacks in subsidies by the State."[36]

We have deliberately dwelt in such detail on events in the life of the lyric theaters at the end of the first five years of their existence under Soviet power. The threat of closing the institutions, which once again arose

---

*Kalinin was the chairman of the Central Executive Committee (TSIK). (Ed.)

†Vladimir Nemirovich-Danchenko was a teacher and director in the theater. Among his students were Olga Knipper, Vsevolod Meyerhold, and Evgeny Vakhtangov. With Stanislavsky, he co-founded the legendary Moscow Art Theater, where he served as dramaturg and encouraged Chekhov and other playwrights. In the early 1920s he founded the Moscow Art Musical Studio. (Ed.)

after the theaters had managed to survive for a number of years under the more difficult conditions of the Civil War, attests to the fact that the reasons that gave rise to this threat were not only of a financial nature.

During the 1921–22 season the Bolshoi and the former Maryinsky theaters were subject to extremely harsh criticism. This is clear from materials on the discussion concerning the lyric theaters and from the press. "Yet Once More Regarding the Bourgeois Heritage" is the title of an article in which the magazine *Vestnik teatra* expressed its attitude toward academic ballet.[37] "Should the Bolshoi Theater Exist?" was the title of Leonid Sabaneyev's article that expressed the opinion that this theater had already died in the prerevolutionary period.[38] "Is the Bolshoi Theater Necessary?" asked the critic of *Teatralnoe obozrenie*.[39]

In Petrograd the situation was even more complicated. Here the ballet was subject to attack from two sides. It was criticized for backwardness, and those who did not believe in the possibilities of renewing the genre devoted ironic obituaries to it:[40] "The ballet is not sick . . . it is senile. Classical ballet as a form has become obsolete."[41] The ballet was attacked on the other side by the supporters of classic dance headed by Akim Volynsky. It was not just legitimate concern over a drop in the level of the prime Russian ballet company that brought on a torrent of critical articles, which appeared in 1920–22 in the Petrograd press. Any moves by the new management of the ballet were subject to sharp criticism, because the company was not headed by those whom the critics would have preferred.

The threat of closing the theaters was finally set aside in 1922 through a number of administrative and financial measures (reduction of production costs, cuts in credits for repairs, raising ticket prices, et cetera).[42] But it was clear that even more intensive work was demanded of the theaters, above all a renewal of the repertory.

In the Bolshoi Theater such a restructuring had already begun during the 1921–22 season. Concert performances were regularly given in the Beethoven Hall, and performances in the Hall of the House of Unions included ballet. At the end of 1921 the New Theater was opened; it allowed for an increase in the number of new productions. The repertory of the New Theater showed that its staging was somewhat experimental. "The New Theater is indispensable . . . as a laboratory for the Bolshoi," wrote Malinovskaya.[43] Here the operas *Manon*, which previously had not been in the repertory of the Bolshoi, *La Bohème*, which had been performed infrequently, and, later, productions by Stanislavsky's studio, such as *Evgeny Onegin* and *Werther*, were staged. During the first season, the ballets *La Fille mal gardée*, The *Nutcracker* (in a new production), *Love is Quick!*, and *Stenka Razin*, which had not been performed since 1918, were transferred here. Finally, in the fall of 1922 *Ever-Fresh Flowers* was presented, the first ballet on a contemporary theme.

In a letter to Lenin dated November 10 Lunacharsky set forth as the main argument in defense of the Bolshoi Theater the creation by the company of a "children's revolutionary ballet." He wrote: "Perhaps having seen with your own eyes the significance of this theater, which my colleagues and I have saved, and how it has moved in the direction of serving the revolution, you will understand with what deep sorrow we react to the current attempt to strangle it."[44]

By the end of the first five years after the October Revolution the Petrograd ballet had also begun to summon its strength. The stage finally hosted productions that had been planned as far back as 1917, such as Stravinsky's *Petrushka* (1920) and *The Firebird* (staged by Lopukhov, 1921). The full-length ballet *Solveig* (1922), to the music of Edvard Grieg, was rather disappointing but served as the basis for a truly important work, Lopukhov's *The Ice Maiden* (1927). The revival of old ballets was encouraged. Starting in 1921 a program of reviving the best ballets of the past, whose choreography had become distorted over the years, was begun. This work was done by Lopukhov with the assistance of the dancers of the older generation.

On October 23, 1922, the first open meeting of the ballet company took place in the building of the Petrograd Museum of State Academic Theaters. Representatives of other theaters and of the Theater School, the press, and the public also were present. "The organizers of this meeting wished to give a wide range of information, both to the artists themselves and to all interested in the fate of Russian ballet, on the present state of choreography and through an exchange of opinions arrive at a clear understanding of the true artistic level of our ballet, in light of persistent attacks and sharp, biased criticism by the press."[45]

After a thorough report by Leonid Leontiev, with additional explanation by I. V. Exkusovich, the head of the state theaters, most of those present expressed support for the policy of the theater management.

The *Ezhenedelnik* published in its November anniversary issue the declaration "Goals and Objectives of the State Academic Ballet." It stated that the ballet, "following the course of its natural and legitimate evolution" must "be in a position to meet the needs and demands of contemporary art."[46]

After the end of the civil war a new stage of development began in the Soviet theater. By this time the composition of the ballet company had stabilized and a considerable number of young people had joined it.[47] Work had become more intense;[48] people capable of taking on administrative leadership had been found. The danger of losing the valuable heritage of the past had been averted; the best ballets were regularly performed. And most important, in both Moscow and Petrograd innovative artists had appeared, possessed by a thirst for creation, who sought new content and new forms.

Boris Georgievich Romanov

The 1917–18 season did not see any new productions in Moscow or Petrograd. Concern over administrative and political questions and also economic difficulties pushed purely artistic problems into the background. This seriously disturbed such artists as Gorsky and Fokine. Fokine had long been well known in foreign theaters, where he had worked before the war. He had been repeatedly invited to Sweden for a production of *Petrushka*. And now, without waiting for the end of the season, in the very beginning of March 1918, when life in the Maryinsky Theater was just starting to settle down, Fokine left for Stockholm. He had planned to return by fall, but the beginning of the civil war upset his plans. Later, circumstances were such that the choreographer ended up permanently cut off from Russia.

The new ballet season in the Maryinsky Theater had already begun without Fokine. Yet the management considered that it was he who headed the company. In an interview published in December 1918 the chairman of the ballet company's committee, Leonid Leontiev, said, "Our main problem is that with Fokine abroad we are left without a choreographer. We have concluded a contract with the composer Tcherepnin to stage his ballet *Narcisse et Echo*. The ballet (music) is wonderful; but alas, there is no one to stage it! Our *Petrushka* is quite ready, but again, because of Fokine's absence we cannot stage it."[1] The same interview mentioned the postponement of the premiere of Boris Romanov's *Solveig*.

At that time Romanov was working actively outside of the Maryinsky Theater. Newspapers mentioned his name in connection with a production of *Oedipus the King*, by Yuri Yuriev, shown May 21–27, 1918, in the Ciniselli Circus. But apparently this collaboration did not actually take place; during the rehearsals (May 14–20) Romanov was on a trip to Moscow and during the play's run the choreographer and his wife, Elena Smirnova, gave a concert in the Maly Hall of the Petrograd Conservatory. When in June 1918 the so-called "Comradeship of Labor" was formed to manage the Theater of Tragedy, which had been designed to continue the work begun by Yuriev in *Oedipus the King*, Romanov was included in it, possibly at the suggestion of Boris Asafiev, who had worked a great deal with him.

Asafiev wrote the music for *Oedipus the King* and for *Macbeth*, the first production of the Theater of Tragedy, performed on August 23, 1918, in the Ciniselli Circus. Romanov was co-director, with the stage director Alexei Granovsky, and, according to the memoirs of Yuriev, staged the mass scenes.[2] The poster for the premiere stated "Stage movement by B. G. Romanov." Alexander Kugel commented on the choreographer's work: "The groupings, like everything B. G. Romanov has a hand in, were very good. The circus arena provided a great deal of space, and there were some interesting toad-like jumps by the witches."[3]

The choreographer's inclination toward the grotesque made itself felt here, too. Yuriev describes the witches' appearance thus:

At first they all sprawled and crept along the ground, huddling tightly against each other in a solid mass, barely moving, like a curled-up octopus. But gradually their individual features emerged. First just one bare arm of the first witch was raised. The crooked wrist and bent fingers looked like tentacles, gloating in anticipation over their victim. Then she straightens up to full height and before you is a dried-up, hideous old woman in gray rags with long, matted hair bristling messily in all directions. And to top it all off—a beard.[4]

Romanov was also involved with the Theater of Artistic Drama, which opened in 1918. He staged the dances to Asafiev's music in Tirso de Molina's comedy *El Burlador de Sevilla y convidado de piedra*. After the merger of the Theater of Tragedy with the Theater of Artistic Drama and the formation of the Grand Dramatic Theater (GDT), this collaboration continued. *Macbeth* was included in the GDT repertory; in 1919 Romanov took part in staging Shakespeare's *Much Ado About Nothing* and then Arvid Järnefelt's *The Destroyer of Jerusalem* (in the former he worked with the composer Yuri Shaporin and in the latter with Asafiev). Artists from the Maryinsky Theater appeared in the dances; the Nubian dance in *The Destroyer of Jerusalem* was performed by Smirnova, and Romanov himself performed in the bacchanale of the third act (to the music of Charles Gounod). The critics praised his choreography.

Romanov's popularity grew quickly. He was invited to work in other theaters as well: In July 1919 he was asked by the Bolshoi Kommunalny (Communal) Theater to stage "Walpurgisnacht" in *Faust*, and in October he was invited to join Sergei Radlov, who was staging Vasily Kamensky's *Stenka Razin* at the Theater of the Baltic Fleet for the second anniversary of the October Revolution. With Olga Preobrajenska, Romanov took part in organizing the Union of Ballet Artists and with Asafiev and Smirnova he organized the ballet studio of the Section on Theatrical Education. Mikhail Kuzmin noted the participation of "the tireless Romanov" in a program at The Comedians' Rest.[*][5]

Romanov was also building a new concert repertory. On May 26, 1918, Romanov and Smirnova presented an evening of work including *Warrior (Pyrrhic Dance)*, choreographed to a Rachmaninov prelude. "His warrior of antiquity, armed with sword and spear, fighting for his fatherland and dying on the battlefield, captivated the audience," wrote the critic of the *Novaya petrogradskaya gazeta*.[6] At the same concert Smirnova danced *The Swan Princess* to Tchaikovsky. "The costume, with its wings around the arms (designed by Dobujinsky), carried the viewer off into the realm of a fantasy by Vrubel.[†] There was something sinister in the bends and *terre-à-terre* poses of the ballerina."[7] Smirnova also performed *The Ice Maiden* to the music of Edvard Grieg. Another concert by Smirnova and Romanov took place on the stage of the Grand Dramatic Theater on June 10, 1919. The correspondent for *Zhizn iskusstva* wrote that "the 'core' of the ele-

---

[*]The Comedians' Rest was an artists' cabaret. (Ed.)

[†]Mikhail Vrubel (1856–1910), the influential Russian painter, was well-known for his satanic themes. He designed the decors and costumes for several operas, including four by Rimsky-Korsakov, at Mamontov's Moscow Private Opera. Theatrical images and characters pervade his paintings and other art works—notably the Ostrovsky-Rimsky-Korsakov *Snow Maiden* and the Swan Princess from Rimsky-Korsakov's *Tale of Tsar Saltan*. (Ed.)

gant program . . . was Glazunov's *Dance of Salomé*, staged for the first time by Romanov."[8] Glazunov himself conducted.*

And yet such random, haphazard work—mostly outside the professional ballet stage—could not satisfy the choreographer, whose ambition was to stage full ballet productions. He prepared a one-act ballet, *La Carmagnole*, with Asafiev for the first anniversary of the October Revolution but was able to perform it only on the stage of a workers' club to a piano accompaniment. The ballet *Our Lady's Juggler* (based on Anatole France's story), which he planned with Shaporin, was not produced. The production of *The Choice of a Bride* with music by Kuzmin, which was to be danced by the artists of the Maryinsky Theater, was announced but never staged.

The spirit at the Maryinsky Theater was dull. Romanov was valued there and in spring 1919 was even elected to the administration. But for the most part he had to work on reviving old ballets choreographed by others. His only new ballet consisted of dances to a pastorale by Gluck, *The Queen of the May* (1919). The premiere of *Solveig* was put off from month to month and work on a new version of *Swan Lake* with decor by Dobujinsky was not even begun.

Earlier, in 1918, Romanov had intended to move to Moscow. He began with a visiting tournée. In spring, in the Zon Theater, he presented *Andalusiana, Gudal's Feast* (to Anton Rubinstein's music from the opera *The Demon*), and also a concert program with Smirnova, a number of dancers from the Maryinsky Theater, and the Moscow corps de ballet. The performances received good reviews. Lev Nikulin described *Andalusiana* as a "triumph,"[9] and Nikolai Zborovsky wrote: "Looking at the animated faces of the Spanish gypsies, it was hard to believe that these were the familiar, usually so inert dancers of the Bolshoi Theater corps de ballet."[10] In June, Romanov again came to Moscow for talks about performances at the Aquarium Theater; in addition to *Andalusiana, The Dream of Pierrot*, with Smirnova and the Moscow dancer Laurent Novikov, was proposed. At the same time, talks were held with the Bolshoi Theater, but they were unsuccessful. Yuri Bakhrushin wrote on June 16, 1918, to the Petrograd ballet critic Denis Leshkov: "According to the rumors I hear, Bobisha

---

*Romanov had choreographed *The Tragedy of Salomé* in 1912, to music by Florent Schmitt, for Diaghilev, with whose company he danced 1910–14. (Ed.)

did not sign a contract—a pity! Both for him and for Moscow." And, apparently thinking of Romanov's dissatisfaction with his work on the small stages of Petrograd and his plans to leave, Bakhrushin added: "And the 'stray dog' is in danger of becoming homeless, if not a dead dog!"[11]

Romanov did not stay in Moscow. But the Moscow trip was extremely significant for him. In Moscow's Literary-Theatrical Museum of the Russian Academy of Sciences, Romanov became acquainted with Petipa's archives, which for him shed new light on the choreographer's art. Bakhrushin wrote to Leshkov: "Yesterday I spent the entire evening, the entire night in the Museum digging in Petipa's archives with Bobisha Romanov, and we found truly fascinating material whose existence I had not suspected. For example, we found an enormous 'dossier' on the staging of *The Sleeping Beauty*. The tiniest details of the ballet had been carefully noted down by Marius Ivanovich . . . Bobisha was ecstatic and filled half a notebook with references."[12]

Romanov expanded on his study of the Petipa archives in his article "A Dancer's Notes":

> The choreographer is like a composer. He must compose great numbers of choreographic themes that can develop in accordance with the nature of the dance and the musical rhythms, forming an entire gamut of consistent movements. . . . In Petipa's papers we find many pages of geometric designs in his own hand—circles, pyramids, ellipses, multigons, triangles, et cetera. These drawings clearly show us the great creative process of a choreographer at work beyond the limits of the stage. This means that the artist, already inspired by the musical themes of the dance, composed dance themes in front of a mirror, that is, made up the steps and then, with a pencil, created the designs for the choral movements.[13]

These notes bear witness to an emergence of interest in problems of pure dance expression. Romanov, famous for expressive dances in which the illustrative element predominated, felt an attraction to other dance forms; that is, not to forms based on human, real-life movements— even if they were theatricalized, amplified, and intensely performed— but rather to movements that were abstracted from life, generalized, and made into a dance melody analogous to a musical melody.

At the same time work was proceeding on *Solveig* to the music of

Edvard Grieg. As the proposed choreographer, Romanov worked together with Andrei Shaikevich and Piotr Potemkin in writing the scenario, which was finished by the end of 1917. At the beginning of 1918
Asafiev selected and orchestrated the music and Romanov listened to it
and gave his opinion.[14] Alexander Golovine was very active in the preparations for the production.

Romanov's *Solveig* expressed a search for a different path than the one
followed on the eve of the revolution. The full-length ballet, built on
juxtapositions between classical and character acts, differed from the picturesque miniatures of Fokine and were closer to the structure of the
"grand" ballets of Petipa. Classical dance was to have been the major
means of characterization. Shaikevich, recalling Smirnova's performance
of the concert piece *The Ice Maiden*, which doubtless was a sketch for the
future ballet, wrote: "In this *Solveig* one sees supreme virginity, the highest achievement and tension of classical dance, its frozen transparency,
and its brilliant dissolution into the pathos of moral ideas."[15]

Leshkov notes that during these years Romanov was thinking about
the expressiveness of dance movement per se and was creating "dance
without music, décor, and even the conventional costume." In the critic's
opinion, "his idea is interesting, . . . however, it was not successful."[16]
The turning point in the choreographer's consciousness was also noted
somewhat later by Shaikevich, who was closely linked to Romanov's foreign troupe. "Fokine's precepts, which at one time were so fused with
his entire being, have now been pushed into the background. He is concerned neither with the clarity of naturalistic, exotic movements, nor
with a psychological solution in the scheme of the dance, nor with the
complexity and intensity of the music. . . . For him dance is a symphony
of rhythm, movement, and expression."[17]

There is a certain logic in Romanov's "metamorphosis." Most followers
of Fokine, having mastered his achievements, sooner or later became
convinced that it was necessary to transcend the limits of his reforms.
Vaslav Nijinsky went from mere description to a clarifying of the inner
essence behind appearances, guided by the new painting of the French
Post-Impressionists. In their own ways, Goleizovsky and Lopukhov
transformed the "Fokinesque" element. At first Romanov was clearly attracted to Expressionism, but then he made a shift; perhaps this was due
to the influence of Asafiev, who in these years had devoted quite a lot of

effort to the study of Tchaikovsky and Glazunov, or perhaps it was due to the ideas of the Grand Dramatic Theater, "a theater of high drama: high tragedy and high comedy," which considered its repertory as "a great school of noble will, musical will, which could help rally, organize, and put in order the externally and internally diffuse, lax people of our time."[18]

One can only guess what *Solveig* would have brought Romanov, for it was finally staged several years later, by others. In January 1920 a note appeared in the press that "the choreographer B. G. Romanov has resigned his duties as manager of the ballet company of the Maryinsky Theater." At the same time there were reports that his wife, Smirnova, planned to join the troupe of the Bolshoi Theater. Romanov and Smirnova went to Moscow, but did not stay there long. During the summer of 1920 news came of their tour to the Ukraine, to Nikolayev, Kherson, and Odessa. In 1921 they performed in the Opera Theater in Bucharest, and the following year they settled in Berlin. Here Romanov organized a troupe with a telling name—the Russian Romantic Theater.

Ballet had almost ceased in postwar Germany. Shortly after the war a new tendency was born, and in the 1920s it began to develop rapidly; it was given the name "expressive" or "new artistic" dance (*Ausdruckstanz*, *Neue künstlerische Tanz*). Its theoretician was Rudolf von Laban, and its most distinguished representative Mary Wigman; both of them had numerous followers. The art of the German dancers was linked to Expressionism. They did not seek beauty and harmony in dance, and they rejected the traditional forms of classical dance, considering them unsuitable for the expression of that intensity of experience to which these artists aspired. Tension, convulsive movements, and an exalted pantomime were their method. Their favorite themes were fear and suffering, despair and death. Most of the dancers of this school gravitated toward social themes, making use of sarcasm, the grotesque, and caricature to criticize contemporary society.

Romanov himself was no stranger to this kind of quest. But despite all the high-strung emotional excitement of his ballets, they were based on that academic school without which the art of any ballet artist—classical or character—is unthinkable. The resources of the academic ballet are so enormous that each protestant and reformer, having recovered from the disease of total abnegation, sooner or later becomes convinced of the value of its traditions. The fact that he returns to them enriched by his quest and thus enriching the tradition itself is another matter. Therefore, paradoxical as it may seem, when Romanov found himself in Germany and truly in touch with Expressionism in dance, he adopted a totally contradictory position at first. The critics saw the Romantic Theater as a reaction against "world pessimism" and "naturalism"[19] and described its goal as follows: "Its motto is not adaptation to the rhythm of the contemporary world, not a play for vulgar and easy laughs . . . but a renascence of that fragile and at the same time powerful world-view that has been cruelly strangled by years of struggle and violence—Romanticism."[20]

The Russian Romantic Theater included in its repertory *Harlequinade; The Boyar's Wedding*, an ethnographic production with sets by Pavel Tchelitchev; *Giselle* (in a cut version); *The Queen of the May*; and a number of Romanov's Petrograd productions (*Andalusiana, Gudal's Feast, Dance of the Warrior*, and others). Among the new productions were two with music by Prokofiev: *Trapeze*, on circus life, and a dance suite.

In 1923–24 the troupe travelled through Europe and performed in Paris in April 1924 in the Théâtre des Champs-Élysées, where Diaghilev's Ballets Russes held its season in May and June, featuring new works by Bronislava Nijinska, *Les Biches* and *Le Train bleu*. As Serge Grigoriev, régisseur of Diaghilev's group, recalls, "Though this season of ours in Paris met with an appreciative response from the public, Diaghilev began at this time to be more and more frequently attacked for deflecting the ballet from its proper course. He was reproached for abandoning the classical tradition."[21] The Paris correspondent of the journal *Novy zritel* wrote of Romanov's troupe: "As opposed to most Russian émigré ballet companies, the Romantics do not take up the latest art, but rather gravitate toward tradition and academicism."[22]

It should not be thought, however, that the evolution of Romanov's creative work was exhausted with his return to Romanticism. The ballets he created during the course of the next thirty years bear witness to the struggles between different aspirations. The line of *Andalusiana* was reborn in *Amor brujo* (music by Manuel de Falla), a ballet that made Romanov famous in Spain and Latin America. This was only natural, since he lived for several years in Argentina, where from 1928 to 1934 he staged exotic, dynamic folkloric ballets. Stravinsky's *Pulcinella* and Prokofiev's *Chout* were doubtless in keeping with his inclination toward comedy and the grotesque. Romanov also worked with Anna Pavlova's troupe, in Milan's La Scala, and in Yugoslavia. He composed new works and revived old ones, including Tchaikovsky's ballets. But the individual details of the descriptions of his ballets reveal Romanov's earlier biases. Thus *The Nutcracker* (1936), in the words of one viewer, the French ballet historian Pierre Michaut, opened with a prologue in which the sorcerer Drosselmeyer was "studying the secrets of children's souls in his laboratory." The guests at the Christmas party "were shown in caricature." The artist Alexei Alexeyev, the creator of several puppet films, was invited by Romanov to make the heavy masks and costumes, cut as though intended for wooden marionettes. "The whole ballet had a burlesque tone," wrote Michaut.[23]

In the 1940s Boris Romanov settled in the United States.* He died in New York on January 30, 1957.

Leonid Sergeyevich Leontiev and
Alexander Ivanovich Chekrygin

After Romanov's departure in January 1920 Leonid Leontiev was appointed head of the ballet company. A student of the Petersburg Theater School, starting in 1903 Leontiev was a dancer at the Maryinsky Theater, playing comic and character roles. A participant in the first seasons of Diaghilev's Ballets Russes, he was well acquainted not only with the traditional repertory of the Maryinsky Theater, but also with Fokine's ballets. Therefore, when after the revolution it was necessary to reconstruct and rehearse a number of old ballets, Leontiev was brought in.

Leontiev's first significant work in the theater was a restaging of Fokine's *Petrushka* (the premiere was on November 20, 1920). When it became clear after Fokine's two-year absence that there was no sense in waiting for his return, it was decided that the ballet would be put on by the company without him. One of Fokine's coauthors, Alexandre Benois, was at that time a member of the administration of the former Maryinsky Theater; of course, his participation was not limited to merely creating the sets. Leontiev relied on Benois's advice in restaging the ballet

---

*In the United States, Romanov choreographed at the Metropolitan Opera House and for various ballet companies, and he taught in New York at the School of Ballet Repertory. (Ed.)

and tried to revive the production, which he remembered from Paris, as exactly as possible.

The very fact that *Petrushka* appeared on the Russian stage was considered a great event bearing witness to the fact that the Petrograd ballet was once again gathering strength. The critics reacted positively to Leontiev's staging and to his performance in the role of Petrushka. The spirit and style of Fokine's production were preserved, and yet the ballet of 1920 was not merely a copy of the Paris one. Asafiev wrote: "In the details of the production and particularly the working out of the next to last scene (the mummers and the revellers' dance) . . . Leontiev invented witty and intriguingly innovative combinations of dance rhythms without losing the integrity of the structure."[24] André Levinson characterizes these scenes as "a dance *lubok** with comically stressed accents and broken movements."[25] By working out the details of mass scenes in his own style, to a certain extent Leontiev moved away from stylized refinement toward a greater, life-like authenticity. There was a cruder look, and in some ways the ballet was more down-to-earth. This was also brought about by Leontiev's interpretation of the character Petrushka. Asafiev considered it an achievement that Leontiev was able to "preserve himself, his 'ego,' in creating a unique personality for Petrushka, which was unforgettable and impossible to ignore, despite the striking contrast between this character and the one formed in Fokine's imagination." The performer's appearance—his short height, his face with high cheekbones, short pug nose, and bulging eyes, as well as his age (Leontiev had been dancing for nearly twenty years) predicated a different interpretation of the character than that presented by Nijinsky. Describing Leontiev's performance, Levinson wrote (in the article cited above): "There are no features here of that genius of movement, that hidden grace, which never deserted Nijinsky, even in *Petrushka*." Leontiev stressed the homeliness, the ordinariness of the puppet's appearance, but the gaze of his big sad eyes revealed his suffering. Thanks to Leontiev, *Petrushka* became part of the repertory of the Russian theater. The ballet was performed in Leningrad until 1928 and was also staged in Moscow.

Leontiev's independent productions were less successful. *Salomé*, to

---

*A *lubok* is an illustrated popular print or broadside, originally a woodcut, usually in a primitive, colorful style and often incorporating language. (Ed.)

the music of Glazunov, was shown only once, on April 24, 1922. His concert numbers, to use Volynsky's imagery, "were strewn over the accumulated snowdrifts of ballet material like unnoticed snowflakes, melting on the spot."[26] On the twentieth anniversary of Leontiev's work he was described primarily as an "honest and above all, cultured reconstructor,"[27] a champion of the classical heritage and an administrator.

Indeed, Leontiev was one of those whose efforts helped support the activity of the Petrograd ballet even in the most difficult years of destruction and famine. Right after the October Revolution he first took upon himself the duties of secretary of the ballet troupe, then chairman of the committee of the troupe; in 1919 he was appointed assistant manager, and in 1920 director of the company.

His statements in the press help us in part to understand the conditions under which he had to work and create. An interview given in December 1918 to a staff member of the journal *Biriuch* draws a convincing picture of the difficulties encountered by the Petrograd ballet. A debate he had with Volynsky and Nikolai Legat in 1920 and 1922 reflects the clash of opinions about the future course of ballet's development that was taking place within the troupe and around the theater. In 1920 Volynsky published a series of articles in the newspaper *Zhizn iskusstva* in which he criticized the Petrograd company and school. In an open letter to Lunacharsky he wrote of the necessity of "radically reforming the state ballet and providing the Maryinsky Theater with a flow of new creative forces that have grown up in conditions of a different, higher type of culture."[28] Volynsky thought a future dancer should not only *master* but also learn to *understand* the forms of classical dance while in school. He insisted that "the ballet must enter into the second stage of its development," requiring "a conscious attitude towards this art," and to this end he projected a program of study for ballet artists that included courses on the theory of movement, the aesthetics of classical dance, the movements of the ancient Greek chorus, and a number of disciplines of a "sociocultural nature." These views of Volynsky's are linked to the themes of his research, reflected in the lectures that he gave at the School of Russian Ballet, which he organized (1921), in articles published in the newspaper *Zhizn iskusstva* (1922), and in *The Book of Exultations* (1925). In this connection, we should briefly summarize Volynsky's theoretical views.

A well-known scholar of art and literature, Volynsky had been extremely interested in the ballet for many years. Before the revolution he regularly wrote reviews of performances at the Maryinsky Theater and at the same time, with Legat's assistance, he became acquainted with classical dance technique. This motivated Volynsky to study the general rules of classical dance, the principles on which his system is based, from an aesthetic perspective. In generalizing, Volynsky's observations went beyond the boundaries of art, revealing the same regularities in all the phenomena of life. For example, in discussing the significance of the *croisé* and *effacé* as a concentrated, condensed quality in the one case and an openness and freedom in the other, he pointed out the existence of these opposing states in nature, psychology, and human physiology.

Many Soviet art historians (in particular Ivan Sollertinsky) were inclined to reject anything Volynsky did in the field of ballet theory, attentive as they were only to the metaphysical quality of his statements. This is partly a result of his ornate, bombastic style, with its abundance of foggy metaphors which clouded his ideas. His abstruse discourses on the vegetable nature of female dance and the animal nature of male dance and his mystical glorification of classical dance as a supra-real language of the soul seem far-fetched.

But certainly Volynsky alone among the scholars of classical dance gave at least an approximate basis for the laws of this art. His opponents limited themselves to refuting his ideas without proposing anything positive in return. As a result, everything true and valuable in Volynsky's ideas was discarded and forgotten, and for all practical purposes the theory of classical dance in our day remains at the same level it had been before him. The significance of Volynsky's ideas was for the most part correctly understood by Fedor Lopukhov, who wrote after the publication of the scholar's articles: "He was the first to try to explain the meaning of each dance movement, which I, as a representative of choreography, welcome enthusiastically . . . while disagreeing with the critic Volynsky in the details of explaining dance movements, I could not fail to welcome his explanation—the first such explanation—of the great essence of choreographic art." [29]

Turning to the arguments between Leontiev and Volynsky, it should be said immediately that Leontiev was not concerned with theoretical questions. The struggle flared up on another beachhead. Putting forth the idea of the reform of ballet dancers' education, Volynsky simultaneously pointed to the flaws in the study programs at the Petrograd School, where Leontiev had worked for many years, and wrote of the catastrophic decline of the level of performance in the company, which Leontiev then headed. In the article "In Defense of the Deteriorating State Ballet,"[30] Leontiev argued with Volynsky's open letter to Lunacharsky, cited above, and in his article "A Soggy Lump of Sugar" he criticized the repertory and the performance at the graduation concert by students of the Theater School as "crumbling and pitiful, like a soggy lump of sugar."[31]

Volynsky's criticism had a basis in real fact. The Petrograd troupe, whose numbers had been significantly reduced, which had lost almost all its premier dancers, and which was exhausted by hunger, cold, and overwork, had to a great extent lost its former sparkle in performance. In individual roles the choreography was distorted, simplified, and cut. In the group and ensemble dances the reduction of the cast ruined the logic of the dance design. Sometimes entire dances were eliminated from the ballets—very important ones at that. Thus, from the comments of the Petrograd critic Denis Leshkov one can conclude that the ballet *Coppélia* was presented in October 1919 "with simplifications"; *The Sleeping Beauty* in February 1920 without the Bluebird; *The Little Humpbacked Horse* in March 1920 with the role of the Pearl omitted, and so on. However, Volynsky's reproofs did not take into consideration the general situation, the fact that the management of the ballet was doing all in its power to preserve both the group and the repertory. At that time survival was the main thing. Survival was crucial so that after the civil war when material and financial problems would gradually begin to wane something new could begin to be created.

Leontiev wrote about just this. He reproached Volynsky, who "like a 'bourgeois' in a sheepskin coat and felt boots comes to the theater when it is two degrees above zero, as was the case this winter, and is surprised that people on stage, half-dressed in thin pieces of fabric, have become inert and out of tune, dancing without temperament or imagination." Leontiev hotly defended the students of the Theater School:

It wasn't "soggy lumps of sugar" we saw before us on May 30 at the graduation performance, Comrade Volynsky, but little heroes who stoically bore the difficulties and deprivations of last winter, who are eager to learn and were deeply saddened when the bitter cold forced them to break off their studies for a while. During the entire theatrical season of 1919–20 they also served the performances of the ballet troupe without a murmur, changing clothes in dressing rooms where water had frozen in the pipes and on the floor.[32]

Volynsky criticized the leadership of the company, pointing to the fact that there were no people among them with creativity or initiative capable of leading ballet in a new direction. Leontiev defended the "volunteers" who did all in their power to preserve the ballet "not . . . for the sake of their careers but solely out of love for their own art." Nevertheless, it was impossible to dispute Volynsky's basic point. And he was not the only one to express warnings. While Volynsky spoke from a primarily academic position, others too were concerned over the impasse in the ballet. Like many others, Dominique Platach called for a radical renewal of the repertory, a restoration of Fokine's ballets (incidentally, Leontiev worked passionately for this), and the promotion of young dancers, in the article "Before It Is Too Late."[33] Indeed, the "headless" Petrograd ballet was in a state of confusion. Among those engaged in the work of staging ballets, no one had yet been able to gain authority.

The productions of Alexander Ivanovich Chekrygin staged at the Maryinsky Theater turned out to be not very successful. In his new version of *Bluebeard* (November 17, 1918) he made such extensive cuts that, according to the review by Leshkov, the ballet was devoid of any sense.[34] Leshkov assigned the staging of the ballet *The Romance of the Rose* at the farewell benefit for Drigo to "the category of accidents." He wrote:

> One can't blame the choreographer, for in the time given him and under the circumstances it was impossible to stage even a divertissement tolerably, let alone a three-act ballet. Incidentally, the audience did not even see any real "acts," could not comprehend the plot, and merely watched, puzzled, while for fifty minutes various "flowers," thrown together in a clump, bumped into each other and vainly tried to find their places on the stage, forming a crowd full of helpless, frightened faces.[35]

The *Schubertiana*, Chekrygin's only independent production at the Maryinsky Theater, was also shown only once, on April 23, 1922. "Pure" classics were not Chekrygin's forte. Assisting Sergeyev in notating dances according to Vladimir Stepanov's system, he studied the traditional repertory, and he mastered the teaching of classical dance, but his predilections as an actor and choreographer were different. A superb performer of the roles of the evil fairy Carabosse, the maniacal old visionary Coppelius, and the character roles of comical old women, Chekrygin was drawn toward sharp, sometimes grotesque forms. It is no accident that his talent as a director emerged in the second half of the twenties on the stage of the Maly Opera Theater, in operas and in the operettas *Die gelbe Jacke* by Franz Lehár, *The Clown* by Michael Krausz, and *Jonny Spielt Auf* and *Der Sprung über den Schatten* by Ernst Křenek, which used Western European revue, jazz, and eccentric dance forms.

We have Volynsky's stinging reaction to the *Schubertiana*: "This is a bad reworking of Fokine's *Chopiniana*. . . . The figures are Fokine's. The lines are all deadly straight and unbearably monotonous. . . . Even the tutus come directly out of *Chopiniana*, though covered with yellow, for appearance's sake, to distinguish this ballet from the badly stripped and ransacked original."[36]

Volynsky's biting tone was not only the result of the drawbacks of the ballet, whose unsuccessful staging is indubitable. In criticizing the choreographic attempts of Chekrygin and Leontiev, Volynsky again pointed to the lack of authoritative leadership in the Maryinsky Theater company and thus paved the way for his own candidacy. In June 1922 there appeared an article by Legat devoted to the Theater School in which he called for a merger with the School of Russian Ballet "under the authoritative leadership of A. L. Volynsky."[37] To a great extent this article coincided with the memorandum sent by Legat to Lunacharsky, excerpts from which were published in *Materials on the History of the Russian Ballet* by Mikhail Borisoglebsky.[38] Volynsky repeatedly expressed the opinion that of all of the balletmasters who remained in Russia, only Legat was competent to head the Petrograd Ballet. For his part, Legat pushed Volynsky forward as an ideologist. Both were opposed to Fokine and his followers, seeing in their experiments only a digression from the true course of the development of Russian ballet. Even when Legat had already gone abroad, Volynsky returned to the question of the leadership of the Maryinsky Theater company and wrote, "I cannot see any other as balletmaster except N. G. Legat, whose activity in Russia was interrupted only by the malicious intriguing of unscrupulous, ignorant opponents."[39] By opponents he meant, above all, Leontiev and Chekrygin.

Solveig by Pavel Nikolayevich Petrov

During 1918–19 preparations were going on for staging the ballet *Solveig* to music by Grieg. The idea for this ballet had developed gradually. From a letter written by Grieg, dated 1902 and published by R.-Aloys Mooser in 1907, we know that the Board of Directors of the Imperial Theaters invited Grieg either to write a new ballet score or to compile a score from his works for the Petersburg theater. The composer declined but wrote that he would not object if someone else made a selection of his music for the project.[40] Denis Leshkov maintains that in 1907 Fokine was attracted to this idea and worked on the plans for this proposed ballet in collaboration with the composer Nikolai Tcherepnin.[41] The versions of a scenario entitled "Trolls," preserved in Fokine's archives in Leningrad, may be connected to this project.[42] In 1918 Asafiev began to compile a score from Grieg's music, but this was for Romanov.

By the end of 1918 all the orchestra parts were written. In the spring of 1920 it was announced that Golovine had finished sketches for the sets and costumes. However, by that time the proposed choreographer, Romanov, had left Petrograd. A replacement was found a year and a half later. In the fall of 1921 the newspaper *Zhizn iskusstva* reported that Pavel Petrov had begun rehearsals.

Since 1910 Petrov had been a dancer with the Maryinsky company, but his work as a choreographer took place mostly outside the Maryinsky Theater. In 1918–19 he staged a number of dance miniatures (*Fantasy* in the Grotesque Theater, *Pepita Rosa* to the music of Paul-Jean-Jacques Lacôme at the Luna Park) and dance episodes in dramatic productions (*The Torn Cape* by Sem Benelli at the Grand Dramatic Theater, 1919), but he was invited more often by opera and operetta theaters. The choreographer of the Bolshoi Opera Theater, in 1921 he participated in staging *The Triumph of Bacchus* by Alexander Dargomyzhsky and *The Maccabees* by Anton Rubinstein, both of which were recognized as significant achievements in the theater, and also Rimsky-Korsakov's *The Tsar's Bride* and *Le Coq d'or*. Petrov worked in the Mikhailovsky Theater starting in 1919 and for four years created dances for all its theater, opera, and operetta productions. His work includes the first small pure dance productions in this theater: *Promenade* to the music of Johann Strauss, and *The Choice of a Bride* by Mikhail Kuzmin. Drigo's *The Enchanted Forest* and Glazunov's *Salomé* were never performed.[43]

Petrov was also known in the Maryinsky Theater for his stagings of the dances for the operas *Faust* (1919), *Evgeny Onegin* (1920), and several separate dances: *Schön Rosmarin* to Fritz Kreisler, *Romance* to Drigo, and *Valse-Caprice* to Rubinstein, all of which everyone danced in variety concerts. More interesting were his character dances, in which he himself often performed. The folk dances in Rimsky-Korsakov's *Mlada* were an example of this category of Petrov's work. The press gave somewhat positive reviews of these, but was rather equivocal: "The dances and groups staged by Petrov are entirely traditional, although a great deal in the performances seems interesting. Only the hellish kolo, with music that should provide inexhaustible possibilities for the choreographer, is not at all developed and, despite the fussy circling about, is not dynamic."[44]

In April 1922 Petrov organized a demonstration evening in the former Merchants' Club in which the Maryinsky Theater dancers performed three of his small ballets: *Promenade valsante* (or *Promenade*), *Pepita Rosa*, and *Suite de ballet* by Drigo. The reviewer was of the following opinion of the choreographer's work: "All of P. N. Petrov's productions display a loving attitude towards art, but lack any kind of individuality."[45] Half a year later, on September 24, 1922, the premiere of *Solveig* took place. It was then that Asafiev's article on the music for this ballet appeared, showing not only that the musical plan had been made by the composer with Romanov, but also that by the end of 1917 Romanov had worked out, as Asafiev writes, "the choreographic mise-en-scène."[46] Thus one can assume that in general the choreographer's interpretation had been defined before Petrov began to stage the work.

The ballet *Solveig* was in three acts and its structure was similar to that of nineteenth-century ballet productions. It is easy to understand why Romanov was interested in the archive of Petipa, which contains the choreographer's sketches, while he was working on *Solveig*.

The elegiac "Solveig's Song" (Opus 55, no. 4), which appeared in the prologue and the epilogue, served as a frame. It seemed to be an introduction to the world of the heroine, this "Norwegian Snow Maiden," charming in her purity, femininity, and simple-heartedness.

The first fairytale act showed the beautiful, mysterious world of Norway, her snowy mountains and forests that Grieg loved so much. The pieces "Gnomes' Tune" from "Three Pieces for the Pianoforte" (No Opus, no. 2), and "Puck" (Opus 71, no. 3) revealed the magic beings of the popular imagination—trolls, kobolds, and forest spirits. Solveig appeared surrounded by the moon maidens and youths ("Notturno," Opus 54, no. 4). She danced to the music "Folksong" (Opus 38, no. 2). Ice maidens and icicles, performed by children, took part in the dances of the winter characters ("Melodie," Opus 47, no. 3), as did the forest maidens ("Album Leaves," Opus 28, no. 3), and the northern birds ("Little Bird," Opus 43, no. 4). They all surrounded Solveig in a general dance of the forest spirits ("Temple Dance" from *Olav Trygvason*, Opus 50). In the first dances of the ballet Solveig was still part of this winter nature, this fantastic world. She was radiant, calm, and cold. Everything changed with the appearance of the hunter, who chased after the bird and wounded it ("Intermezzo," Opus 56, no. 2).

Asafiev recounted his intention in the first act as follows: "This suite tells in sounds the arrival of a man in the world of the trolls and the birth of feeling between him and Solveig, the ice maiden, whom only a kiss can bring to life. The essence of the action, both in music and in dramatic movement, is the shift from icy numbness and cold gloom to trembling life, to the ecstasy of love, falling gradually, endlessly in love."[47]

In the scenes with Solveig and the wounded bird and her meetings with Hans and their exit into the world of people the "Valse-Caprice" (Opus 37, no. 2) was used with Asafiev's orchestration accompanied by a chorus heard from behind the stage, as well as the romance "I Love Thee" (Opus 5, no. 3). This music expressed all-consuming love.

The second act was realistic: In a Norwegian village Hans's and Solveig's marriage was celebrated. Here Asafiev drew material from the enormous wealth of Grieg's folk wedding and dance music. "This act presents a vast ground for musical ethnography, for orchestrated flashes of folklore."[48] After the wedding march ("Wedding Day at Troldhaugen," Opus 65, no. 6) followed the scene of congratulating the newlyweds ("Triumphal March," Opus 56, no. 3), and the folk suite consisting of a farandole ("Norwegian Melody," Opus 12, no. 6), the Norwegian dance with the ensemble ("Norwegian Dance," Opus 35, no. 2), the dance of the two girls and two boys, friends of the newlyweds ("Norwegian dance," Opus 35, no. 3), the duet of the newlyweds ("Scherzo-Impromptu" from the cycle *Moods*, Opus 73, no. 2), and the final ensemble dance ("Norwegian Dance," Opus 35, no. 1). But here the merrymaking abruptly broke off. The piece "From Years of Youth" (Opus 65, no. 1, part 3) was heard. An icy wind began to blow; this was the fatal breath of winter coming toward the people, the appearance of the ice maiden Oze to take Solveig back to the mountains. Solveig fell unconscious. She was picked up and carried away by the trolls. The act ended with the "Funeral March in Memory of Richard Nordraak."

The third act returned to the scene of the first act. Once again, to the music of the piece "Mountain Tune" (from the suite "Pictures from Life in the Country," Opus 19, no. 1), spirits, monsters, and snow youths danced. And, like Orpheus, a man appeared to claim his kidnapped beloved. Here Asafiev used the music of the romance "You grasp not the waves, eternal motion" (Opus 5, no. 2), one of Grieg's most inspired love songs, and the lyric poem "Erotik" (Opus 43, no. 5). Oze challenged the youth to recognize Solveig among twelve identical forest maidens. The maidens danced to the "Valse-Caprice" (Opus 37, no. 1), which Asafiev orchestrated "in muffled, dead tones," to give the episode a hint of lifelessness, of slowing down; the dance of the maidens was not warmed by feeling. And Hans could not recognize his bride.

The mistake cost the youth his life. "Peer Gynt's Homecoming" (from the *Peer Gynt Suite*, Opus 55, no. 3) served as the background to the scene of Hans's death, for he was handed over to the vengeance of the whirlwinds. The act ended with the same "Solveig's Song," which brought reconciliation and a mood of radiant sadness. One of the comparatively earlier variants of the ballet's scenario states: "The sun has risen. Happiness has returned to the land of the Solveigs. The forest is filled with the hubbub of morning and through the mountains go the shepherds, welcoming the spring sun."[49] In other words: Hans has perished, and Solveig has once again become an ice maiden, cold and unfeeling; still, spring has come to the people. The list of characters attached to the scenario includes shepherds and Norwegian girls, who were supposed to appear at the end of the production. However, as is clear from the programs published after the premiere, the finale was subsequently rejected. A review points out that the plot "ends as it were with a full circle, returning in the finale to the original scene and musical leitmotif: the song of Solveig, who sits in a tree, surrounded by gnomes."[50]

Apparently, in putting together Grieg's pieces for the music of the ballet, Asafiev, Romanov, and Golovine proceeded from the traditional structure of Romantic ballet. The notion of the contradiction between the spirit and the flesh, the ideal and the material, the heavenly and the earthly were the basis for many ballets in the era of Romanticism. Fantastic scenes alternated with realistic ones. Conflicts arose through the encounter by the hero with a spectral being—a spirit, a fairy. These incorporeal creatures longed for earthly love and wanted to know the joys and sorrows of earthly life. The Sylphide, Ondine, and La Péri strove for human love; the Sylphide died of that love; Ondine sacrificed her immortality, but could not live on earth; La Péri took on the appearance of an ordinary slave to be reunited with her beloved. The union of a supernatural being and a human brought misfortune to both. Youths chasing after a spirit set out for a river bed (*La Fille du Danube*), went to their deaths (*La Péri*), or renounced their former loves (*La Sylphide, Ondine*). All of these motifs are present in *Solveig*.

Such a conception is not at odds with the outlook of Grieg, the poet of northern nature. In the north, nature is magnificent and powerful. People who live in the mountains and the forest groves of Norway, on the shores of its cold sea, also grow up to be strong and proud. They seem to merge with nature and at the same time they resist it. Nature jealously guards its secrets from man, and when he forces his way into its forbidden bounds, its inexorable laws confront his bold aspirations. The hunter Hans brings the forest maiden to life through the force of his love. However, since she herself is a part of nature, she must inevitably return to her own natural element. Summer must give way to winter, and man has no power to resist its advent. But just as inevitably, winter yields its place to spring. And with spring, warmth returns and love is reborn.

In selecting the music, Asafiev tried on the one hand to avoid monotony and on the other to avoid creating a mosaic in which the various pieces seemed artificially joined together. Working with Romanov, Asafiev tried to prevent *Solveig* from turning into a divertissement; it contained a progression of musical thought. "The instrumental movement was equal to the line of development of the drama, and the dynamics of a purely orchestral nature fully and organically blended a mechanical combination of separate numbers."[51]

Nature in the north, perceived directly through Grieg's music, also inspired the artist Golovine. Sketches for the winter scene (the sets were used in the first and third acts) and for the second act are preserved in the A. A. Bakhrushin Theatrical Museum. The first shows an impenetrable forest thicket, which the rays of the northern sun penetrate with difficulty. Pale pink reflections on the snow relieve the dense blackness of the entwined branches of the crowded trees. This is a gloomily romantic fairytale world. And among the trunks and branches in the foreground are three absurd gargoyles, like tree stumps come to life—the trolls. The sketch for the second act shows a Norwegian landscape. At the foot of a cliff, behind which are snowy peaks, is a village hidden in greenery. To the right is a two-story red brick building trimmed in white. Its glass terrace, with steps leading to it from the porch, and the tower with a spire recall Grieg's house in Trollhaugen, which is well known from photographs. The porch is covered with a rug, and the terrace is strewn with garlands and wreaths of leaves. Around the house, tables are set, groups of peasants in national costumes lead a choral dance, and in the distance are seen barrels, set aflame, which will be jumped over as part of the wedding ritual.

Like Asafiev, Golovine saw the basic theme of the ballet as the victory of spring over winter and the exaltation of nature, eternally alive and eternally renewed, despite the tragic climax. Incidentally, the above-mentioned scenario of the ballet with the "spring-coming" finale is preserved in Golovine's archive. Asafiev wrote of his collaboration with the painter and of his sets for the first act:

> When I had to work with Golovine on *Solveig*, for which the musical basis was Grieg's poetic northern spring refrains (this was still before the later "crude" version), I saw the first sketches and heard the beautiful tales of Alexander Yakovlevich [Golovine] about nature and folklife in Norway; the northern spring in its earliest stage particularly caressed and enchanted his imagination. Golovine valued my idea of gradually introducing animation into the orchestra, adding the organ and then the human chorus. In a word, this new quality made one feel that spring had come. And the set of the springtime

rebirth of nature in *Solveig* is beautiful in the subtlety of its observation of that precise moment: the *coming* of spring.[52]

The music and decor of the ballet shared a single conception. Judging from a few reviews, Petrov departed from this conception, unable to do the most important thing—to create, as Asafiev wanted, dances "tightly linked to the dramatic action." The critics wrote that *Solveig* was not a "*unified* artistic work," but "*separate* dances, scenes, and groups, totally unconnected, sometimes even contradictory."[53]

The fairytale characters of the first act were not portrayed through dance, and they did not create the image of a winter fantasy, the cold glitter of ice. Volynsky was surprised by the bacchic nature of the dances of the ice and moon maidens, "a completely unmotivated transplant of the Seville seguidilla to the snowy peaks of the fjords."[54] The gnomes were more reminiscent of comic monsters in the retinue of the fairy Carabosse than of the characters in Scandinavian myths. On the other hand, in the second act, in the wedding scene, Petrov tried to stick as closely as possible to ethnographic authenticity. He reproduced folkgames onstage: youths jumped, trying to knock down with their knees a hat hanging on a pole, little boys somersaulted. But although he tried to be scrupulously authentic, he was not able to create a dance interpretation of folk holiday pastimes.

Platach[55] and Leshkov[56] called Petrov's production "purely classical," an epigone of Petipa's ballets. For the critics of the twenties, this meant a rejection of any *modern* values of choreographic productions, since "Petipa is entirely in the past—in the museum province" (Platach). They saw the link with Petipa in the divertissement-like construction and the superficial quality of the spectacle. In reality, classical forms in the best of Petipa's works were imbued with profound meaning. Apparently Petrov utterly failed in this. Noting that Petrov's staging was "out of touch with the work of Golovine," and that he was a "helpless choreo-dramatist and something of a dilettante," a witness to one performance, Yuri Slonimsky, made an exception for the dance of the whirlwinds of the last act, in which sixteen men took part, including Piotr Gusev, Georgi Balanchivadze, and Vasily Vainonen. "Using this dance as a springboard, Lopukhov later found the image of the finale in *The Ice Maiden*."[57]

The production of *Solveig* ran only during the 1922–23 season, and was performed six times altogether. It was not successful with the audience. "The second performance of the new ballet *Solveig* in the Maryinsky Theater earned 2½ billion, the third performance (on Sunday) 3½ billion, the fourth performance 1½ billion, and next to this, *Sleeping Beauty* earns 8½ billion, that is, practically a full house, while the new ballet— in the best of cases!—fills *one-third* of the house."[58]

But the extraordinary music of Grieg, selected and orchestrated by Asafiev, remained. Golovine's costumes and sets remained. All of this was used again five years later in Lopukhov's ballet *The Ice Maiden*.

As for Petrov, in 1924 he left Leningrad and settled in Lithuania. There in 1925 he staged *Coppélia* with the students of the local ballet studio and with dramatic and opera artists. This was the first ballet performance in Kaunas. Later, Petrov produced *Swan Lake* (1927), *The Nutcracker* (1928), *Lithuanian Rhapsody*, to the music of Jurgys Karnavičius (1928), and *Harlequinade* (1929), and he taught many performers, laying the foundations for the Lithuanian Ballet Theater.

Georgi Melitonovich Balanchivadze and the Young Ballet

Strictly speaking, *Solveig* was the first fully independent full-length ballet by the Petrograd company after the October Revolution. However, the flaws of the production on the one hand and a distrust of the possibilities of an "outdated" classic on the other led to the fact that no one considered *Solveig* an innovation—rather, it was felt to be in the same class as Lopukhov's restagings of the ballets of Petipa and Fokine.

In 1922, toward the end of the first revolutionary five-year period, something new was quite clearly emerging on the ballet stage. The first ballets by Fedor Lopukhov were staged (see Chapter 6). In fall 1922 the visit to Petrograd of the Kamerny Ballet (Chamber Ballet) of the Moscow choreographer Kasian Goleizovsky provoked a stormy exchange of views (see Chapter 4). Then talk began about performances by the dancers from the Maryinsky Theater, recent graduates of the Petrograd School, who had formed an association known as the Young Ballet. During its early period (1922–24), the animator and initiator of all the group's experiments was Georgi Melitonovich Balanchivadze (later known as George Balanchine), who graduated from the school in 1921.

While still in school, Balanchivadze did not limit his interests to dance. A talented musician, he was at the same time a student at the Conservatory. He had several times tried his skills in staging program numbers at student concerts. Balanchivadze's first such work was a love duet to Rubinstein's music *La Nuit* (1920). One of the performers, Olga Mungalova, recalled that "For the first time, acrobatic lifts appeared in our school."[59] Balanchine later told the British critic Arnold Haskell that some of the teachers considered this piece not academic enough, and, most importantly, "scandalous." They talked about its "eroticism." "As I remember it today," said Balanchine, "it would be perfectly suitable for a presentation in a young ladies' seminary."[60] The dissatisfaction of his teachers did not stop the sixteen-year-old choreographer, for young people sympathetic to his quest began to collect around him. The costumes for these works were designed by the choreographer and sewn by the performers themselves. Sometimes Balanchivadze also composed the music: *Waltz and Adagio*, danced by Mungalova and Piotr Gusev, was his composition. Contemporaries remember yet another duet—*Poème*, performed by Balanchivadze and Alexandra Danilova to the music of Zdeněk Fibich. Mikhail Mikhailov also cites *Hungarian Gypsy Dance*, to the music of Johannes Brahms, and the dance miniature *Orientalia*, to the music of César Cui.[61] From all accounts, these numbers did not contain any choreographic innovations.

In the theater Balanchivadze danced both in the classical repertory and in Lopukhov's productions. "*Dance Symphony* [*The Magnificence of the Universe*] became the major stimulus in the life of the young generation and for Balanchine personally. The same was true for other ballets by Lopukhov, and for the resurrection of the full *Sleeping Beauty*," writes Slonimsky, who at the time was working with Balanchivadze.[62]

Balanchivadze began working steadily as a choreographer during his second year at the theater in the 1922–23 season. He was in part influenced by Goleizovsky's Chamber Ballet. The group's concert made such an impression on Balanchivadze that he rushed backstage to express his enthusiasm to the choreographer. "Seeing Goleizovsky was what first gave me the courage to try something different on my own," Balanchine told Bernard Taper, his American biographer.[63]

"To seek something unusual, something of one's own"—many attempted this at the time. Working with Balanchivadze were the young dancers Danilova, Lidia Ivanova, Mungalova, Gusev, Nikolai Efimov, and others, and also the visual artists Vladimir Dmitriev, Boris Erbstein, Tatiana Bruni, the art scholar Yuri Slonimsky, and the musician Vladimir Dranishnikov. With the artist Dmitriev, Balanchine staged not only the Young Ballet productions but other works as well. For N. A. Shcherbakov's production of Arthur Schnitzler's pantomime *Der Schleier der Pierrette* (Columbine's Scarf) in 1923, Dmitriev created interesting movable sets and Balanchine composed the dances.

One of the first memorable performances of the Young Ballet took place on June 1, 1923, in the Experimental Theater (the hall of the former Municipal Duma).* Then, during the year prior to the departure abroad of Balanchivadze, Danilova, Efimov, and Tamara Gevergeyeva (Geva), concerts took place fairly regularly in various venues in Petrograd, Pavlovsk, and occasionally Moscow.

Performances of the Young Ballet and in particular Balanchivadze's ballets provoked conflicting reactions. Volynsky and the critic Yuri Brodersen, who sided with him, immediately attacked the Young Ballet. Brodersen called the June 1 concert "a solid evening of theatrical vulgarity."[64] Anatoly Kankarovich and Boris Erbstein welcomed the birth of the young group "thirsting for new forms, new content, seeking new music to embody its ideas,"[65] but pointed out its lack of knowledge, experience, and most importantly of clear goals. Alexei Gvozdev, who wrote several articles on the problem of establishing an experimental studio, which was indispensable for further development of the ballet, pointed out both the merits and flaws in the work of the Young Ballet.

Apparently the haphazard nature of the Young Ballet's concerts permeated all aspects of its activity. Concern for box office success gave rise to a lack of selectivity regarding music, which Gvozdev noted. "Here are works by Arensky and Rubinstein that have been played to death, there is a Vilbushevich polka, and there's an amateurish foxtrot."[66] Costumes and sets were handmade. Despite the participation of talented young people, plans were not always carried out successfully. Apparently Gvozdev had grounds for writing that "the performances take place with a background

---

*The program included *La Mort du cygne, Adagio, Romance (La Nuit), Waltz and Adagio, Matelotte, Spanish Dance, Marche funèbre, Waltz,* and *Extase.* These are documented in *Choreography by George Balanchine: A Catalogue of Works* (NY: Eakins Press Foundation, 1983). (Ed.)

of utterly preposterous sets."[67] In conclusion, the critic called on Balanchivadze to discard outside influences and to "find himself."

> I heartily welcome the attempts by the leader of the group, Balanchivadze, to pour new wine into old wineskins. I value his ability to refresh the outlines of classical dance with new lines, clear positions, and unexpectedly daring transitions. But his efforts at imitating [Lev] Lukin* and Goleizovsky I considered a fundamental error which at some point I shall try to explain clearly, for I am sure that the young choreographer will be able to extricate himself from this state of rebellious restlessness and will fulfill his talents without the assistance of the Moscow decadents.[68]

The programs of the Young Ballet remained mixed; they included pas de deux by Petipa and dances by Fokine. This implied, incidentally, that Balanchivadze was not planning to renounce the legacy of the past completely. But in his own works of those years, he was indeed oriented toward Goleizovsky. Mikhailov, recalling the first concert in the hall of the former Duma, writes, "When . . . the concert was ready it became clear to many of us that it smacked terribly of the current programs of the talented Kasian Goleizovsky."[69]

In fact, Balanchivadze used the same music as Goleizovsky. He was attracted by the Romantic and Impressionist composers, such as Chopin and Ravel. His fascination with Chopin even affected the young choreographer's physical appearance; photographs of 1923 show a pale, long-haired youth dressed in black, with a tragic, passionate gaze. The resemblance was striking. Influenced by Nikolai Medtner's funeral march danced by the Chamber Ballet, Balanchivadze put on Chopin's *Marche Funèbre*. Photographs show him in various positions: on the knees with the arms extended, in profile on pointe with the legs parallel, and in clearly unclassical positions of the arms, with the hands held flat. Later Balanchivadze returned to the theme of death in a piece staged for Lidia Ivanova to the music of Jean Sibelius's "Valse Triste." It attracted attention on tours, and a Moscow critic has left us a description of a few moments:

---

*Lev Lukin, like Goleizovsky, used music by Scriabin as well as classical music in an austere, eroticized style of choreography. (Ed.)

The dancer, conveying a rising sense of horror, and moving, in a kind of emotional crescendo, along a straight line from the back of the stage to the footlights, at the last moment—obviously, at the peak of emotion—suddenly turns her back to the audience with a quick movement. And at that instant she freezes. This fermata is enormously impressive. . . . And further on in the same dance, the final emotional tension is superbly conveyed through a totally new device—the silent scream of a wide-open mouth.[70]

Balanchivadze also freely made use of acrobatics. A four-line verse is addressed to him:

> I've lived for thirty years, o gods divine,
> And never knew until today
> That to break one's legs and spine
> Is a search for a new way.[71]

It should not be forgotten, however, that at that time Balanchivadze was still under twenty and was just beginning to grope his way in art.

Another experiment is also extremely interesting. At the end of 1923 the Young Ballet staged a pantomime number that was done to the background of a chorus reciting Alexander Blok's poem "The Twelve." Then it was announced that the troupe was preparing the ballet *Pulcinella*.[72] According to Balanchine, the administration of the Maryinsky Theater expressed dissatisfaction with these experiments. They not only refused to support his proposed staging of *Le Sacre du printemps*, but also forbade the dancers to take part in the Young Ballet concerts.[73]

Balanchivadze searched for a way to use his talent outside the Young Ballet as well. He staged the dances for the opera *Le Coq d'or* on the stage of the Maly Opera Theater. In the production, which was staged by Nikolai Smolich, the choreographer designed the "Procession" and the "Oriental Dances." The reviewers, criticizing the production, in which the music was split up into a number of revue-style episodes, also disliked the work of the choreographer. Nikolai Strelnikov expressed amazement that "such a capable and musically gifted choreographer as Balanchivadze could have omitted a clear alternation of groups in the procession of all those separately characterized warriors, retinues, fat men, and giants, and how could he so confuse the designs of the music in the dancing"; he wondered why the Russian G-major theme was performed by "four frail bayadères."[74] It would seem that the choreographer interpreted the music the way the director Smolich saw fit. In any case, Asafiev, who also considered that there were many controversial points in the opera's staging, wrote: "There are witty details, and the procession in the finale of the second act is an enchanting sight."[75]

At that time Balanchivadze rehearsed, but never staged, Darius Milhaud and Jean Cocteau's pantomime *Le Boeuf sur le toit* in the Petrograd Free Theater. He also produced dances in two productions at the Alexandrinsky Theater: *Caesar and Cleopatra* by George Bernard Shaw, and *Eugene the Unfortunate* by Ernst Toller. Sergei Radlov, the director of *Eugene the Unfortunate*, put music by Kuzmin into the production and created a number of episodes in which dance played an important role. Balanchivadze staged the dances in the cafe, which was two stories high, with moving figures appearing in silhouette. Cripples begged for alms to the background of a mechanical dance by chorus girls. Reviewers did not fail to note the "choreographically interesting part conceived and executed by Balanchivadze."[76]

With each new work the talent of the choreographer defined itself more and more clearly, and his productions aroused ever greater interest. Those who at the beginning of the twenties had predicted a brilliant future for the youth were not mistaken. However, fame came not to Georgi Balanchivadze, but to Georges (later George) Balanchine. Everything the choreographer did after 1924 became the property of France and then of the United States, where Balanchine continued to work until his death in 1983.

Mikhail Mikhailovich Mordkin,
Lavrenti Lavrentievich Novikov,
Vladimir Alexandrovich Riabtsev

In the prewar years all the ballet productions on the Moscow stage were done by Gorsky. By the beginning of World War I the situation had begun to change: Dancers gave many concerts outside the theater, presenting separate pieces, whole programs, and then full ballets as well. Kasian Goleizovsky won considerable popularity with his works at The

---

*The Bat was a cabaret theater, organized by Nikita Baliev in Moscow in 1908, originally as an actors' after-hours club. After Baliev moved to Paris in 1920 the group was known as the Chauve-Souris. (Ed.)

Bat* and other small theaters.[77] Other dancers at the Bolshoi Theater were also attracted to choreography—Mikhail Mordkin, Lavrenti (later, Laurent) Novikov, Vladimir Riabtsev, Vasily Tikhomirov, Lev Lashchilin, and others.

Mikhail Mikhailovich Mordkin was the romantic hero of the Moscow stage. Of magnificent physique, with a beautiful, refined face and an inspired gaze, he danced in the Bolshoi Theater from 1900 to 1908 in ballets from the classical legacy and in Gorsky's productions. At the same time, beginning in 1909, he toured abroad, in particular as Anna Pavlova's partner.

Mordkin's dancing was passionate and powerful, and his poses and gestures were expressive. The fusion of dance and pantomime, something not all ballet artists can achieve, was his specialty. One of the particularly successful numbers he staged for himself was his *Italian Beggar*, a solo scene in which he portrayed a ragged, starving man seeking sympathy in vain from passersby.

As a choreographer Mordkin was attracted to the romantic and exotic. His first major production, *Aziade*, to the music of Josef Hüttel, was staged in 1912. *Aziade* was an Oriental legend of a beautiful girl who poisoned a sheik when he forced her to become his concubine. This ballet had the exotic elements of Fokine's *Schéhérazade* but without the intensity of passion and color that lay at the heart of Fokine's and Bakst's work. The plot was didactic and watered down by dramatic meanderings. A novella had become a melodrama.

In 1918 Mordkin revived this ballet in the Nikitin Circus. The performers were from a private ballet company and the soloists from the Bolshoi Theater. Up to two hundred supernumeraries took part in the production. The action was not only in the arena, but also on stairs covered with rugs, and on a specially constructed stage located on the level of the lower balcony and joined to the arena. Projectors with colored lenses were used to help show strikingly animated scenes with silhouettes on a curtain. In the scene where the captive Aziade is brought to the sheik, horses pranced around the stage.

The public responded well to the production. The idea of using ballet in the circus interested Lunacharsky, who championed mass spectacles and performances. He saw the production and said that he favored such experiments.

For a while Mordkin was close to Tairov's Kamerny Theater. Working in 1917 on dance and stage movements with the performers, he collaborated with Alice Koonen on the dance of Salomé in the performance of the same name, for which Hüttel, the composer of *Aziade*, whom Mordkin knew well, wrote the music.* In December 1917 Mordkin worked on a production of Debussy's *Boîte à joujoux*; the critics wrote of the success of the stylized dances of the Negro, the Sailor, the Doll, and so on.

After leaving the Bolshoi Theater in 1918 Mordkin put on a few performances in the Theater of the Council of Workers' Deputies (formerly the Zimin Theater). Here he produced *Aziade*, the program "Choreographic Etudes," and the children's ballet *A Dream on Christmas Night*. During 1918–23 he performed in concerts in various Russian cities. In 1919 he worked in Kiev, where he staged "The Dance of the Capes" in Konstantin Mardjanov's production of *La Fuente Ovejuna*. An eyewitness asserted that this dance evoked "youth, power, and the strength of a victorious people." It alternated with scenes of pantomime and was quite far removed from a ballet divertissement, as it "was subordinated to dramatic action."[78]

In 1921–22 Mordkin had a ballet studio in Tiflis (Tbilisi). In August 1922 he was invited to the Bolshoi Theater, where he was offered work as a choreographer (including work on a revival of the ballet *The Sleeping Beauty*). But he held the position of head of the ballet company for only twelve days and then left to return to concert performances. In December 1922 after a four-year hiatus, Mordkin's first Moscow performance took place. Then for a year and a half (until the spring of 1924) performances by a group of artists who had united around Mordkin were held in Moscow, Petrograd, and in the major provincial cities.

In his concert programs Mordkin avoided divertissements. Thus he created *Le Carnaval*, in which he tried to fuse new dances with numbers from classical ballets. The devices he used were quite naive: "The odalisques rocked back and forth to the beat of a Hungarian dance, Spanish women created a background for the dance of the Persians, and during the classical pas de deux from *Raymonda*, young Spaniards joyfully threw a ball back and forth."[79]

Imitating drama directors, the choreographer introduced such "contemporary tricks" as having the performers run through the audience.

---

*Alexandra Exter designed the sets and costumes. (Ed.)

The critics rightly objected to such attempts to "turn the classics to the left,"* considering that the dancers should be given the opportunity to present the dances staged by Mordkin without doing any sly tricks, all the more so since they actually "have not departed much from the academic cliché."[80]

Mordkin was one of the greatest performers on the Moscow stage. His achievements as a teacher in Moscow and abroad, where he settled in the middle of 1924, are also unquestionable. But clearly he did not have talent as an expressive choreographer; his subjective biases as an actor prompted him to dramatize dance along the lines of romantic melodrama. Moreover, he imitated Fokine and Gorsky, but his works did not contain any new ideas at all.

A number of staging experiments were carried out by Lavrenti (later, Laurent) Novikov, who was a leading soloist of the Bolshoi Theater from 1906 to 1918. "As opposed to Mordkin, who is simple and clear and knows how to please the crowds, Novikov is completely involved in his quests and doubts," the critics wrote.[81]

In 1915–16 he staged productions in variety theaters (the ballet *The Paper Ballerina* and others). In April 1918 he presented in the Kamerny Theater the ballet *The Great Pan Is Dead*, inspired by a poem by Ivan Turgenev to the music of Anatoly Kankarovich, and in the summer of the same year at the Aquarium Theater he presented Tcherepnin's *Narcissus*. Using Fokine's inventions, he built the dance in flat groups, with profile movements copied from Egyptian frescoes and Etruscan vases. The critics noted the affected quality of the dance design, its artificiality. "There was a mannered quality in the movements and dances, a certain angularity and brusqueness, particularly as concerns the arms."[82] Stylistically this contradicted the monumental, deliberately primitive decor by Ivan Fedotov. It was also noted that dance was used by the choreographer in an especially ornamental way, that he did not reveal any content in the image, and that it was difficult for the performers (in particular, for Elena Adamovich in the role of Echo) to "warm and animate this whole lifeless, syrupy choreographic picture."[83]

After *Narcissus*, Novikov presented at the Aquarium Theater the dances

---

*Those who wanted to interpret the classics from a contemporary, avant-garde, experimental approach were considered "left-wing" in their aesthetic. (Ed.)

inserted in the ballet *Thamar*, staged by Gorsky, and *Bacchanale*, to the music of Glazunov. In the same year, he left the Bolshoi Theater and subsequently worked abroad, mostly as a dancer, teacher, and répétiteur, for the most part producing other people's works.

Mordkin and Novikov left Moscow without staging a single production in the Bolshoi Theater. Meanwhile, right after the revolution, noises were made in the theater to the effect that an end should be put to the monopoly of the chief choreographer. "Recently the Artistic Council of ballet artists came to a positive decision regarding the question of those members of the company who themselves wish to participate in staging ballets, which was not permitted under the old regime. This is an extremely serious decision, opening the way for developing the creations of artists aspiring to work as choreographers,"[84] wrote Pleshcheyev before the opening of the 1917–18 season. Beginning in 1918–19 newspaper reports of plans by the Bolshoi Theater mentioned more and more new names. "A number of choreographers in addition to A. A. Gorsky will be involved in staging ballets. Thus Debussy's *Awakening of Spring* will be staged by Nikolai Legat, *The Red Masks* by Mr. Goleizovsky, and *Nur and Anitra* by Vasily Tikhomirov."[85] This was also noted in the records of the administration's meetings. For example, on June 20, 1919: "For one of the new productions it would be desirable to bring in someone from the outside, for example, someone from Petrograd. Work on the staging of the new ballets should be divided between Gorsky, Komissarzhevsky, Riabtsev, and Tikhomirov; moreover, Komissarzhevsky is to be involved as a director-consultant in all ballets that are being newly restaged."[86]

Vladimir Riabtsev was one of the first to become involved in production work. Since 1898 Riabtsev had been an outstanding character dancer and mime at the Bolshoi Theater and a performer of such roles as Ivanushka in *The Little Humpbacked Horse*, Marcelline (Madame Simone) in *La Fille mal gardée*, and Sancho Panza in *Don Quixote*. In addition to ballet, Riabtsev also performed in the theater and on the music-hall stage; as a student he acted at the Maly Theater and later was a director at The Bat and in the theater of Yakov Yuzhny (1917).

Riabtsev was particularly attracted by vaudeville. He was a great expert on this genre, owned an excellent collection of texts, and at the beginning of the twenties he organized in Moscow the Theater of Old-Fashioned Vaudeville; the bills and posters read, "What our grandmothers and great-grandmothers laughed at." Riabtsev worked here as an actor, director, and producer of the dances with which vaudeville teemed. However, he never broke with the ballet.

After the revolution, continuing to appear onstage, he also took up a number of administrative posts, taught pantomime at the school of the Bolshoi Theater, and organized his own studio, where in 1918–19 he staged the children's ballets *Little Red Riding Hood* and *The Snowflake*. But in the theater Riabtsev's work for the most part was rightly reduced to reworking the ballets in which he himself had played major pantomime roles. Thus, working in the Ukraine in the twenties, he mounted *The Little Humpbacked Horse*, *Coppélia*, and *Le Corsaire*.

In 1921 he produced Fokine's *Petrushka* in the Bolshoi Theater. The theater copied the sketches for the sets and costumes that Benois had done for the Paris premiere. This defined not only the style of the production, but also the nature of the dances. In Fokine's *Petrushka*, the music, the sets, and the dance movements are so closely interwoven that, in keeping the costumes and decor, it was impossible to stray from the original choreography.

The crowd scenes became a topic of particular concern to Riabtsev. In the fairground episodes he set up the ensemble sections first, trying to have the characters behave as naturally as possible. In a speech to the dancers, Riabtsev said that "an unusual number of details requires the most careful attention and nervous tension if they are to be understood." [87] While rehearsing the ballet he carefully worked on each gesture of the characters in the crowd, demanding that they all act and not simply stand around. This is clear even from the notes of the meetings of the Artistic Council: "In the fourth scene—the laugh of the whole crowd should be stronger"; "They don't act around the samovar enough," et cetera. [88]

Apparently the Moscow production of *Petrushka* was more ethnographic than the Petrograd one. In it, life at the fair was shown more authentically, more directly, and in a more lively manner, with a particular gusto, and all of this resulted in a swarming, resounding, incredibly colorful commotion. One of the performers in the role of the Ballerina, Margarita Kandaurova, went to Petrograd to see *Petrushka* and recalls that there the ballet seemed to her more "faded." [89] The traditions of the Moscow ballet made themselves felt, leaning toward a folkloric piling up of images, the tradition of both Gorsky's and Riabtsev's own inclinations as directors.

That same year, 1921, saw yet another project, this one unrealized: the one-act ballet *The Zaporozhy Cossacks*, with music by Reinhold Glière, based on Repin's famous painting.* [90] In May 1924 Riabtsev staged *Le Carnaval*, a dance suite consisting of separate numbers to selected music. Iving wrote of Riabtsev's *Le Carnaval* that it was made "with this choreographer's customary level of realism," when he "is able to make the crowd come alive on the stage, to link it through a single rhythm." [91] But it was pointed out that the dances themselves were wanly staged "in an old-fashioned way." Pierrot's dance owed its success for the most part to the "sparkling mimic performance" of Riabtsev himself. Later, in December of the same year, his reworking of the comic ballet *Harlequinade* (*Les Millions d'Arlequin*) by Drigo, with new decor by Aristarkh Lentulov, was not much acclaimed.

---

*Repin's painting *The Zaporozhy Cossacks Write a Letter to the Turkish Sultan* (1891), a work contemporary with Borodin's opera *Prince Igor*, was an important example of Russian nationalist art idealizing the people resisting foreign power. (Ed.)

Plans

In the first months after the October Revolution, life in the Bolshoi Theater settled down with difficulty. Gorsky did not hide his dissatisfaction. In an interview given to a correspondent of the newspaper *Rannee utro* he said: "What was this season like artistically? Boring. Nothing new, nothing outstanding. *Raymonda*? It isn't new, and the newspapers were much mistaken in considering it new; I won't talk about the rest."[1] These words of Gorsky's aroused a storm in the theater. Leonid Zhukov spoke at a meeting of the dancers. It was said that "Gorsky rejects the masses in the company," that he had "dried up." At the same time, his personal biases were brought up. In an explanatory letter dealing with that interview, Gorsky wrote to Tikhomirov, chair of the committee at that time: "Having once more studied it, I find nothing offensive in it either to the company or to our art. The truth cannot be offensive, and the truth came out under the influence of the grief that haunted me all season. I love art, it is my life, and I felt that it was escaping us."[2]

In Gorsky's interview, along with the critique of the Bolshoi Ballet, he once again expressed his ideas regarding the democratization of the theater:

Democratization of choreography means, of course, its potential wide penetration into the broad working masses. But to this end it must be comprehensible and faithful in its conception of the epoch shown on stage, down to the last details, and faithful not in an absolute manner but in terms of artistic truth, yet still faithful ethnographically, and, in any case, it cannot be absurd. This is the thesis of my plans for the future, but my future is obscure, for my colors are living, free people, who do not always understand the truth, ethnography, and the epoch the same way I or someone else does—each one does so in his own way, particularly when they are finding themselves. This is a factor in a period of development, or fermentation, and how it will all end is uncertain.[3]

We cited earlier Gorsky's statement on the same question in spring 1917. A year had passed, much in the country had changed, and now he was thinking not only of the necessity of returning to the people their accumulated treasures, but also of creating a new repertory. It is significant that he warned against accommodating to the tastes of inexperienced audiences and insisted on fidelity to "artistic truth"—that new truth which, as Gorsky correctly noted, at the time was still understood in different ways. And he himself did not hide his doubts and hesitations ("my future is obscure").

Gorsky's interview and letter also attest to the complicated situation in which he had to work. The letter complains that recently the troupe's interpretation of his ballets was "incorrect, distorting them until they are unrecognizable and depriving them of any artistic quality."[4] Gorsky mentions that his best ballets had fallen out of the repertory (*Gudule's Daughter, Salammbô, Nur and Anitra, Schubertiana, Love is Quick!, Eunice and Petronius, Fifth Symphony*), and that he simply could not "stage for nearly the tenth time the dances from *Sadko* and perform every other kind of work as well, turning from an artist into a dance machine."[5]

In fact, Gorsky was having a hard time. It was true that most of the dancers were involved with questions of self-management, the struggle between the "shops" (opera, orchestra, ballet, and others), and setting up councils, committees, meetings, and conferences. At the same time, the very artistic differences that had existed even earlier between Gorsky and those dancers who remained in the company after the revolution (Geltser and Tikhomirov) were exacerbated. They stemmed from a differing understanding of ballet's course of development. Like Fokine, Gorsky considered that ballet could survive only if it became an art of its time. He felt keenly the need to renew its themes and its language. Contemporary direction and principles of set design had to help in transforming the appearance of ballets. The development of pantomime had to give the dancers new expressive means. At the same time dance itself was subject to reform. Gorsky used free dance movements in contrast to the academic, frozen forms. Yet, as usually happens during the first stage of any reform, he did so to a needlessly dogmatic degree. Fokine himself also went through this stage.

Geltser and Tikhomirov took a strong stand on guarding tradition. And while the intensified emotional quality of Gorsky's productions and his quest for life-like truth did not run counter to Geltser's aspirations—for she had a clear dramatic temperament—as a rule she objected to his dance innovations. Tikhomirov, too, was a devout champion of the academic ballet, but he lacked Geltser's dramatic talent. This struggle, which had apparently quieted down during the years of creating *Le Corsaire* (1912) and *Eunice and Petronius* (1915), intensified after the revolution. Geltser and Tikhomirov did not participate in a single one of Gorsky's new productions in the Aquarium Theater (1918), the Bolshoi Theater Studio (1919–21), or in the Novy Theater (New Theater) (1922). And, as we shall see, when he staged *The Nutcracker* in 1919, Gorsky himself rejected Geltser's candidacy.

Reminiscing about Gorsky, Geltser later wrote: "He became excessively attracted by the new, sometimes forgetting about the old classical heritage."[6] Now, looking back and judging from a contemporary perspective, we must conclude that to a great extent the famous ballet dancers of the Bolshoi Ballet were right. In fact, it was fidelity to its academic foundations that helped ballet to survive. This served as the base for the growth of Soviet ballet. But we cannot forget something else: Modern ballet could not have emerged directly from nineteenth-century ballet without passing through the stages of Fokine's and Gorsky's creative work. These experiments were an absolute necessity. To end them would have meant to stop the very development of ballet. The breakdown of old forms, the temporary rejection of turnout and of pointe technique, and the use of Duncan's movements on the ballet stage—this was a natural, inevitable stage of development. What happened afterward seemed, to many, a step backward, toward nineteenth-century forms, but in fact it was an emergence of a new ballet on the basis of a modified, enriched old ballet.

Geltser and Tikhomirov were right to defend the foundations of classical dance, but they forgot that preservation also implies development, that preservation without enrichment means the arrest of development.

Gorsky himself was easily carried away and at times did not realize the extent of his enthusiasm; sometimes he was ready to subvert and destroy that which only yesterday had seemed unshakeable. In the last analysis, no one was absolutely right in this argument, but the truth emerged in the course of the dispute.

After 1917, when people of various tastes and interests were included in the administration of the company, it became even more difficult for Gorsky to carry out his policy. For certain people he was too much of a "leftist," a dreamer, who not only dressed ballerinas used to traditional tutus in rags or in floor-length dresses, but even made them dance barefoot. For others he was too much of a "rightist"; after all, he presented art that the new system had inherited from the past, while young people aspired toward the new, toward that which had never been before. For the young generation, Gorsky's quest was a search for yesterday.

A war on two fronts was too much for Gorsky. Gradually he began moving out of the company's administration; he worked less and less on the main stage of the theater and more with students in the studio, in the New Theater, and in private schools and troupes.

In discussions of the repertory, *Nur and Anitra* and *The King's Feast*, the ballets proposed by Gorsky, were mentioned several times. But their rehearsals never even began. When Gorsky engaged the artist Anatoly Arapov to make sketches for the décor, he incurred the dissatisfaction of the company administration. Attached to Arapov's report of the work he had done there is a resolution: "Find out from A. A. Gorsky on whose authority he put in this order."[7] The report for 1917–18 states: "The following productions—ballets—have been removed from the repertory: 1. *Eunice and Petronius, Le Carnaval*,"[8] without any explanation of the reasons.

Gorsky's original ballets were gradually pushed out of the repertory. Despite the attempts of the choreographer to at least present them on stages other than the main stage (for example, *Eunice* in 1919 in the Studio, and in 1922 in the New Theater), at the end of Gorsky's life not one of his productions, aside from reworkings of other people's ballets, was running in the theater.

In the spring of 1918 the fate of the Bolshoi Theater and the problems of its repertory were discussed at a specially convened meeting of theater employees and workers' organizations. The archives of the Bolshoi Theater contain notes on Gorsky's report, which we assume dates from the fall of 1918. Gorsky here summed up work done in the spring of 1918 and at the beginning of the next season. "The Bolshoi Theater is a stone box with chaos inside. . . . There was no answer to the bombs thrown at the Bolshoi Theater in the spring," wrote Gorsky, evidently having in mind the criticism of his theater's work and the embarrassment of the theater administration after this attack. He made a number of concrete suggestions: to stage *The King's Feast*, Stravinsky's *Firebird*, and Tchaikovsky's Third Suite, which he presented in the summer of 1918 in the Aquarium Theater; to present *The Masque of the Red Death*, on which Goleizovsky had worked; and to invite Legat to work in the theater.[9]

The ranks of Gorsky's supporters were thinning. In February 1918 Mordkin left; he felt he had been unjustly fined by the committee of the ballet company. Thus the Bolshoi Theater was forever deprived of this remarkable performer, an extraordinary interpreter of Gorsky's ideas.

Margarita Frohman left the group along with him. A nervous breakdown interrupted the stage work of another of Gorsky's favorite dancers —Sofia Fedorova. Goleizovsky left the theater in the fall of 1918, having quarreled with Tikhomirov, the director of the company. And many other dancers first toured the country and then went abroad and never returned: Gorsky's protégée Vera Karalli, Laurent Novikov, Viacheslav Svoboda, and Elizaveta Anderson. Now the choreographer had to rely primarily on his young students, whose authority of course still did not have much weight with the theater administration. The dancer Vera Svetinskaya recalled: "Gorsky was only an artist. . . . He was not involved in the revolutionary cause . . . and he was not an administrator by nature. . . . Things began to fall apart on stage. People said, 'Musically things are not the way they should be.' He wasn't a strong person, he wasn't firm, and he restaged things several times . . ."[10]

All this explains why as early as the summer of 1918 Gorsky took his experiments out of the Bolshoi Theater.

The Summer Season in the Aquarium Garden Theater

In 1918 there was no time for the dancers to rest. The summer months had to be spent working. Life had become more and more difficult, and everyone needed additional earnings, especially the young, poorly paid dancers. Meanwhile, three and a half months' time off was still given, according to the old rules—from the middle of May to September. Therefore, when the entrepreneurs Fedor Thomas and Boris Evelinov decided, since the interest in ballet was enormous, to organize a ballet season instead of presenting the operettas and "fantastic amusements" with which they usually entertained summer audiences, they were able to attract a large group of dancers and choreographers from the Bolshoi Theater. Their company was headed by Gorsky and Novikov. The leading roles were danced by Maria Reisen, Elena Adamovich, Ekaterina Dévilière, Novikov, Ivan Sidorov, Viacheslav Svoboda, Anastasia Abramova, who had just joined the theater, and also Nina Podgoretskaya and other students in the senior classes. For three months (from May 28 through August 27), on Tuesdays, Thursdays, and Sundays, programs were presented that included several ballets (mostly one-act), concert pieces, and dance scenes from operas.

Despite the fact that material difficulties forced the dancers to continue work during vacation time, the performances at the Aquarium Garden Theater should not be lumped together with the ordinary "hackwork" performances that were widespread at the time. These performances gave the dancers a chance to test their skills in new roles, and Gorsky was able to carry out some of his plans that had not been supported in the Bolshoi Theater. "The entire company was split into two camps (in connection with the Aquarium productions)," wrote Bakhrushin to Leshkov on June 16, 1918.[11]

The conditions for ballet performance in the theater at the Aquarium Garden were far from ideal: the stage was small, not intended for complex theatrical sets, and half open; the productions were hindered by daylight; and in bad weather (the summer turned out to be rainy) the dancers nearly froze in their light clothing. Nevertheless, the young performers eagerly threw themselves into the work. Olga Nekrasova recalls how enthusiastically they prepared the sets and costumes. "He [Gorsky] gave advice and himself painted the sets with the dancers, gave them everything he had; his only wish was to have things work out well. The entire floor was covered with paint, a whole shop was set up, we made the flowers ourselves, and did everything with our own hands."[12] The contract required a new production each week. Only a few of the productions came from the Bolshoi repertory: *Love is Quick!*, the suite *Études*, and dances from the operas *Prince Igor* and *Khovanshchina*. *Giselle* was also presented, but in the revised version, with modernized sets by Ivan Fedotov. Everything else was new work: seven one-act ballets, six of which were staged by Gorsky and one, *Narcissus*, by Novikov, and a concert program to the music of Johann Strauss waltzes (*Tales from the Vienna Woods*).

The press welcomed the undertaking, calling it a new Moscow Ballets Russes. "The heads of the company, A. A. Gorsky and L. L. Novikov, have shown that they are trying to get away from the clichés of the old ballet both in their choice of repertory and in bringing in such interesting artistic talent as I. Fedotov and A. Lentulov."[13] In his search for the new, Gorsky tried to rely on artists. He sought out those young rebellious artists with revolutionary inclinations whose primitively crude and daringly sweeping painting seemed to reflect the era. The first productions in the Aquarium were designed by Aristarkh Lentulov (*Lyric Poem*, "Polovetsian Dances") and by Ivan Fedotov (*Giselle*, *Narcissus*).

All of Gorsky's prerevolutionary productions had been created in close collaboration with Konstantin Korovin. Theirs was a fruitful collaboration, since it was based on shared creative convictions. Gorsky now felt that a new era needed new themes and new forms. He felt this, but did not actually visualize them. And the artists clearly were generally not interested in the problems of the ballet; it is telling that later neither Fedotov nor Lentulov designed for dance productions. Their Futurist décor spoke for itself. Fedotov's sets "have nothing to do with the given ballet," reported the critic of the newspaper *Nashe vremya*.[14] Therefore such a union between the artist and the choreographer came to nothing. And it is not accidental that the ballets later included in the repertory were presented with sets already designed by Korovin (*Spanish Sketches*, *La Péri*), Vasily Diachkov (*En blanc*), and Gorsky himself (*Thamar*).

Lyric Poem is one of the many variations on the theme of Pierrot and Columbine that were widely produced on the Russian stage on the eve of World War I. In Fokine's *Le Carnaval* (1910) Columbine mischievously and tenderly flirted with Harlequin, and the clumsy Pierrot, always late everywhere for everything, grieved submissively. In the same year Vsevolod Meyerhold staged the pantomime *Columbine's Scarf* (based on Schnitzler's pantomime *Der Schleier der Pierrette*), in which the lyric element yielded to the tragic grotesque and *bouffonnade*. And later the theater directors Nikolai Evreinov and Alexander Tairov and the choreographers Romanov and Goleizovsky treated the same topic in different ways.

Gorsky brought the same characters onto the stage in similar situations: Pierrot, who has been killed in a duel, reproaches Columbine, who is responsible for his death. But in Meyerhold's pantomime and in Romanov's ballet there was a tense passion, an almost deliberately crude coloring; the fantastically ugly bordered on the comic, and the awkwardness of this combination evoked a sense of nightmare. Gorsky's ballet had neither the irony, the grotesque, nor the "sadism" of which Romanov was accused. Such an understanding of the theme also conditioned the choice of music: it was impossible to imagine that the bright grotesque of Meyerhold or Romanov could be combined with the serene grandeur of Glazunov's *Lyric Poem*.

Gorsky achieved the necessary atmosphere not through contrast but through a monotone construction. "Gorsky has made this tiny theme for an intermezzo in graphically cold, condensed tones," wrote the critic of *Teatralnaya gazeta*.[15] Pale as an otherworldly phantom, Pierrot and the languid Columbine were dressed in black and white costumes. However, here too the choreographer did not come to a meeting of minds with the artist. "The very nature of the characters, the contrast of the black and white patches on the costumes, cries out for a similar background in the 'blanc et noir' style, although the primitive sets of A. Lentulov are done with taste and serenity."[16] *Lyric Poem* was presented several times in the Aquarium, and then Gorsky no longer revived it.

Another ballet of Gorsky's, *Night on Bald Mountain*, met the same fate. The announcements and reviews make it clear that Gorsky had first intended to stage a bacchanalia of evil spirits, a witches' Sabbath in the spirit of the Italian Middle Ages, inspired by the images of Dmitri Merezhkovsky's novel *The Romance of Leonardo da Vinci, or The Resurrection of the Gods*. Some characters were kept—the black werecat, the witch riding a hog, the naked redhaired witch, the shaggy incubus, and the nun. However, the main characters and the time and place of the action were changed. Instead of the beautiful Italian lady Cassandra, engaged to Hircus Nocturnus (the Night Goat), Gorsky had Hanna and the Devil; instead of the patriarch of the sorcerers, the high priest of the Holy Inquisition, he had Chernobog; instead of the canon, a sacristan. In Merezhkovsky's original, during the wedding ceremony the Night Goat took on the form of the young, beautiful Dionysus, while in Gorsky's production it was the god Yarilo.* Thus his satanic Sabbat was transformed not into a divine orgy of Bacchus but rather into a scene of adoration of the ancient Slavic god who incarnates the life-giving force of the sun. Apparently the critic who wrote ironically about the performance was right when he asserted that in it the "little Russian" element dominated, pushing all the literary allusions into the background.[17] But even within these limits Gorsky's success was minimal. The critics, pointing out that this theme had great potential for dance, reproached him for the lack of temperament necessary to translate Mussorgsky's powerful fantasy. "The whole externally colorful picture is internally pale."[18] Six years later Fedor Lopukhov would find a new, modern incarnation for this music.

For *Spanish Sketches* Gorsky used Glinka's *Capriccio brilliante* and *Recuerdos de Castilla* (First and Second Spanish Overtures). In *Don Quixote* (1901) Gorsky had tried for the first time to break with the clichés of "balletic pseudo-Spain." His major success, as Asafiev noted, was the fact that the dancing was born "from emotional states that kindled a consuming need for dance."[19] Later, in the Spanish ballets of Fokine and Romanov, the dancing kept this quality and also gained a number of new ones. First of all, it was now born from the music: Minkus was replaced by Glinka and Bizet. Secondly, it was enriched with ethnographic details. And finally, it was freed from outdated conventions, whose power Gorsky continued to feel.

Fokine went further than anyone else. In *Jota Aragonesa* (1916) he created a model of character ballet in which the dancing in all its richness of colors and nuances, unburdened by dramatic conflict, reveals the content of Glinka's work. Such a solution was alien to Gorsky; he rarely got by without a plot as the basis for action. *Spanish Sketches* gave grounds for complaints that "the presence of a plot is oppressive and the realism of the images weighs heavily."[20] The choreographer sought refuge in melodrama, and in doing so came close to Romanov. The critics noted a common thread in their productions; *Andalusiana*, which Romanov had presented in Moscow in the spring of 1918, was still fresh in everyone's

* Yarilo is the ancient Slavic sun-god.

memory. The action of *Spanish Sketches* also took place in a tavern. The focus of attention was also a young beauty, for whose love a young man and an old one sparred. But Romanov's version had "nerve on stage, had intensity,"[21] while Gorsky's had "a kaleidoscope of colors but a lack of colorfulness."[22]

The same accusations could have been leveled at the ballet *Thamar*, to the music of Mili Balakirev. In the A. A. Bakhrushin State Central Theater Museum are sketches for the decor and several costumes for Gorsky's *Thamar*. The decor is crude in its color combinations: A pink alcove is framed by bright blue columns, which support a green arch; Thamar's couch is bright yellow, the rug yellow, and so on. The multicolored bright costumes, in the style of the old *luboks*, also transcend the usual spectrum. Judging by reviews, the production did not have the sense of mystery and uneasiness, evoking the feeling that evil spirits lurked, that made Diaghilev's production of *Thamar* in 1912, with choreography by Fokine and designs by Bakst, so distinctive. Once again, for the *n*th time, there were frenzied dances, the flash of daggers, and the tearing away of veils—all the attributes of romanticized eroticism well-known since Fokine's *Schéhérazade*. In 1918 all of this was perceived as an anachronism. The same outdated language appeared in *La Péri*, to the music of Paul Dukas: the spicy East and fuzzy philosophizing on love that spoke simultaneously of death and immortality.

The ballet *En blanc*, staged to the music of Tchaikovsky's Third Suite, was considerably more interesting. The suite is a long (more than forty minutes) four-part work. Its first part, both in terms of form and depth of content and emotional intensity, could have been part of a symphony. But the last part is extremely unusual, composed in the form of a series of variations and notable for its length; it is as long as the other three put together. It is precisely the lack of obligatory unity and balance characteristic of symphonies that prevents the Third Suite from belonging to that genre. Its individual parts are perceived as completely independent works, distinct in mood, principle of construction, and intention.

The first part of this suite, "Elegy," is dramatic. It opens with a lyric theme, but gradually its intonations become more tense, and notes of pathos toll. The music sounds like a human voice, now grieving, now inquiring, now triumphant. It is not accidental that choreographers always use the "Elegy" in the most emotionally charged scenes. In *The Snow*

Maiden (staged by Vladimir Varkovitsky in 1946 and by Vladimir Bur-meister in 1963), the duet of the Snow Maiden and the youth, which ends with her melting away, is set to this music.

"Theme and Variations" has a completely different character. Here the composer sets himself a formal task: Having first presented the theme, he goes on to show it in twelve different variations so that it resounds in a dark chorale, then in a vivacious dance, and lastly, in the finale, in a gala polonaise. "Theme and Variations" has been used for dances by George Balanchine, Walter Gore, and Janine Charrat abroad, and by Robert Gerbek and Feya Balabina in Leningrad. It is a suite of varied dance numbers, fast and slow, gay and sad—a parade of dancers showing off their technique.

Fifty years after Gorsky, Tchaikovsky's Third Suite was staged in its entirety by Balanchine (1970). He not only did not seek a single choreo-graphic solution that would be appropriate to all parts of the work, but deliberately contrasted the first part to "Theme and Variations." Gorsky tried to find a unifying principle in the "whiteness" of the production (hence its title, *En blanc*). The costumes of the soloist (Adamovich), of the performers of the variations, and of the corps de ballet were white, and pure classical dance served as the vocabulary. But this was not the whiteness of the "ballet blanc" that had become a symbol of choreo-graphic academicism. The dancers appeared not in tutus, but in light-weight dresses. According to the original plan, they were to wear white wigs, but for reasons of economy these were replaced with bows. The dancing was also different from the old ballets. As Nikolai Markvardt put it, "stiff classicism" was combined with free groupings "in the spirit of the 'new school.'"[23]

The major roles in "Elegy" were danced by Adamovich and Svoboda. The female role, for all of its elegiac quality, was built on quite com-plex movements of classical dance: The reviews mention turns on pointe, leaps, and complex lifts. The corps de ballet now entered into the dance, now formed separate groupings. "The elegant muslin dresses of the bal-lerinas, like snowflakes flitting by in graceful pas de chat, frozen in im-passive arabesques, as in old prints, the general style of the staging and its disciplined execution—all of this produces an impression of unity," wrote Markvardt.[24] In the last part of the suite, the young dancers from the theater and students in the senior classes, Nina Podgoretskaya and

Elena Ilyushchenko, had individual dances (duos and trios) on an equal footing with the leading performers, such as Svoboda, who performed the virtuoso variations. Even the male corps de ballet joined in the finale. Gorsky introduced this additional coloring apparently in order to convey the spectacular tones of the brilliant polonaise. Here the principle of "en blanc" was violated; the men danced in multicolored frockcoats à l'Empire.

In setting *En blanc* to the music of Tchaikovsky's Third Suite, Gorsky staged a ballet to a major symphonic non-program work for the second time (after Glazunov's Fifth Symphony [1916]). However, in the first case he was trying to adapt a plot based on life in ancient Greece to the music, while here he was looking for its expression in pure dance. Soon (in 1923) Lopukhov's dance symphony *The Magnificence of the Universe* would be staged, and later this type of ballet would become one of the most widespread. Here choreographic themes would express corresponding musical themes, and choreographic form would become analogous to musical form.

Gorsky was far from reaching this stage. For him music merely accompanied the dancing, which coincided with it in rhythm and duration and reflected its general mood. One cannot call the ballet *En blanc* a dance symphony, yet it is a milestone on the road toward the eventual creation of the dance symphony.

Apparently the choreographer himself considered that this ballet had been more successful than his other productions in the Aquarium Garden Theater. He continued to work on it in a studio at the Bolshoi Theater. For a concert in the House of Unions on December 19, 1921, Gorsky prepared "An Evening of Symphonic Ballet," which included Tchaikovsky's Third Suite, Franz Liszt's Second Rhapsody, and Karl Maria von Weber's *Invitation to the Dance*. He hoped to include these productions in the theater's repertory. However, as Adamovich notes, Gorsky's studio works were all vetoed by the theater directorate.[25] Along with these new works, Gorsky also presented *Giselle*, which he had reworked, with sets by Fedotov, in the Aquarium.[26] (This production will be discussed later.)

Thematically, musically, and choreographically, Gorsky's productions continued his prerevolutionary practice. At the same time, by inviting Futurist artists to be his partners, the choreographer was trying to approach contemporary art movements. Such stylistic discord gave rise to eclecticism. The press accused Gorsky of simultaneously trying to make his ballets "sensational" and "brazenly popular," and yet of being totally bogged down in routine. Gennady Geronsky, who saw in the production *En blanc* "a mixture of dead old devices and new, not fully thought through ideas"[27] expressed the general opinion not so much of this ballet as of the season as a whole.

Yet Gorsky was honestly trying to keep abreast with contemporary life. He welcomed the revolution, which for a while created hopes of "working on that which was close to his heart,"[28] and he paid close attention to the new events that were emerging all around him. At the same time, Gorsky's worldview and artistic beliefs were organically linked with the ideals of the preceding epoch. Hence his constant turning towards the choreographic achievements of the first decade of the century and his attraction to the free movements of Isadora Duncan.

The new season lay ahead, a responsible and difficult one. He had to lead it with a company weakened by the departure of many dancers. In keeping with the demands made on art by the revolutionary authorities, new productions were also expected from Gorsky. Anticipating impending changes, Gorsky showed his own strength and the strength of the young members of the ballet company in the Aquarium Theater.

Stenka Razin

In the fall of 1918 the new regime was preparing to celebrate the first anniversary of the October Revolution. "The ceremonies will begin at twelve noon on November 6 and will finish the night of November 7. Dancers should participate in two ways: First of all there will be a number of street performances on specially erected stands; representatives of all the arts, including the ballet, will take part in these performances. . . . Secondly, performances will be given in all the theaters, for which tickets will be extremely inexpensive, and the repertory will be appropriate to this historic moment."[29]

A commission was entrusted with running the ceremonies. It included Konstantin Stanislavsky, Vladimir Nemirovich-Danchenko, Alexander Sanin; the artists Konstantin Korovin, Piotr Konchalovsky, Aristarkh Lentulov; the conductors Émile Cooper, Viacheslav Suk, Andrei Arends;

and others. The ballet was represented on the committee by Gorsky. The ceremonial performance was planned for November 6 at the Bolshoi Theater. Discussion of its program began in mid-October, and on October 30 the project was approved by the administration.

It was of course impossible to prepare a totally new production during the time remaining. Therefore, selected works were chosen from the repertory of symphonic music and from the opera theater that differed in content and style but were linked by a common theme of popular uprising and the struggle for justice and freedom. The performance opened with the newly adopted Soviet anthem, "The Internationale," performed by the chorus and orchestra of the Bolshoi Theater.

Next on the program was Beethoven's Ninth Symphony. Beethoven's music was particularly popular. On November 6 and 7 the SRD Theater presented the opera *Fidelio*. On the eve of this celebration, November 2, Lunacharsky gave an introductory address on the Ninth Symphony at the second symphonic concert of the Moscow Professional Union of Musicians and Performers. In the Bolshoi Theater the text of Friedrich Schiller's "Ode to Joy," inviting people to unite in the name of happiness and brotherhood on earth, was to be sung by Antonina Nezhdanova, Nadezhda Obukhova, Andrei Labinsky, and Vasily Petrov, along with the chorus.

The works of Alexander Scriabin were also heard throughout these concerts, and this was quite understandable. The bold innovations in his music and his mystical aspirations to penetrate the secrets of creation were bound to strike a chord in the soul of people who had witnessed such monumental dramatic events. In the future, as we shall see, all the choreographers seeking new dance forms, such as Goleizovsky, Lev Lukin, the representatives of various studios of free dance, and even Gorsky, were also attracted to the works of Scriabin.

The program of the gala performance included Scriabin's poem *Prometheus*. Nemirovich-Danchenko took the initiative in deciding not to perform the Ninth Symphony this time. *Prometheus*, a poem about fire, was performed on the holiday program right after "The Internationale."[30]

The lighting for this passionate, tragic poem personifying man's revolt against darkness and the power of matter was done in accordance with the composer's original specifications. At first the stage was engulfed in violet-gray twilight; then it was illuminated by bright blue rays which changed to blood-red. Finally, at the climax, when the chorus sang, everything was flooded with a dazzling white light.

The second half of the program opened with a scene from Rimsky-Korsakov's opera *The Maid of Pskov* (also known as *Ivan the Terrible*), in a naturalistic staging by Alexander Sanin, which served as a contrast to Scriabin's mystical symphony of color and sound. Bonfires burned, lighting up the square of ancient Pskov; bells sounded the alarm, and the people proclaimed their determination to resist Ivan the Terrible.

In the repertory of symphonic music and in opera it was relatively easy to find works in keeping with the contemporary era. Things were more difficult with the ballet. In the Bolshoi Theater productions there were no dance scenes appropriate to the holiday program. Therefore it was decided to stage a new ballet. Its protagonist was Stenka Razin.*

Fokine had already staged Glazunov's symphonic poem *Stenka Razin* for a charity benefit evening on the stage of the Maryinsky Theater in November 1915. In 1916 the ballet was performed in Moscow during the tour of Fokine and his wife Vera Fokina. Moscow dancers participated in the ensemble scenes. The ballet had more success in Moscow than in Petrograd.

The famous sculptor Sergei Konenkov was also attracted by the figure of Razin. One of his drawings of 1916 shows Razin and the Persian princess, the traditional characters of the well-known folksong. Later, in 1919, he made a wooden statue of the hero, surrounded by comrades-in-arms, intended for Red Square. In 1916 the poet Vasily Kamensky wrote a poem and later a play about Razin.

After the revolution, Razin became one of the most popular historical figures. He appeared in mass pageants; in the scenario for the production *Hymn of Liberated Labor*, mention was made of the "onslaught of peasants in red shirts, armed with staves and axes, led by Stenka Razin."[31] Plays about Razin succeeded each other in rapid succession. Aside from Kamensky, Andrei Globa, Ilary Shadrin, Ivan Novozhilov, and Yuri Yurin dealt with this theme. Several operas appeared. In 1921 Maxim Gorky wrote the scenario for a full-length film, *Stenka Razin*. Even in the circus Razin appeared in the pantomime numbers.

---

*Stenka Razin led a peasant uprising in 1667–71 and became an important Russian folk hero, a symbol of populist revolt. (Ed.)

The figure of Razin was particularly frequent in the Moscow festival performances marking the first anniversary of the October Revolution. Fedor Komissarzhevsky staged Kamensky's play with Nikolai Znamensky and Alice Koonen in the leading roles at this time. The artists decorated holiday streets with portraits of the famous rebel. On Theater Square, bedecked with flags, garlands, and placards, were hung huge panels, the work of Lentulov, Robert Falk, Alexander Osmerkin, and others. "The revolution calling to the leaders of the proletariat" was next to the reapers and the trees weighed down by fruit on the building of the Maly Theater, whose facade was decorated for the holidays by Pavel Kuznetsov and Nikolai Rosenfeld; next to it hung a "picture showing the popular hero Stenka Razin."[32]

The Bolshoi Theater decided to glorify him in dance. Gorsky had to work under difficult conditions. The time available for preparing the ballet was very short. The newspapers announced the production of *Stenka Razin* on October 17. At first it was assumed that the main female role of the Persian princess would be played by Geltser or Alexandra Balashova. But the leading ballerinas apparently refused to take part in the production. Therefore a new candidate was proposed—Maria Reisen, with whom Gorsky had just worked extremely successfully in the Aquarium. The sets were done in a hurry; only on October 24 was the money necessary for purchasing paint allocated.[33] There is little information available on the ballet *Stenka Razin*. There are no materials on it in any of the theater archives. The majority of the participants and audience cannot remember the ballet. In the view of Maria Reisen, the dancing was less outstanding and less elegant than Fokine's production. In a later study of *Stenka Razin*, Slonimsky cites Goleizovsky's opinion.[34] The choreographer believes that the difficulties Gorsky encountered and, above all, the monotony and insufficient dance quality of the music prevented him from achieving the desired effect. At the time of the premiere there was only one press notice. An article on the festival evening devoted only a few lines of criticism to it.[35]

This critic wrote of a "slapdash, clichéd" scenario. This reproach is hardly fair. Gorsky, like Fokine before him, was forced to follow Glazunov's program. The content of the poem was stated by the composer as follows: "The calm breadth of the Volga. For a long time the Russian land around it lay quiet and undisturbed until the terrible ataman, Stenka

Razin, appeared. With his fierce gang he began travelling up and down the Volga on rafts, and he pillaged cities and villages. . . ." Further on, the Persian princess, kidnapped and taken prisoner by Stenka, tells of her dream: "The ataman will be shot, the Cossack oarsmen will go to prison, and I will drown in the Mother Volga. . . ." Surrounded by tsarist troops, Razin decides to give to the Mother Volga "the most beautiful thing in the world" and throws the princess into the waves. "The wild gang began to sing his glory and then joined him in fighting the tsar's troops." [36] Gorsky followed this program; that is why the focus of attention was the banal episode with the Persian princess.

And yet, Glazunov's poem does have its merits, justifying its selection for the revolutionary anniversary production. The basic musical theme that characterizes Razin's troops is the melody for the well-known song of the Volga boatmen, "Ei, ukhnem." The theme "Ei, ukhnem" develops throughout the poem. It is stated in the introduction ("The calm breadth of the Volga") and has further variations in the middle part, where it characterizes Stenka's troops, the wild temper of their chief, and the rakish boldness of his company. It also occurs in the last part of the poem and in its powerful finale. Here the image of the river in revolt merges with the longing of the soul, the desperate determination of Razin making his sacrifice, and the triumph of his reckless, unrestrained companions.

In the second part of the nineteenth century "Ei, ukhnem" was taken up by the Russian revolutionary movement, transcended its significance as bargehaulers' folklore, and became known as a song of social protest. During the revolution of 1905 it was disseminated on a mass level, and after the October Revolution it became a popular favorite. The fact that the melody was heard in the ballet made it to some extent in tune with the era, even if social motifs were not in the foreground of the scenario.

The review says of Gorsky's production: "Purely choreographically speaking there was nothing new or interesting here." Following Glazunov's music, Gorsky, like Fokine before him, put the wild dances of Razin's companions at the center of the production; this contrasted with the mood of the dances of the Persian prisoners. For Fokine's production, Glazunov conducted the premiere and wrote additional music. The dance of the Cossacks was set to this music. Judging by the program and by the memoirs of Yuri Faier, this dance was not included in the Bolshoi Theater production. Probably this weakened the choreography.

Critics asserted that the revolutionary theme was treated "with the help of the conventional forms of the old ballet." Gorsky's ballet really had little in common with the new revolutionary art that during those festivities powerfully made itself known through the language of colorful posters and Futurist portraits. The ballet showed a completely different Razin than the one the viewer knew from the square in front of theater. The dances did not at all portray the episodes from the life of Stenka Razin "painted in the style of an old Russian showbooth" which were displayed on the walls of the Maly Theater.[37] In the hall of the Bolshoi Theater, draped with red calico and adorned with the slogans "The revolution is the locomotive of history" or "Long live the union of workers and poor peasants of the villages!," Razin, as Gorsky was able to show him, looked obsolete. In terms of style, Gorsky's ballet was, of course, linked to prerevolutionary choreography. Having broken with the traditions of the old character dancing of the corps de ballet, Fokine and Gorsky systematically turned to dance folklore, singling out in it features of raging spontaneity, of orgiastic intoxication in the dance. Eastern dance movements—the play of the hands and torso—had an equally important role in their ballets. This time it was used in the scenes with the women prisoners.

The critic of *Izvestiia* was also dissatisfied with the sets for the ballet: "Konchalovsky's decor was not pleasing to the eye; the grey sails were absolutely unsuccessful."[38] The draft sketches for the sets, which are now in the A. A. Bakhrushin State Central Theatrical Museum, give another impression; they are dynamic. The colorful pile-up of cliffs and the sails blowing in the wind seem to embody the dashing, daring, free spirit of Stenka's rebels. The costumes, which had been selected from the theater's wardrobe for various ballets and perhaps from opera productions as well, were not appropriate to the sets; "this created an unharmonic mixture, giving the viewer a feeling of disorder."[39]

Gorsky's position was not enviable. Once again, as during the days of the performances in the Aquarium Garden Theater, he was subjected to simultaneous fire from both the "right" and the "left." The supporters of "new forms" in art found the ballet old-fashioned. But the devotees of the old academic ballet also reacted negatively; a few years later, when the ballet was revived in the New Theater, the Petrograd reviewer Alexander Kleiman wrote a devastating review of it. Incidentally, he was sharply critical of all Moscow productions.[40]

And yet, for all that, the ballet *Stenka Razin* marks a new stage in Gorsky's creative life. It is precisely with this production and not with the Aquarium season that the new, Soviet period of his work begins.

The ballet recalls the heroic qualities of Gorsky's early productions. The audiences of 1918 saw in Razin the leader of insurgents and not the head of a "wild gang." Recalling the production of November 7, 1918, Pavel Markov wrote that Alexei Bulgakov interpreted the image of Razin "as clearly positive, as the image of a popular hero who has sacrificed his love."[41] *Stenka Razin* is the first attempt by the Moscow ballet to react to the demands of a revolutionary people. This in itself makes it an event in the history of the Soviet theater.

Gorsky's ballet strengthened yet another tendency that was very important for the further development of Soviet ballet: that attention to dynamic crowd scenes from which the later collective heroic image arose. Gorsky's *Stenka Razin* was the first such statement. The dances of Pugachev's supporters in Andrei Pashchenko's opera *Revolt of the Eagles*, staged by Lopukhov in 1925, comes closer to the mark. But Lopukhov, too, apparently not without reason, was accused of putting a rowdy horde on the stage instead of a revolutionary people.

The flowering of the heroic dance was still to come in Soviet ballet. Some features of the new element would be noticeable in the famous dance "Yablochko" ("Little Apple") in *The Red Poppy* (1927). But mass heroic dances were to appear only later, when the style of male classical dance performance changed and ballet began even more intensively to absorb folklore. Strictly speaking, we will see these only in the ballets of Vainonen and Chabukiani.

The ballet *Stenka Razin* was staged with the anniversary program in mind. After the ceremonial premiere it was shown three more times and then disappeared from the repertory. But apparently Gorsky did not want to let the production die. In 1922 he took *Stenka Razin* to the stage of the New Theater, where he had the opportunity to revive a number of his experimental works. Here the ballet was shown fairly regularly for some time.

The Nutcracker

The next ballet premiere at the Bolshoi Theater was Tchaikovsky's *The Nutcracker*. Before the revolution *The Nutcracker* had not been performed in Moscow. Gorsky had planned to produce it in 1912; before that it had been impossible to stage it, for from 1905 to 1910 the ballet department of the Moscow Theater School did not accept students and there would have been no one to dance in the children's scenes. Enrollment resumed in 1911.

In April 1912 the Bolshoi Theater asked Tchaikovsky's heir, Modest Tchaikovsky, for permission to make a number of changes in the ballet. These changes included dividing the first act into two (making the scene in the winter forest a separate act) and transferring into it the pas de deux of the Sugarplum Fairy and her Cavalier from the last act. The last act was supposed to include a new pas de deux from Tchaikovsky's works. Andrei Arends orchestrated the pieces "Mazurka," "Snowdrop," and "Tendres reproches" for it. The directorate explained that these changes "were prompted by the desire to let the ballerina lead the entire ballet," while "the score has only one pas de deux in the last act."[42] Geltser was the proposed performer. In September 1912 the newspaper *Russkoe slovo* reported that Korovin was working on the decor for *The Nutcracker*. In May 1913 the artist signed an agreement to finish the decor by November. In 1913–14 sketches were drawn up for the costumes, which is attested to by the pages dated by Vasily Diachkov in the archives of the Bolshoi Theater. The outbreak of the war put a stop to this work; at that time it seemed awkward to stage a ballet based on a plot by the German writer E. T. A. Hoffmann.

Work on *The Nutcracker* resumed only after the February Revolution. In May 1917 Gorsky granted an interview to Alexander Pleshcheyev and mentioned *The Nutcracker* among the productions planned.[43] Soon afterwards, Korovin too resumed his work. In July sketches for the first scene and for "The Kingdom of Snow" were finished. Then again there was an interruption: revolutionary events put off for a time the plans for a new production. Finally, in 1918 Georgi Golov, Mikhail Yakovlev, and Larisa Golova began painting the sets. But vacation time and then preparation for celebration of the first anniversary of the Soviet Republic again delayed their completion. The premiere finally took place on May 21, 1919.

In staging other ballets drawn from the classical heritage Gorsky usually took as a basis the accepted version and reworked it, making the ballet more modern. His production of *The Nutcracker* was entirely new. This is probably explained by the fact that he considered the old production unsuccessful and therefore did not see any grounds for keeping even individual fragments, as he had done in other cases.

The libretto of *The Nutcracker* is attributed to Ivan Vsevolozhsky and Marius Petipa, who had produced a detailed staging plan, on the basis of which Tchaikovsky worked. This plan divided the ballet into two distinct halves. It opens with the children's Christmas celebration, where the little girl Clara receives a gift of a toy nutcracker. Then there is a nighttime battle between the toys and the mice, and the Nutcracker, transformed into a Prince, sets off with Clara on a fairytale journey. The dramatic action ends with these events, and the production then turns into a *féerie*. The first act ends with the scene in the winter forest, and the second shows Konfitürenburg, where all possible kinds of confections, endowed with the ability to dance, appear before Clara and the Prince. Thus the gala divertissement, with which Petipa customarily ended his productions, expanded here to formerly unheard-of proportions, constituting half the ballet.

Tchaikovsky's music formally met the demands made by the libretto, but in fact its content is far more profound. *The Nutcracker* is a children's fairytale and at the same time a work of great psychological depth. In it Tchaikovsky spoke of children with love, insight, and seriousness, expressing in music their real experiences and fantasies. The music depicts the gaiety around the Christmas tree, children's happiness at bright lights and gifts, and then their fears at night, when all things come to life and tin soldiers have to fend off attacks by evil mice. But at the same time, the music reveals the spiritual world of the heroine, the little girl who loves the toy despised by all—the ugly Nutcracker. By defending him she is able to overcome her fear of the terrible Mouse King and thus wins the right to have her dreams come true. Selfless love is the key to all the beauty in the world, to all the hopes; it is the way to great achievements.

Thus the simple fairytale plot line was interpreted by Tchaikovsky's music, which, as conceived by the scenarist and choreographer, was only an excuse for the gala divertissement and *féerie*. Tchaikovsky not only transcended the boundaries of the children's fairytale ballet, but, revealing in the music an enormous emotional tension, departed so far from the fairytale that at times he completely lost the plot line. The andante in the scene of the winter forest, some parts of the battle, and, in particular, the majestic adagio of the last act present difficulties even for contemporary choreographers who are forced to stick to the scenario. And at the end of the nineteenth century such an interpretation of a fairytale, one which raised it to the level of a philosophical abstraction, was all the more difficult to produce.

In addition, it was impossible to imagine a ballet without a role for a ballerina that was rich in strong dances. Any Petersburg prima ballerina or famous guest artist was by right entitled to perform several virtuoso variations or a striking pas de deux in a ballet. Thus the 1892 production was built around two main characters. In the first act, at the Christmas celebration, it was the little girl Clara, performed by a small student from the ballet school. In the second act it was the Sugarplum Fairy, who welcomed Clara on her arrival at Konfitürenburg. Here she became the major character of the ballet. Petipa gave her a large classical duet with Prince Coqueluche, and the entire dance suite revolves around her.

Gorsky found the flaws of the 1892 production particularly annoying, since they were the results of precisely those conventions of the "old" ballet that he opposed. A supporter of dance-drama, he dismissed the achievements of the first version of *The Nutcracker*, for here what was of greatest value were not the plot episodes, but the large classical ensemble —"The Waltz of the Snowflakes." At the time when Gorsky was staging his ballet, it was still being presented on the Petrograd stage; Volynsky's well-known articles, on which all scholars are obliged to rely, since they give the most precise and careful description of this dance, were written in 1922 and 1923.

The scene in the forest was intended by Petipa as a grandiose spectacle—a féerie. In the original plan, the "Waltz of the Snowflakes" was called *"tourbillonnant"*—sixty dancers were to perform it, and electric lighting was to be included in the finale. For Tchaikovsky the Waltz expresses considerably more. It is Clara's dream, full of sweet and alarming forebodings. Lev Ivanov sensitively caught the lyricism of the image and conveyed it by means as simple as they were expressive: the uncomplicated movements of classical dance, varied in different combinations and repeated over and over; the severe white tutus and the hair decorations made of trembling white bits of fluff. The patterns the dancers formed —lines that intersected and separated, circles and crosses—created the impression of whirling snowflakes, melting little snow stars. The striking musicality and formal perfection of the dancing gave it the depth and penetration that characterized the music.

However, in staging *The Nutcracker* Gorsky did not retain the discoveries of his predecessors. He sought his own solution. As always, the choreographer strove for a unity of impression, a single style for the production. In this case, for him the key to the ballet became the theme of childhood. From the first scene to the last the plot revolved around one character—the little girl. Gorsky eliminated the Sugarplum Fairy and gave her role to Clara, casting Valentina Kudriavtseva, a student in the senior classes, rather than a very young student, in this role. He categorically rejected all the claims of the leading ballerinas. An open conflict broke out with Geltser, who insisted up to opening night on her right under contract to participate in all new Bolshoi Theater productions.[44] But Gorsky did not give in. When after the premiere the question again arose of replacing the student with an adult dancer, the administration of the Bolshoi Theater, having discussed the question, "expressed the opinion that in creating this role the choreographer had in mind a specific image and when Gorsky's plan was being approved he fully sketched out the artistic framework this image fit; the student Kudriavtseva has fully met the demands of this image." The opinion was then stated that "in this role it would be desirable to see a performer even younger than the student Kudriavtseva, to create the image of a very young girl, who experiences childish happiness and grief, the basic motifs running through the entire fairytale."[45]

Everything that happens in the ballet was seen by Gorsky from a child's point of view. The dominant feature was a naive faith in the reality of the fairytale element, where magic takes on fully tangible features and all the familiar concrete phenomena turn into a fairytale. Gorsky changed the traditional division of the ballet into two acts, dividing it now into three. The action of the first act took place in the living room of the Silberhaus family, whose decorations made the room look somewhat like a hall in a hunting lodge. The walls were hung with deer antlers. In the foreground on the left was an enormous clock as tall as a person. On it sat an owl, a gloomy, sulking bird with round eyes. When the clock struck, the owl flapped its wings. Next to the Christmas tree was a tea table and on it a coffee set, a tea kettle, and a Chinese tea set. And here the toys were set out: dolls, dancers, *polichinelles,* toy soldiers, cannons, and a whole toy fortress.

The lighting was muted. The costumes of the dancers were all in dull "autumn" colors. The master of the house wore a brown evening jacket, beige pants, and a vest embroidered with lilac flowers. The mistress of the house was in a brown and beige dress with pale green sleeves, trimmed in the color of fading roses. The costumes of the older guests were in appropriate tones: brown, yellow-green, yellow, and lilac shades, with brown and grey for the men. Some of the guests were grey-haired or bald old men and old women in lilac dresses and caps. The sketch that shows a decrepit old woman in an enormous cap with lilac ribbons involuntarily brings to mind the old Countess from Pushkin's "The Queen of Spades." The younger guests—young ladies and little girls—wore light-colored dresses: pink, light blue, greenish, lavender. But even here there were no joyous, sunny hues or sharp contrasts of color.

This was not a triumphant gala ball, but rather a domestic holiday, and it was run by very ordinary adults who had their daily concerns, people who did not dream. The image of the grown-up guests around the tree was very carefully thought out. In the forefront stood a card table, and the old men were sitting down to play cards. They argued energetically. Standing next to them, a young man in a bright checkered suit with a monocle on a large red ribbon (Leonid Zhukov) observed the game with a dull expression. The choreographer and the dancer worked out all the details of the young dandy's behavior in this act—his foppish manners and mincing gait. The young man tried to court Drosselmeyer's haughty wife (Elena Adamovich), but she coldly refused his invitation to dance; he had no choice but to choose as his partner the withered old lady, played by Antonina Shalomytova.

Gorsky's Drosselmeyer did not have an aura of mystery. He was not a sorcerer, a master of magic games, but one of the guests. The sketches show a middle-aged, stout man with sideburns and round glasses. It is true that participants in the ballet say that Alexei Bulgakov added a particular elegance to Drosselmeyer that set him off from the others around him. He was more aristocratic and refined, a graceful dreamer who stood at the very threshold of that world of poetry the other adults did not enter. But even if Bulgakov's Drosselmeyer was not as prosaic as the other guests, he was still quite different from the Drosselmeyer of the Petersburg production—the frightening one-eyed old man, the herald of evil events. In Gorsky's ballet, Drosselmeyer is a kind godfather who has appeared laden down with toys; here are dolls, *polichinelles*, a cannon, and, hidden in his pocket, the Nutcracker and a package with his bed. Behind him a fat bald servant carries an enormous doll, human size, all wrapped up. At the height of the festivities Drosselmeyer shows his fantastic wind-up toys: a toy soldier who dances with a vivandière, Harlequin and Columbine. So far there was nothing mysterious in these tricks of Drosselmeyer's. He was just a kind godfather amusing the children.

But Clara did not perceive things this way. In the gloomy Silberhaus home, with its dull, humdrum life, lived a little girl who was not like those around her; she was able to draw a spark of poetry from everything.

Gorsky wanted Clara to look like a child, but at the same time he needed a performer who could fulfill rather complex acting and dance tasks. The choice of Kudriavtseva, who was then fifteen, created the possibility of enriching the dancing in this role. Playing Clara, she admired the Nutcracker, defended him from the bold, mischievous Fritz, caressed him and put him to bed, but her small dance numbers were more complex than they were for the young performers of this role in other productions.

In the second scene after the departure of the guests Clara quietly came back into the moonlit living room for the Nutcracker. Now, instead of a splendid lace dress, she wore a long nightshirt and cap and held a candle in her hands. The clock struck midnight and in the place of the owl Drosselmeyer appeared with his reddish sideburns, glasses, and eyes as round as the bird's. (On the sketch there is a note by Gorsky explaining that the clock's body should be constructed so that Bulgakov, who played Drosselmeyer, could hide in it.) Gorsky did not invent this scene. Petipa's plan already had a note for Tchaikovsky: "Clara looks at the clock and sees with horror that the owl has turned into Drosselmeyer, who looks at her with his mocking laugh."[46] But he made use of every possible means to show the shift from the real to the fantastic. Yuri Bakhrushin, who saw this production, confirms that the scene "was totally confused and unclear, exactly the way things happen in a dream."[47]

Then the wonders began. The Christmas tree grew and so did the toys along with it. A comparison of the sketches of the props and costumes reveals that each toy corresponded to a dancer's costume: small eight- to ten-inch dolls, dancers, and *polichinelles* "came to life"—that is, were replaced by performers. Special seats were built for them on the Christmas tree. When the battle of the tin soldiers and the mice started, the dolls came down from the tree and watched the battle with Clara. The toy cannons and fortresses also grew, along with the Christmas tree, until they were big enough for the toy soldiers, played by students from the ballet school, to enter the fortress and shoot the cannons. The Nutcracker's little bed also grew. At the height of the battle, when the mice repelled the tin soldiers, the Nutcracker appeared, transformed into a prince in a white uniform embroidered in sparkling gold, wearing a fur-lined dolman and a white busby with a red feather. With his sword he immediately chopped off all seven heads of the enormous white Mouse King, who had appeared from below the earth. The toys rejoiced at the victory. The Nutcracker Prince invited Clara to travel with him. She was dressed in a fur coat and hood, seated on a litter, and carried away, and the dolls accompanied the travelers. This was the end of the first act of Gorsky's ballet.

The action of the second act took place in a winter forest. The wanderings of Clara and the Nutcracker Prince began. The living room in the first two scenes of the ballet had a large window covered with icy designs. The decor for the following scene showed the same window, but increased to the size of the stage, and the ice patterns had been transformed into fantastic snow-covered trees. When the curtain opened, rows of Grandfather Frosts came out from each side of the stage with little Christmas trees in their hands. Then the extraordinary snowflakes appeared. Yuri Bakhrushin wrote that the choreographer's intention conflicted with the artist's idea. Korovin had indicated that "on the background of this set the snowflake dancers, in whimsical, varied tutus, perform a waltz." Meanwhile, Gorsky "dressed all the snowflakes in uniform costumes: Over ordinary tutus, the dancers had short little grey fur coats and winter hoods. Thus the entire effect of Korovin's design was lost."[48] Elsewhere Bakhrushin explained: "The lack of tarlatan in those years forced him to reject the idea of sparkling costumes for the snowflakes and to replace them with the ill-suited fur coats and hoods."[49] However, a study of the costume sketches seems to show that the problem was not just the lack of material.

In the Bolshoi Theater Museum there are sketches for the dancers' costumes in "The Kingdom of Snow" scene which show nine variants of tutus with the captions "frost," "hail," "snowflakes." These are indeed "glittering tutus" (on the sketches there are notes—"bright sparkles," "made of foil") in very soft, iridescent tones of pink, pale blue, and green. There are tutus and headdresses in a prickly, angular texture ("frost") and soft fluffy ones ("snowflakes"). These sketches from 1914 were not used; unlike other sketches, they do not bear the names of the dancers. But from 1914 as well there is a sketch for the "snow maidens"—that same bluish mother-of-pearl fur coat lined with white fur of which Bakhrushin wrote and the accompanying hood, white muff, and silver fur-trimmed boots. As is clear from the list of names, this costume was intended for all forty dancers in "The Kingdom of Snow" scene, as well as for Clara. On a sketch for Clara's costume for the first act, Gorsky wrote: "For the second act, a silvery fur-trimmed coat is needed, and also a hood and muff (like the drawings of the snow maidens). It will also be used in the third act." Thus it is clear that Gorsky quite deliberately dressed the snowflakes in fur coats and hoods; the same coat was brought to Clara at the end of the first act. In the little girl's mind, the snowflakes are connected to the Christmas party. For her they are visiting little girlfriends, very like herself—in other words, the fairytale again grows out of that reality with which the child is familiar. Probably the original idea was that in the second act, possibly before the adagio, the snowflakes were to throw off their fur coats, revealing their sparkling tutus. But this transformation did not take place in the performance.

The appearance of the snowflakes determined the very nature of their dances. The movements of the snowflakes were in keeping with their childish, almost toy-like appearance. Gorsky did not put a large classical ensemble into these scenes, in the spirit of Petipa and Lev Ivanov. He did not even use pointe technique. The snowflakes moved around in tiny *pas de chat*, knees forward, holding their hands, which were thrust into their muffs, to their faces. Gorsky asked the dancers to draw an even circle of rouge, a toy-like blush, on each cheek.

In making "The Kingdom of Snow" an independent act Gorsky made changes in the music, as had been intended even in 1912, to intensify the poetic quality of the scene in the forest, "putting into it the duet from the third act, where it serves no purpose."[50] The long adagio section, whose lyric theme becomes highly dramatic in its culminating moments, contrasts with the majestic, radiant andante movement that opened the act. Here the man's tarantella and the ballerina's variation written for the celesta were performed. Thus Gorsky put together all the music designed to reveal the internal world of the protagonist. Through these rearrangements, as well as by dividing the ballet into three acts, he achieved a more harmonious structure. Thus, if the external action was limited willy-nilly to the first act, the internal action—the spiritual growth of the heroine, which was revealed in her resistance to evil, in her love, and in her communion with nature—continued, reaching its apotheosis in the second act. And only the third act was given over to a divertissement.

The changes Gorsky made in the composer's score could have been justified if the dances of the second act had indeed expressed the profound content of the music he had put together there. Yet in animating Clara's childish fancies Gorsky did not go beyond the bounds of a naive childish idyll. The andante, in which Tchaikovsky depicts the joyous excitement of the soul that has fought its way to freedom, featured a procession of the thirty-two Grandfather Frosts and dwarfs. They also participated in the adagio and, during the moments of highest emotional tension, raised Clara high above the ground. Soaring in the air, she feasted her eyes on the beauties of the winter forest. However, no matter how high the Grandfather Frosts threw Clara nor how sweetly she rejoiced in the view of nature spread out before her and the touching little-girl snowflakes, these devices could not express the essence of the lofty adagio, in which triumph and grief merge.

Gorsky consistently developed his pet theme of a toy-like children's ballet, and, as usual, the libretto and not the music served as the basis for ballet action. The choreographer reproduced the meanderings of the plot onstage and gave the music an interpretation suggested by the logic of the children's fairytale. But he was not able to penetrate the depths of the content of the music and to embody it in dance form. The heights to which Tchaikovsky led were for him unattainable.

From the musical point of view, Gorsky's interpretation of "The Waltz of the Snowflakes" was also wrong. The image of Russian winter and of snowy expanses sketched out by Tchaikovsky was contrasted to petit bourgeois, everyday German life. The new world that opened up to Clara was a world full of alarming and joyous forebodings. Gorsky did not sense this, and he staged a dance of amusing snowflake-sisters dreamed up by a little girl. In this sense the choreographer not only went no further than his predecessor Lev Ivanov, but entirely lost the latter's achievements.

Apparently the audience was aware of this drawback in the ballet. The author of the only surviving review wrote that Gorsky staged a ballet that gave nothing to the mind and heart of the adult viewer.[51] Nevertheless, Gorsky himself at first was looking for something different and specifically imagined the dance of the snowflakes differently. This is proved by the sketches dated 1914.

When he revived the ballet in 1922 Gorsky redid the second act. The performer in the role of Clara, Anastasia Abramova, and her partner here executed a real pas de deux with pirouettes and high lifts. Abramova wore the usual costume of a classical ballerina, a light-blue spangled tutu. The dancer herself thinks that this innovation was not good for the production, since its stylistic unity and childlike charm were lost. But Gorsky apparently made these changes because he was aware of the difference in the scale of musical and dramatic images in the first version.

The third act was in sharp contrast in terms of mood and color to the previous ones. In the first scene, Clara and the Nutcracker sailed the sea. It was a joyous journey. In his review of *The Nutcracker* during its 1922 revival Gennady Geronsky said that "the bright colors of Fedorovsky . . . made one recall Sudeikin and Sapunov at the time of the flowering of The World of Art, particularly the scene at sea."[52] It is true that in the New Theater *The Nutcracker* already had other sets (the earlier ones had burned in the spring of 1920), but the basic idea of the production had not changed.

The second scene was unusually vivid. Recalling it, a participant in the production of 1919, Vera Svetinskaya, expressed her feelings thus: "Such happiness! So much light!"[53] The stage showed a tea table covered with a white tablecloth. On it was the coffee set and teapot from the first act increased to such a size that the dancers for Coffee and Chocolate could hide behind them. In the teapot, which had been transformed into a little Chinese house, were hidden the performers for Tea. On the backdrop was drawn an enormous Christmas tree (the same one that had stood in the Silberhaus living room) and under it sat the dancers who had played the Christmas tree toys, their legs spread apart like dolls. Clara and the Nutcracker Prince ran onstage, and recognized the familiar toys and objects with amazement. All the characters introduced themselves to them. Then a general waltz began. (Having taken the pas de deux out of the last act, Gorsky was forced to make rearrangements in the third act as well:

The waltz was performed before the divertissement, which went directly into the coda.) It was danced by various Christmas tree toys: colorful *borstentänzer*,* the elegant porcelain dolls who had accompanied Clara in the first act, folkdancers, and *polichinelles* glittering with gold braid. In between them four soloists in magnificent tutus (Christmas Tree Flowers) swept by with high leaps. The Spanish dance ("Chocolate") was performed by two couples. Adamovich and Alexandra Shelepina wore gold dresses with wide skirts, decorated with appliqués of shiny brown satin; Lev Lashchilin wore brown and Mikhail Fedorov wore white. The Oriental dance ("Arabian Coffee") was performed by Ekaterina Dévilière (known in the West as Catherine Devillier) with six female dancers. The movements of "Tea" were reminiscent of the familiar Chinese dance in the Petersburg production. In addition to the soloists, Viktorina Krieger and Vladimir Kuznetsov, there were four more dancers. The costumes, with their decorations and shiny metal ornaments, were very colorful.

In general, as opposed to the first act, here the designers did not spare their colors. The muted tones of the previous scenes were replaced by clear, strong hues, like handmade folk toys, a sparkle of Christmas tree decorations. The *Matrioshka*** (Alexandra Balashova), all in spangles and a foil *kokoshnik*,† hung with bright beads and silken ribbons, rode out on a painted sleigh harnessed to a troika of wooden horses. She danced a *trepak* with the coachman, the comic bumpkin Vanka (Zhukov). The dance of the shepherds was staged as an ensemble scene. Four soloists and six couples from the corps de ballet took part in it. The gracious, curly-headed shepherds, in white stockings adorned with ribbons and knickers, held up garlands of flowers; pink, light blue, and pistachio shepherdesses in farthingales held elegant baskets of flowers. Shaking their hoops, the hunchback *polichinelles*, in colorful gold-embroidered uniforms adorned with an incredible quantity of ribbons, bobbed up and down. The entire act should have been viewed as a single crowd dance. "What was most important here was the crowd. Everything blended into

---

Borstentänzer were nineteenth-century German folk puppets, mounted on flexible bristles (*borste*), which allowed them to dangle and dance. (Ed.)

**A *matrioshka* is a hand-made Russian peasant doll carved from a single block of wood and brightly painted. (Ed.)

†A *kokoshnik* was a woman's traditional Russian headdress. (Ed.)

one festive scene,"[54] recalls Svetinskaya. The choreographer's task was to make everything come to life, to move. Later, in reviving the production in the New Theater (1922), Gorsky tried to solve this problem with the artist Fedorovsky. "The 'crowd' here doesn't stay on the stage, doesn't wait with blank, dull faces for its 'mass' number—the coda,"[55] wrote the critic. Everything—the virtuoso dance, the leading soloists of the company—lent a festive air to this act.

Leaving all trouble behind, Clara and the Prince celebrated their victory. Like the children in Maeterlinck's play *The Bluebird* they found friends in the things that surrounded them. And now, when the heroes themselves were transformed both externally and internally, when all fetters and masks were thrown off, even their formerly silent fellow travelers found souls. "The Christmas tree decorations, flowers, porcelain statuettes, *polichinelles,* and wooden toys interlace in the dance, and like a glittering garland encircle the pedestal on which the happy Clara and the Nutcracker are crowned," according to the program.

In 1919 and 1920 Gorsky's ballet was performed in the Bolshoi Theater seventeen times. But in spring 1920, during a fire in the theater's warehouses, the sets burned up and the ballet was taken out of the repertory. *The Nutcracker* was revived in 1922 in the New Theater (the premiere was on February 24) and was performed eleven times in one season. With that, the short stage-life of the production ended.

And yet it would be unjust to consign it to oblivion. Gorsky's achievements in *The Nutcracker* did exist side by side with its shortcomings. Tchaikovsky's philosophical generalizations were not fully buttressed by the imagery of the dance, and the composer's profound ideas were not brought to life. Although Gorsky created a charming fairytale about children for children, he was not able to create a "symphony of childhood" (Asafiev). All this is true. But in Gorsky's production we see tendencies that were developed by later directors.

Gorsky was the first to give the ballet integrity of plot and stylistic unity, eliminating the contradictions between two acts in two different genres. In Vasily Vainonen's production, staged fifteen years later, Gorsky's suggestions that the ballet be built around a single character ultimately triumphed. But in Vainonen's ballet the transformation of little Masha (as she was called) occurred mechanically: The little girl of the first scene was replaced by an adult dancer. At the same time, Vainonen in some ways went further, trying to subordinate external action to the internal content of the music: He resolved the adagio in the forest scene in dance terms. In Grigorovich's multilayered, poetic production, the music is interpreted in an incomparably more profound way than in Gorsky's version, from a different, more contemporary point of view, but the external course of action often coincides. Like Gorsky, he takes a single dancer through the entire ballet, and like Gorsky, he surrounds his protagonist with toys that have come to life and that accompany her throughout the ballet; also like Gorsky, he builds up to the final wedding scene.

Swan Lake

In August 1919 Vladimir Nemirovich-Danchenko, who had recently come to the Bolshoi Theater to reorganize it on a new basis, wrote to Malinovskaya: "We got together, had a discussion, and came to the decision—Tikhomirov, Gorsky, Riabtsev, and I—to open the season with *Swan Lake*; but having gotten thoroughly involved in it . . . all of us, having looked at the ballet together, will come to an agreement as to what has to be done to create a fresh production. Perhaps we will have to make a whole new act and redo a great deal of the mise-en-scène . . . I promised to get away from the Moscow Art Theater for three or four days just now for discussions of *Swan Lake* with the choreographers, lead dancers, and even the corps de ballet. . . . Here in general the mood is business-like and energetic."[56]

This was not the first time Gorsky turned to *Swan Lake*. In 1901, while transferring the Petersburg production by Petipa and Ivanov to Moscow, he partially reworked the dances. Individual changes were also made in 1906, and then in 1912, when the ballet was totally restaged with new decor by Korovin (in 1901 the artists for the production were Korovin and Golovine), and in 1916–17, when it was revived after a warehouse fire. Thus, by 1920 the Moscow version of *Swan Lake* was already considerably different from the canonical Petersburg version. The peasants' waltz from the first act was redone. Gorsky did away with the sedate formation of straight frontal lines and added character dancing, ending the act with a vigorous, somewhat medieval-looking farandole with torches in the dancers' hands. "The finale of the first act of *Swan Lake*, listless and sloppy in the St. Petersburg production, in Gorsky's version has become an artistic, vigorous torch procession of medieval fantoccini."[57] In the third act, the waltz of the prospective brides by the corps de ballet was given to the soloists, and the dances of the character divertissement were restaged. One of Gorsky's achievements was the "Spanish Dance," which during the 1913–14 season was included in the Petersburg version as well and is preserved on our stage to this day.

Gorsky did not limit himself to redoing the two realistic acts. Gorsky's second—swan—act was more dramatic than the classical Petersburg version. His swans ran in circles in a confused flock, frightened by the stranger's arrival. The mise-en-scène rather expressively communicated their fear and excitement. But the drama and realism of details reduced the abstract quality of the images. Here proportion and symmetry appear in the same order as in architecture. Lines of figures coordinated with each other create the impression of a single whole; fragmenting them here is inappropriate and individualization intolerable. The harmony of the entire construction lies in its monolithic quality: Here to split, to crumble, means to destroy, yet this is precisely the way both the corps de ballet and the group dances were reworked.

The critics, noting the various prerevolutionary stages of Gorsky's reworking of *Swan Lake*, assert on the one hand that he "does not succeed with classical dance," and on the other that he seems to have preserved too much of the old. In fact, in the new production the scenes with the swans, deprived of the clarity and severity that in Ivanov's version of the dances was enchanting, no longer satisfied the audience. Having lost their abstract quality, they were also stripped of their inherent internal drama. Gorsky was attracted to a different kind of drama, true to life and expressed in external action. The production of 1920 was a natural continuation of Gorsky's earlier experiments, except that a great deal that earlier had merely been hinted at was expressed here in extreme form.

In this work fate brought Gorsky together with Nemirovich-Danchenko, whose participation in the staging of *Swan Lake* was not accidental. In the first years after the revolution, the lyric theaters were continually subject to attack as "belonging to the imperial courts." Then the idea arose of turning toward drama directors, which Lunacharsky, in particular, supported. It was assumed that Stanislavsky and Nemirovich-Danchenko, who in the past had been reformers in the dramatic theater, could also help the musical theater find new paths. The Moscow Art Theater in its turn was going through a period of doubts and upheavals; its directors were seeking new types of activity and gladly sought a rapprochement with the lyric theater (though, to be sure, primarily with the opera). Thus, in the beginning of 1919 the Moscow Art Theater and the Bolshoi Theater entered into a union: ". . . The Moscow Art Theater company received a proposal that it take in hand the responsibility for the directorial work of the Bolshoi State Theater. V. I. Nemirovich-Danchenko has already worked out the plan in general terms for the impending task."[58]

In the fall of 1919 Nemirovich-Danchenko and Gorsky began their joint work. Both were full of optimistic hopes. Gorsky, a long-time admirer of the Moscow Art Theater, could not fail to be attracted by the prospect of working with the famous director. And it would seem that Gorsky's aspirations had long found favor with Nemirovich-Danchenko.

None of Gorsky's plans for the staging and no interpretations by Nemirovich-Danchenko have been preserved. The archives of Yuri Bakhrushin contain individual notes made by Nemirovich-Danchenko during the rehearsals. These are directed against one or another incongruous element that characterized the old ballet and they attest to a desire to stage a production as truthful as possible; on the whole, however, they deal with secondary aspects. Nemirovich-Danchenko demanded darker lighting for the stage as night approached and more fluid movement for the prop swans.[59] He approved of the fact that in the new version of the ballet all the entrances and exits of the dancers were logical: "It does not have that incoherent rushing on and off into the wings."[60] Such comments allow us to understand the director's line of thought as he tried to reform the ballet on the basis of the Moscow Art Theater method. But it would seem that Nemirovich-Danchenko's participation in the production did not stop here.

One of the important features of the production was the idea of dividing the single role of Odette-Odile into two opposing roles. This immediately provoked the resistance of the company. Most of the performers and contemporaries of the production (in particular, the first performers Elena Ilyushchenko and Maria Reisen) are inclined to ascribe this innovation to Nemirovich-Danchenko. To what extent can we consider this innovation justified? Musicologists and scholars of the ballet insist that these roles should be played by a single dancer, because Odette and Odile seem to be two sides of a single character. But something else is also indisputable: Having one artist play the two roles makes it difficult for an untrained audience to understand what is happening onstage. Thus one spectator of *Swan Lake* wrote a letter to the magazine *Vestnik teatra* to complain that most people in the audience could not grasp the content of the production. In his view, one should "before the ballet production explain the plot to the audience or provide the viewers with published or written program notes (or at least hang them in the corridors). . . . Otherwise," he concludes his letter, "once again we have the situation that this is not for us, but for the masters!"[61] Perhaps in introducing changes into the plot of the ballet, Nemirovich-Danchenko was to some extent proceeding from the interests of this new democratic audience. But one would think that this was not the main reason.

In dividing the role of Odette-Odile in two, it was possible to contrast more sharply one group of characters in the production to another group, and consequently to show two hostile worlds: the role of those who love, who embody the good (Odette, the Prince, the white swans), and the world of those who hate and sow evil (Odile, Rothbart, and their retinue—the guests at the ball). The role of Odile was no longer limited, as it had been, to her appearance in the third act, when through deceit she extracts the Prince's oath. Odile also followed the Prince and Odette in the second act, and in the end became a witness to their triumph. The desire to stress who was good and who was evil, to show the victory of the positive characters and the defeat of the negative ones doubtless is a tribute to the times.

The new interpretation required a new, straightforwardly happy ending. Before that, the ballet had ended with the death of Odette and the Prince and their subsequent triumph beyond the grave. In the first production of the ballet (1877), Tchaikovsky had devoted a great deal of attention to the final scene, which showed a thunderstorm coming from the shore of the lake and the death of Odette and Siegfried in the waves. After that, "for the apotheosis, dawn came and, just before the curtain fell, trees were illuminated by the first rays of the rising sun."[62] The final idea of the scene was that the lovers triumph, even in death, because they did not give in to evil.

In the next variant of the libretto, written for the 1895 production,

Siegfried "rushes to help Odette and throws himself into the lake with her." In addition, the self-sacrifice of the hero brings death to Rothbart. It is true that the last, lucid bars of music were accompanied by a tasteless apotheosis—the underwater kingdom where "nymphs and naiads meet the lovers and carry them off into the temple of eternal happiness and bliss." But the theme of love faithful even unto death was preserved. Beginning in 1901 all of Gorsky's productions also unfailingly ended with the heroes drowning in the lake.

The 1920 production for the first time changes this tradition. Odette and the Prince triumph over Rothbart and Odile. This again was an aspiration toward didacticism, a direct graphic expression of the idea of the victory of the cause of the just. Incidentally, as soon as the theater rejected Nemirovich-Danchenko's production, the finale too was changed. The production of 1922, which in essence was a return to the former version, although it preserved certain innovations from 1920, again ended tragically. The definitively happy ending—liberation from the spell of the magician and the joyous wedding to come—ultimately triumphed in the 1937 Moscow production.

Having worked out a plan for the staging, Gorsky and Nemirovich-Danchenko started work in September 1919. A new decor was ordered from the artist Anatoly Arapov, and rehearsals were scheduled. From the very first day, resistance began to grow and make itself ever more clearly felt within the theater. The reports of the regisseur Vladimir Vorontsov attest to this. On September 5 Tikhomirov did not appear at an emergency repertory meeting, which resulted in the cancellation of rehearsals, since no decision had been reached as to whether the role of Odette and Odile would be performed by one dancer or by two. "The choreographer A. A. Gorsky refuses to take on personally the discussion of casting after the directives given by V. V. Tikhomirov verbally to the ballet regisseur," reported Vorontsov.[63] Finally, on September 12 Gorsky's and Nemirovich-Danchenko's plan was accepted.[64] On October 13 Tikhomirov, who at the end of September had left the administrative staff, responded with his "A Dissenting View":

> I believe it is my duty to express the following views regarding the *cleaning up* of the ballet *Swan Lake*. As I understood from preliminary discussions with competent people regarding the question of

cleaning up certain ballets, it seems to me we are talking *not of a radical* break with already formed works, but only about those places in the given ballets that are not clear enough. . . . Now from the discussion of the question at the last meeting of the administration, I found out that we are talking about a total break with the choreographic part of *Swan Lake*. In particular, the role of Odette and Odile is being so reworked that it has been transformed from one of the most difficult roles in the choreographic repertory into a simplified version that could well be within the range of even a beginning dancer. . . . I simply cannot reconcile *cleaning up* with a reworking of the already formed, superb roles of the old ballets.[65]

Soon the controversy about *Swan Lake* became known outside the Bolshoi Theater. The Supreme Choreographic Council of the Central Committee of the All-Russian Union of Artistic Workers convened a special meeting on October 27 devoted to the restoration of *Swan Lake* in connection with the resurgence "of all kinds of suggestions, rumors, and idle talk, which are circulating around this production."[66]

A report was given by Ilya Schneider. He recalls that after the report there was a stormy meeting "which Gorsky left in a fury, after he protested against the interference in the creative laboratory of an artist at work. The Supreme Choreographic Council passed a decree forbidding Gorsky to experiment with *Swan Lake*."[67]

At about the same time, preparations were going on for a ballet conference (at first planned for October 16–18). Here such questions as the defense of the "author's rights" of the choreographer and the establishment of artistic control in the area of staging were to be discussed. These questions were closely linked to the problem of the relation to the classical heritage, insofar as the author's rights implies preservation of the author's version of the ballet, while artistic control should put an end to any attempt to distort works of art. At the end of October an article by the choreographer Mikhail Dyskovsky was published. Disputing those sections of the codex being prepared for the conference that were devoted to problems of artistic control, Dyskovsky criticized the old production of *Swan Lake* and demanded a radical review of those ballets kept in the repertory.[68]

Meanwhile, Gorsky and Nemirovich-Danchenko had begun work.

Newspapers published reports that Ekaterina Geltser, Alexandra Bala-shova, and Margarita Kandaurova were to take part in the production. But in fact the ballerinas did not take part in the rehearsals for the ballet. Typhus fever was raging in Moscow. First Elena Adamovich, who was about to start work on the production, fell ill, and then Kandaurova. The meeting of the administration on December 9 passed a special resolution —to ask Nemirovich-Danchenko to "renew discussions with Balashova and persuade her to play the role of Odette."[69] But even after that she did not become involved in the work. Gorsky's opponents were happy to take advantage of the situation to force the producers to renounce their intention: ". . . In my view, due to Kandaurova's illness and absence, the ballet should be postponed for some time if the meeting does not come to the conclusion that it will change its idea (of having two performers) and present *Swan Lake* as it has been presented up to now," wrote Tikhomi-rov in his statement.[70] Then Gorsky decided to bring into the work on the production a group of young people, including Nina Podgoretskaya and Elena Ilyushchenko, just out of school.

The winter of 1920 was one of Moscow's most difficult. Transporta-tion stopped; there was no fuel, and it was cold everywhere. There also was no electricity, and the newspapers suggested limiting the work of theatrical enterprises to three days a week. The question arose of closing the Bolshoi Theater once and for all. Many members of the *Maly Sov-narkom* * considered it criminal to throw valuable fuel into the furnace of a theater that was still so weak in its propaganda of new ideas. But Lenin's decisive words, "It is too early for us to hand over the heritage of bourgeois art to the archives," are well known.[71]

Work on *Swan Lake* continued in unbearably difficult circumstances. The dancers, forced to earn extra pay outside the Bolshoi, where they were paid not in money but in food products, missed rehearsals. Voron-tsov reported: "The sets were not ready, the floorboards were set up in a very approximate fashion . . . there are not enough colleagues present. . . ."; "The props crew worked unwillingly and listlessly after two o'clock in the afternoon, saying that they were cold, hungry, and tired."[72] On December 1 Riabtsev reported the cancellation of rehearsals

---

* This was from 1917–46 the highest organ of executive and administrative power in the U.S.S.R. *Sovnarkom* is an acronym that stands for the Soviet of People's Commissars. (Ed.)

in the school "because the temperature in the rehearsal room was two and half degrees."[73] Around that time (more precisely, on March 1, 1920, that is, the day after the premiere of *Swan Lake*), a general meeting of the ballet dancers discussed the situation: the salaries "were not enough to buy a pound of bread a day."[74]

However, this was not the major obstacle. On December 21 Gorsky spoke at a meeting of the directorate and recounted in detail all the difficulties he had faced. He talked about the cold which forced them to rehearse in street clothes and even in fur coats, about the illnesses of the dancers, and above all about the atmosphere he had to work in. He spoke of the resistance by "the representatives of old classical ballet to those new undertakings necessary for the revival of this ballet, because for the most part attention was paid to general artistic construction, to the detriment of individual interests."[75] He pointed out the "abnormal relations" established by casting a young dancer in the role of Odette.[76] Indeed, Victor Smoltsov stopped rehearsals, declaring that "he had absolutely no feeling for his role when danced with Ilyushchenko,"[77] and Bulgakov made an effort to refuse the role of the evil genius, but the directorate did not accept it. The date for the production was continually delayed—at first December, then January, and then February.

The premiere took place on February 29, 1920. The performers were: Odette—Elena Ilyushchenko; Odile—Maria Reisen; the Prince—Leonid Zhukov; his friend—Lev Lashchilin; his tutor—Vasily Chudinov; the Evil Genius—Alexei Bulgakov. Andrei Arends conducted.

No published reviews of this production exist, and therefore we must rely on the reactions of eyewitnesses, the memoirs of the participants, and a small number of unpublished reviews. In the first act, there were no significant innovations, only a heightening of those tendencies existing in earlier variants. Instead of a holiday celebration on the palace grounds, there was a hunting scene in a natural setting. The servants laid down animal skins and set up wine jugs. The peasant waltz was turned from a "toe" dance into a "heel" one, that is, it became more down-to-earth. In the pas de quatre (the former pas de trois), the Prince and his friend danced with the peasant girls. According to the recollections of Anastasia Abramova, until 1920 the participants in this dance played the roles of courtiers dressed up as peasant girls. They ran out dressed in cloaks and threw them off, showing their little dresses with farthingales. Now they played real peasant girls, and their variations were also "heel," rather than "toe." At first both made a deep curtsey to the Prince, and then one, dancing, threw him a bouquet while the other flirted with him, arms akimbo.

For the dancer Vasily Efimov, Gorsky invented a new character, introduced for the first time in *Swan Lake*—the Jester. The Jester made the action of the first act more lively. As Abramova recalls, his role was not as technical as it has become in our day. "He was funny, impudent, and hit everyone with his scepter."[78] The Jester wore a black and white costume and a black cap with many long ribbons, hung with little bells.

An unpublished review signed E. Rensil, dated March 1, 1920, says of the dancing in the first act: "Throughout the first act, the corps de ballet crowds onto the stage like a disorderly mass. The waltz, usually so pure and elegant, is lost in this disorganized bustle."[79] This accusation was not new. It was leveled many times at Gorsky in connection with his other productions, when instead of the former groups and ranks moving in strict order he created a dancing, milling crowd. In the new production, Gorsky followed the same path. Bakhrushin confirmed that the first act "was almost the same in tone as formerly. Even the dancing in it came alive and to some extent so did the act itself."[80] However, the reworking was done primarily in the three following acts, for which Arapov made new sets.

The decor for the second act was a backdrop showing a light blue sky and green water. On both sides of the stage were daises—the refuge of the Evil Genius and the hill on which Odette appeared. This allowed the mise-en-scène to be built on a principle of contrasts, the confrontation of two opposing forces, which was noted in Rensil's review. In reworking the second act the directors went even further in dramatizing the dancing and in rethinking it than Gorsky had done in the previous variants. As Bakhrushin recalls, Nemirovich-Danchenko did not quite understand that a ballet can not be judged by everyday common sense, that it has its own poetic logic. For example, a question that had not been raised since the time of the Reisinger production of 1877 now became a primary focus of attention: When do the dancers appear on the stage as maidens, and when do they appear as swans, and how should the transformation be shown? The desire to think through and justify everything inevitably led to a renunciation of Lev Ivanov's psychological images. To Ivanov, the music suggested another interpretation: Profound human feeling is endowed with a sense of "wingedness," of flight, like that of a bird. The swan's regal bearing becomes a characteristic of the imprisoned queen.

Ilyushchenko says that the new costumes were not like the earlier, poetically abstract costumes of the swan maidens. Odette wore not a tutu but a longer dress, full at the bottom. On her head were a heavy crown and two long braids. According to Ilyushchenko's account, Nemirovich-Danchenko told her that her character seemed close to that of the enchanted queen in Georgian fairytales. Sketches of the costumes for Odette and Odile by Vasily Diachkov have been preserved, in which both are shown with enormous wings on their backs. These same wings, which were removed at the moment of the transformation, were also to have been given to the corps de ballet. Bakhrushin reports that, because of their unwieldiness, after the dress rehearsal the wings were dropped.[81]

In the Bolshoi Theater Museum there are many sketches of the characters in *Swan Lake* done by Gorsky himself. There is reason to think that they were from the 1920 production. In one of the drawings Odette is shown in a costume somewhat reminiscent of the one Ilyushchenko mentions. It is a rather long dress with a puffy skirt, in gentle colors, flowing from greenish to pinkish. (Ilyushchenko describes the color of her costume as mother-of-pearl.) On the drawing small wings are visible, stitched to the waistline, but they lie flat and are tightly attached to the skirt, not behind the back, as in Diachkov's sketch. According to Ilyushchenko, Odile's costume in the second act was similar to Odette's costume, but was adorned with bright colors. In Gorsky's drawing this is not quite so. Odile's dress is longer in back and shorter in front, in dark blue and dark red hues, gradually changing to yellow-green, then to yellow-orange, and has large wings on the back. Odile raises her hand to her face and inclines her head slightly, as though listening. Perhaps Gorsky wanted to depict the moment when she follows the Prince and Odette. Of course, Gorsky's drawings are not the sketches according to which costumes were sewn, but it would be wrong to wholly reject their link to the production.

Like many other choreographers, Gorsky was in the habit of sketching out the future ballet before beginning work. He worked in close contact with Diachkov, who designed the costumes for almost all of Gorsky's ballets. The choreographer drew things as he imagined them, while the artist, working from these rough drafts, created the final sketches. Apparently the designs for the costumes of Odette and Odile in Gorsky's archives belong to the category of such preliminary sketches.

The reviews and reminiscences of the participants provide little material useful for an understanding of the choreography of the second act. Bakhrushin considers the second and fourth acts not so much ballet as a "kind of unsuccessful transition from ballet to cinematography" (he had in mind silent films and their pantomimes). All the eyewitnesses, participants in the production, and reviewers point out the paucity of dancing in the swan scenes. Rensil writes of the second act: "As for the dances, they are reduced to a minimum." Bakhrushin asserts that this is "a kind of pantomime with inserted dance numbers. In the second and fourth acts you can barely count up five dances!" He particularly notes the unsuccessful interpretation of the waltz in the second act, and complains of "the criminal wastefulness" of the choreographer, who allows the music, which was made for dancing, to play on for no reason. This was the consequence of Gorsky's dramatization of the ballet. The number of episodes that served to develop the plot line were increased; here mime play dominated, especially dance pantomime. Deprived of their concrete representational functions, the number of dances decreased.

But the question was not only one of the quantity of dances. Rensil speaks of their simplification—their reduction to "hopping." At the beginning of the work on the ballet, Tikhomirov also protested against the "simplification" of the dances. Ilyushchenko recalls that the adagio and variation for Odette in the second act were very simple. Rensil expressed the following views in regard to this: "One is inclined to think that the choreographer consented to such simplification because of the limited abilities of both interpreters, Ilyushchenko-Odette and Reisen-Odile." There is some truth in this. Ilyushchenko was a quite young beginning dancer, while Reisen, for the most part, was always a stranger to classical dance. For Geltser and Balashova Gorsky probably would have staged the dances differently. On the other hand, Tikhomirov's "Dissenting View" had already been sent to the directorate on October 13, a month after the beginning of rehearsals, when the young ballerinas had not yet begun to work; Kandaurova and Adamovich were preparing for the production, and negotiations were being conducted with Balashova. Therefore, changes in the choreography were made not only because of the performers' insufficient experience; complex dance forms, requiring a high level of technique, were lacking in this production, because here the dancing was the expression of an immediate situation or mood. After all, even simple movements can express a mood; all of Duncan's art is based on this—when the choreographer needs abstractions, dance appears, in all its richness. All the instruments of the orchestra are, so to speak, put to use. Ilyushchenko says that Odette's companions led the round dance around the prisoner, consoled her, rejoiced and grieved with her. Like the princesses in Fokine's *Firebird*, they were touching but simple. The multifaceted image of the swan corps de ballet that for Lev Ivanov had been the means of expressing the protagonists' feelings had disappeared.

The third act, the scene of the ball in the palace, was the most interesting. "This is one of Gorsky's best achievements in recent times," writes Rensil. "The lively excitement and the flash of the colorful ballroom were beautifully conveyed." Gorsky staged a "masked dance," during which one of the masks told fortunes. The Jester also took part in this dance. The masked dance and the role of the Jester were kept in 1922 when Gorsky again reworked the ballet, bringing it closer to the pre-1920 version. Apparently, for Gorsky this episode was not simply one more divertissement at a ball. It helped create the atmosphere of mystery that accompanies the appearance of Rothbart and his retinue. For Odile is also "masked," as Odette, and the forced gaiety of the guests helps to implement the treacherous scheme. Against the background of the radiant costumes of the courtiers, the black and white finery of the masks and the decidedly gloomy black and green costumes of Rothbart's retinue stood out. This was Diachkov's last work, for he died two weeks before the premiere.

Among Gorsky's drawings are those for Odile's costume in the third act. Gorsky's version, of course, could not be used in a ballet built on classical dance. It is a heavy garment with skirts reaching nearly to the floor, with colors like those of a peacock, blending dark green, gold, and rich blue highlights. Despite all its heaviness and splendor, this costume partially echoes Odette's costume, but here everything is exaggerated, overdone: the same wings, caught at the waistline, lying flat on the skirt, the same positioning of the spots of color, scattered on the dress like peacock's eyes. This costume may have had little in common with the one the dancer actually wore on stage, but it does give us some idea of

Gorsky's intentions. He would hardly have begun drawing such a sketch if, as was the case in the old productions, he had intended to characterize Odile through virtuoso classical dance. Contemporaries recall that at the beginning of the production, Gorsky sought out old people who remembered the Moscow version of *Swan Lake* in the 1880s.

To this day historians have not discovered how the role of Odile was done in the first production. There is a theory put forward by Bakhrushin that Odile was played by an obscure dancer, a supernumerary, and that therefore the name of the performer was marked on the program with three asterisks. In his book *Tchaikovsky and the Ballet Theater of His Time*, Yuri Slonimsky rather convincingly rejects this point of view. The performer in the role of Odette, according to the premiere program, took part in three dances in the third act: in two groups (one of them was a sextet with Siegfried) and in the "Russian Dance." Regardless of all the awkward things that took place in the ballet during those years, it still would be difficult to assume that she did all this as Odette. Even the libretto of the first performance clearly states that at the ball Odile captivates the Prince. Odette only appears at the finale, after the Prince has taken the fatal oath. It follows that the "Russian Dance" in the 1877 version was performed by Odile, who became one of the participants in the character divertissement. Twice—in the duet and in the "Russian Dance" —a leading ballerina appeared in Joseph Hansen's 1880 production. And only in 1895, in Petipa's staging, did the famous classical pas de deux appear (to the music from the first act, with additions). Thus even before Gorsky there were various interpretations of the role of Odile, including those that took a form close to character dance. Gorsky went further, dressing Odile in luxurious "peacock" plumage. He wanted to see in this character a mysterious being with an unusual appearance, a kind of heavenly bird, fascinating and deadly. About this change in Odile's usual appearance, Adamovich recalls, "Gorsky took the tutu off Odile and put horns on her head, because Odile came with the enchanted Evil Genius."[82]

Odette's participation in the third act was limited to one appearance at a window behind the princess and courtiers sitting at the table, at the moment when the Prince declares that Odile is his chosen one.

The central episode of the fourth act is the second meeting of Siegfried and Odette on the lake shore when he rushes off to win her forgiveness.

One of the elements of the dance designs in this section was, according to the recollections of Ilyushchenko, a circle formed by the swans, who hid Odette from Siegfried at the moment he appeared, and his subsequent search for her among the other swan maidens. In this act, the performer of Odette acted more than she danced. This is noted by the critics and by Ilyushchenko herself. Rensil, recalling "several beautiful moments created by Ilyushchenko in her final dance," later complains that everything was limited to these two or three "graceful movements." Bakhrushin, praising the performer, who in his view created "a remarkably touching image, permeated with a certain romantic sadness and lyrical reverie," writes: "Her dance . . . but we have to be silent about the dances, for she hardly dances at all." In all of her behavior, Odile-Reisen had to appear in total contrast to Odette-Ilyushchenko. This was a contrast of characters with a certain similarity in appearance: as Ilyushchenko recalls, the role of Odette was given to her because she was the same type as Reisen—a dark-haired, dark-skinned girl from the south. Odile, for Nemirovich-Danchenko, had a "totally demonic nature." He reproached Reisen for not being able to fully free herself from any lyricism, and insisted that in this role there "should be only an enigmatic smile and dark passion."[83]

Reisen recalls that Nemirovich-Danchenko himself went over the fourth act with her. He wanted to stage a mad scene and tried to convince Reisen that this scene would be just as successful for her as the similar episode in the first act of *Giselle*. Meanwhile, Reisen was naturally puzzled as to how feelings could be expressed in the ballet that were not backed by the music: After all, Tchaikovsky has no scene here of Odile's madness. "Act in contrast to the music," insisted Nemirovich-Danchenko.

The lack of understanding between the ballet dancers and the theater director made Nemirovich-Danchenko's and Gorsky's work even more complicated. Jokes, caricatures, and mocking verses were declaimed behind the backs of the directors and, more important, the dancers showed an inability to meet their demands. In the last analysis, Nemirovich-Danchenko was disappointed in the results of his work, all the more so since things were going no better with his staging of an opera. Vasily Luzhsky, who had begun to work in the Bolshoi Theater together with Nemirovich-Danchenko, wrote in his diary on February 20, 1920 (nine days before the premiere of *Swan Lake*), "Yesterday it was a year since Nemirovich-Danchenko and I came to the Bolshoi Theater for the first time, with the production of *The Snow Maiden*. So many fine words were spoken and so little has actually happened."[84] According to the performers' recollections, Nemirovich-Danchenko did not come to the premiere.

The ballet was shown a total of sixteen times during the 1919–20 and 1920–21 seasons. On June 14, 1922, the Artistic Council passed a resolution to rework the second, third, and fourth acts of the ballet. In the reports summarizing the season, it was said of the production of *Swan Lake*: "In the lengthy work process designed to 'refresh the old ballet' the views of various groups and conflicts of interest were revealed, and the resistance of the conservative part of the ballet company considerably interfered with the work."[85]

Gorsky's letter to the administration is an even more eloquent document. It is written in pathetic tones: "Directorate, I appeal to you as an artist. Arise, throw off for a while your everyday concerns," wrote Gorsky, and he drew a picture of the intratheater struggle as "the so-called classical school insisting on its rights, influencing the youth," which "finds itself between the devil and the deep blue sea." He blamed the directorate for wanting stellar names that had proved themselves "solely on the basis of the traditional old ballets" and complained of the tenacity of the old, against which "he had been *struggling* for the best twenty years of his life," and which was now perishing "in a swamp of stagnating water." Disturbed over the fate of the young dancers, Gorsky contrasted the atmosphere in the theater with the enthusiasm of the studios, where "desires are burning, even though they are desires without any support, without the necessary base, with feeble means." He was disturbed by the self-satisfaction and conservatism shown even by the young members of the company. Recalling Smoltsov's refusal to dance in *Swan Lake*, he wrote, "Smoltsov himself is not strong, he is still in an embryonic stage, but it is already hard for him to get away from the old forms." He called on the youth to follow the path of "new quests for artistic truth," "to throw off the shackles of the cheap success of the traditional *Don Quixotes* and *Little Humpbacked Horses*," forgetting in the heat of his polemics how much he himself had put into these ballets.[86]

The work on *Swan Lake* once again emphasized the differences in the Bolshoi Theater Company between Gorsky and the leading dancers of the older generation. In the postrevolutionary years, when there were constant appeals in the press to put an end once and for all to *The Little Humpbacked Horse* and *Giselle*, fears for the future of ballet made Geltser and Tikhomirov insist even more strongly on the necessity of preserving the old. In revolting against the destruction of these treasures they were unquestionably right, but their conservatism hindered them from seeing that not everything old is valuable. Gorsky for his part tried to move the ballet away from positions of ossified academicism; here he was also right, but the path he chose was not always true.

In turning to *Swan Lake*, Gorsky and Nemirovich-Danchenko wanted to create a ballet logically justified in all of its links, and they tried to bring democratic ideas into this classical work. However, in introducing into the ballet the realism of drama they scorned the specific quality of choreographic theater, and, most important, they destroyed everything that did not fit in with their intentions. The classical dance variations and ensembles were not in keeping with the goals of the director and choreographer, and were therefore thrown away. But what they created to replace them with was considerably weaker, all the more so since the directors did not take into account the content of the music.

The production did not survive long. However, to say that it left no traces would be untrue. It is not only a question of the few details preserved up to now in the Bolshoi Theater production—the Jester, the vestiges of the masked dance, and some details of the ensemble dances in the first act. The idea of redoing *Swan Lake* (and incidentally, other classical ballets as well) from a position of "realistic action" attracted choreographers from then on. In this they found support from literary experts, artists, and particularly from theater directors, who, like Nemirovich-Danchenko, went into the ballet to help it embark on this new course.

The tendencies in the staging of *Swan Lake* in 1920 can be followed in the Vaganova production of 1933, although here the dance values were preserved. But the plot was transferred into the nineteenth century and was built around the experiences of a romantically inclined youth who mistook a swan for a girl. When the mistake became clear and the swan died, the youth committed suicide.

The desire to emphasize the plot, which revealed itself in Gorsky's and Nemirovich-Danchenko's production, became the basic method for reworking old ballets in the 1930s to the 1950s. In the production of

Swan Lake by Vladimir Burmeister in the Stanislavsky and Nemirovich-Danchenko Theater (1953), the major goal of the director was to clarify and logically streamline all the ups and downs of the action. Hence, specifically, the emergence of the prologue, in which the viewer observes the transformation of Odette the maiden into Odette the bird. The theme of the masquerade, where lies prevail over truth, where false faces and false feelings dominate, stressed by Gorsky in the scenes with the Jester and the masked guests, was also taken up by Vaganova and Burmeister.

Chrysis and Other Works
of 1921–1922

Gorsky's creations from 1921 to 1923 (during the last year of his life he could no longer work) are by no means equal in value. There were productions that not only added nothing to what had already been said but that, even in what was old, resurrected the outmoded and sterile. *The Dance of Salomé* to the music of Richard Strauss, staged in February 1921 for Balashova, went completely unnoticed. Gorsky's sketches in the Bolshoi Theater Museum show variants of her costumes and give an idea of the nature of the dance. One of them makes the dancer look like a butterfly: she wears a blue and green leotard, a yellow scarf like wings behind her back, and a high headdress decorated with sharp spikes. A second consists entirely of leaves and large flowers encircling the body and carefully layered on the chest. The saccharine prettiness of the dance was particularly intolerable compared to the staging by Goleizovsky for his Chamber Ballet on a similar theme.

At the same time, work was in progress on the three-act (in twelve scenes) ballet *Chrysis*, to music by Glière. The ballet was based on two works by the French writer Pierre Louÿs, *Les Chansons de Bilitis* and *Aphrodite*, written in the 1890s. Louÿs, whom Lunarcharsky called a "coldly depraved pornographic stylist,"[87] imitated in his works the Greek poets of the Alexandrine period. The theme of his poems and prose is love, but this love is primarily carnal and therefore does not bring joy or elevate man, but rather enslaves him.

In the ballet, Glière showed the evolution of sensual love from the awakening of the flesh in a very young girl to the despair of an aging woman who recognizes that her body has lost its allure. In the first act,

Chrysis gambols with her girlfriend at a brook and catches a butterfly —in other words, she indulges in innocent pastimes. A passerby kisses her and then leaves, laughing. For Chrysis this is the end of childhood, the powerful awakening of a need for love that leads her into the embraces of the shepherd Lykas. Lykas, however, betrays Chrysis with her girlfriend Psophis. Despair prompts Chrysis to leave her homeland. The second act is devoted to her wanderings. Again and again, love appears to her in various manifestations. Chrysis comes to the Lesbians, and the mad bacchantes rush past her. In the temple of Alexandria, Aphrodite introduces her to the "mysteries of love"; Chrysis becomes a hetaera. Years pass in banquets and the amusements of love (the third act). But the day comes when the aging Chrysis is rejected for the first time by a passerby to whom she offers herself. The ballet ends with the scene of a curse. Chrysis blames the goddess of love for not having given her servant happiness. Infuriated, Aphrodite punishes her with death.

What motivated Gorsky in 1921 to resurrect this ballet, written in 1912? Apparently the same reasons that made him stubbornly insist on the production of *Eunice*, first staged in 1915. In 1919 he gave the role of Eunice to a new performer—Adamovich. The dancer was very successful in this role. The ballet *Chrysis* was also staged for her. It is not accidental that Adamovich's biographer called her role as Chrysis another variant of Eunice.[88] Glière himself reacted to Adamovich's performance in the role of Chrysis with great praise.[89]

As staged by Gorsky, the ballet had little in common with its original source. Gorsky was attracted here not so much by the sexual theme as by the theme of discontent and the destruction of hope. In *Eunice* he showed the death of beauty, in *Chrysis* the degradation of beauty that cannot find a place in this terrible world. In *Chrysis* another theme apparently also interested Gorsky—the fear of the onset of old age. It is not by chance that in those years he spoke several times of the possibility of staging Adrian Shaposhnikov's ballet *The King's Feast* (also written in 1912), the tragic tale of the spiritual loneliness of an old man.

Work on Glière's ballet *Chrysis* doubtless attracted Gorsky. The Bolshoi Theater Museum and the Central Theatrical Museum contain many of his sketches, including a portrait of the sumptuous beauty Chrysis, blue-eyed and golden-haired, with bare shoulders. And although there is more of a crude thoroughness here than artistic temperament, as is usual in Gorsky's drawings, they attest to the care that Gorsky devoted to this production.

The preview was shown on May 12, 1921, to representatives of the Moscow artistic world. This performance took place in a totally unfinished form. The rehearsals were insufficient and the dancers saw the costumes for the first time on the day of the performance. The group evidently worked enthusiastically. In any case, in a letter of May 14, 1921, Gorsky expressed his gratitude for their self-sacrificing attitude, ending his letter with these words: "And so, comrades, until autumn; the beginning has been completed and success lies ahead."[90] In the fall they did not return to the ballet. The production was already doomed to failure by the selection of the topic and its interpretation—at least that is how contemporaries perceived the failure of the ballet: "For her realistic acting Adamovich received signs of the greatest approval from the audience, but the ballet itself, particularly its subjects, was defective. The Bolshoi Theater could not fail to see the discrepancy between the primitive plot of the ballet and the present historic epoch."[91]

Wolfgang Amadeus Mozart's ballet *Les petits riens*, staged by Gorsky on October 27, 1922, also did not survive. The critics thought the gallant pastorale *à la* Watteau was highly stylized in the manner of fashionable Paris magazines of the 1910s and was not in tune with the spirit of Mozart's music.[92] However, two ballets shown in 1922 aroused unquestionable interest—*Giselle* and *Ever-Fresh Flowers*.

Giselle

Like the *Swan Lake* staged two years earlier, *Giselle* completed the series of experiments conducted by Gorsky from the beginning of the century with this well-known Romantic ballet. The classic version of *Giselle* remained on the stage of the Bolshoi Theater until the end of the nineteenth century. In 1901 Gorsky revived it for the Italian ballerina Enrichetta Grimaldi. The ballet was produced with the old sets. Later, from 1904 to 1907, the ballet was dropped from the repertory. In 1906 Vera Karalli graduated from the Moscow school. It seems that the young dancer had many gifts that made her a good candidate for Giselle. She had a superb physique and was able to bring out the beauty of the poses in the Romantic ballet; she was also a good mime and could play the dramatic scene of

Giselle's madness. Karalli's drawback was her weak technique. But this did not bother Gorsky. For Karalli he again staged *Giselle* in 1907.[93]

By this time Gorsky already had some solid experience in reworking old ballets. Turning to the choreography of the past, Gorsky viewed his task differently from those reconstructors who concentrated on simply preserving the old: In other people's ballets he tried to assert his own ideas. In *Giselle*, Gorsky continued to struggle for a real-life, authentic quality in the ballet performance and for the elimination of all the conventions that seemed to him to be out-of-date.

To add a more genuine quality to the events in the first act, the choreographer transferred the action to an era not far removed from our time. All the characters wore the fashions of the Directoire, and the Duke was dressed as an *"incroyable"* in tails, a waistcoat, and a cocked hat. Gorsky tried to achieve greater realism in the actions of the crowd. The participants in the crowd scenes were individualized, with specific behavioral types. For example, curious old women appeared who hopped about and stole sly glances from behind the fence at Giselle and Albrecht. Thus the ballet was transferred from the level of a stylized romantic drama to a drama of everyday life.

Psychological authenticity was combined with a desire to reproduce features of the era in which the action of the ballet had been placed. Gorsky simplified the dances considerably. Later, Alexander Tcherepnin wrote that Gorsky "succeeded in the simple-hearted naiveté of the ensemble in the first act and in the dances of the soloists, done in the spirit of the old ballets—*en face*, with a cavalier behind them . . ."[94] This return to the forms of the past was not through stylization, as in Fokine's *Chopiniana*. Reanimating the motifs of the Romantic ballet, Fokine admired the old and at the same time sought that which brought it closer to the present. Here Gorsky used antiquated dancing as an element of everyday life. Moreover, he ignored the stylistics of the old *Giselle*. The spirit of the 1840s had vanished; the quality of an old engraving had disappeared; the veneer of "fake peasantry" was removed. The new production was a real drama of French life at the end of the eighteenth century, and Gorsky tried to reveal all the inner mechanisms of this drama. The characters were also revised. Karalli was the sole performer of the title role from 1907 through 1913. The critics several times noted her weak dancing and her desire to reduce the entire role to dramatic play. In the review quoted above, Tcherepnin wrote: "The level of the quotidian has so engulfed Miss Karalli that, for example, she permits herself to step clearly beyond the boundaries of ballet style, as in her expression of fatigue after the dance with the Duke in the first act." The fact that in Giselle's mad scene Karalli began to laugh loudly was also deplored.[95]

The second act, too, was changed. In the several decades of the ballet's life on the Russian stage in the nineteenth century it underwent a steady process: The lyrical element was winning out over the dramatic. The emphasis on the vengefulness of the Wilis was lost—for example, the scene of the peasants' arrival at the beginning of the second act and their frightened flight. The gloomy attributes of the cemetery also disappeared. But the lyrical abstract quality of the *ballet blanc* was always alien to Gorsky. The Wilis' passionlessness seemed to him unfounded and the traditional tutus outmoded.

Most of the critics condemned Gorsky's innovations. Mikhail Likiardopulo complained of the "crude *féerie* quality" of the second act[96] and the reviewer of the magazine *Rampa i zhizn*, particularly unfavorable in his attitude, wrote: "one has to be completely devoid of any sense of style to replace the dance of the Wilis with chaotic running about on stage, to replace the white tutu with some kind of nightgown (even the little that remains of the true classical dance is lost because of these disgraceful gowns), and to transform the poetic, seductive Wilis themselves into crude wenches."[97] But in other reviews there is an obvious desire to get to the heart of the choreographer's intentions. N. Churikov points out the Duncanesque features in the second act of *Giselle*. The dances of the Wilis, which he compares to light butterflies and sad anemones, apparently acquired that immediacy of feeling that the famous "barefoot dancer" herself professed. In the view of the critics, the scene of the parting of Giselle and Albrecht was close to *Orpheus and Eurydice*, a painting by the pre-Raphaelite Watts: Throwing away his lyre, the singer clasps the dying Eurydice in despair.

The need to fill any dance with acting explains most of Gorsky's innovations. "In Gorsky's production, practically all that remains of the old *Giselle* are the dramatic scenes," wrote one critic.[98] Such innovations clearly did more harm than good.

In 1913 Sofia Fedorova danced the role of Giselle. She was one of the most expressive character dancers in the Bolshoi Theater. This was the old production: The staging, direction, and dances were the same. But Fedorova's interpretation so strongly changed the ballet that future performers—and even the choreographer himself—could no longer free themselves from her influence. In the opinion of André Levinson, Fedorova "brings to [the ballet] the anguish and pathos of psychological tragedy."[99] In the first act, with her cruel, truthful portrayal of Giselle's madness, she was astounding. "It was painful to see that face distorted by mortal suffering, the movements out of control, the attempts to bind the chaos of fragmented thoughts and feelings, the struggle of a soul with impending darkness. . . ."[100] Sergei Savvich Mamontov, who was at the premiere, wrote: "All of this is so horribly truthful that it fascinates you and sends a chill down your spine. You want to shake off this nightmare, to remind yourself that you are at the ballet . . ."[101] This picture of degradation, the disintegration of consciousness, was naturally incompatible with the reconciliation of the second act. It had to be changed. Therefore although Fedorova's "crowning number" remained the mad scene, for the very sake of which she who was so far removed from the classics had decided to dance Giselle, the second act was of greater significance for the fate of the ballet.

Viacheslav Ivanov wrote of Sofia Fedorova: "Her province is the dark mysticism of the soul." He confessed that Fedorova awoke in his soul vague recollections, even fear; unable to resist, he yielded to her fascination.[102] In entering the performance, such a dancer subordinated everything to her own view of the world.

Gorsky's original rejection of tutus and the introduction of chitons was brought about by the desire to avoid the cliché of the *ballet blanc*. None of the reviewers had earlier written that the Wilis brought to mind the dead, risen from their graves, but with the arrival of Fedorova, the same dances acquired, in the words of the ballerina's biographer, "an eerily prophetic, mystical character."[103] In the traditional *Giselle*, the Wilis are from "another world," but it is the world of poetry, and not the darkness beyond the grave. "As a Wili, Fedorova gave a total impression of the other world as she understood it," Olga Nekrasova, a participant in the production, writes in her memoirs.[104] Fedorova renounced earthly existence and was moved to forgive Albrecht not by true love but by somber self-sacrifice. Fedorova's interpretation influenced the style of future performances.

In 1918, during the season at the Aquarium Garden Theater, Gorsky staged yet another production of *Giselle*. The ballet was unexpectedly added to the season's repertory: The previous program, which had consisted entirely of new productions, was not successful, and the entrepreneur demanded that the next program be sure to include a "real classical ballet." A performer had to be found, and quickly. So Gorsky suggested to Reisen that she play the role of *Giselle*.

"*Giselle* with M. R. Reisen! There's no denying that's daring!" the critic of the newspaper *Nashe vremya* began his review.[105] For the second time, it was not a lyric dancer who appeared in the role of Giselle, but a temperamental performer of bacchic dances, who brought a shade of realistic exultation even to classical dance.

The *Giselle* shown in 1918 was a sharp break with tradition. Markvardt complained that Gorsky had "cleaned up a passionless, naive little ballet from the fairytale cobweb of sweet Romanticism and colored it with vaguely bacchic, stormy tones."[106] The reviewer was puzzled: "What . . . is there in common between a character ballerina with bacchic outbursts, a strongly realistic cinematographic quality, and that barely perceptible image of the original Giselle, who dissolves into clouds of tutus . . . ?"[107] The accusation that Reisen was "cinematographic" is found in other reviews too. Apparently what was meant was the over-abundance of exaggeratedly "passionate" mimicry in silent films.

According to Reisen, in the first act Gorsky stressed the tragedy of class prejudices. The dancer had to remember that Giselle was poor and looked frightened and awkward next to the elegant Bathilde. Reisen recalled that during the first postrevolutionary years this interpretation made a great impression on the broad democratic audience. Here is Viacheslav Ivanov's impression of the dancer's performance in the Aquarium Garden Theater on July 23, 1918: "The first act is well thought-out and executed. . . . Personally, I like a different Giselle, more symbolic. . . . Ballet, as a higher form of art, will not be fully satisfied with your realism."[108]

In the second act of *Giselle*, Reisen also stressed the earthly element. She saw in the Wili a soul that had not yet departed from the earth and still lived with its former passions. Death transformed Giselle's love and gave it a tragic quality. Descriptions of Reisen's performances by Viacheslav Ivanov also make one think of the influence of Sofia Fedorova. "In her soul one feels the glitter of ominousness. She restored to Giselle that gloom inherent in a Wili." [109] In the Aquarium, *Giselle* was staged with new decor by Ivan Fedotov, which Markvardt called "the deliberately crude spittle of Futurist painting." [110] In a letter to Leshkov on June 10, 1918 (old style), Bakhrushin gave his impression of the staging of *Giselle*:

I. Fedotov's sets, done under the influence of leftist tendencies in modern art, were striking. When the curtain rose, a tense bewilderment reigned. The audience did not know how to take the sets —as a joke or seriously. But after a few moments, one's eye got used to them and began to make out individual details, and when the dancers filled the stage, the scene became animated and sparkled with color. The old costumes were sharply dissonant with the general background of the sets; one wanted to see innovation in them too. [111]

In conclusion, Bakhrushin assessed the production as follows: "In general, the production of *Giselle* deserves special attention because of both the bold sets (perhaps from another point of view somewhat inappropriate in this echo of the age of Romanticism), and the efforts of the dancers to create with the old something new and original. . . . Loud debates about the production went on during the intermission." [112] After *Giselle* had been performed at the Aquarium Garden Theater it was shown again in the Bolshoi Theater in the fall of 1918 and was kept in the repertory for one season with Reisen in the major role and with the old decor.

During the 1921–22 season, when the Bolshoi and Maly Theaters were using the stage of the New Theater, Gorsky returned to *Giselle*. The production was shown on January 9, 1922, with Fedor Fedorovsky's sets.

The designer at the New Theater was faced with the problem of creating a simplified and economical stage set, "out of the ever-present canvases, with the addition of expressively highlighted parts of the movable sets." [113] But Fedorovsky was trying for a massive scale. A critically inclined reviewer wrote that "the sweep of his brush would have been more appropriate for the new building of the Kazan railroad station than for the always intimate *Giselle*." [114] In the decor of the first act, there was something of Gustave Doré. On the backdrop were mighty, hollow trees with branches bending like giant snakes. Over them, at an incredible height, were the barely visible towers of the castle. On the right and left sides, near the wings, were several more trees, and in the background a small arched bridge. This created the impression that Fedorovsky wanted to deprive the first act of *Giselle* of its usual intimacy and give it greater drama. He did not construct on the stage the usual little houses—Giselle's home and the hut in which Albrecht changes into peasant clothing. Probably on the small stage of the New Theater they would have taken up too much room, and a "mundane quality," which Fedorovsky disliked, would have cropped up.

But judging from photographs, the scenic action had a different character. Here is one scene: In the center stands Giselle, her legs slightly apart, fists firmly held against her sides, her gaze mockingly coquettish, even challenging. She wears shoes with heels, like the other dancers. Opposite her, in an awkward position, obviously not knowing where to place his hands, is the embarrassed Albrecht. Boys and girls are grouped around them. All of them hold themselves "like plain folk," arms akimbo and legs apart, slightly pigeon-toed; one pair is embracing, someone is giggling and slapping his thighs. From this photograph it is clear that Gorsky had returned a realistic quality to the "classicized," stylized peasant dances of *Giselle*'s first act. The lendler performed by Giselle and Albrecht lost the character of a lyric ballet dance and was once again transformed into a lendler. Gorsky expressed his concept of the character of Giselle in a note he gave to Kandaurova on the day of the premiere: "To Rita Kandaurova. Be a temperamental wench—don't dance on pointe (too sugary). Jump like a young little goat and really do go mad. Die with your legs apart, not placing one on the other. A. Gorsky." [115]

The village crones, in long heavy dresses, big caps, and striped stockings, peeped out at the young people amusing themselves. An elderly peasant, sitting on a bench, sipped from an earthenware jug. The appearance of the forester (Ivan Sidorov) was unusual. One could not even suspect the actor of belonging to the ballet; he was a gloomy-looking person with a beard and shaggy, dishevelled hair, slovenly and badly dressed. In all the photos he is standing near Giselle, but still a little bit off to the side, as though unable to make up his mind to approach her. The production stressed the drama of this already middle-aged man who has fallen in love with a young, slightly frivolous girl, and who becomes a witness to her death. As for Albrecht himself, it was not accidental that one of the performers of this role in the New Theater was Lev Lashchilin, who as a rule did not dance classical roles; Gorsky's production required a character actor. The reviewer called Lashchilin "a roué duke,"[116] for apparently the dancer was not inclined to justify Albrecht.

The decor for the second act showed a cemetery with identical wooden crosses leaning in various directions. Groups of low thick bushes, drawn in a non-realistic style, served as a background. Their snake-like branches, interweaving, formed a solid wall. In the openings in the decor, among the branches and roots, one could see here a woman's face, there an outstretched arm or the edge of a white bridal veil. The Wilis, who inhabited the cemetery, were waiting for their queen to summon them from their graves.

The Romantic ballet transformed the mystic horror of the German legend of vengeful dead women who killed tardy travelers into a certain lofty personification of the forces of nature. To some extent Gorsky brought *Giselle* back to its original source, rethinking the plot in the spirit of the twilight moods characteristic of prerevolutionary poetry. Instead of the former meadow, flooded with moonlight, there was the blackness of the cemetery. One might think Gorsky wanted to make visible and tangible the image of Nikolai Gumilev's reverie.*

> In this forest whitish trunks
> Suddenly appeared from the shadows,
> Root after root sprouted from the earth,
> Like the hands of the graves' inhabitants . . .

In this forest, instead of light-winged sylphs, gloomy shadows flashed by, apparitions, suffering and indignant souls. The Wilis appeared after the bell struck midnight. White veils fluttered by in wreaths of mist, which gradually covered the floor of the stage.

Gorsky dealt with the corps de ballet completely differently from the classic version; there the dancers, standing in even ranks, were seen as an echo of the central theme, the theme of Giselle. They embodied a collective Wili image. In Gorsky's production, there were groups of mourners, both sad and menacing, and each lamented in her own way and menaced on her own behalf. In the photographs all the dancers are in various emphatically dramatic positions—there are many extended arms and heads

---

*Nikolai Gumilev (1886–1921) was a major Acmeist poet (one of the post-Symbolist literary movements in St. Petersburg). (Ed.)

tossed back; one sits on the floor, her head bent over to her neighbor's knees, another one is half-reclining. The Wilis' costume is a wide gown hanging down to the ankles, with unevenly torn hems, and a very thick veil caught at the brows, covering the head, arms, and almost the entire body. The Wilis were made up to look deathly pale, with tragic black circles under their eyes.

The staging of *Giselle* in 1922 was a logical continuation of Gorsky's previous experiments. Creating one variant after another, he moved further and further away from the classic version. Beginning in 1907 he built up features of realistic drama in the first act. This helped to accent the motif of social inequality, which was the reason for Giselle's death. In the second act Gorsky emphasized the gloomy details from which *Giselle* had been freed in the course of the nineteenth century, and he gave the ballet back its former fantastic quality. But he lost the lucid lyricism of the old production, which yielded to different interpretations and thus had more depth than the somewhat sinister, ghost-like 1922 production.

At the same time, the dramatic element won out. "In Gorsky's new production, Théophile's Gautier's *Giselle* was for practical purposes no longer a classical ballet, so little room was given here to 'pure' dance. . . . Now everything is built on mime,"[117] wrote one viewer.

Gorsky's production of *Giselle* ran in the New Theater and then, beginning in 1924, in the Bolshoi Theater. Sooner or later, however, the Moscow ballet had to return to the traditional version. In 1934 Viktor Iving wrote: "The present choreographer, Monakhov, was completely right when he refused to revive Gorsky's modernized production, which had been on the Moscow stage, in the latter's attempt to rehabilitate the old version by Petipa."[118]

Ever-Fresh Flowers

While reworking the classical heritage, Gorsky was simultaneously thinking about works that directly expressed the spirit of the times. In those years, everyone was similarly preoccupied. But few believed that the ballet, a relic from the past, could reach a rapprochement with the contemporary period.

Defending the academic theaters, Lunacharsky considered it possible to preserve the opera and the ballet "not so much for their own sake, as for what would doubtless emerge from them."[119] That was what he wrote in "Why Are We Preserving the Bolshoi Theater?" (1925), dreaming of festive pageants, popular revolutionary ceremonies, and gigantic "oratorios" with singing, declamation, and dancing, which would replace the opera and the ballet.

Five years earlier, Lunacharsky had recommended that a ballet be staged based on Ilya Schneider's libretto, *The Golden King*. Schneider suggested that Scriabin's *Poem of Ecstasy* be used to depict a symbolic scene of slave labor, the revolt of the oppressed, and the downfall of the "golden idol." A scenario for this same music has been preserved in Gorsky's archives. Here also a popular uprising was shown allegorically: "From the abysses of high mountains hands are outstretched, hundreds and thousands of them, clenched into fists and with palms spread, white and black"; Then "the whole earth becomes alive through this living mass of people, who have come out onto the highest places and straightened out their limbs from the tiredness of heavy slave labor." Above is the fantastic castle—the center of earthly riches and nest of debauchery. "And the crowd of half-naked workers rushed at this monstrous palace. . . . The palace threw its riches into the crowd, its glittering mantles and precious gems. But the ecstasy in the soul of the people helped them plunge the traitorous, monstrous palace into dust." Finally, "a universal fire was burning. The monstrous palace was devastated, and a new temple to an unknown god appeared on a white cliff. And the light of truth and freedom filled every space."[120]

Perhaps this image of mountain heights and human crowds appearing from abysses was inspired by the performance of Scriabin's *Prometheus* on the first anniversary of the October Revolution: "Silhouettes were seen on the background of other-worldly, unearthly mountains, far-off people, the masses of the chorus; and further on rose up images of flaming banners, and even higher up were colorful boulders whose forms were unreal."[121]

The abstract allegory, sometimes touched with mysticism, characteristic of these early attempts, brought them close to the quest of playwrights and stage directors before World War I. The hands reaching from the abyss that Gorsky envisaged were reminiscent of Max Reinhardt's *Oedipus the King*.

At the same time, new efforts to bring explicit revolutionary emblems into ballet appeared. In Gorsky's papers are two scenarios that were never staged, written by Georgi Rimsky-Korsakov, who worked with Gorsky from 1919 to 1921. The first, *Red Star* (to the music of Frédéric Chopin), told of a deserter who was persuaded by his bride to return to the front. In the finale the Red Star glowed, and the hero rushed after it. The second, *The Third International* (to music by Richard Wagner), was divided into two scenes: First, in "the prerevolutionary era of mankind," hard work, grief, and deprivation were depicted, and then mankind, turning toward two figures standing on pedestals—the Peasant with the sickle and the Worker with the hammer.[122]

The link of the scenarios with Soviet revolutionary posters, in which the images were distinctively schematic, is obvious. Allegory and hyperbole were also characteristic of the work of the proletarian poets called Cosmists, who wanted to "build a Palace of Universal Freedom on the canals of Mars" and who sang of "the fiery smiths of the future," and "the burning maiden freedom." In the dramatic theater, as well, particularly in mass pageants by the *Proletkult*,* there were symbolic representations of the struggle of the working class, its cosmic scope, and its destructive, elemental force. Here the hero was presented as a smith stripped to the waist, in a leather apron; a half-naked youth encircled by a hammer and sickle; or a woman in loose, flowing clothes with a banner in her hands. Here the actions of allegorical characters—Wisdom, Thought, Evil, and so on—were shown. In the triumphant apotheosis, Freedom shattered its shackles and youths and maidens in white clothes sang hymns and performed a Dance of Labor.

Something similar happened in ballet too. Lopukhov's *The Red Whirlwind* (1924) and Goleizovsky's *The Whirlwind* (1927) are phenomena of this type. But even earlier, Gorsky had staged a children's ballet, *Ever-Fresh Flowers*, where there was unique combination of the forms of traditional ballet and the devices of revolutionary festivals.

The ballet *Ever-Fresh Flowers*, shown in November 1922 in the New

---

*The *Proletkult*, or Organization for Proletarian Culture, wanted to break with bourgeois art and build a new proletarian art. Founded by A. Bogdanov in 1906, it became active after 1917 in fusing art and industry. In terms of theater, the *Proletkult* organized readings, plays, and pageants in Petrograd and in Moscow, where Sergei Eisenstein became director in 1922. Supported by Lunacharsky, *Proletkult* was seen as a threat to party hegemony by Lenin and abolished in 1923.

Theater, was about children; it was staged for them and performed by them. The interest in the theme of children in the first postrevolutionary years was not accidental. Aside from Gorsky, Riabtsev staged ballets for children in his studio, as did Goleizovsky and the Petrograd choreographers. Ballet productions for children were only a small part of the work in children's theater begun in those years, when a great deal of attention was paid to everything that had to do with children. People who were laying down the foundations of the new society gave a great deal of thought to the problems of educating future generations.

In addition, day-to-day problems required a particular concern for children. After the civil war, destruction, and famine, orphaned children as well as street urchins had to be cared for, and a struggle was launched against juvenile crime. In 1922 many thousands of children lived in orphanages. And there were quite a few children who spent the night in boiler rooms or gateways, hiding from roundups.

Hence the keen interest that Lunacharsky showed in art for children, and specifically in children's theater; not only in dramatic theater, but also in the ballet. He became involved in the affairs of the ballet schools, firmly objecting in particular to the closing of the ballet school of the Bolshoi Theater, and he assisted Goleizovsky's Children's Ballet.

Ever-Fresh Flowers is not only a ballet for children, it is also a ballet whose subject is children: children as the future of the country, as that "ever-fresh treasure" that the country is obliged to protect. In terms of genre, Gorsky's children's production is a choreographic presentation with singing and verbal text. The text was written by Vladimir Marz, a specialist in children's theater.[123]

In the prologue, two children—a little boy and a little girl—came into the hall and, turning to the audience, said that they had left home searching for ever-fresh flowers. The leader, Uncle Volodya, asked the audience for advice. They suggested that he call the Magician. The Good Magician appeared, saying:

> There are ever-fresh flowers in the world, but only he who himself is honest, just, and loves all children can see them. Those people who live by their own labor, wish good for all, and call their neighbors their comrades see them. These flowers grow beautifully in our country, and five years have now passed since everyone was driven out who did not love his country and his people, who lived by some-

one else's labor, and had an abundance of everything. And soon in our country there will be no poor people at all, there will be no idle or evil people, because people here struggle and toil for the common good.[124]

Dwarfs and giants brought in a talisman. The Magician presented it to the children and explained that the talisman would light up on encountering the ever-fresh flowers. All the participants in the prologue went onto the stage. The curtain opened and the sea and a ship could be seen; the children got into the ship and sailed off on a journey (first scene). Music depicting a thunderstorm was heard, lightning flashed, thunder growled, the trees shook, and rain began to pour. The second scene of the first act took place in a forest, where the tired travelers appeared. Animals entertained them, performing a grand "nighttime" dance in which baby bears, little rabbits, grasshoppers, beetles, fireflies, night butterflies, tiny frogs, and foxes all took part. The performers were the younger students of the ballet school. After talking to the travelers, who tried to find out whether the ever-fresh flowers grew in the forest, all the little animals said goodbye to the children in a cheerful "morning" dance.

The third scene began with a joyous musical introduction. The curtain opened to reveal a flowerbed. The flowers woke up and began to sing. Two flowers, a rose and a peony, danced an adagio. The grasshoppers invited everyone into the garden. The two children appeared: they were welcomed by the rose, and then the autumn leaves, varicolored butterflies, field flowers, some toys forgotten in the garden (a doll, Sonya, with a little bear in her hands, and a doll called Kurilka), bluebells, and wild pansies all danced for them. At the end of this divertissement, the flowers began to fade. The children looked at the talisman; it did not light up.

In the second act (fourth scene) a field was shown on the stage. An old peasant came out and with him the sowers, who sowed the fields. The stage was filled with the corps de ballet, dressed as wheat, cornflowers, and poppies. Forty-eight junior students of the ballet school performed a waltz. Among them fluttered a golden butterfly and a dragonfly— older students. Then reapers came from the audience onto the stage and began to reap; behind them were threshers, who represented the harvest. Millers brought out sacks. Two lit stoves rolled out onto the stage, and bakers danced around them with two enormous frying pans. Real cakes and buns appeared in the pans and twenty bread hawkers gathered them into baskets. At the same time, the stoves moved around and apple trees grew up on the stage. The little students did an apple-picking dance. The apples were also put into the baskets and the hawkers carried them into the auditorium.

In the third act (scene five), six smiths stood at a forge on the stage with six anvils. Here other workers were also laboring, digging tunnels, raising brick walls, planing, sawing, and painting. At the same time that the smiths were forging a sickle, hammer, and the number five (representing the fifth anniversary of the October Revolution), the other workers formed from glittering letters the word International. The workers sang a well-known song, "We Are the Smiths," which was taken up by the audience. At the end of the song, the travelers went out into the audience. They asked the Old Smith a question: "What are these people doing?" "We are forging a new life," answered the old smith. "We want happiness and joy for everyone." [125] He told the children how terrible life was before the revolution; he showed them the hammer and sickle and explained the meanings of those emblems. The children asked whether the ever-fresh flowers were here. The Old Smith replied, "In our country, the children of the workers are called flowers." The walls of the smithy moved apart, a meadow was revealed (scene six), and on it a choral round dance of the field flowers took place. Meanwhile, the talisman brought by the children began to move quickly and lit up brightly. The two children became convinced that they indeed had found those ever-fresh flowers of which the Magician had spoken. Then the little boy pointed out to the Old Workers the children sitting in the audience. "And these children, right here, who came to us on this holiday, are they also 'ever-fresh flowers?'" [126] The worker replied affirmatively. A glowing sign appeared at the footlights: "Children are flowers of the sun, the joy of life." Garlands fell from the boxes and were thrown onto the stage. The smith suggested that they form a procession. The children-actors and children-spectators formed a line headed by a military band and went out into the lobby to the sounds of a march. Having gone through the building singing revolutionary songs, they came back into the auditorium.

During that time, a kind of apotheosis had appeared on the stage ("Hymn to Labor"). "At the back of the stage was a staircase, and in the center of the stage was a shield made by the smiths, with a hammer and sickle on it. Higher up the children held flashing letters, The International. On the background of a reddish gold gleaming sun, along the sides of the stage were grain reapers with wheat and fruits, craftsmen, and workers." [127]

The music for the ballet was selected from various sources. Most of it was taken from Asafiev's ballet *The White Lily*. The performance opened with the musical introduction to this ballet. The music describing the storm was also taken from this work: gusts of wind, thunder, falling rain, then a gradual calm. The dances of the little animals (in the second scene of the first act) and the dances of the flowers (in the third scene) were also for the most part from *The White Lily*. In the third act, the dances of the flowers in the field, the flight of the golden butterfly and the dragonfly, the entrance of the millers, the dance around the stoves, the apple-picking dance, and the final scene with the grand waltz (before the apotheosis) were also set to Asafiev's music.

Individual numbers taken from works of other composers were also used in the ballet. The entrance of the Good Magician in the prologue was accompanied by music from Gounod's opera *Faust*. The gnomes, giants, and monsters carried out the talisman to the March from Rimsky-Korsakov's *Le Coq d'or*. The dance of the flowers made use of the Adagio from Pugni's *Le Roi Candaule*, Chopin's Mazurka (Opus 47), the "Harlequin Dance" from the first act of *The Nutcracker* ("Kurilka") and the trepak from the same ballet ("The Dance of the Wild Pansies").

The third act introduced popular children's and revolutionary songs: "Boldly Keep Abreast, Comrades," "Song of the Flowers," "Song of the Reapers," "We Are the Smiths," "The Children's Internationale," "The Internationale," and others. The future spectators learned them beforehand in schools and orphanages so that they could sing along with the dancers at the performance. The full text of a song written by Lunacharsky is appended to the manuscript of the play:

> We are children, the pink buds,
> We are drawn to the light and we wait,
> Morning has come, the small leaves have opened,
> We will blossom into roses in the afternoon. . . .

One of the initiators of the production was the artist Fedorovsky. He participated in making up the plan and he created the decor and costumes. A backdrop was done for each scene. The backdrops showed drawings that were brightly colored in a single hue, like appliqués on children's clothing or rugs. On one were fir trees with mushrooms and forest flowers underneath them on a green hummock; on another, blue-bells, cornflowers, and still more flowers drawn with colorful squares and circles, half the height of the sets. On the third was an apple tree with a big trunk and, on its strong branches, apples shown as large circles, clearly divided into two halves, bright red and green.

The costumes did not seem so much ballet costumes as masquerade ones. The flower performers were dressed not in traditional tutus, but in a type of overalls, with a headdress in the form of a little daisy head or other flowers. The animals wore the same type of overalls: the little rabbits had white ones and hats with ears; the fox had red overalls and a rather realistic mask. The fireflies had lanterns hidden in their costumes that were lit up and extinguished when necessary. The costumes of the human characters (peasants, smiths, etc.) were true-to-life but brightly colored.

Aside from Gorsky, the director Andrei Petrovsky and two assistants who had created individual dances—the dancers Konstantin Baranov and Asaf Messerer—took part in the production. The performers were almost all children from the ballet school and chorus. There were few adults in the production. The role of the "leader" who talked to the audience was played at the first performance by Marz, the author of the text, and after his tragic death on the day after the premiere it was taken over by the ballet dancer Riabtsev. The role of the Good Magician was played by Pavel Tsaplin. The hawkers who carried the cakes and apples around the audience were played by artists from the mime ensemble.

The children each played several roles. The older ones danced the following roles: Sofia Lifshitz played the rose, Shulamith Messerer—the peony, Minna Shmelkina—the Golden Butterfly, Tamara Tkachenko—the dragonfly, Alexei Zhukov—Kurilka, Vasily Matorin and Lev Pospekhin—the wild pansies. But the "soloists" also took part in the ensemble scenes; the older girls, for example, played the bakers, the younger children little animals and insects in the first act; Irina Charnotskaya danced the fox. They also played the field flowers in the third act.

Serafima Kholfina, who took part in the field scene, recalls that the old peasant, played by Sasha Rudenko, came out and plowed. He was followed by three sowers. "They scattered seed from their bags with measured movements to a generously flowing melody." A dance of the grains followed. "Two lines, sixteen people." At first "the crops knelt on one leg, then 'rye' began to 'grow.' Gorsky showed us how the rye should grow and sway. 'A breeze meanders gently across the field, plays with the grain, and the friendly sun blazes with his fiery rays,' he told the performers. He knelt, bent pliantly to the side, and, over his head, his hands moved almost imperceptibly. . . ." Forty-eight junior students from the ballet school danced the waltz of the grains, poppies, and cornflowers. Kholfina remembers that Gorsky demonstrated the dance of the butterfly. " 'The butterfly is tender and light—very light . . .' He flew among the 'grains' and 'flowers' with broad jumps in arabesque and sang, 'Taiya! Taiya!' He fluttered along the stage as lightly as if he had just graduated from the ballet school. We clapped our hands with delight." [128]

The authors of the few published reviews gave high praise to the children's performances: "I have not seen such a well-organized production for a long time, such a careful attitude on the part of the performers, such efforts . . . I saw not amateurish amusement that no one assumed responsibility for, but a carefully thought through production with children who showed me something completely unexpected, for, in addition to the dancing, there was also excellent acting and mime." [129]

In creating a children's fairytale ballet in the Bolshoi Theater, Gorsky primarily made use of the experience of the old ballet-féeries. Each act was a dance divertissement, framed with mime scenes (and in this case with conversation as well). Such divertissements included appearances by soloists and dances by the corps de ballet. Neither the compulsory march-processions nor the triumphant apotheosis of the finale was left out. As regards the dancing, all the variations for the roses and butterflies, the dance of the four grasshoppers, six little leaves, and sixteen cornflowers were traditional in the most primitive sense of the word— they were composed of movements familiar from dance classes and easily performed by children.

But the tradition of the old divertissement ballet was joined to a new and different tradition in *Ever-Fresh Flowers*. For five years quite a few agitprop performances, pageants, festivals, and parades had been put on. Contemporary ideas found their most direct expression in these productions; here the appropriate production devices were worked out. Gorsky and the director Petrovsky made use of them in staging a production that

1

2

1. Costume design for a snowflake in "The Kingdom of Snow" dance from Alexander Gorsky's *The Nutcracker*. Bolshoi Museum.

2. Drawing of Odette by Gorsky for his *Swan Lake*, 1920. Bolshoi Museum.

3. Drawing of Odile by Gorsky for his *Swan Lake*, 1920. Bolshoi Museum.

**4. Drawing by Kasian Goleizovsky for his *Snow White*,
1919. Bakhrushin Museum.**

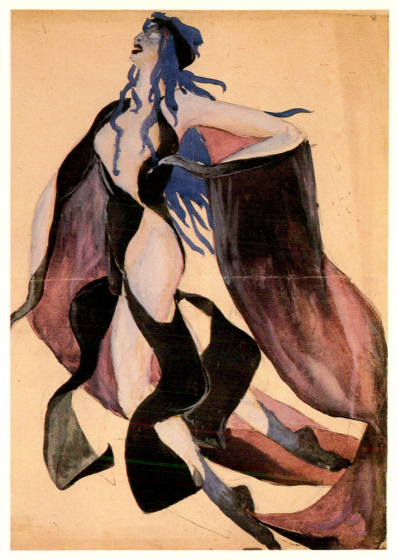

**5. Drawing by Goleizovsky for his Scriabin *Etude*, 1924.
Bakhrushin Museum.**

6. Costume design of a man for Goleizovsky's *Joseph the Beautiful*, 1925. Bolshoi Museum.

7. Set design by Alexander Golovine for act 2 of Pavel Petrov's *Solveig* (1922) and Fedor Lopukhov's *The Ice Maiden* (1927). Bakhrushin Museum.

6

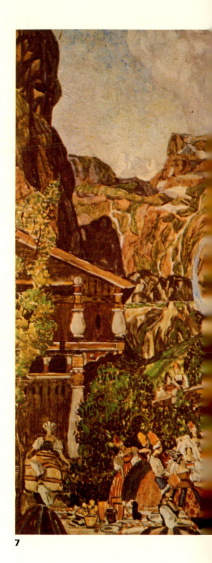

7

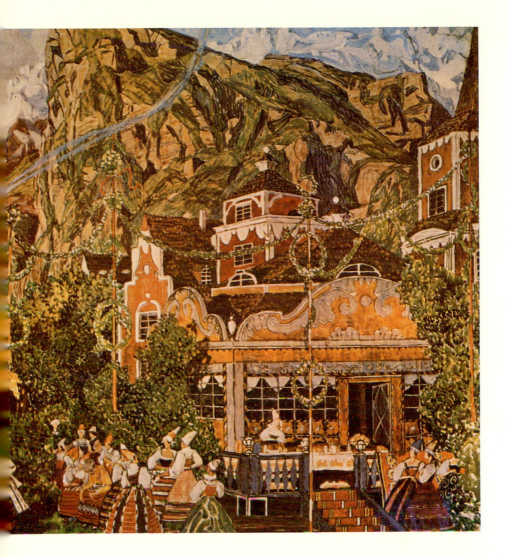

8. Set by Mikhail Kurilko for Lev Laschilin's ballroom scene in *The Red Poppy*, 1927. Bakhrushin Museum.

9. Drawing by Nikolai Musatov of the Ruler ("Vladyka") in Goleizovsky's *The Whirlwind*. Bolshoi Museum.

10. Costume design by Kurilko for a Zephyr in *Red Poppy*, 1927. Bolshoi Musuem.

9

10

11. Drawing by Musatov of the Victory Group in Goleizovsky's
Whirlwind, 1927. Bolshoi Museum.

featured modern people. In the course of the action's development, the new imagery pushed out the clichés of the fairytale ballet. The appearance of the smith in the second half of the production was not accidental. The smith holding the hammer, the emblem of the Soviet Republic, the smith "forging happiness" and "forging the future" is probably one of the most widely disseminated images of those years: He appeared in poems and songs, on posters and postage stamps, on dishes, designed by Sergei Chekhonin, and on book covers. *The Smithy* and *The Forge* were names of writers' unions and journals. The figure of a man stripped to the waist with a hammer in his hands, wearing a long apron, appeared in performances as well. Mass spectacles continually resorted to such means of poster expression. Wide use was also made of all kinds of emblems and slogans. The hammer and sickle, which in Gorsky's production were forged by the smiths, the words "The International," which the workers pieced together from gleaming letters, the slogans that were illuminated onstage—all of this was drawn from agitprop productions, from posters, and from festival decorations for streets and squares. Thus the apotheosis of the old ballet merged with the apotheosis of revolutionary spectacles.

The idea of bringing together performers and audience was also new. Many directors then tried to use this device, not only in open-air mass pageants, but also in ordinary theaters. They wanted to destroy the footlights, tear away the curtains, and unite the stage and the house in one burst. In a children's production, when one is dealing with a viewer who so directly and actively reacts to what is going on on stage, this was easier to do than anywhere else. The authors of *Ever-Fresh Flowers* made use of the rather rich experience of the children's theatricalized games that existed by 1922. There is a direct link between *Ever-Fresh Flowers* and the scenario of the New Year's play *The Fairytale and the Truth* (1920), also written by Marz. Not only are the courses of the plots similar, but the two works were based on similar structural principles.

In *Ever-Fresh Flowers* the major characters asked questions of the audience. The little boy and little girl asked the viewers how to find the ever-fresh flowers; Uncle Volodya asked them, after they had listened to the music, to say where the two children had ended up—in a forest or in a field? He consulted with the audience as to how the little boy and the little girl should act later; he asked their opinion as to whether the talisman would light up or not, and so on. Of course, for the most part people who had been deliberately placed there answered these questions

—young dancers seated in the orchestra and in the balcony (they were listed in the cast). But as is always the case with children's productions, the little spectators could not remain indifferent and also entered in the discussion.

The ballet turned into a game. The director's plan shows that in the intermission between the first and second acts the game "Peasants" was played, and during the next one the audience was given cookies "freshly baked" on the stage and apples "picked" before their very eyes. The finale was structured with the participation of the entire audience taken into account. The viewers were included in the apotheosis: The director's plan provided for garlands and ribbons thrown down from the upper tiers that were then taken by the children and "formed a single pyramid with the audience."

The ballet *Ever-Fresh Flowers* was shown for the first time in a matinee performance honoring the fifth anniversary of the October Revolution on November 7, 1922. This was a free performance with an audience of almost one thousand five hundred children from schools and orphanages. The production was repeated on November 11 and then again during the Week of Assistance to Schools on December 4. It was staged five times altogether during the 1922–23 season, and according to data from the reference book *Moscow Theaters*, 4997 viewers saw it. The critic from *Izvestia* noted that of all productions done for the anniversary of the revolution, the greatest interest was aroused by *Ever-Fresh Flowers*.[130] The *Pravda* reviewer wrote: "Despite its fully understandable flaws, *Ever-Fresh Flowers* is the first truly revolutionary children's production of the last five years."[131]

Lunacharsky was interested in this ballet. Of course, he could not fail to see the naiveté of a spectacle in which butterflies fluttered in a classical dance while next to them smiths made speeches about the revolution. And yet, the production to some extent was in keeping with his dreams of a mass spectacle involving the viewer in the action. This prompted Lunacharsky to write to Lenin and to invite him to the second performance of *Ever-Fresh Flowers*: "I would very much hope that you and Nadezhda Konstantinovna could come to the Bolshoi Theater on Sunday at one o'clock in the afternoon, when there will be a repeat performance of the experimental and enormously successful revolutionary children's production," he wrote on November 10, 1922.[132]

Ever-Fresh Flowers was Gorsky's last major production. In the winter of 1922–23 his illness worsened. His relationship with the administrators of the theater also became complicated. Malinovskaya, director of the theater from 1920 on, and Viktor Kubatsky, head of the musical division, did not believe in his talent and preferred to rely on other choreographers, such as Riabtsev and Zhukov. In 1921 the ballet *Chrysis* was not performed. "An Evening of Symphonic Ballet," which had also been prepared that year by the theater studio, was not shown: At the last minute, when the Hall of Columns of the House of Unions had already been booked for the production, the administration refused to provide costumes and sets. According to Nekrasova, "Everyone stopped taking Gorsky seriously. Kubatsky made totally intolerable, sharp comments to him in front of everyone . . . at one point Gorsky wanted to leave the theater altogether." She tells of the ballet *Capriccio Espagnol*, which was being prepared in 1923: "He [Gorsky] worked on the score of *Capriccio*, spent two or three nights on it, and came to the rehearsal. And they said to him, 'No, it is not you who are staging *Capriccio* but Zhukov.'"[133] The choreographer had a difficult time in terms of his material situation. Salaries were still paid in the theater, but to get firewood and rations it was necessary to find other work. During his last years, Gorsky taught and even staged concert programs in Edward Elirov's studio, though its reputation was not the best.

Gorsky rehearsed the ballet *The Grotto of Venus* to Wagner's music from *Tannhäuser* while he was already quite ill. Adamovich recalls that while creating the poses for the Three Graces, to everyone's embarrassment he began looking for a fourth.[134] In Viktor Iving's view, the disorderly movements of the ensemble onstage utterly failed to create an impression of frenzy and wildness. He also complained about the banality and saccharine quality of the general staging. "Sickly-sweet sets with nice little pink flowers, a sugary knight with a harp, Venus in a blonde curly wig—all this recalls the apotheosis of some 'luxurious' operetta production from the good old days, as staged by Briansky and Bauer."[135]

By the beginning of the next season Gorsky was no longer able to work. Nevertheless, he came to the theater every day, wandering in confusion down the corridors and halls, and soon had to be sent to the Usoltsev mental hospital. Gorsky died there a year later, on October 20, 1924.

In Moscow, Goleizovsky was the leader who attracted the younger generation to experiment. Kasian Yaroslavich Goleizovsky had been a student at the Petersburg Theater School; he was accepted in 1902 and spent seven years there along with the future participants in Diaghilev's Ballets Russes abroad. At that time, Fokine was already working in the Maryinsky Theater with students and young dancers. In the school, he conducted the women's class parallel to the one in which Goleizovsky was studying. For the examination performance, Fokine presented *Les Saisons* to the music of Tchaikovsky, in which Goleizovsky appeared partnering Fokine's student Elena Lyukom.

In 1909 Goleizovsky was accepted into the Moscow ballet company. Until 1918 he was a dancer in the Bolshoi Theater and took part in Gorsky's experimental productions. Thus the future choreographer's youth was linked with both reformers of the Russian ballet stage. From them he inherited, on the one hand, a profound knowledge of classical dance and respect for it as the professional basis of the art of ballet, and on the other hand, a mistrust for the immutability of academic canons. Goleizovsky understood that Fokine was asking his students to swim "against the current." Therefore, when he matured, he himself began to reexamine critically the ideas of his teachers.

Work in the Imperial Ballet—whether in Petersburg or in Moscow —was not completely satisfying. Goleizovsky was eager for everything new. He was attracted by concerts and exhibitions, he studied the violin, drew, attended lectures on art and political economy, took part in student debates on social issues, and he wrote poems (which Vladimir Maximov read at concerts) and ballet libretti in verse—at first composed for other choreographers, for example *Aziade* and *The Flowers of Granada* for Mordkin.

At the same time, working in a theater where he had to dance in everything being presented became a habitual but depressing duty. When he got a role in an experimental presentation, the desire to work rekindled. Giving Goleizovsky the part of the god Komon in *Salammbô*, Gorsky enthusiastically explained how he had thought up the scene in the temple and helped him with an unusual design for the make-up. But mostly Goleizovsky had to dance totally identical variations in totally identical ballets: friends of the prince and noble knights who were as similar as peas in a pod.

Goleizovsky recalls his performance in the role of a butterfly in *The Goldfish*. Having run offstage to applause after a successful number, he suddenly stopped dead upon catching sight of his reflection in the mirror: doll's make-up—bow lips, languidly made-up eyes—"romantic" black curls down to his shoulders caught up in a golden band, silk tights generously decorated with velvet appliqués, multi-colored wings on his back. . . . No, he had to either abandon the stage or make ballet into something else! Gorsky's attempts at transforming ballet without transgressing the limits of the old forms were not producing tangible results; his reform of the dance vocabulary was indecisive; his philosophic tinkering with the old ballets was compromising.

Goleizovsky immediately took on several tasks. He opened a private school (1916) and began to stage dances and sometimes even small ballets outside the Bolshoi Theater, at The Bat, the Mamonovsky Theater of Miniatures, and other places. In B. S. Nevolin's Intimate Theater in 1916 he presented *Japanese Dance* and the ballets *The Goatlegged*, by Ilya Satz, and *The Choice of a Bride*, with music and verse prologue composed by the poet Mikhail Kuzmin. The dancer Pipetta, the Sultaness Guilnar, and the bold Mirliton were part of the plot. Their affected grace revived the style of the conventional Oriental ballets of the eighteenth century, but all this was presented as if with a light ironic smile: "The comic element was interwoven with a tender pastoral feeling."[1] Apparently the production was not entirely without merit. Otherwise it would be difficult to explain the stubborn desire of one of the most capable dancers of the Bolshoi Theater, Adamovich, to play the role of Pipetta. Breaking the rule forbidding dancers of the Imperial stage to appear elsewhere, she had to remove her name from the billboards of the Intimate Theater, but she continued to dance there.

Work in the Theater School,
Children's Productions,
The Masque of the Red Death

By 1917 Goleizovsky was already very popular as a choreographer on the cabaret stage. The revolution immediately opened other prospects for creativity. The ballet, that stronghold of tradition, slowly and arduously began to turn toward the new. Therefore, when an obviously talented young man appeared and announced that his goal was to "bring the art of ballet closer to the broad democratic masses,"[2] he was welcomed. In the spring of 1918 Goleizovsky was invited to head the studio of the Bolshoi Theater School.

He spent his days and nights at the school. He dragged his books, notes, and pictures to a storeroom next to the dance studio. In the rehearsal hall he hung a curtain procured somewhere with the help of the performers, and he convinced the workers to erect a stage from old boards. Here he worked on dances to the music of contemporary composers (Scriabin, Rachmaninov) and those of the past (Rameau, Lanner). The young dancers from the theater and the students at the school, including Nina Podgoretskaya, Elena Ilyushchenko, and Liubov Bank, performed.

The first program was shown on May 30, 1918, at a dress rehearsal. It included a section called *The Evolution of Dance* (dance stylizations after the art of different epochs, from ancient Greece to modern America), divertissements, the ballet *The Goatlegged* by Satz, and *The Sonata of Death and Movement* to the music of Scriabin's Tenth Sonata. The dance to Scriabin's sonata aroused the greatest interest.

This piece was performed by six men and twelve women, led by Podgoretskaya. The soloist who, in the words of Pleshcheyev, had to "rush about, spin, and bend," demonstrated "a free plasticity of gesture, spirit, and lightness in flight."[3] She remained, in Bank's memory, a "heroic bird," and the corps de ballet "was always flying off somewhere."[4] The ensemble dances were built around complex groupings, which in Pleshcheyev's opinion were distinguished by "fancifulness of design" and "acrobaticism," while to the anonymous reviewer in the newspaper *Velikaya rossiya* they suggested "gymnastic exercises in the spirit of the Sokol

League* with its diverse pyramids."[5] Not all the critics approved of the idea of dancing to Scriabin's music. There were even those who called the production "the ravings of a madman" and pointed out "its inadmissibility in an academic institution."[6] Others, on the contrary, rejoiced at the unconventional decision that "an expression of pain, struggle, and despair could replace the cold and stern smile of the ballerina,"[7] and at the unconventional music; "there were even moments of penetration into the elemental force of Scriabin's dreams, which hardly yield themselves to dance."[8] In accustoming the ballet audiences to Scriabin's work and showing them that one could dance to a new type of music, Goleizovsky was also seeking new means of expression, something unusual for those who were raised with the principles of academic ballet.

Goleizovsky had long been interested in Scriabin's music. He said that he first dealt with it around 1910 or 1911. The dance fragments that he was then creating were never performed in public, but there were sometimes unexpected guests at the rehearsals, which took place in the Slavic Bazaar Hotel. Scriabin, who had heard from someone that "ballet people were mutilating his music," was one of them. After watching the rehearsal, however, he did not protest the use of his works in dance, but merely indicated which of his compositions were suitable for choreographic adaptation and which were not. Goleizovsky also made use of Scriabin's music when he was working in Baliev's theater, The Bat. In the postrevolutionary years in particular, Scriabin seemed especially important to Goleizovsky—and not only to him, but to many others who were trying to understand the grandeur and contradictions of the age— as an artist who "through the portrayal of passion depicted or predicted the revolution."[9]

At the beginning of the new season in 1918–19 Goleizovsky left the

---

*The Sokol League was a group in Czechoslovakia, founded by Miroslav Tyrs in 1862, that used gymnastics and plastique for covert political, nationalist organizing under Austrian rule, especially during World War I. Their activities included revived Greek games, living tableaux, and mass exercises. According to W. G. Raffé, in *Dictionary of the Dance*, Émile Jaques-Dalcroze and Rudolf von Laban were interested in the Sokol League, which held international conferences, and which also influenced Russian physical culture. The Nazis abolished the Sokol League but used some of their techniques. (Ed.)

Bolshoi Ballet in order to devote himself totally to choreography. In the spring of 1918, a children's division had been organized in the Theatrical-Musical Section (*Temusek*) of the Moscow Soviet of Workers' Deputies. Ballet dancers often participated in its concert programs. They performed individual dance numbers from popular ballets, but as yet there was no specific repertory for children. For the programs designated as "children's mornings," Goleizovsky, as Natalia Satz recalls, "produced . . . several little ballet scenes with students from the Bolshoi Theater School —the audiences were ecstatic." [10] At the same time, the children's ballets *Little Red Riding Hood* and *The Snowflake* were performed in Riabtsev's studio. Goleizovsky too was thinking of the possibility of staging a full-length ballet for children.

At this time, he was working with the members of his own studio (which had grown out of the school he had opened in 1916) and a group of children. Goleizovsky related that he had succeeded in acquiring for the studio a private residence abandoned by its owners; it consisted of twenty rooms with ceilings decorated with stucco friezes. Shortly after, during one of the dreadful freezing winters of the Civil War, this private house would share the fate of many of Moscow's wooden buildings at the time: It was pulled down for firewood. But there, in 1918, Goleizovsky began to gather young people together. The times were hard: many children were orphaned and starving. In the studio they were warm, they washed, and they got down to business with enthusiasm: learning to dance, rehearsing, sewing costumes after the sketches made by Goleizovsky himself, and painting scenery. That autumn, with these children and a group of older dance students, Goleizovsky produced his first ballet for children—*The Sandmen*.

It was a three-act ballet to an assortment of music, mostly Robert Schumann's pieces from *Album für die Jugend*. Its plot, which Goleizovsky took from his son Dima's brightly illustrated picture book, was not complicated: The little girl Olya for a long time didn't want to go to sleep, but the old men from the fairytales threw sand in her eyes, and they closed of their own accord. Then "the sandmen left with Olya on an interesting journey in which the little girl's favorite toys came to life, and mushrooms, animals, and birds all danced." [11] Satz noted the musicality of Goleizovsky's production, considering it the chief merit of the work.

The Sandmen was performed several times on the premises of the Vvedensky People's House (Narodny Dom) (the premiere was October 13, 1918) and later in many district clubs. Beginning at the end of 1918 the Children's Theater of *Temusek* began to operate in Mamonovsky Lane under Natalia Satz's direction. Its structure also included Goleizovsky's school-studio which, as of May 1, 1919, had come under the jurisdiction of the TEO of the People's Commissariat for Education. Here Goleizovsky produced *Snow White* to music by Vladimir Rebikov. According to Satz, the fragments of the ballet that were shown were very interesting. Goleizovsky's sketches for the costumes are preserved in the A. A. Bakhrushin State Central Theatrical Museum. They are executed with unusual care; every detail of clothing, hair style, and ornament is thoroughly planned. But the full *Snow White* was never performed in public.

Another ballet that Goleizovsky was then producing led the choreographer to break with Satz's theater. Goleizovsky was attracted by the idea of making a ballet intended not only for girls who loved fairytales, but also for boys who were indifferent to them. The plot of the ballet was adapted from a book by the famous German humorist and caricaturist Wilhelm Busch, *Max and Moritz*, which described the tricks of two indefatigable pranksters. The études of Ludwig Schytte were the musical basis for the ballet. Goleizovsky's wife, Nina Sibiryakova, designed the scenery and costumes. Leonid Matskevich, Alexei Serlov, Alexander Bryndin, and the brothers Georgi and Ivan Tokarev were the adult dancers, and the children who were studying at the ballet studio also performed. Children liked the merry ballet but, according to Satz, the managers of the theater gradually began to get the idea that from an educational point of view it contained serious flaws. Ultimately the Commission for the Organization of a Children's Art Theater, together with Lunacharsky, removed the ballet from the repertory.

Judging from the comments in print, two accusations were leveled against this work of Goleizovsky's. The first concerned the source: According to Satz, after having seen the ballet, Lunacharsky called Busch "a witty but unkind artist, undoubtedly harmful to children's education."[12] In point of fact, in Busch's *Max and Moritz* one does sometimes feel a certain no-nonsense cruelty, a blunt straightforwardness. Many of Max and Moritz's pranks are not particularly humane, and the ending of the whole story is downright bloodthirsty: A baker, after an unsuccessful attempt at baking the pranksters in an oven, sends them off in sacks to a mill, where the boys are ground up by millstones and the flour is tossed to ducklings as food.

But Goleizovsky was by no means trying to emphasize all these cruelties. At the end of the ballet, when the naughty boys are caught, they are picked up by their ears and spanked. Even in this ballet version the pranks of Max and Moritz were not always good-natured, but only to the degree to which many comic situations are offensive: laughter at a person who has slipped, is drenched with paint, is caught on a nail, and so on. Of course it's not funny for the victim, but in vaudeville as well as in the circus ring, this type of slapstick humor is used incessantly. And it would seem that Goleizovsky's ballet was no more "cruel" than clowning in general or the comic films of Max Linder and other famous comedians.

The second—and major—accusation was that Busch's little book, and Goleizovsky's ballet as well, were anti-educational. In the theater they were afraid that children would imitate "the not entirely innocent pranks they had seen."[13] The Commission also expressed the same apprehensions. In the report on the meeting of the organization called Theater Center (*Tsentroteatr*), mention is also made of "anti-educational" and "anti-artistic" tricks and episodes.[14] Unfortunately, this report was written so that Lunacharsky's negative opinion cited in it is expressed both categorically ("a dispirited impression," "absurd music") and without convincing proof.

Satz defined her position much more precisely; she did not consider the work of the choreographer weak at all: "Goleizovsky staged the ballet with his customary inventiveness." But it did seem to her nevertheless that he was carried away by "his individualistic visions" and had forgotten about "the future audience."[15] In other words, he had forgotten that his ballet must "instruct." Apparently, in Satz's soul the artist had struggled against the pedagogue and the pedagogue had gained the upper hand. But here doubts automatically arise about the correctness of the educational theories of those who were so seriously frightened by the pranks of Max and Moritz. To the minds of these people, the children's perception of the ballet would be uncritical and unthinking. They imagined that the young spectators would immediately try to "realize" any situation seen on stage: They would begin to saw the piles off bridges, throw gunpowder into stoves, and so on.

Meanwhile, the choreographer only wanted to produce a merry, dynamic ballet with some buffoonery. In Goleizovsky's archives there is a scenario for a ballet apparently intended for a circus, *The Redheads' Pranks*, where there are two clowns in place of Max and Moritz. As is apparent from a scenario dated 1923, he intended to use a chase scene with comic effects in the ballet *The City*.

Finally in 1928 Goleizovsky produced the ballet *The Imps* to the music of Franz Schubert at the Moscow Studio of Dramatic Ballet. Jumping ahead, we note that even here he was criticized on the same grounds.

This production is a staging of the well-known German children's book, *Max and Moritz*, by Busch, which has been removed from our children's libraries because of the negative influence it has on children. Thus the very thing that teachers and librarians are fighting against is being popularized on the stage of the Music Hall in the attractive form of a theatrical spectacle. The entire ballet is sheer propaganda for mischievousness and forms of hooliganism accessible to children.[16]

Again the ballet was considered not as a work of art that the audience enjoys through its merry mood and dynamics but as a theatrical moral admonition. It was as if what the child sees and hears remains stagnant in his mind and does not become food for thought. This is a particularly utilitarian view of the theater, which admits only the right to establish norms of behavior.

Most likely, both of Goleizovsky's ballets were far from perfect. The staging of Busch's book was more successful in the puppet theater. In Evgeny Demmeni's production in 1927, every time Max and Moritz overstepped the bounds of the permissible and their joke threatened to cause real harm, they themselves were entrapped and became the laughingstock of the audience. Goleizovsky's solution was much more primitive. His 1928 ballet is a clown show. In the words of one viewer, the "imps" Max and Moritz constantly create trouble; they grab and ruin other people's things, trip up passersby, pull chairs out from under people, put tacks on chairs. The entire comic aspect of the production that attracts children lies in these "pranks": the falls, throwing things around, the endless shoves in the behind, the tongues stuck out, and so on. All this concludes with an "ideological" colophon: A placard appears—"You've had your fun, and that's enough!"—after which the chase after the "imps" by everyone who has suffered from their tricks begins. Goleizovsky was unable to find a finale that would have destroyed the troublemakers in the eyes of the audience, so he limited himself to punishing them. "Pioneers appear and seize the pranksters; Max and Moritz are put behind bars." [17] Indisputably, this is not the best of conclusions. And yet, Goleizovsky's comic children's ballet hardly possessed the dangerous power the reviewer ascribed to it. It seems to have been a funny, dynamic, and colorful production in keeping with children's eternal need for laughter.

On December 24, 1919, Goleizovsky announced his departure from the Children's Theater, and on January 14, 1920, the ballet troupe was disbanded. Many plans remained unfulfilled. Among them were the revolutionary programs which Satz had discussed with him. There was talk of a show for adolescents, depicting "an episode from the French Revolution in the form of a ballet or pantomime." [18] In Goleizovsky's archives there is a scenario written in collaboration with Grigory Pozhidayev—*Gamelin, or The Revolution Will Be Victorious*. The individual details, such as the suite of French folk dances, the final celebration of the Revolution, and the use of the music of the times, anticipate the future ballet *The Flames of Paris*.

Goleizovsky's work was not limited to the productions at the Children's Theater. He was constantly expanding the repertory of the studio,[19] and in 1919–20 he also worked at the Bolshoi Theater and at the circus.

In January 1919 Goleizovsky was invited to stage *The Masque of the Red Death* in the Bolshoi Theater. The basis for the ballet, for which Nikolai Tcherepnin wrote the music in 1912, was the fantastic, sinister story of the same name by Edgar Allan Poe. The composer wrote, "The music in my ballet *Le Pavillon d'Armide* is as sunny and joyful as the music in this ballet is nightmarish and gloomy. In order to give the music a gloomy tinge, I significantly increased the size of the orchestra, introducing completely new instruments into the score. . . . And I myself was very happy when I was finally rid of this nightmarish work and immediately devoted myself to 'lighter' creative work." [20]

The theme of this ballet is the inevitability of approaching catastrophe, the inexorable movement over the earth of a threatening force, before which pathetic, insignificant man is helpless. As with many works of an allegorical nature, the ballet admitted of an interpretation that was to some degree "consonant" with the October Revolution. The death of the prince could even be interpreted as the overthrow of the autocracy.

The plot of the ballet is as follows: A party is going on in the castle of Prince Prospero, while at the gate a terrible guest is already knocking—the Plague. Everyone knows that this uninvited guest is nearby, but no one can recognize it, for the masks on the faces of the merrymakers hide the grimace of horror. And when it is midnight, the Plague, who has penetrated into the palace under the mask of the red death, triumphantly announces itself.

Judging from the materials in his archives, in Goleizovsky's version the masquerade ball took place around an antique clock and the ballet was divided into three "hours" (scenes). In the first scene, the masks of commedia del l'arte predominated, alternating with ancient Greek characters. Gradually the ball was transformed into an orgy. Here (the second hour) the specific motif emerged—later developed by Goleizovsky in *The Whirlwind*—of the monks who turned into satyrs and danced with bacchantes. When the clock struck the third hour, the atmosphere of terror thickened. "Living dreams" appeared, then "masks of horror," and finally, three consecutive forms of the red death—"in the clock, in the center of the group, and in the orchestra."[21] The Prince's encounter with it led to his death.

Nemirovich-Danchenko, at that time the head of the directorate of the Bolshoi Theater, supported Goleizovsky's ballet. At one time he had planned to direct it, but he subsequently entrusted the work to Vakhtang Mchedelov. Gorsky was also sympathetic to Goleizovsky's production, although he could have considered himself insulted; everyone knew that he was interested in Tcherepnin's ballet and had even signed an agreement for its production in 1913 with Serge Diaghilev. However, Gorsky sincerely tried to help the young choreographer in his fight with the conservative members of the company, led by Tikhomirov, who opposed this production. Gorsky wrote in one of his letters: "Goleizovsky complained to me last night about the prejudice of the company against his staging, but I advised him to pay no attention to them. I experienced the same thing whenever I succeeded in carrying out something of my own. But he is nervous."[22] Nemirovich-Danchenko reported the same thing to Lunacharsky on April 15, 1919: "Goleizovsky's work on *The Masque of the Red Death* is being held up by outside circumstances. In any event,

I will do everything I can so that Goleizovsky's artistic plans will be fulfilled, even at the risk of failure."[23]

The work, which was begun in January 1919, continued to the end of the season. In June, the majority of the sketches for the decor and costumes were completed by the set designer, Grigory Pozhidayev.[24] Nevertheless, Goleizovsky's production never reached the stage. The report of the theater concerning the fulfillment of the repertory plan for the 1918–19 season contains a specific point concerning the production by the Moscow Art Theater's directors of the opera *The Snow Maiden* and the ballet *The Masque of the Red Death*: "This work did not go forward largely as a result of a hidden but stubborn opposition on the part of the Bolshoi Ballet."[25]

The plan for staging *The Masque of the Red Death* is connected with prerevolutionary ideas; the presentiment of grandiose cataclysms found expression in the tragic images of Leonid Andreyev's works and in such ballets as *Pierrot and the Masks* by Boris Romanov (1914). The motifs of the tragic masquerade, the unmasking of the mendacity of what is presented as truth, and the transience of principles considered immutable also arose in other works by Goleizovsky. This was how he interpreted the commedia del l'arte. While he was still working in the Children's Theater, his *Harlequinade*, to music by Cécile Chaminade, was produced (the premiere was on June 8, 1919). Here, in the framework of a stylized representation of Italian masks, a melodrama was played out about the abandoned Pierrot and Pierrette, who has been debauched by the lying Harlequin and dies when she discovers that Columbine is Harlequin's bride. Later this plot, somewhat reminiscent of a parody on *Giselle*, was transformed. In one of the variants of the scenario found in Goleizovsky's archives, it had acquired the character of a sinister phantasmagoria. Harlequin (he is Duke Noss) feasts in a tavern in the company of monsters and werewolves. Here the Unknown Woman (Pierrette) appears to him as the embodiment of purity and light. Goleizovsky wrote in the introduction to the script: "The mood of the whole thing is rather tragic. It must accelerate . . . nervous, broken off, like the breathing of someone who is sleeping, drugged with some sort of narcotic. A nightmare that will never end."

It is true that the variant of the pantomime *Harlequinade* (*Pierrot and Columbine*) that was shown in the autumn of 1920 in the Second State

Circus did not contain such motifs. But other miniatures with masks (*The Tragedy of the Masks* and *Tombeau de Columbine*, to the music of Boris Beer) also dealt with the theme of masks hiding reality, although in a less sinister aspect than had been planned. According to Goleizovsky's account, in *Tombeau de Columbine* Pierrot and Harlequin meet at the grave of Columbine. Like a vision from the other world, the deceased appears to Pierrot "in a nimbus of beauty" (Goleizovsky's expression), but at this point she sees Harlequin. And everything changes before Pierrot's eyes: with Harlequin, Columbine behaves provocatively, like a common prostitute. Thus his illusions are destroyed.

Goleizovsky's Studio,
The Moscow Chamber Ballet

From the moment he left the Bolshoi Theater in 1918, Goleizovsky's main activity centered around the school-studio he had created. It might temporarily join with the Children's Theater, the choreographer might use it for productions in the circus, but its fundamental importance lay in the work he did which was directed toward the creation of his own dance theater. There was a large group working in the studio (in 1921 there were 72 people)—students and those who thought the same way as Goleizovsky: members of the studio (Sofia Bem, Dmitri Dmitriev, and others), as well as dancers from the Bolshoi Theater (Elena Adamovich, Liubov Bank, Alexander Bryndin, Nikolai Gerber, Vasily Efimov, Olga Martynova, Leonid Matskevich, the sisters Maria and Sofia Nevelskaya, Vera Svetinskaya, Nikolai Tarasov, the brothers Vladimir and Igor Shokorov, Viktor Tsaplin, Sergei Chudinov, and others).

The dance studios of the 1920s contributed significantly to Soviet choreography. During this period, when the lyric theaters were mainly biding their time, experimental work was conducted primarily in the studios. One after another, various dance classes, workshops, schools, studios, and circles began to open. There was an especially large number of these in Moscow. By no means all of them were truly professional; often what was taught in the studios was the sheerest dilettantism, if not charlatanism. In September 1924 an investigation of the Moscow private studios and schools was launched, after which only a few studios where young people were really educated creatively remained. Individual studios headed by talented people grew into independent dance collectives that presented entire programs and sometimes even ballets. People were thinking about the future of the art of choreography and trying to make dance modern.

Among the leaders of the studios were several followers of Duncan. Duncan's own school opened in Moscow in 1921. Isadora herself and her adopted daughter Irma performed together with the students from the studio; their repertory included Tchaikovsky's *Marche slave* and *Symphonie pathétique*, and dances to the music of revolutionary songs, including "The Internationale." In the studios of Inna Chernetskaya and of Vera Maya, the "free," "natural" dance of Duncan gradually became more complex. Chernetskaya produced stylized dances; Maya produced national and comic ones, and, in the late 1920s, satirical genre sketches (*Masks of the City*, among others). Classical music was also used in the productions of Lev Lukin, creating harsh, sensual compositions with a tendency toward eroticism.

It was in the studios and on the vaudeville stage, which was more mobile than the theater, that the first attempts were made to portray modern people in dance. There were experiments in various directions. The leaders of the studio *Drambalet*, having lost faith in the possibilities of dance, advanced pantomime as the major expressive means. Several tried to convey the buoyant tone and impetuous rhythm of the age through gymnastics and acrobatics. A unique outgrowth of gymnastic dance included Valentin Parnakh's and Nikolai Foregger's "machine dances," in which people imitated the motions of pendulums, pistons, and wheels. Goleizovsky's studio was distinguished from the others by its professionalism, which brought it closer to the academic ballet.

After the break with the Children's Theater, the studio for some time was without a stage. On December 28, 1920, the studio members—a group of 56 people, headed by Goleizovsky—wrote a letter to Meyerhold.* They briefly outlined the history of the studio, its goals ("the search for new forms and paths"), listed their productions, and complained that the public was unable to acquaint itself with the studio. They begged Meyerhold: "Make us a theater."[26]

---

*Meyerhold was at that time the director of the theatrical department of the People's Commissariat of Enlightenment. (Ed.)

The appeal was not heeded, but in 1921 Goleizovsky succeeded in organizing a number of concerts: "The First Evening of Dances by Kasian Goleizovsky" (in May), "Second Evening" (in October), and a concert in the Hall of Columns of the House of Unions (in December). They immediately attracted attention. As serious a scholar of ballet as Yuri Bakhrushin wrote in January 1922 to Leshkov in Petrograd, "As regards new ballet, we have nothing and don't foresee anything; the only interesting thing is the series of private evenings arranged by K. Goleizovsky. He has now embarked on a course of very serious work and has already done a great deal in this direction."[27]

The programs for these three evenings consisted of dances primarily to the music of modern composers, including Nikolai Medtner (*Prologue*, *Funeral March*, Études and Préludes) and Scriabin (*Guirlandes*, *Flammes Sombres*, Études and Préludes). In early 1922 the program of Scriabin's music was enriched by *The White Mass*, as the new choreographic version of the Tenth Sonata was called. This was the beginning of the studio's intensive work; for the next four years (1921–25) Goleizovsky did a great deal of experimenting.

In 1922 a cycle of works appeared whose scope was similar to that of a one-act ballet: *Faun* to the music of Claude Debussy and *Salomé* to the music of Richard Strauss. This program, as well as the *Medtneriana* and *Scriabiniana*, was shown in the autumn of 1922 in Petrograd and met with a heated response. There were arguments about the dances to Scriabin's music, about the faithfulness to the composer's style, and about whether this was decadence or whether the searches were fruitful. There were arguments over the choreographic language: in what its novelty lay, in what ways it depended upon the classics.

Meanwhile, a new task had preoccupied the choreographer. In the spring of 1923 a series of "eccentric" dances emerged: a foxtrot, a two-step, and a tango, which Goleizovsky "reshaped" and "reworked imaginatively."[28] By no means all of the critics were favorably inclined toward them, all the more so because the program was called an "eccentric erotica" and contained more than a few risqué moments. And then, in the autumn of the same year, as if to specially prove his seriousness of intent and the wealth of his possibilities, the choreographer showed études to the music of Chopin, in which again "he approached the semi-classical compositions from which he had departed the previous year,"[29] and Spanish dances marking "an obvious change from mannered posing to real dancing."[30]

During the Chamber Ballet period, the basic lines along which Goleizovsky's quest proceeded began to show through more clearly; his choreographic signature took shape, and his biases became evident.

The revolution inevitably had to be reflected in the theater. The experiments of all of the artists of the period, even the most dissimilar, were ruled by a desire for modernity. Still, they saw the path to this modernization and, consequently, to the renewal of choreography in different ways. Having fallen by the wayside of the Bolshoi Theater, Goleizovsky joined with those who intended to "make a revolution" in ballet, breaking with the old art. Many limited themselves to a negative program, rejecting everything created before the revolution just because it had existed under a different social system.

Goleizovsky had other views. True, even he declared academic ballet anathema several times in articles and speeches. He was devastatingly critical of the repertories of the theaters which continued to show only *The Little Humpbacked Horse* and *La Bayadère*. He wrote in sharp terms about the clichéd manner of performing. He fiercely attacked the conservative leaders. And yet there were essential differences between Goleizovsky's aspirations and the demands of many of those who also wrote declarations and manifestos. Goleizovsky had his own vision of the new forms that would replace the old ones, and at the same time he had a solid professional base, without which all searches are fruitless.

The connection between Goleizovsky's art and the age of the revolution is not established by means of direct and obvious analogies, but in a more complex, roundabout way. It does not lie in comments on the news of the day, or in the depiction of everyday life, or in a view of society. Goleizovsky was neither involved in the theatrical "Left Front," nor in "industrial" agitational art, nor in the "collective creation" of the Theater of the Masses, which lived the same life as the masses. He came from those tendencies which, born in innovation and protest during the prerevolutionary years, continued to survive even after the revolution by trying to apply their aesthetic to new social tasks.

In the ballet, these tendencies proved even more vital than in other forms of art. The entire complex of ideas about the "new" ballet that had taken shape in the prerevolutionary years, as opposed to the dance academicism of the nineteenth century, retained its effect on the audience after the revolution as well; this is explained by the fact that the revitalization of the ballet undertaken by Fokine had relatively little effect on the imperial stage. He produced most of his innovative ballets for Diaghilev's Ballets Russes abroad; those ballets that were shown in Russia, primarily as charity performances, were by no means always included in the repertory. And outside the limits of the formal stage, there was practically no place for ballet choreographers to work; there were no ballet companies other than the imperial ones. Therefore, under the new conditions, when at least a broad field had opened up for all sorts of undertakings, it was completely natural for the experiments to continue what had already been begun. The first Soviet choreographers sought support in the slogans advanced by Fokine.

Many studios that announced their hatred for ballet and also their intention of creating a new choreographic art had their origins in Isadora Duncan and Émile Jaques-Dalcroze, that is, in the prerevolutionary experiments in the realm of "free" dance. But Duncanism, to which in their time both Fokine and Gorsky had already paid tribute, was a completed step by the Soviet period. The various gymnastic-acrobatic forms and the Foregger "machine dances" enriched choreography with new expressive means, but could not serve as the basis for a new, contemporary dance art antagonistic to the ballet. To put it briefly, the renewal of ballet came not from without but from within—primarily in an evolutionary, not a revolutionary manner.

Goleizovsky's art was born in protest. The choreographer rebelled against the old morality, against the stagnant forms and the stagnant content of the old ballet. But in his protest Goleizovsky directly continued the investigations of those who fought for the renewal of choreography even before the revolution. Goleizovsky's repertory, especially during the first half of the 1920s, was connected by many threads with the innovative tendencies of prerevolutionary art, which was ultimately the fruit of the Russian intelligentsia's frame of mind during the prewar years.

Goleizovsky was attracted by the theme of the mirage-like illusion of phenomena, the masquerade world with its deceptive happiness, where love revolves around death. Eroticism, raised to a metaphysical level, also occupied a large place in his work. The classical and Biblical themes of his works were not accidental. Like many representatives of Russian modernism, he perceived the heritage of the ancients symbolically, which opened the way for various, primarily subjective, interpretations. But as a man of another age, he naturally lent a different interpretation to these themes.

The love theme is undoubtedly the most developed in Goleizovsky's work. The majority of his dances reflect a meeting or a parting, mutual attraction, the ecstasy of love, a fight over a woman. Fokine touched on the same themes. But his eroticism was enveloped in an exotic, stylized shell. Recluses in a harem and fierce Oriental warriors also figured in the poetic scenario of *Aziade*, written by Goleizovsky. But he himself did not produce it; Mordkin did (1912). In his productions, Goleizovsky easily managed without the luxuriant Oriental background. He did not drag oriental rugs onstage, as in *Schéhérazade*, nor did he hide the pair of lovers under a canopy or cover them with large fans, as in *Cléopâtre*. Spain was also presented differently in Goleizovsky's ballets. Romanov, Gorsky, and Lopukhov succeeded in producing scenes of Spanish and Mexican *tabernas* where liquor was consumed and men stabbed each other with daggers as they fought for the possession of beautiful women. For Goleizovsky the heat of passion was no less, but it was expressed only through dance, without support from an external plot. For Goleizovsky emotion was not dressed up in the colorful clothing of far-off times or of strange lands. Emotion interested the choreographer in and of itself. This is the reason that Goleizovsky worked primarily in the sphere of small forms. He was a miniaturist, as was Fokine. But while Fokine leaned toward the one-act ballet, Goleizovsky was closer to the dance piece, the dance miniature. Fokine sketched out the plot at hand in order to evoke a stylized appearance of the epoch and the country. Goleizovsky did not need an external plot at all; his dances are the dynamic, plastic expression of emotion.

The emotionalism peculiar to Goleizovsky's dances served during the 1920s as the key to approaching the modern world. He belonged to that part of the artistic intelligentsia that accepted the revolution. He could not help being attracted by the possibilities the revolution opened up to artists, but he, like most artists, understood politics poorly. The decisive things for him were not social or political problems, but aesthetic ones. Everything that could facilitate the freedom to search, every attempt at self-expression was greeted enthusiastically. Hence the rejoicing in the days of the overthrow of absolutism when it seemed that prospects for the development of art were opening up, independent of any power, and governed by no one; hence the confusion, which sometimes grew into resistance, with which the October Revolution was greeted. "The bloodless revolution," born to "the ringing of old bells" merging with the "majestic outpouring of trumpets" singing "how glorious," and then "The Marseillaise,"[31] proved to be a mirage. Freedom was won through blood and suffering. It was accompanied by the violence and cruelty inevitable in a class struggle, and the meaning of what had happened became clear to many people only much later. For the majority of the artists of the time, the ideology of the revolution remained a riddle; only its emotional elements were perceived. Putting the exciting and tragic themes of the revolution on the dance stage at first seemed an insoluble problem. Artists tried to convey the feeling of reality on an emotional plane.

It was at this time that the art of the revolution was born. It resembled a political demonstration: It agitated, exhorted, made demands, and sloganeered. It was based on the poster and used its bright, garish colors as well as its laconic style. Like political demonstrations and posters, the art of the revolution was monumental and massive—the art of collective actions and collective feelings.

Goleizovsky approached the new world in a slightly different manner. He was interested not in the masses, but in the individual person. He had protested against the lack of rights of the individual in the old society. Hatred for the bourgeois way of life, its hypocrisy and lies—this was the basis for the "revolutionism" of many of the artistic intelligentsia during those years. By freedom, they understood primarily freedom from restrictions and prejudices, from the moral fetters that weighed people down in the old society. The eroticism in Goleizovsky's art also bore the imprint of individualism; it stood in opposition to bourgeois sanctimony.

But the soul of an individual reflects what is happening around one; one's experiences are an echo of social events. Therefore the times themselves, with their burdens, upheavals, hopes, and discoveries, appeared in Goleizovsky's productions. Goleizovsky perceived the new in life through the emotions, figuratively and intuitively. He was not the only one to take this path; after all, even in drama, which reacted far more sensitively to contemporary events than did ballet, there were artists who saw the point of contact with the revolution precisely in its emotional, elemental force.

Goleizovsky repeatedly spoke and wrote about dance as an art that celebrates the "might of human passion and heroic achievement." But in his early productions, the content was sometimes in conflict with the artistic style. The productions of 1921–22 were distinguished by grandiloquent beauty, affected and recherché, and by stylized exultation, which connected them with prerevolutionary decadence.

In 1921 Goleizovsky produced *Prologue* ("Along the midnight sky an angel was flying") performed by Adamovich and Tarasov to the music of Medtner. It was a duet in which a man in red flowing clothes suggesting wings led a woman and lifted her toward the sky. The lifts in this piece were unusually high for those times, but they were perceived not as a show of virtuosity but as an expression of upward aspiration; this created an illusion of soaring. Fluidity of movement was emphasized by a long scarf that floated along the ground. In the finale, after the dancer lifted his partner, he carried her offstage; the scarf hovered behind them along the floor of the stage, even after the dancers had disappeared. The theme of the duet, as is clear from the subtitle of the piece, came from the poem by Lermontov. But contemporaries read it slightly differently. "A strong principle draws after it an inert figure: a thought, a dream, perhaps a soul; and shows her, the timid one, who goes astray, suffers, and stops to rest, the path ahead to the inevitable, to the exalted." [32] This is what Georgi Rimsky-Korsakov, the biographer of Adamovich, wrote about the piece. A reflection of the moods of the people of the time was seen in the dance.

Medtneriana also included another dance, *Funeral March*, danced by five women. In the beginning the dancers moved slowly, with heavy steps and bowed heads, forming a compact group; then their tight formation broke apart. The dance was constructed of fluid movements of the arms and body, accompanied by the waving of ribbons. "The arrangement of the figures, the individual movements—all this was remarkable for its beauty and especially for its drama," a Petrograd critic wrote. "The final figure of the piece was amazingly conceived and executed—this final sigh is full of truth and the impression is unforgettable!" [33]

The final grouping made an impression on many people. Leonid Entelis remembered it many years later: "I recall how in the finale they slowly lay down, forming a black cross, and with the concluding *morendo* the cross barely rose and fell, like the chest of someone expelling the final breath of his life." [34] Maria Gorshkova also wrote about it. She too recalled the cross, very clearly outlined by the costumes, which were black with white—the ballerinas wore black caps—and the finale, during which the center of the cross rose slightly.[35]

Like many in those years, Goleizovsky felt a particular attraction to the exalted music of Scriabin. The tragic pathos of *Flammes Sombres* (performed by Efimov) and the wild joy of *Guirlandes* (performed by Grigory Polivanov and Viktor Tsaplin) found a clear response in the souls of his contemporaries. It is no coincidence that the choreographer several times returned to the Tenth Sonata, refining the content of the production each time. The dance was performed to the accompaniment of a piano, which sounded from the darkness. On the stage male and female figures moved in long white costumes. With a change in the mood of the music, the composition of the dance suddenly broke as well. The lines became uneasy, the groupings asymmetrical. The rows swayed: First the center rose, then the edges. In the finale all the dancers formed a tall, narrow pyramid, crowned by a figure with wide-spread arms borne high above the ground. Dressed from head to toe in white, clinging close together, they pushed toward the center and upward simultaneously, in a common movement. Those who stood at the top seemed to embrace the body of the hero; the following row reached toward him in prayer; and those at the bottom lay on the floor as if frozen in a final outburst, like a person who has lost all strength but stubbornly struggles onward. In Goleizovsky's archives there are sketches and a photograph that has fixed this final scene, suggesting the worship of one who was crucified. But according to Goleizovsky, the mood was not one of sorrowful prayer. "He is not crucified, but appears to soar up into the sky." And yet apparently there was in this production a certain sense of exultation peculiar to many of the productions of the early postrevolutory years.

One of the most significant works of the Chamber Ballet was *Faun*, to the music of Debussy's *Prélude à l'après-midi d'un faune* (1922). Boris Erdman built a wooden set painted in white enamel: several platforms arranged with their ledges one above another and, on the sides, two sets of steps. It was an absolutely utilitarian construction, not claiming to represent a hill, a spring, or anything else. Its steps and platforms allowed for the formation of unique vertical groupings. But the audience, free to fantasize, could imagine a hill, green slopes, and a torturously hot sun. Several reviewers found something in common between the open-work design of the white sets and the subtle tracery of Debussy's music.

The costumes Erdman planned were equally non-realistic. They were made of cord wound tightly around the head like a turban for the faun, and close-fitting caps for the nymphs. Round discs of cord coiled into spirals, fastened at the ears, completed the headdress. Cords encircling the naked body similarly formed the costume. They circled the chest, crossed over the abdomen, and hung from the hips in a thick fringe like a skirt. There were no tights or shoes.

The ballet had no clear-cut plot and was built not on the actions of characters but on sensations. Its content was revealed through abstract, symbolic images. The meaning of this dance miniature was the affirmation of the power of love over everything alive: "The earth is in love with the sun, but the sun passes over the earth. The earth lifts mountain-knees, and they blush with shame." [36] Here the choreography proclaimed fantasy and poetry the greatest human achievement. It was not accidental that Goleizovsky qualified as "prosaic" the two satyr spies who, after finding places for themselves on the stairs, commented on the action with ironic movements. They jeered at the faun, contemptuously calling him "a dreamer": "This dreamer embraces her scarf!" The principal characters of the ballet were the gold-horned faun in love, a mysterious being, enigmatically beautiful ("It is not for you to understand my staccato and my Mandarin eyes"), and the nymph Ualenta, "born of two beautiful fairies," a changing and elusive dream. Turning to her, the faun said, "Just once, Ualenta, fairy of the mountains, your heart is not crumpled by prose. I, the gold-horned faun, am in your dreams." At the end Ualenta disappeared, leaving the faun her scarf as consolation.

Acrobatic and gymnastic elements were widely used in the dance; it was built on shifting poses that were extravagant, affected, tense, and unfamiliar. A photograph has preserved the following moment: two platforms of the set are visible; on the upper one, Ualenta (Adamovich) is standing in a mannered pose; the faun (Leonid Obolensky) supports her with one hand. The ballerina's bare leg is lifted and forms a sharp angle; her bare foot rests on the head of another dancer (a nymph), positioned a step lower. The latter is half-reclining, lifting a bent leg upward and resting the other on a lower step of the set. On the lower step, yet another dancer repeats this pose, slightly altered. Alongside stands a fourth, grasping her lifted bare leg in her hand. All this together forms a complex, interwoven pattern of lifted legs, arms, heads, and bodies wound and braided with cord. In the dance, this pattern constantly changed, although the dancers almost never left their places; the faun and Ualenta were on the upper platform the whole time, the nymphs on the lower. The design was without dynamics; there was not even a precise line to the immobile forms. Everything was swaying, bending, and flowing, as if its contours were blurred. This voluptuous dance, pervaded with languid laziness, undoubtedly expressed the qualities of Debussy's meditative, sensual music.

Somewhat different was the symbolism of *Salomé* (1922). Goleizovsky took the entire music of Salomé's dance from Strauss's opera. To this music he made something like a dance of seven veils, but in no way connected it to the story of Salomé and John the Baptist.

A high scaffold was built onstage. When Salomé (Zinaida Tarkhovskaya) appeared on it, a huge moon shone behind her and the dancer seemed to be surrounded with radiance. Young men stood below, by the scaffold. The lighting of this scene was designed so that, according to Goleizovsky, "it was as if the radiance came from the ballerina herself, and her hands were illuminated by another color." She began her "conversation" with the youths with her arms, spreading them wide apart and moving them smoothly, "creating the impression that her fingers were growing infinitely longer"; then the ballerina rushed down from the scaffold and the youths all caught her as she leaped. She wore multi-colored veils ("all colors, from black to white") and each of the veils corresponded to a specific movement of the body and a specific set of gestures. While dancing, Salomé went to each of the youths in turn; for each of them was destined one of the veils and the movements associated with it. The youths encircled her in a frenzy of passion and ecstasy, catching her every gesture, every glance. When the dancer tossed out a veil, the youth would catch it and disappear with it. And then, still dancing, Salomé would give another part of herself to the next youth, the gift of a whimsical, fantastic pose, the harmony of the body. By the end of the dance, Salomé was almost completely naked. The youths gathered together again and lifted her to the upper platform, where the moon was shining once again. Then darkness gradually fell; Salomé disappeared with the moon, and the figures of the youths also dissolved in the darkness.

A great deal has been written about the eroticism that saturated this dance. Many were embarrassed by the almost complete nudity of the dancer; others tried to find an analogy to this dance in ancient rituals.

According to the choreographer himself, the veils of Salomé embodied the fullness of the life force and the joyful emancipation of man. Of course the sensual, even sexual, principle is powerful in this dance, as in many of Goleizovsky's other productions as well.

The relationships between partners in his ballets was completely different from what they had been in the old ballet. They appeared on stage neither to demonstrate the gallantry of the cavalier toward his lady, nor to lure the spectator into the world of fleshless visions and ideal incorporeality, nor even to demonstrate the marvels of dance technique. On the stage were men and women—the wonderful female body, which attracts through its earthly material beauty, and man, for whom woman is an object of worship, naturally attractive. In Goleizovsky's dances the poetry of real human feelings, of the rapture in life, reigned supreme. Sometimes these feelings were colored by a certain mysticism. At times decadent mannerism peeked through as well. Sometimes—especially in the NEP years*—there was a desire to shock the audience, which saw in these productions only nudity and voluptuous movements. Many critics were irritated by "the twisted poses, the everlasting embraces of legs."[37] They warned the choreographer that he "was balancing on the very edge of the precipice called pornography."[38] Lopukhov also wrote about Goleizovsky's "excessive eroticism." Such criticism had some basis. But gradually, without compromising what was most important, Goleizovsky freed himself from decadent tendencies and moved on to brighter, more noble images.

These images were sometimes tragic. "Goleizovsky introduced into his Chopin ballets features of the stern tragedy of ancient Greece, not of Euripides, but of Aeschylus, and B. R. Erdman, with his Hellenistic costumes, further intensified this impression of ancient tragedy,"[39] Iving wrote about the dances Goleizovsky showed in the autumn of 1923. The designer dressed the performers in regal mourning clothes. The veils falling to the shoulders were black; the helmets, manacles, and belts were gold. But this gold did not shine with brilliant patches of sunlight; it was dark and dull. Iving's article conveys the tragic nuance of Goleizovsky's dances:

*The NEP years saw the rise of a new class, the nouveau riche, as well as the introduction (after a hiatus of several years) of Western art and entertainment, including jazz music and associated social dances. (Ed.)

They struggle but are always defeated, because they know of their defeat beforehand. Hence this depression, this inconsolable languor of doom. Hence the aspiration, the warlike waving of the arms, the sharp thrusts of the legs, the gloomy faces with lengthened brows, the frenzied tension of the poses. And they inevitably end with a fall to the floor. This is not the Greece of marble and sun, the Greece of wise, powerful men, as clear and stoic as the columns of its temples. This is the sad, eternally humid land of the chimera of which Homer spoke with secret horror, the extreme West of the earth, which could only be reached on a black boat at sunset.

In characterizing Goleizovsky's work of 1924 Tcherepnin noted that he "gradually replaces tired lyricism with strong gusts of passion." [40] He wrote about the Spanish dances: "Instead of the intimate sensations proper to intellectuals there is a sweeping, full-breasted feeling of life; instead of mental considerations—elemental force; instead of refinement —the brutality of spontaneous emotion. . . . All this is done in a broad, hitherto unprecedented dance-poster manner, economically, clearly, and without little flourishes and bows." [41]

The expressive means were sharply modern regardless of the choice of theme. Goleizovsky's revival of form preceded a revival of content. In this he was not alone. For the majority of the artists of the 1920s, a new "language" in and of itself was a sign of being revolutionary. During the first postrevolutionary years there were fierce arguments in the ballet and on the variety stage about what new choreography should be. There was much publicity for the rhythmoplastique, the eccentric, the acrobatic, and the Duncanist dance. It was thought that these systems were fated to force out classical dance entirely.

Those who wrote about Goleizovsky at times maintained that he sided with those who were overthrowing the foundations of dance. However, in rereading Goleizovsky's articles of those years, which are confusingly written and full of unconvincing declarations and contradictions, in examining his extensive correspondence with the directorate of the Bolshoi Theater, and in speaking with the dancers who worked with him, one comes to the conclusion that this is not so.

In those years Goleizovsky was fighting a battle on two fronts. His enemies were the academic ballet on the one hand and dilettantism in the art of dance on the other. Many times he spoke out sharply against the old ballet theater, which seemed to him rigid, monotonous, and stagnant. He wrote about dance that was "devoid of thought," about "bare, boring technique," which had been adopted by those whom he called "fanatics of the past."

While lamenting the backwardness of the ballet theater, he tried to explain it by the fact that "the funds for ballet were allocated only to the academic theaters, where *The Little Humpbacked Horses* and *La Bayadères*—those common graves of ballet artists—are still being cultivated."[42] Reading such statements, the leaders of the Bolshoi Theater for their part rushed to label Goleizovsky a malicious destroyer of ballet's foundations and forbade dancers to take part in his productions under threat of being fired.

But in reality the furious philippics that Goleizovsky addressed to classical ballet had its clichés as their target. He took up arms against antiquated forms that had been preserved and artificially protected for decades. And he correctly maintained that devices with origins in the remote past could not serve as a means for the expression of newly arisen images and concepts.

Yet at the same time Goleizovsky did not at all reject classical dance and was delighted with its innumerable possibilities, primarily with the system of educating the performer. He was a supporter of professionalism in ballet and a supporter of the school, and he did not sympathize with those experimenters who rejected the fundamental, constructive resources of dance art for the sake of innovation. This is why he did not join the Duncanists, the rhythmicists, the plastiquists, and the other representatives of the so-called "free" dance. More than anything he hated dilettantism and battled against the ignoramuses "who set about resolving the problems of higher mathematics after just barely learning to count to 100,"[43] against "millions of all sorts of harmful bacteria-studios."[44] In a letter to Lashchilin on June 10, 1924, Goleizovsky lamented the fact that such leaders of the Bolshoi Theater company as Tikhomirov and Riabtsev "do not want to and cannot understand that my orientation has a strictly academic foundation, that I am only using what they have given me, and that despite myself I have become their successor. . . ."[45]

After criticizing the leaders of the Bolshoi Ballet for being bogged down in routine, Goleizovsky's firm conviction that without professionalism there can be no art prompted him to write: "Everything new will come only from the state theater, because that is the only place where there is consistent skill."[46] He believed in the resourcefulness of the experts at this theater: "Ballet dancers at the academic theater are not to blame for the fact that they are vegetating in the 'joys of yesteryear,' but the true great choreographic revolution sooner or later will come from them, because they possess the real mastery of pure dance."[47]

But the point, of course, is not only what Goleizovsky wrote; more important, the new dance forms he created on the basis of classical dance rested upon an absolute knowledge of all the fine points of centuries-old ballet technique. This is true even in relation to those productions where it seemed as though the external signs of that dance were rejected. Even in composing risky, unprecedented movements, he took off from the ballet technique that the classical school had given him. Many critics in those years were able to grasp this. One of them wrote, "In Goleizovsky's rebellious experiments there is more love for the captivating art of the classical dance than in many orthodox *pas d'action,* worn out —alas!—on the hackwork variety stage."[48] Another, examining in 1922 such works of Goleizovsky's as *Prologue, Visions Fugitives,* and *White Mass,* insisted that even Goleizovsky's boldest poses "are built on classical technique."[49] The majority of the critics upheld the same point of view during the tours of the Chamber Ballet in Petrograd in October 1922. One of the participants in a discussion in the *Krasnaya gazeta* stated categorically, "The revival of the cult of classical dance and its coming into harmony with our era will come from the theater group called the Moscow Chamber Ballet."[50]

But while acknowledging classical dance as a necessary basis, Goleizovsky did not think it possible to limit himself to established forms. By discarding the customary combinations and devices which had grown into clichés from constant use, Goleizovsky was able to see old movements in new ways and, by watching them intently, he turned them in an unexpected direction and put them together in unprecedented sequences. Bold variations on traditional positions were created. The ballerina executed arabesques and attitudes not standing up, but up in the air, in the arms of her partner, and sometimes sitting or lying down. Generally, in contrast to "pure classicism," Goleizovsky made extensive use of prone positions, which gave the choreographer's opponents occasion to grumble about "lolling about on the floor." In the meantime, the new style of performance changed the very meaning of the movement. "An unexpected function has been given to the leg—to serve not as support for the body, but as an independently expressive factor. In order to free the leg, the body is flung onto a platform or held in a lift. The leg 'gesticulates.' Through the interweaving of the lines of the arms and legs, new and unusual effects are obtained."[51]

Thus new qualities emerged, seemingly incompatible with the "legitimate" emblems of classical ballet: the positions fluctuated; straight horizontals and verticals disappeared. The dance consisted of a smooth alternation of undulating movements flowing from one into another. Gusev thought that "for Goleizovsky . . . the line is broken, curved, softened, with no inner strength, as it would have in circus or acrobatics, but refined and delicately bizarre, with a persistent rejection of everything resembling the classical."[52]

Nevertheless, this was not a repudiation of the school of classical dance. After all, the dancer was not deprived of all of the expressive means available to him through his command of classical dance. But at the same time, even more possibilities opened up for him.

In broadening the sphere of movements used in dance, Goleizovsky went still further. He combined classicism with other methods of bodily expression. The choreographer was indignant when "one of the pundits of the Bolshoi State Academic Theater," upon seeing a somersault in his production, "grimaced contemptuously. 'Is this really dance?' "[53] He insisted that in dance there were no "illegitimate" movements; one needed only to be able to use them appropriately.

Goleizovsky found support for his ideas in productions by the directors of the dramatic theaters. Meyerhold, Tairov, and Vakhtangov demanded from the actor not only verbal, but also physical expressiveness. In working with Meyerhold, especially on the production *D. E. (Give Us Europe),** Goleizovsky was amazed by the care with which the actors' movements on stage were developed. Still closer to him was the Kamerny Theater, with its inclination toward the emotionally intense spectacle, where music, dance, poses, groupings of human figures, and the rhythm of movement were of primary significance. Goleizovsky saw in *Prin-*

---

*D. E. (Give Us Europe), based on Ilya Ehrenburg's novel *Trust D. E.*, was staged by Meyerhold as a political revue, with a jazz band and cinematic live effects. (Ed.)

cess *Brambilla* and *Phèdre* "genuine, beautiful ballets; to reach them, *The Little Humpbacked Horse* must grow a long time." He wrote, "Tseretelli's monologue in the play *King Harlequin* is imbued with dynamic movements. . . . Really, this is a beautiful, meaningful variation."[54]

All his life Goleizovsky was a creator and an inventor of dance "words." His imagination was inexhaustible. Not long before his death Goleizovsky wrote in an unpublished article, "If the artist (in this case the choreographer) does not experiment and always uses only something old and outdated, if he does not live in a state of constant longing for revelations and creative ecstasy, he kills the feeling of inspiration and enthusiasm in himself. He loses his love for form (that powerful means of expressing thought), for color, and for beauty, which knows no limits or bounds in its development."[55]

The new form Goleizovsky valued so highly did not exist for him in and of itself. His experiments were not born of a capricious desire to contort the human body as no one had previously done; his poetic, emotional perception of the world demanded appropriate devices, and these devices were born of images of reality, portrayed just as poetically and emotionally. Goleizovsky kept this emotional vision of the world throughout his life. The young choreographer of the 1920s and the master grown wise from experience as we knew him only recently are certainly different people in many respects. But the ability to ferret out the unusual in the everyday, to see the soul of a thing under the covering in which it appears to everyone—this poetic gift can be discerned in everything that Goleizovsky did: in his old verses and drawings, reeking of decadence; in his book about Russian dance; and in his remarkable wooden sculptures, which populate his house. The curves of the branches, the snakelike roots, the pattern of the leaves—images of the Russian forests, which Goleizovsky loved so much—are perceptible in his productions, in the bodies sprawled on the floor, raised to the sky, and clinging to each other, in the bends and twists of the torsos, and in the intricately entwined arms.

In enriching dance and trying to make it still more eloquent, the choreographer devoted special attention to such secondary means as costumes and decor. In dance, where the main creative material is the body of the performer, the goal of the costume is to make the body more expressive. Therefore, for Goleizovsky, the costume existed neither for its own sake, nor as an identifying sign of a country or epoch; it was a means of creating an emotional image. In Goleizovsky's productions, the costume was a continuation of the dance and, as a rule, was born together with it.

Often, especially in the early years, Goleizovsky himself drew the sketches for the costumes, but dilettantism in all its aspects irritated this great master. Therefore, he saw his task as a starting point for the designer, which professionals could develop and fully realize—still, he collaborated only with those designers who thought the same way he did. In the 1920s this was most often Erdman; sometimes it was Nikolai Musatov and Anatoly Petritsky.

For all their variety of color, material, and detail, the costumes in Goleizovsky's productions were intended to reveal as much of the body as possible. There were of course also costumes that, when Goleizovsky's intention demanded, covered the body completely, for example the long robes suggestive of monastic garb in *White Mass*. But generally, Goleizovsky was a proponent of the idea that harmony of movement had its own influence. In the article "The Bare Body on Stage," he wrote that a young, beautiful, nude body is a highly moral and aesthetic sight.[56]

Incidentally, what Goleizovsky said was not new. The idea of "nudity on the stage" was proposed by many people in prerevolutionary years; a number of articles about this idea were published in theatrical journals. In 1911 Evreinov published an anthology containing the opinions of various people active in the arts. Here different motives came together: the taste for the racy and erotic, the cult of "the natural," and the desire to shock the petit bourgeois. As a rule, sculptors and artists cited the experience of their art and spoke of a purely aesthetic attitude toward the naked body. But the question also aroused the interest of those who linked the future of society with the harmonious development of man as a biological individual. Even Lunacharsky took part in this polemic, announcing that "the battle for nudity is a battle for beauty, health, and freedom."[57] Goleizovsky also saw in nudity a means for challenging the old "hypocritical" morality, but he was even more interested in the artistic aspect of the question.

Dance costume had changed over the course of the centuries, along with the evolution of aesthetic principles. At the end of the nineteenth century it responded to the demands dance technique made on the female dancer in the academic ballet. Legs covered in pink tights demonstrated

1. Caricature by M. Linsky of Lavrenti Novikov in Novikov's *Narcissus*, 1918. *Rampa i zhizn*, 1918.

2. Scene from Mikhail Mordkin's *Aziade*, 1917. *Center*, Mordkin. Bakhrushin Museum.

4

3

5

3. Costume design by Alexandre Benois for a Masked Merrymaker in Michel Fokine's *Petrushka* (used at the Petrograd Theater of Opera and Ballet in 1920 and at the Bolshoi in 1921). Bolshoi Museum.

4. Caricature of George Balanchine. *Zhizn iskusstva*, 1924.

5. Lidia Ivanova in Balanchine's *Valse triste*, 1922. Leningrad Theater Museum.

«ЭЛЕКТРИЧЕСКИЕ ТАНЦЫ».
Н. М. ФОРЕГГЕРА.

7

6. Drawing by Boris Erdman of "Electric Dances" from Nikolai Foregger's *Machine Dances*. *Zrelishcha*, 1923.

7. Drawing by Erdman of Foregger's *Machine Dances*. *Zrelishcha*, 1923.

8. Children from the Isadora Duncan School, 1923. *Zrelishcha*, 1923.

8

9

11

10

9. Drawing by Alexander Gorsky for his *Lyric Poem*, 1918. Bolshoi Museum.

10. Costume design by Konstantin Korovin and Diachkov for the Snowflakes and Clara in the snowflake scene from Gorsky's *Nutcracker*. Bolshoi Museum.

11. Act 1 of Gorsky and Vladimir Nemirovich-Danchenko's *Swan Lake*, 1920. Bakhrushin Museum.

12. Drawing by Vasily Diachkov of the little Grandfather Frosts in the snowflake scene from Gorsky's *Nutcracker*. Bolshoi Museum.

12

13

13. Costume design for the Matrioshka Doll in Gorsky's *The Nutcracker*. Bolshoi Museum.

14. Drawing by Gorsky for his *Salomé*, 1921. Bolshoi Museum.

15. Drawing by Gorsky for his *Chrysis*, 1921. Bakhrushin Museum.

16. Act 2 of Gorsky's *Giselle*, 1922. Bakhrushin Museum.

14

15

16

17   18

19

20

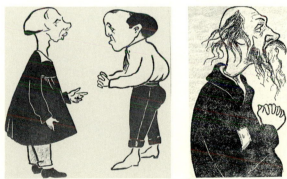

17. Drawing by Kasian Golei-
zovsky of Columbine in his
Harlequinade, 1919.
Bakhrushin Museum.

18. Drawing by Goleizovsky of
Harlequin in his *Harlequinade*,
1919. Bakhrushin Museum.

19. Scene in the fields from
Gorsky's *Ever-Fresh Flowers*,
1922, a dance-play for children.
Author's collection.

20. Drawing for *The
Goatlegged*, 1916. Goleizovsky
archive.

21. Caricature of the choreographers Goleizovsky and Lev
Lukin. *Zrelishcha*, 1923.

22. Caricature by Radimov of
Gorsky. *Ekran*, 1922.

21   22

23

23. Drawing by Goleizovsky for one of his ballets, ca. 1919–20, perhaps *The Tragedy of the Masks.* Bakhrushin Museum.

24. Drawing by Goleizovsky of Little Red Riding-Hood in a dance at the Moscow Ballet School, 1918. Bakhrushin Museum.

24

25. Drawing by Deni (Viktor Denisov) of the First Imp for Goleizovsky's *The Imps* (*Max and Moritz*), 1928. *Sovremennyi teatr*, 1928.

26. Drawing by Deni of the Professor for Goleizovsky's *Imps*. *Sovremennyi teatr*, 1928.

27. Goleizovsky's *Faun*, 1922. *Echo*, 1923.

Московский Камерный балет.

28. Drawing by Mampus of
Leonid Obolensky as the Faun
in Goleizovsky's *Faun*, 1922.
Goleizovsky archive, unidenti-
fied clipping.

29. Drawing by Piotr Galadzhev
of Zinaida Tarkhovskaya in
Goleizovsky's *Faun*. *Zrelishcha*,
1923.

30. Drawing by Galadzhev of
Goleizovsky's *Faun*. *Zrelishcha*,
1922.

31

31. Drawing by Galadzhev of Goleizovsky's *Tombeau de Colombine*, 1922. *Hermitage*, 1922.

32. Drawing by Goleizovsky, 1923. Goleizovsky archive.

32

33. Drawing by Galadzhev of Goleizovsky's *Salomé* with Tarkhovskaya, 1923. *Zrelishcha*, 1923.

34. Drawing by Erdman of Y. Lenskaya, Z. Drutskaya, and L. Gai in Goleizovsky's *Spanish Dance*, 1923. *Zrelishcha*, 1923.

34

35

35. Goleizovsky's *The White Mass*, 1922. *Iskusstvo i promyshlennost*, 1924.

36. Goleizovsky's *Visions fugitives*, 1922. *Iskusstvo i promyshlennost*, 1924.

37. Liubov Bank as Lisette in Goleizovsky's *Teolinda*, 1925. Goleizovsky archive.

38. N. Miroslavskaya, Y. Ivanova, and D. Dmitriev in Goleizovsky's *Spanish Dance*, 1923. *Iskusstvo i promyshlennost*, 1924.

36

37

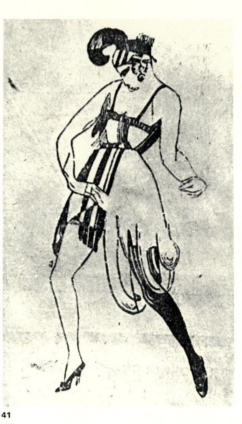

39. Drawing by Erdman of
D'Arto and Goleizovsky in
Goleizovsky's *Foxtrot*, 1923.

40. Drawing by Erdman of Y.
Lenskaya, D. Dmitriev, and Z.
Drutskaya in Goleizovsky's
Cakewalk, 1923. *Zrelishcha*,
1923.

41. Y. Lenskaya in a dance performed by Goleizovsky's Chamber Ballet, ca. 1923–24. Goleizovsky archive.

42. Dance performed by
Goleizovsky's Chamber Ballet,
ca. 1923–24. Goleizovsky
archive.

42

43

43. Scene from act 1,
Goleizovsky's *Joseph the Beautiful*, 1925. Bakhrushin
Museum.

44. Scene from act 2,
Goleizovsky's *Joseph the Beautiful*, 1925. Bakhrushin
Museum.

44

45. Drawing by Nikolai Musatov of a jailer for Goleizovsky's *The Whirlwind*, 1927. Bolshoi Museum.

46. Costume design for a shepherdess in Goleizovsky's *Joseph the Beautiful*, 1925. Bolshoi Museum.

47. Drawing by Musatov of the Seven Deadly Sins for Goleizovsky's *Whirlwind*, 1927. Bolshoi Museum.

45

46

47

48

48. Drawing of a monk turning into a satyr for Goleizovsky's *Whirlwind*, 1927. Bolshoi Museum.

49. Drawing by Musatov of the musicians for Goleizovsky's *Whirlwind*, 1927. Bolshoi Museum.

49

50

52

51

50. Ekaterina Geltser as Esmeralda in Vasily Tikhomirov's *Esmeralda*, 1926. Bolshoi Museum.

51. Set by Mikhail Kurilko for Lev Lashchilin and Tikhomirov's *The Red Poppy*, 1927. Bolshoi Museum.

52. Act 1 of *Red Poppy*, 1927. Bolshoi Museum.

53

54

55

53. Costume design by Kurilko for a dancer in the ballroom scene in *Red Poppy*, 1927. Bolshoi Museum.

54. Costume design by Kurilko for a poppy in *Red Poppy*, 1927. Bolshoi Museum.

55. The ballroom scene from *Red Poppy*, 1927. Bolshoi Museum.

56. Geltser as Tao-Hoa in *Red Poppy*, 1927. Bolshoi Museum.

57. Costume design by Kurilko for Tao-Hoa in *Red Poppy*, 1927. Bolshoi Museum.

58

59

60

58. Manuscript of Fedor Lopukhov's movement score for *The Magnificence of the Universe*, 1923. Lopukhov archive.

59. Rehearsal of Lopukhov's *Giselle*, 1922, with Olga Spessivtseva (*center foreground*), Mikhail Dudko, and Nikolai Soliannikov. *Far right*, Lopukhov. V. Ghil photo collection.

60. Elena Lyukom and Boris Shavrov as the Firebird and the Prince in Lopukhov's *The Firebird*, 1921. Leningrad Theater Museum.

61

61. Costume design by Mikhail Domrachev for the Devil in Lopukhov's *Night on Bald Mountain*, 1924. Leningrad Theater Museum.

62. Costume design by Domrachev for the Sweeper in Lopukhov's *Night on Bald Mountain*, 1924. Leningrad Theater Museum.

63. Act 1 of Lopukhov's *The Red Whirlwind*, 1924. Leningrad Theater Museum.

63

62

64

64. Final scene of Lopukhov's *Red Whirl-wind*, 1924. Leningrad Theater Museum.

65. Costume design by Leonid Chupiatov for act 1 of *Red Whirlwind*, 1924. Leningrad Theater Museum.

66. Costume design by Chupiatov for act 1 of *Red Whirlwind*, 1924. Leningrad Theater Museum.

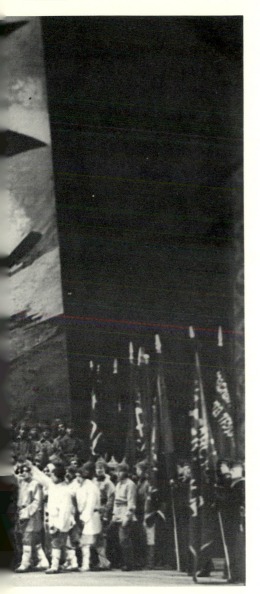

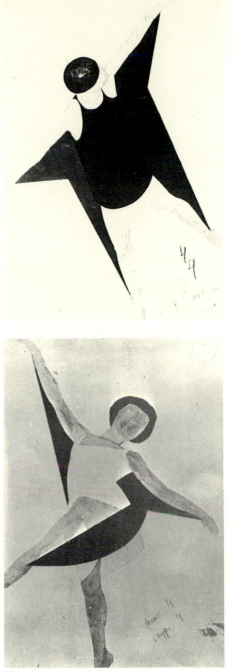

66

67

68

70

Пульчинелла П. М. Бакланов. Л-град.

69

71

67. Elizaveta Gerdt as Smerald-ina in Lopukhov's *Pulchinella*, 1926. Leningrad Theater Museum.

68. Boris Komarov as *Pulchi-nella*, 1926. Leningrad Theater Museum.

69. Piotr Baklanov as Il Dottore in Lopukhov's *Pulchinella*, 1926. Leningrad Theater Museum.

70. Act 2 of Lopukhov's *Red Whirlwind*, 1924. Leningrad Theater Museum.

71. Costume designs by Vladi-mir Dmitriev for Il Pantalone and Il Dottore in *Pulchinella*, 1926. Leningrad Theater Museum.

72. Lopukhov with the performers in his *Pulchinella*, 1926. *Seated, left to right*: Leonid Leontiev (Pulchinella), Lopukhov, Taissia Troyanovskaya (Smeraldina); *standing, left to right:* Pavel Goncharov (Il Sbirro), Yosif Kschessinsky (Il Pantalone), Rostislav Slavianinov (Il Capitano), Piotr Baklanov (Il Dottore). V. Ghil photo collection.

73. Final scene from Lopukhov's *Pulchinella*, 1926. Leningrad Theater Museum.

74. The little Pulchinellas in Lopukhov's *Pulchinella*, 1926. Leningrad Theater Museum.

Балет: „Пульчинелла." 1926 г. Л-град.

74

76

75

75. Costume design by Alexander Golovine for the Old Women in Pavel Petrov's *Solveig*, 1922, and Lopukhov's *The Ice Maiden*, 1927. Bakhrushin Museum.

76. Old Women in Lopukhov's *Ice Maiden*, 1927. Bakhrushin Museum.

77. Costume design by Dmitriev for the Ram in Lopukhov's *Le Renard*, 1927. Leningrad Theater Museum.

78. Costume design by Dmitriev for the Rooster in Lopukhov's *Le Renard*, 1927. Leningrad Theater Museum.

79. Costume design by Dmitriev for the Fox in Lopukhov's *Le Renard*, 1927. Leningrad Theater Museum.

80. Scene from Lopukhov's *Le Renard*, 1927. Leningrad Theater Museum.

77 78 79

80

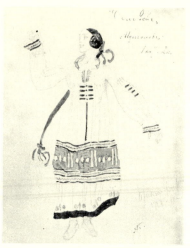

81

82

83

84

81. Costume design by Golovine for Olga Mungalova as Solveig in Lopukhov's *Ice Maiden*, 1927. Bakhrushin Museum.

82. Costume design by Golovine for Piotr Gusev as Asak in Lopukhov's *Ice Maiden*, 1927. Bakhrushin Museum.

83. Costume design by Golovine for Asak's father in Lopukhov's *Ice Maiden*, 1927. Bakhrushin Museum.

84. Scene from Petrov's *Solveig*, 1922. Leningrad Theater Museum.

85. Scene from act 1 of Lopukhov's *Ice Maiden*, 1927. Leningrad Theater Museum.

86. Mungalova and Gusev as the Ice Maiden and Asak in act 1 of Lopukhov's *Ice Maiden*, 1927. Leningrad Theater Museum.

87. Mungalova as the Ice Maiden in act 1 of Lopukhov's *Ice Maiden*, 1927. Leningrad Theater Museum.

86

87

88

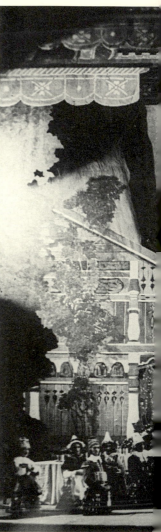

90

88. Mungalova and Gusev as Solveig and Asak in act 2 of Lopukhov's *Ice Maiden*, 1927. Leningrad Theater Museum.

89. Gusev as Asak in act 1 of Lopukhov's *Ice Maiden*, 1927. Leningrad Theater Museum.

90 . Scene from act 2 of Lopukhov's *Ice Maiden*, 1927. Leningrad Theater Museum.

89

91

93

92

91. and 92. Mungalova as the Ice Maiden in act 1 of Lopukhov's *Ice Maiden*, 1927. Leningrad Theater Museum.

93. The Snowflakes in Lopukhov's *Nutcracker*, 1929. Leningrad Theater Museum.

94. Scene from act 1 of Lopukhov's *Ice Maiden*,
1927. Leningrad Theater Museum.

the beauty of the straight line and the arched instep. The short skirt allowed one to follow the complex movements of the legs, and its fluffiness imparted a graceful quality to the female figure, evoking comparison to a luxuriant flower; it also looked effective during turns. The smooth, closely fitted bodice emphasized the ideal straightness of the spine. The blunt-nosed hard slipper permitted the demonstration of stability and the strength of the "steel pointe." Gorsky and Fokine rejected this ballet "uniform," insisting that the costume should always correspond to the era. The magnificent attire created from the sketches of Bakst and Benois were works of art in their own right. These costumes merged with the dance image and supplemented it, but also had an independent value as one of the details of the scenic background.

Goleizovsky tried to express the image of the epoch primarily through movement. In his productions, costume was only remotely associated with a concrete environment and period. It did not "act" separately from the performer, outside of the link with movement. All those ribbons, fillets, braids, plaits, badges, discs, and strips of fabric didn't look at all like costumes by themselves, but as part of a performer's attire they fulfilled their major function: They revealed the meaning of the movement.

It is not surprising that Goleizovsky's dances were often performed by almost naked dancers. After all, the choreographer sought the utmost freedom of movement. He wanted to reveal to the audience the body of the dancer as a whole, unencumbered by any extraneous details. Hence his urge for local coloration and laconicism of form. Nudity, in Goleizovsky's opinion, met all these demands. When the dancer is naked, nothing interferes with seeing the movement and perceiving its meaning. In point of fact, Goleizovsky never resorted to complete nudity; he came closest to it in *Salomé*. Nevertheless, the form of the costume was determined by these experiments.

The standard costume-uniform in the early productions of Goleizovsky and the designer Erdman was a pair of briefs and a narrow band. At first they were of one color; then the designer began to use colorful combinations of fabrics and new, sometimes unexpected materials. The costumes in *Faun* were made of cords wound around the body. As Markov wrote, "From the interweaving of lines it (the body—F. S.) emerged full of life, and the black shadows only emphasized its vital force."[58]

Erdman created an effective "Spanish" costume for Vera Drutskaya.

"A fine net of black lines on the naked body—and somewhere, just here, a free wave of material that flawlessly accompanied the movement."[59]

The function of scenery also changed in Goleizovsky's productions. A new attitude toward set design could already be seen in the productions of the Moscow Chamber Ballet, in which there was no scenery as such—the set design was treated as part of the dance composition. In Medtner's *Funeral March* and Scriabin's Études, there were only "three large panels of canvas in indefinite tones onstage. Shafts of light replaced the usual theatrical decor."[60]

As early as 1922 Goleizovsky was thinking of a stage platform where "every unexpected turn, bend, rise, step" would serve the choreographer "as an object of reflection, as a chance to amplify (intensify) his movement."[61] This is why he joined ranks with Tairov, who insisted on an alteration in the very nature of the stage in the ballet theater, and he dreamed of Constructivist sets. For one of Goleizovsky's productions to Scriabin's music, Alexandra Exter planned such decor in 1921–22. In 1924, for the unproduced ballet *The Death of Isolde* to the music of Wagner, Petritsky made a Constructivist model. The design of the ballet *Faun* described above was also Constructivist.

In principle, this new concept of stage space in the ballet theater rejected the pictorial logic of Fokine's ballets. In Fokine's approach, ballet decor ceased to exist as a neutral, non-expressive background. In contrast to the general conception of the ballet, to Fokine, the scenery affected the audience as much as the music and dance. It soon became clear that this principle of equality did not entirely suit the artist. He was no longer a collaborator, for all practical purposes, he was gradually becoming the main partner. The stage was perceived as a gigantic picture put into the gilded frame of the proscenium; in the final analysis, the dancer was only a detail in this picture. In the interests of creating a picture, the choreographer sometimes agreed to sacrifice the dance itself—the movement yielded its place to a colorful palette (as in the ballet *Petrushka*). In individual instances, he resolved the contradiction between the flat forms of painted scenery and the three-dimensionality of human figures by constructing the dance design according to the principles of bas-relief and making the dancers' bodies seem to lie flat on the surface of the picture (as, for example, in *Une Nuit d'Égypte*).

For Goleizovsky, scenery was not a background for action, but one of the means for constructing it. The set, for him, revealed the possibility for a variety of compositions and their various rhythmical combinations. In explaining his intentions while producing the ballet *The Whirlwind* in 1927, Goleizovsky wrote, "The artistic set design is built on the principle of realistically filling out the painted image of human bodies."[62]

Joseph the Beautiful

On November 26, 1924, the Bolshoi Theater signed a contract with Goleizovsky and Erdman to produce the two-act ballet *La Sylphide* and the one-act *The Legend of Joseph the Beautiful* within a month and a half. Later, the plans were somewhat changed. *La Sylphide* (a reconstruction of the second act of Taglioni's ballet) was staged not by Goleizovsky, but by Tikhomirov, and was shown on February 2, 1925, for the 100th anniversary of the Bolshoi Theater. Geltser danced the Sylphide, and it is possible that this was the reason for handing over the production to Tikhomirov, since Goleizovsky had never worked with Geltser. He wrote, "Ekaterina Vasilievna Geltser repeatedly tried to rehearse with me and each time our rehearsal did not work out."[63] Goleizovsky and Geltser must have had completely different ideas about the style of Taglioni's ballet and about how to perform the role of the Sylphide. Apparently, just to demonstrate how he imagined Romantic ballet, Goleizovsky made *Teolinda*, to the music of Franz Schubert, instead of *La Sylphide*. The premiere of Goleizovsky's program, which comprised *Teolinda* and *Joseph the Beautiful*, took place in the Experimental Theater (a subsidiary of the Bolshoi) on March 3, 1925.

Joseph the Beautiful was the culmination of all the experiments Goleizovsky had conducted in the Chamber Ballet. The first act took place in Joseph's native land. The decor was an installation made of several small platforms, straight and sloping, positioned at various levels and connected by little bridges. It seemed to suggest the hills of Canaan. The figures were sharply outlined on a black velvet backdrop, which helped to create an impression of limitless distance and empty spaces. The musical introduction was built on a simple, conventional, Oriental-style melody and concluded in pianissimo.

In the beginning of the first scene Joseph was alone on stage, playing on a reed pipe. Lost in reverie for a minute, he stretched his arms toward the sun and danced dreamily. Then he took up the pipe again. Thus Joseph's first appearance characterized him as a poet with a sensitive feeling for nature, responsive to beauty and goodness. This made crude souls—first and foremost, his brothers—hate Joseph. Their entrance followed upon Joseph's variations.

The music sounded threatening; there was something predatory in the grotesquely angular movements of the brothers. They ambushed Joseph from behind, as the ominous intonations of the music grew, reaching a fortissimo. At this point, the oldest had already raised a club. The blow accidentally missed, and Joseph turned around. The embarrassed brothers surrounded him, flatteringly shook hands, and assured him that they were just joking. The tension decreased with the appearance of youths and maidens. They danced their first (so-called "bucolic") dance, a lyric round dance, which seemed to return the audience to Joseph's poetic world.

In the photographs that have been preserved, the 28 dancers, holding hands, form a winding garland, which spreads along the floor, crosses over the lower platforms of the set, winds along the inclined, gangplank-like planes, and finishes on the farthest crest, the highest platform. The formation is asymmetrical. The fanciful pattern rises in zigzag lines, formed by the standing figures, and spreads, gently sloping, from one prone body to the next, as the dancers' hands connect them, stretching from the lowest platform to the highest. The poses are varied and expressive. In one place a leg is thrown over from one part of the set to another; in another a reclining woman seems to hang from the very edge of the inclined bridges. She is held from above and below, so that her body connects the loops of the round dance. All the figures are holding hands and are also united by the ornamental decorations on the costumes: large and small discs hang from the women's arms and are sewn to the men's chests and fastened at the waist. The principle of asymmetry is maintained in the costumes, too: black and white stripes and circles, with a trace of green, cross, merge, and diverge.

In the next dance—a Jewish ritual dance—motifs of worshipful concentration appeared. An ordinary dance grew into a sort of dance symbol. Here a stylized device was used: The soloist did not enter from the ranks of the female dancers, but appeared in the center of the stage from underground, as if she were not a real woman but a personification of the mood of those surrounding her.

The action switches from concrete reality to the psychological plane completely naturally and organically. . . . The ribbon game on which the dance is built symbolizes the psychological split of the human personality, the existence in the soul of eternally warring, contrasting principles. Goleizovsky uses the symbolic meaning and the brilliant imagery of the movements of the ancient ritual dance. The downcast gazes of the women, the soft inaudible step, and the lithe, careful movements of the body imbue the dance with the aura of a religious rite. The shepherds who sit around it accompany the movements of the soloist with a dreamy rocking of the torso. This rocking motif becomes dominant in the poetic dance-song.[64]

Offstage a single female voice was heard, reinforced by the solo oboe, and then the female chorus entered. This was the musical theme familiar from Joseph's first dance, which had emphasized his spiritual kinship with the inhabitants of Canaan. Sitting on the floor, with half-closed eyes, the maidens rocked evenly from side to side, as if merging with nature, imbibing the surrounding beauty and calm, the breathing of the sky and the fields. The lyrical mood lingered in the next scene, the sunset. Gathering in groups, the youths and maidens gazed at the evening star and then slowly dispersed; after first threatening Joseph, the brothers also left. With darkness approaching, Joseph was seized by terrifying premonitions. Evil, unexpectedly revealed to his gaze, filled him with confusion. His brothers' hatred depressed him. Sorrowful complaints gave way to a stormy dance—despair. Then came tranquility; the light of the moon poured down on the hills, as, downcast, Joseph exited.

Quietly, as if from afar, a monotonous theme was heard. Gradually growing, it captured the attention of the listener and dominated. The monotony itself gave birth to the image of a long procession through the fields and the deserts, where the landscape does not change for days— always the same sand, hills, and sky. A caravan approached. On the crest of a hill the angular, predatory figures of Joseph's brothers were starkly outlined as they came toward the caravan. Merchants in bright clothes and young slave women appeared. They brought onstage a gaudy kaleidoscope of colors, sharp movements, and a headlong change in rhythms. The sweeping gesticulations of the merchants and the bustle of the drivers were in direct contrast to the dreamy dances of the Jewish maidens. The Eastern-sounding musical theme which characterized the foreigners was interwoven with the threatening theme of Joseph's brothers. Both groups met and quickly came to a mutual understanding. During the dances of the slaves, the merchants noticed Joseph, and the brothers joyfully agreed to sell him, but at this point the caravan again prepared to take to the road. The drivers assembled the slaves. Meanwhile, the brothers had already been keeping a watch on Joseph, gradually surrounding him and forcing him into a corner. And as soon as the merchants gave the sign, the slaves dashed forward with lightning speed; pinioning his arms, they seized and bore off the captive.

The last episode of the first act—the departure of the caravan—was always performed to applause. Again the same dejectedly monotonous melody was heard. Above the hills, the dawn was barely breaking, and in the first rays of the sun the silhouettes of the drivers appeared. With one hand they were holding the reins and in the other they held short whips, which they waved evenly in time to the music. The caravan proceeded across the desert. There were many days ahead before they would reach Egypt.

Thus two worlds collided in the first act of the ballet. On the one hand, an artist, a dreamer, a poet, a character exceptional both in his sensitivity to the beautiful and his defenselessness; on the other hand, very primitive and crude people, whose spiritual world was barren, whose weapons were deceit, slyness, and physical force.

In the second act, the contrast was still more glaring. Joseph was pitted against an unconquerable force—the despotic power of the Pharaoh. Goleizovsky and Erdman made the pyramid the symbol of the Pharaoh's immutability. The pyramid embodies the idea of eternity: It is fated to stand for centuries, just as, at first, the kingdom of Potiphar also appeared to be eternal.

This identification of the world of Potiphar with the pyramid was quite directly and graphically expressed in the production. The first scene of the second act, which was preceded by a pompous musical introduction, opened with a triumphal march of warriors and courtiers, crowned by the entrance of the Pharaoh. Queen Tayakh was carried in on a shield. Each group—the guards with their spears, the warriors with their shields, and so on—took its place and was illuminated by a spotlight. Gradually the light covered more and more of the space and, finally, the entire stage. The composition suggested a gigantic triangle: in the center towered the powerful figure of Pharaoh Potiphar, with a tall tiara on his head and widespread arms, like the carved image of a gigantic bird; at his feet was the white kneeling figure of Queen Tayakh; the groups were positioned around her in profile. The harpists laid their hands on their harps; the warriors raised their spears and shields, forming a severe, symmetrical figure. The ranks of the courtiers formed along both sides of the stage on the stairs. Their arms, raised up and held close together over their heads, formed yet another straight line directed toward the figure of Potiphar. The black slaves leaning on the proscenium also stretched their hands toward the Pharaoh. All the groups were frozen in triumphant immobility, tightly filling up all the space and forming a composition of many figures. The monotony and the abundance of similar forms in this scenario implied the negation of the possibility of any internal contradictions.

The same principle was the basis for the court suite that followed. All the dances were ornamental and devoid of any individualizing features. They did not shine with their own light; the refined beauty of their patterns was the reflection of the glory of the invincible Egyptian king. Garlands were woven of half-naked female bodies. The submissive slaves of Potiphar, they had no feelings of their own; all their desires and bursts of emotion were governed by another's will. The music for the dance of the warriors was somewhat reminiscent of "Polovetsian Dances," but instead of the savage passion of a primitive horde, here there was inexorable brute force. It is not accidental that once again in this scene the musical theme from the introduction to the second act, emphasizing the idea of autocracy, emerged.

At this point, a new slave was led in—Joseph. His despairing complaint was heard, built on the melody of the dramatic variation in the first act. The first part of Joseph's dance musically reproduced the idyllic episode that opened the ballet. But now he had only the memories of his happy youth and his native land. Then the tragic intonations began: The native land was far away, he had been robbed of happiness. . . . And at the end, the first melody, the theme of the land of Canaan, was heard again. This lyrical, simple, clear music accompanied Joseph because it embodied not only the world in which Joseph lived before his captivity, but also his internal world. It was thanks to this internal world that he remained free, even in captivity. Goleizovsky did not give Joseph manliness and energy; fragility and defenselessness remained the basic features of his character. The talent of the first performer—Vasily Efimov—made this possible. He portrayed Joseph as a being doomed to inevitable suffering and imbued each gesture with an intonation of perpetual grief. Nevertheless, the spiritual elements that Joseph embodied in the ballet collided with tyranny—brute physical force—and were conquered.

The new slave attracted the attention of Queen Tayakh; he may have appealed to her precisely because he was not like the others. Sitting in state on the upper platform, the queen watched him greedily during his dance; then she came down the steps. She wanted to look at him more closely, but at the same time she could not resist the temptation of trying out the force of her charms on him. According to the first performer, Liubov Bank, Tayakh's variations were based on broad movements, leaps, and twists. It was a dance of triumph and rapture over her beauty and power. In the first part of the dance, her movements were sharp and imperious: profile poses, abrupt leaps with the knees thrown up at a right angle, and swift strokes of the extended arms that cleaved the air predominated. In the second part of the variation, a different theme arose—the dance depicted the queen's sensuality and voluptuousness. She seemed to demonstrate her provocative beauty with extreme twists, slowly turning her torso. Tayakh's entire costume consisted of a narrow brocade strip on her chest, a loincloth with a short skirt fastened to it, and a diamond thread along the part in her jet-black hair.

When this dance was over, Tayakh ran up the stairway to Potiphar. Aroused by her alluring dance, he was about to reach out to her, but Tayakh pushed her spouse away. She demanded a present: Let Joseph be given to her!—and Potiphar agreed.

The following seduction scene was the central episode of the second act and perhaps of the entire ballet. Here the composer deliberately brought together all the basic leitmotifs: the theme from the introduction to the ballet, the theme of the land of Canaan, and other melodies. According to Bank, the scene was divided into two parts. The first had seven youths in it; it was an adagio to the languid Oriental music from the introduction. The youths lifted Tayakh onto a shield as if showing her to Joseph. Goleizovsky invented complex patterns and lifts, including Tayakh's leap from the high platform into the arms of the youths standing below. Several choreographic motifs suggested the earlier *Salomé*. While Tayakh did not have veils that she could remove, as did Salomé, nevertheless in this scene she appeared even more naked than she had in the previous one: Instead of the little skirt there was only the narrow loincloth. In the semi-darkness, her body, heavily powdered, seemed blindingly white. Joseph only retreated from the queen in horror.

On a sign from Tayakh, harps were brought out onto the set from two sides and young male slaves hid behind them. The queen remained in private with Joseph. The duet of Tayakh and Joseph was built on the contrast of two forms of movement. The inflexibility and power of Tayakh was expressed through verticals and broad movements *en dehors*. Her grand poses and sweeping gestures emphasized her proud, upward surge, and the music acquired a mobile, willful character. But Joseph seemed to shrink into a lump and pressed himself into the earth, as if defending himself against dreadful danger. Fear could be read in every one of his gestures. Despair was written on his face; the performer's eyes were heavily outlined, and on his pale face they seemed huge and mournful. Efimov's partner Bank says that in Joseph's appearance and in his movements there was something of Rublev;* the performer drew his inspiration from the images of Byzantine or old Russian icons.

Sensing Joseph's stubborn resistance, the queen began to get angry. She ordered the young man to rise. Blinded simultaneously by lust and fury, she ripped off his clothes, reached for him, crawled after him, and then sprang on his shoulder like a panther.[65] But Joseph again fled her. Then rage and the consciousness of the insult dealt her as a woman conclusively gained the upper hand over her other feelings, and Tayakh rushed to Potiphar.

Again the giant pyramid was illuminated, crowned by the figure of the Pharaoh. Tayakh ran toward him along the central stairway. An insignificant slave—she pointed downward—dared to offend her honor! "Execute him," ordered Pharaoh. The angry gesture of the ruler was repeated simultaneously by all the courtiers. "Execute him . . . execute him. . . ." There could be no disagreement. The stone colossus moved to crush the little man, driven into a corner. Joseph totally shrank away. The guards already dragged him to the staircase, and in another moment he was at the top. The columns moved together and Joseph appeared to

---

*Andrei Rublev (1370–1430) was an icon painter whose work was distinguished by its spirituality and subtlety. (Ed.)

be squeezed between them, while an abyss opened at his feet; he finally jumped into this abyss of his own accord.

The theme of protest against force and the theme of the freedom of feeling repeatedly developed by Goleizovsky in individual dances and ballet miniatures became the definitive elements in the ballet *Joseph the Beautiful*. However weak Joseph might be—and like a Christian martyr, he seemingly without a murmur gave himself into the hands of the executioners—in reality he did not submit. His was a struggle for his own human dignity. His victory lay in the conscious rejection of what he could not choose of his own free will. Thus, Goleizovsky maintained, the very stability of despotic power is cast into doubt.

He introduced this idea in the concluding scene of the ballet, when Joseph disappeared into the abyss. From the height of their power, Tayakh and Potiphar gazed at the earth, which had swallowed the rebel, and the servants began to dance over the dungeon—Joseph's grave. The former tight ranks of the courtiers had been destroyed. The pyramid had not remained impregnable; it had scattered into pieces. The will holding all the figures in their places likewise had been weakened; thus the force connecting them had dried up.

This ballet, thematically continuing Goleizovsky's early pieces, also further developed the choreographer's formal experiments. "We have before us Goleizovsky as he was when staging *Salomé*, matured and transformed," wrote Alexei Sidorov.[66] *Joseph the Beautiful* was distinguished primarily by well-planned directorial judgment, compositional logic, and stylistic unity. This was unfailingly noticed by contemporaries: "The brilliant inventiveness and, to tell the truth, the directorial talents of K. Goleizovsky, make *Joseph* an elegant ballet, rhythmically austere, imbued with the temperament of the performer and *a great variety of movements*. For a long time we have not had the opportunity to see a ballet with such *choreographic coherence*. It attests to the profound unity of producer, designer, and composer.[67]

Goleizovsky had created a ballet with continuous choreographic action, intending that each dance would either introduce us to a new event or add a new detail to the development of the characters or to the general atmosphere of the action. In this respect he followed Fokine. Also, like Fokine, Goleizovsky was drawn to spectacle. Sidorov wrote of Goleizovsky: "He has long been accustomed to building the visual effects of his productions on principles of picturesque—or rather pictorial—treatment."[68] But despite their common tendencies toward the pictorial, the two choreographers' use of this element in their ballets was different.

With Fokine the stage was often transformed into a gigantic canvas: Along with the motionless spots of scenery, there were moving brush strokes—the performers. In *Schéhérazade* the storminess of the colors of the costumes and scenery corresponded to the storminess of the passions. In *Petrushka* the kaleidoscopic change of characters, noisily multi-colored like the carousel and puppet shows randomly flashing nearby, as well as their very differences (each one was individualized and lived his or her own life) helped to create an impression of the hurly-burly of a fair.

With Goleizovsky the choreography in *Joseph the Beautiful* suggested, rather, a sculpture with many figures. He positioned the dancers in pictorial poses and made complex configurations of groups—living bas-reliefs, in a way. This was noted by Iving, who wrote, "The sculpture is Goleizovsky's, the coloring, Erdman's."[69] The groups moved in strict rhythm. One pose "poured" into another and formed new configurations. Everything was planned, down to the tiniest detail: each turn of the head, each position of the wrist, and each angle of the raised leg. A change in a detail would have led to the destruction of the entire concept; the whole complex of strictly planned, precisely executed movements and poses gave birth to an image. Goleizovsky deliberately used a nonrealistic method of composing dances for large groups, but the stylized quality of his groupings is of a totally different order from the stylized but abstract quality governing the corps de ballet dances of academic ballet.

The meaning of "pure" classical dance lies in the combination of positions and pas, whose forms are polished, carefully tuned, and purged of anything accidental and transient; in other words, classical dance is generalized. The steps of classical dance express abstract thought. The arrow-like line of the arabesque, the flowing movements of the arms, verticals and horizontals, crossings and fractures, spirals, turns, and pauses —all these movements and positions of the body possess their own expressiveness, somewhat akin to the expressiveness of musical sounds. In any given instance, the human body is only an instrument; its strengths and weaknesses are evaluated according to the artistic perfection of the movements it performs and, hence, according to how fully the idea embedded in this movement is revealed. It seems to cease existing in the real sense, since its individual peculiarities have no significance and the moment of sensual perception is rejected.

For Goleizovsky things were different. He was never interested in pure form, and he cared little about bringing out the abstract meaning of a position. The classical arabesque as a symbol of extension and upward aspiration was unnecessary to his productions. A pose in Goleizovsky's dances assumed other criteria. The audience was meant to appreciate the beauty of the dancer's bare legs and delight in the flexibility of her body, feeling its living warmth. From such bodies—bent, straightened out, or pressed against the floor—he formed expressive groups.

In *Joseph the Beautiful* there were no national dances in their pure ethnographic form. For Goleizovsky, work in museums and the study of ancient artworks preceded the production of the ballet. But there was no archaeological verisimilitude either in the dances or in the costumes. Historical documents only suggested individual details to the choreographer, providing him with ethnic motifs which could show through in the dances. The soloists were hardly distinguished from the ensemble and expressed themselves in the same language. The only difference between them was that some had more poses and others more dance movements. Pantomime in Goleizovsky's ballet had its own specific features; it was not contrasted to dance and was indivisible from it. Joseph's brothers were characterized by grotesque gestures, but they were so sharply drawn and so merged with the music that there is no basis for considering such an interpretation a non-dance one. The major female role was not built on academic classicism, although Tayakh's variations demanded of the dancer superb training in classical dance; only many years of comprehensive training could ensure the necessary freedom for control of the body. However, the traditional ballet class did not give the dancer all the knowledge needed to understand Goleizovsky's choreography, which was constantly renewing the expressive means of the ballet. Sergei Chudinov, a performer in all the ballet productions of the Bolshoi Theater from 1907 on, recalls his first rehearsal with Goleizovsky: "For us there was a law: an arabesque is done only this way and an attitude, only that way. But with him everything was different. Everyone was astounded. To many it seemed like something absolutely impossible."[70]

In any case, Goleizovsky's dances demanded a special kind of preparation from the dancers. His opponents accused the choreographer of "destroying the dancers' knowledge of classical dance," and making them "break their legs." Goleizovsky, on the other hand, pointed to the one-sidedness of the knowledge obtained in the ballet school, where the students were educated to be fit only for the old "classics"; therefore even such a capable artist as Bank "had to exert herself to the utmost" learning the role of Tayakh. He maintained that "the dancers and their teachers do not entirely understand or have forgotten what they ought to know and well remember."[71]

The set designer for *Joseph* was Goleizovsky's constant collaborator, Boris Erdman. In creating the costumes, Erdman began with the forms and ornaments of ancient Judea and ancient Egypt, but they were transformed by the imagination of the designer who, like the choreographer, had neither historical nor stylizing goals. Erdman was concerned that the costume reveal the dancer's movement as much as possible. The body of the dancer was free. The costume was reduced to the loincloth and small apron or short skirt characteristic of Egyptian pictures. But in addition to the costume, the designer introduced body make-up. He followed the Egyptian drawings, where the men are depicted in brownish-red and the women in yellowish-pink. In the ballet, brown and orange body make-up was used for the men, while Tayakh was heavily powdered, her whiteness setting her off from the general background. Individual parts of the costumes were brightly colored; the colors harmonized and yet contrasted sharply. Large ornaments in the form of appliqués were widely used. One of the most widespread motifs was the circle. Circles were attached to clothing; they also formed headdresses, imitating the circle at the head of a human or animal often found in Egyptian hieroglyphic writing.

The distinguishing feature of Erdman's costumes lay in the fact that the Egyptian motif here varied in such a way that it unexpectedly turned into an eccentric device in the style of the 1920s. Women's wigs with straight hair and bangs were based on the hairdos of Egyptian women and yet at the same time suggested the short haircut so popular during the twenties. The principle of asymmetry constantly applied by the designer was also modern: the bodice joined to the skirt only on one side or caught on one shoulder (like many ball gowns of the time); the loincloth fastened on one side; the lacing that went up one leg, leaving the other bare, and so on. Even the ornaments were placed asymmetrically, creating the impression of glimpses of parts, unexpected shifts, and juxtaposed fragments. The multicolored details of the clothing contrasted sharply; wide stripes cut across the figure. This gave rise to a dynamism of color and form more like the urban art of the twentieth century than that of Egypt.

The costumes of the extras (for example, the merchants in the first act) were imposing. The cloth was draped in stiff folds; heavy headdresses, solid and inflexible, fell in bristly strips. Every costume was also "included" in the action; it shaped the gestures of the performer and became an element of the dance design. Even the crooks in the hands of the old men, clearly outlined against the backdrop in white lines, filled out the pattern.

The decor consisted of platforms, bridges, and stairs placed against a black or white background. It provided the possibility for quite varied compositions and rhythmic combinations, which helped to create the desired image. The staircases and platforms were positioned differently in the two acts. In Potiphar's palace a symmetrical construction was used, in which the steps of the wide staircase rose majestically and evenly to the central wide, flat platform. Two monumental columns towered on both sides; altogether, it vaguely suggested the entrance to a pyramid. Such a platform was appropriate for grandiose movements. The platforms of various heights and the little bridges in the first act made for completely different constructions. The dancers swiftly rose and fell, and leaped from platform to platform. In the scene of the arrival of the caravan and the capture of Joseph, for example, this helped create a feeling of anxiety; it made the action more dynamic. A new treatment of stage space allowed for dancing that used different planes of the stage without being limited to the surface of the floor.

Teolinda

As part of the same program with *Joseph the Beautiful*, a one-act ballet in three scenes, *Teolinda*, was performed to the music of Schubert. At first Goleizovsky wanted to call it *Teolinda, or the Repentant Brigand*, in order to emphasize the connection with the ballet of the mid-nineteenth century, when such double titles were commonly used. Indeed, he intended to restore "classical dance, like that of the 30s and 40s of the previous century," and he alluded to material at the Bakhrushin Museum "where one may see all the groups, poses, and movements of *Teolinda*."[72]

This time Goleizovsky did not introduce into the ballet elements that could be called "foreign" from the point of view of the champions of the old ballet. It was utterly pure classical dance, but its manner of execution was fundamentally different from that which was generally accepted. Goleizovsky wrote about Bank in the role of Lizette: "For her 'classical dances' in *Teolinda* to be characterized by the enchanting airiness and grace of the nineteenth century, she had to spend many hours 'getting out of the habit' of acting like a court ballerina."[73] Bank herself confirms this. She recalls poses with a finger pressed to her lips and flying arabesques, all reminiscent of engravings.

It may seem strange that an innovative choreographer who was utterly devoted to the newest dance forms would work on the restoration of Romantic ballet. But in rebelling against the academic ballet, Goleizovsky was primarily referring to the numbness of its forms, the loss of feeling in its style. He maintained that it was impossible to express modern ideas through formulas composed for a completely different purpose. The same idea is also applicable to other eras, since each age possesses its own stylistic peculiarities. While *Joseph the Beautiful* demanded of its choreographer a feeling for modern times and a rejection of the devices of late nineteenth-century ballet, in recreating the choreography of the age of Romanticism in *Teolinda*, Goleizovsky also sought appropriate forms and did not use already existing ones. The lexicon of ballet is incomparably more varied, more subtle, and richer in nuances than it seems to "academics," who reduce the concept of classical dance to one single style, Goleizovsky maintained. As proof of this, he composed *Teolinda*.

But for all that, Goleizovsky was not a stylist. He thought that discolored ancient embroidery, faded fabric, cracked porcelain, and tarnished metal, objects once beautiful but now touched by decay, should be preserved in museums, but could no longer occupy a place in real life. He himself lived in the thick of life. The poetry of the airy dances of Romantic ballerinas belonged to another age. The same was even more true of the fairytale plots, the saccharine happy endings, and the exaggerated expression of feelings. These features were intensified in the ballets of the late nineteenth century and, in fact, survive in those that are still staged at the Bolshoi Theater. Fokine had already come out against them, and two decades later Goleizovsky too became convinced of the amazing persistence of many formulas that had outlived their time. Therefore, *Teolinda* was both a glorification of the old ballet and a parody of it.

In the ballet, a group of brigands led by their chief, Raoul, were shown gathering in the woods. Lizette wandered in with her friends. The girls were dressed in costumes copied exactly from nineteenth-century engravings: long muslin Taglioniesque skirts and orange velvet camisoles. The friends frolicked in the meadow, not suspecting danger. A triumphal march was heard, and the brigands jumped out with great leaps, gesticulating threateningly and rolling their eyes fiercely. In vain the girls pleaded for mercy, but they did not succeed in softening the brigands' cruel hearts. The good fairy Teolinda came to the aid of the unfortunate maidens. She ordered the brigands to marry the girls; they responded with mocking laughter. Then Teolinda resorted to magic. She turned the girls into sylphs and they appeared in white tutus with little wreaths on their heads; the brigands became fauns. A scene of the dances of the fauns and the sylphs in the enchanted woods followed. A cupid flew by, pierced the hearts of the fauns with the arrow of love, and notified them that if they "promised Teolinda they would abandon their brigandry, she would again return them to their previous state."[74] The first to show repentance was the chief. Then all the faun-brigands swore to abandon their former sinful way of life. The fairy Teolinda triumphantly returned them to their former shapes. The sylphs turned back into girls. General rejoicing followed.

In *Teolinda*, Goleizovsky used all the riches of traditional classical dance, reviving a number of very old movements, especially in the men's variations. "The part of Raoul is among the most difficult men's parts in the ballet repertory. In addition to the numerous lifts required of the ballet cavalier, there is a lot of dancing. And this dancing is not doled out sparingly, as in the majority of ballets where the man must dance one variation of some kind and a little bit in the coda; here there is dancing all through the ballet," wrote Iving.[75]

According to the recollections of the performers, the ensemble dances were also highly complex, such as the cachucha danced by Lizette's friends, performed entirely on pointe. For Asaf Messerer, who could do astounding leaps, Goleizovsky created the role of "a parody of Zephyr, exaggerating the poses of such a character."[76]

The solo variations, adagio, and group dances, during which the girls tied neckerchiefs on their loved ones, followed one on the other. At times one might believe that all this was in earnest, as in other traditional ballets. But the ironic intention of the choreographer was nevertheless quite obvious. The oversupply of old-fashioned accessories, the emphatically melodramatic gestures, the slightly overacted earnestness, and the obviously exaggerated fierceness of the brigands all testified to this. One of the brigands, so bloodthirsty he always carried a chopped-off human leg with him, became a monk after he repented. The wings of an angel grew on his back and he began to dance with the Gospels in his hands.

Only after he had proved that he could be "more classical than the classics and more romantic than Schubert's romanticism"[77] could Goleizovsky allow himself to poke fun at the high-sounding nonsense of the old ballet.

The "Revolt" of the Younger Generation

The ballets *Joseph the Beautiful* and *Teolinda* were shown on March 3, 1925, in the Experimental Theater and until the end of the season were presented regularly (*Joseph* was performed 17 times), with good box offices. Lunacharsky approved of the new program: "Enumerating only the unquestionably interesting performances of this year . . . one must include . . . the new ballet production of the Bolshoi Theater under the direction of the new choreographer Goleizovsky. . . ."[78] But *Joseph the Beautiful* caused a split in the theater.

In May 1925 an episode occurred that was known as the "revolt" of the younger generation. An order was issued concerning the new composition of the administration of the Bolshoi Theater. Tikhomirov was appointed chairman and also manager of the artistic sector, with Leonid Zhukov and Ivan Smoltsov as members. The younger dancers were concerned that not one supporter of new ideas was among the administrators of the company. "This artists' council is Tikhomirov to the third power," wrote the young dancers.[79] On May 12 seventy-four of the one hundred twenty-five artists in the Bolshoi Ballet signed a petition to review the order. Among them were Mikhail Gabovich, Igor Moiseyev, Asaf Messerer, Nikolai Tarasov, Vasily Efimov, Nina Podgoretskaya, Elena Ilyushchenko, Valentina Galetskaya, Olga Martynova, and Irina Vronskaya—that is, almost all the young people, regardless of the positions they held.[80]

In their statement to the director of the theater, Grigory Koloskov, the performers wrote that "even in his first production (*Teolinda* and *Joseph the Beautiful*), when he had not yet explored all his potential, [Golei-zovsky] immediately gave inspiration to that life, that sense of the new for which we were waiting, toward which we were rushing, and which filled the usually half-empty rows of the theater with a broad, excited audience."

At the same time they discussed Tikhomirov: "We are not opposed to Tikhomirov as a comrade and as a person; we are not opposed to Tikho-mirov as a dancer. But we will fight against Tikhomirov the conservative, the champion of rotting causes; we will fight doggedly, just as he has fought and still fights against everything that is new." [81]

The director called in the "instigators." The conversation that took place between them is summarized in a collective letter from the ballet dancers. "You met with us cautiously, perhaps distrustfully. We remem-ber your question: 'Aren't you playing at democracy?' What could have made you so distrust the younger generation, which *for the first time in an entire century has dared to think and hope, and to honestly and openly talk about that*?" [82] Then the dancers lay out their intentions: "We were only trying to eliminate the oppressive weight of the old tendencies and thereby to open the door to new forces and new productions." In the letter, they speak of the fact that "under the present conditions in bal-let management the possibilities inherent in ballet as a whole and in the younger generation remain hidden and unused," possibilities that must be "revealed and put to use for the ballet and the theater," to ensure "the progress necessary for new productions, without which our ballet is doomed to perish during the very next season." [83]

Both sides stuck to their own opinions. There were new meetings of the company and new resolutions. Then the directors decided to take stronger measures.

And then you summoned us, but only to . . . fire us as an element that agitates and divides the company. . . . We wanted something new, something vital, and right away we encountered a barrier, the old lifeless administration, which inevitably must fight against what we aspire to. . . . If during a weak moment we told you *"we renounce our opinions,"* would you really decide that everything is settled and that the youth movement that is spontaneously tearing down century-old foundations has quieted down? Then what is the reason for this discussion, the threat of firing the youngest and therefore the most sincere, the hush-hush conversation in the directors' box in the presence only of Smoltsov and Tikhomirov, instead of bringing up the question for a broad, thorough discussion before the whole company? . . . In the struggle between two principles—the old and the new—you temporarily, *but* only temporarily, are on the side of those who are implacably hostile to everything truly alive.[84]

This was what the group of young ballet people with initiative wrote to the director.

At this time, the point was no longer merely the leadership of the administration, but also the fate of the new repertory, including the ballets of Goleizovsky, and the right to experiment. The dancer Riabtsev, no longer young but respected by everybody, was selected as arbitrator. The directors gave him the young people's statement. Riabtsev took a quite reasonable position on the question of classical and innovative repertory.

I think that every employee of the theater not only has the right but also the duty, the obligation, to express his opinion about his work —that is an indication of his interest in the field. After studying the present statement in detail, I absolutely do not see that its authors reject the classics or even ballet in its old classical form. I only see the aspiration to build new forms based on this classical, inevitable, immutable foundation. And a move forward in art must always be welcomed. The authors suggest that those not sharing such a view should depart "into semi-darkness." They (the authors) are right.

As regards Goleizovsky's productions, Riabtsev asked, "Is Goleizovsky talented or not?" and answered, "My opinion is—yes. Everything of talent belongs in the Bolshoi Academic Theater." He recalled Gorsky's experiments, which were met with "great protest, but not by the masses; protest by those who headed the ballet. As a result, the masses understood Gorsky and Gorsky understood the masses. In sum, these were brilliant productions, on which the Bolshoi Ballet has gotten by for two decades. . . ." In conclusion, Riabtsev pointed out that the statement of the young people "is the first action by a group of dancers in the Bolshoi Theater concerned with the future of the ballet. . . . If this statement by a group of dancers is a step toward socially useful work, it should be welcomed and forgiven for a few possible exaggerations."[85]

However, the "revolt" of the young did not end here. A new meeting took place under Tarasov's chairmanship on May 29; forty-seven people attended. The most active participants were Gabovich and Moiseyev. On their suggestion, the meeting gave a detailed description of each member of the ballet administration and introduced a resolution stating that people who did not welcome experiments in art and were indifferent to young people (they were referring primarily to Tikhomirov and partly to Smoltsov; Zhukov was accused of a "hackwork attitude") should not have the right to decide on artistic questions; at best, they (in particular Smoltsov) could assume administrative duties. The young people wanted to see Riabtsev as chairman of the directorate.[86]

Nevertheless, the board of directors did not consider it necessary to change the leadership of the company. The instigators of the "revolt" (nine people headed by Moiseyev and Gabovich) were temporarily fired from the theater. These events drew comment in the press: There was an article by Vladimir Blum;[87] Goleizovsky also made a statement.[88] But gradually the passions died down.

At the beginning of the next season, Goleizovsky signed a contract with the Bolshoi Theater accepting responsibility for directing all performances of *Joseph the Beautiful* and *Teolinda* and for producing a new four-act ballet, *Lola*, with the composer Sergei Vasilenko. The text of the contract in the archives of the Bolshoi Theater, covered with Goleizovsky's corrections and Koloskov's remarks, attests to the heated arguments between the choreographer and the administration. Trying to protect his work from outside interference, Goleizovsky demanded authority exceeding the usual rights of a producing choreographer. "Bank, approved for the role of Lola, may not be removed from that role without Goleizovsky's consent; otherwise, Goleizovsky has the right to postpone the date of the premiere," he inserted in the text. Thereupon follows in the margins Koloskov's "retort," "Does he imagine he is also heading the theater?"[89] Goleizovsky insisted on his exclusive right to select the cast and demanded that no one other than himself be permitted to attend rehearsals of his ballets; the director objected.

Formally, Koloskov was right in refusing to grant autonomy to each producer. But Goleizovsky also had cause to take a defensive position in advance. Gorsky was no longer alive; he had supported the young choreographer in his work on *The Masque of the Red Death*. Now Goleizovsky's supporters were primarily the young people, "the nice young opposition," as Lunacharsky called them.[90] Goleizovsky wrote that the leadership of the ballet company was openly expressing "displeasure" with his creative work as early as the production of *Joseph* and *Teolinda*: "It was painful to listen to the accusations of the respected V. D. Tikhomirov, our teacher, a maestro, who had given us so much technical knowledge, when he accused me of pornography. Under the leadership of Gavrilov, the director of the school, first the parent committee, then the pedagogical council, would rush into rehearsals as though trying to defend the children in the cast from the corrupting influence of my productions. . . ."[91] During the entire season of 1925–26 clashes between Goleizovsky and the administration continued unabated.

First of all, Goleizovsky was trying to keep his ballets intact at a time when the leadership of the company insisted on alterations. They demanded that all the "dragging along the floor" in *Joseph the Beautiful* be eliminated, and that the body make-up be changed and the dancers be clothed in knitted tights and jerseys. Extensive correspondence exists on this point. Goleizovsky and Erdman firmly protested, at times evincing extreme irritability. Goleizovsky's threats and ultimata, interspersed with complaints, reproaches, and excuses, exasperated the directorate.

Second, Goleizovsky was trying to get on with the work on *Lola*. At the same time, Tikhomirov was staging *Esmeralda*. As head of the company and choreographer of a ballet intended for Geltser, he naturally enjoyed several advantages. Goleizovsky was nervous and, with the suspiciousness of an embittered man, he was inclined to view any obstacle to his work as a personal insult. It seemed to him that everyone was against him. However, there were also people on the board of directors who understood that the theater needed Goleizovsky. This is evident from the fact that in October 1925, at the height of the disagreement between Goleizovsky and the administration, the music for the ballet *The Whirlwind* was ordered from the composer Boris Beer. At that time the date for the premiere of *Lola* was constantly being postponed. Work was finally completely discontinued. In the spring of 1926 conflicts arose concerning the renewal of the contract for the production. In May Lunacharsky questioned the theater about this.[92] It all ended, however, with Goleizovsky's departure for the Ukraine.

In the ballet *Lola*, the authors (Goleizovsky and Vasilenko) intended to continue and develop what they had begun in *Joseph the Beautiful*.

They intended to present a folk tragedy. The site of the action in the four-act ballet (in eighteen scenes) was Spain at the end of the seventeenth or beginning of the eighteenth century; the heroine was the folk dancer Lola. Lola loved the peasant Phoebus, but she was pursued by the marquis, who was hated by all the inhabitants of the village. The first act was devoted to characterization; here, during a folk festival, a conspiracy against the marquis was hatched. The second act (in the castle) satirically portrayed the marquis and his surroundings. Then folk scenes were interspersed with episodes in the cellar, where Lola's blind father was tortured in front of her, and with scenes of Phoebus' nightmares: He saw dark shadows pursuing Lola. She was meant to dance, mad, before a procession of monks. The plot absorbed many motifs from such works as *Fuente ovejuna* and *Notre-Dame de Paris*. *Lola* was obviously a polemic against Tikhomirov's *Esmeralda*: Goleizovsky particularly stressed the tragic ending.

Vasilenko's music developed in detail the themes characterizing the people and the rebels. Erdman created a set appropriate for a monumental spectacle. It consisted of several platforms and a drawbridge. By lowering a backdrop showing arcs and columns, the site could be changed; it suggested a square, a main hall, or the underground vaults of a prison.

A new theme had appeared in Goleizovsky's creative work. From year to year, he enriched both his forms and the sphere of emotions he expressed in dance. *Lola* was to reveal a new realm of feelings—courageous, powerful, full-blooded. Bank, who worked on the leading role, recalls how Goleizovsky rehearsed the scene of the procession to the execution with her. In her opinion, the choreographer was working toward a ballet of intense action and heightened passions. He could have gone even further, "could have revealed himself in a heroic context."[93] Lunacharsky also had hopes for Goleizovsky. "After the remarkable success of *Joseph the Beautiful*, one expects that the ballets planned by Goleizovsky, *Lola* and *Don Quixote*,[94] will be major events in the life of the Bolshoi Ballet."[95] Bank remembers her conversations with Lunacharsky, who also said that "we may develop a heroic style, not just a poster style."

Unfortunately, Goleizovsky did not succeed then in developing these qualities. His *Lola* was never performed. *The Whirlwind* was shown only two years later, at the end of 1927. Poorly received, this ballet was performed only once; it was severely criticized in the press. Perhaps much would have been different if Goleizovsky had begun work on *The Whirl-wind* after having created *Lola*, but things did not turn out that way.

While working in the Ukraine, Goleizovsky staged a new ballet by Vasilenko, *In the Sun's Rays*, in Odessa and Kharkov. It was a satire on contemporary bourgeois society, anticipating some scenes from *The Whirlwind*. Morality, Public Opinion, Love for Sale, and other characters dance in the light of the streetlamps of a modern city; they are surrounded by faceless "ladies and gentlemen," distinguishable from one another only by the letters on their clothing.

The heroic aspect of Goleizovsky's work came to a halt at this point, just when the ballet *The Red Poppy* was being shown in the Bolshoi Theater. This ballet, in many ways foreign and even inimical to Goleizovsky's quest, was unexpectedly very well received. Goleizovsky, who had just scoffed at the clichés of "old ballet" in *Teolinda*, stubbornly maintaining that the path to modernity lay not through *La Bayadère* and *The Little Humpbacked Horse*, but through a search for new forms, now had something to think about, something to be confused by. This confusion was felt in his new production. It was not by chance that Goleizovsky wrote of *The Whirlwind*: "I had to totally reject the initial plan of 1925. Now it seems too aesthetic to me."[96]

The Whirlwind

The ballet *The Whirlwind* was prepared over a long period of time, and it took shape gradually. Goleizovsky's work in vaudeville, especially *The City* in the Moscow Free Theater in 1924, served as a rough draft. It included a "foxtrot orgy" of the bourgeois, as well as, in contrast, youths with hammers and sickles.

Work on the scenario for the ballet took place in 1925. Goleizovsky's application has been preserved in the Central State Archives of Literature and Art, and his personal archive contains the initial version of the scenario. The distinguishing characteristic of these first versions is their deliberate distance from real life. In the application, the place of action was defined as "the world (partially the USSR)." The time of action is indicated as "outside of time (partially 1917–18)."[97] In the scenario, Goleizovsky was more precise: "It is not necessary to indicate exactly the time and place of the action. The choreographer, the composer, and the designer creating the costumes and scenery are asked to forget about ordinary life and, so to speak, to dissolve in time." Further, "the performers in the group scenes of the first act are not 'workers,' but 'Figures of Protest.'" The central figure in the second scene is not "the tsar of country x," but an "emblem of tsarism." In describing the characters, he wrote, "I am shrouding them in the cover of profoundest fantasy—beyond time and space."

This was how the content of the future ballet was set forth in the application:

> The proletarian revolution has encompassed the world. Palace after palace is consumed by the flames of rebellion. The servants of tsarism, which is dying out and devoured by the indignant people, are hiding in palaces that have been spared here and there. Dread Red Death—the Red Whirlwind—chases them and overtakes them everywhere. One such palace is in our play. Debauchery and decay dance their last dance, arrayed in gold and jewels. The Red Death demolishes the stone and iron vaults. It penetrates inside and destroys this final canker. A new era of a new life dawns over the world. In the place of a morass where vile creatures swarmed, the hammer and sickle restore their crops to life. Great, free labor rules and shines over the entire world.[98]

The connection between the scenarios for *The Whirlwind* and Tcherepnin's *The Masque of the Red Death*, which Goleizovsky staged in 1919, is quite obvious. In both cases, there is a ruler hiding from danger in a palace, hysterical merry-making, a sort of "feast during the plague." In both cases, a death-bearing specter appears in the castle; in one it is the Red Death, the plague, and in the other it is the Red Whirlwind, the revolution. Analogies arise even in regard to secondary characters. In Goleizovsky's ballet, a violinist appears at the ball in the palace (the role was played by a well-known musician, Boris Sibor, a soloist in the Bolshoi Theater Orchestra). Tcherepnin had thought of using the same device and wrote: "Among the characters will be a violin virtuoso who must execute a difficult cadenza on stage, continuing for about ten minutes."[99] The images in *The Whirlwind* also somewhat resemble those in the ballet *The Golden King*, which was once promoted by Lunacharsky. Here too, the Ruler feasting in his castle is swept away by the rebellious people.

Lunacharsky sympathized with Goleizovsky's intention and understood the complex circumstances in which he had to work—all the more so after *The Red Poppy*, when adherents of the academic ballet had come to believe in the universality of tried-and-true formulas. At that time, it was impossible to explain the reasons for the success of *The Red Poppy* and to analyze its strengths and weaknesses. Only one thing was important—the academics had triumphed. It was not by chance that precisely during those days the people's commissar, who had supported the innovators of the ballet stage, considered it necessary to make mention in print of "Goleizovsky's brilliant talents" and to express the conviction that "the directorate of the Bolshoi Theater will soon understand the necessity for giving patronage to our young ballet forces." And at the same time he complained of the dominance in the Moscow ballet of "highly honored artists no longer in their first youth," which was "a serious obstacle to development." [100]

The action in the first scene of *The Whirlwind* took place in a city. As Nikolai Musatov, the set designer for the production, explained, "It is no particular city; it is the silhouette of a city." [101] Stairs and inclined platforms positioned at various angles allowed one to observe the contours of the winding, ledge-like streets. There was a sense of uneasiness in their outlines. This was not a city of spacious, straight avenues; it clearly lacked air. In the beginning of the scene, a glow appeared beyond the horizon and gradually grew. Peals of thunder were heard, at first weak, then louder and louder. Spotlight beams scanned the stage. Lightning flashed.

Goleizovsky called this first scene "an allegorical thunderstorm." He demanded that the composer and designer increase the tension to the point where the thunder became "like continuous boiling." The thunder had to last no less than a minute, until the first running human figure appeared. This was an Aristocrat wearing a top hat, a white shirt-front and gloves spattered with blood, and patent-leather shoes. He ran, looking around and crouching; men in frock coats and women in evening gowns appeared behind him. At the same time, the glow spread and the black crosses of a vast number of gallows were outlined against the crimson sky. The legs of the first hanged men—in Musatov's sketch—are the most noticeable detail in the foreground; farther away, yet another figure appears, hanging with his hands tied behind his back, and behind him are more and more gallows, diminishing in the distance.

While the Aristocrats were running by in the lightning flashes and the rumbling (which could be understood not just as thunder but also as gunfire), the first "Figures of Protest" appeared. These were the people in revolt. They wore torn clothes; their hair was matted; in their hands were hammers, shovels, and clubs. In describing them, Goleizovsky wrote in the notes to the scenario: "The dancers in these groups are portraying exhausted, suffering, tortured, and embittered people whose faces, like all their bodies, are aflame with the idea of liberation and vengeance." Thirty-six dancers and supernumeraries used in mime scenes portrayed the rebels. The scene of their appearance and their dance, which in the scenario Goleizovsky calls "The Whirlwind of Protest," was meant to last ten minutes, that is, it took up more than half of the first scene of the ballet, which lasted seventeen minutes. All that is known of this dance is that the culmination was "a funnel-shaped, gyrating movement of the agitated mass."[102]

According to the initial plan, all the participants in the revolt were abstract "Figures of Protest." No one was to stand out. The positive characters were generally undifferentiated and did not have solo dances or scenes; the soloists and leading dancers did not participate in the revolt scenes. Only in the second scene of the ballet did the "Specter of the Revolution" appear; the choreographer wanted to portray him with a mechanical figure appearing in various corners of the stage.

The ballet went into production in 1927. Apparently, the absence of real heroes leading the crowd gave rise to unfavorable criticism and such characters subsequently did appear in the ballet. They arose at the last moment, before the premiere, which was timed for the tenth anniversary of the October Revolution; even as late as September they were not mentioned in the cast list for the rehearsals. In the dance in the first scene "The Whirlwind of Protest" a soloist (Viktor Smoltsov) appeared in fiery orange garb, with a red flag in his hands. Bank recalls Smoltsov's impressive run across the proscenium with the huge, unfurled banner. The leader "pronounced" a revolutionary speech. "Here there are also moments of dance but pantomime predominates. In his speech, the leader curses the old world and calls for the construction of a new one," wrote Goleizovsky.[103]

The second scene took place in the palace. The symmetrical columns and stairways, the gallery for the musicians, and the dais in the back for the throne created an impression of triumphant luxury. First the Aristocrats ran along the illuminated pale blue hall. They looked around just as anxiously as in the first scene. Then the hall began to fill with the fantastic figures of the courtiers, the orchestra, jesters, guards, and others. The Ruler (Ivan Sidorov) sitting on the throne appeared last. The artist gave the Ruler an Oriental appearance. The plump, sleek, immobile face with half-closed eyes expressed dullness, satiety, and indifference. The monstrously heavy bare belly was adorned by a precious stone in the navel. The Ruler was dressed in fantastic attire made of balls, gilded plates, and chains that hung at his legs. On his head was a tall crown: a ball encircled by pointed, bent strips. This costume was a complicated and luxurious affair, the splendid dress raising the Ruler above all those present. The Ruler was surrounded by retainers who, as Goleizovsky wrote, "are in the full sense of the word an extension of the Ruler." The retainers were also clothed in semi-Oriental costumes. Their naked, egg-shaped skulls were crowned with the same lancet-like tufts of hair as the Ruler's. The women had big, bare, sagging breasts. But among the Ruler's retinue, self-satisfied pomposity gave way to servility and obsequiousness: The heads of the courtiers were fearfully tucked into their shoulders and their hands raised to their faces, like little dogs standing on their hind legs.

The courtiers and guests in the palace were the embodiment of all the vices. In order to emphasize this idea, the choreographer decided to bring onstage the "Seven Deadly Sins." In Musatov's sketch they are standing in a row: Drunkenness with a barrel on his head; Murder with a knife in his teeth, holding a severed head; Indiscretion with an exorbitantly long tongue wriggling like a snake's; Lust serving her naked breasts on a plate along with fruits and berries, and so on.

The first dance was performed by eight male jesters and one female jester (Abramova). The designer wanted to emphasize their connection to our epoch; hence the red and yellow tights juxtaposed with polished boots and the headgear adorned with bells, combined with starched shirtfronts and bowties. The dance was lively, built on a rapid alternation of movements. Goleizovsky wrote in the appendix to the scenario that in this dance there was a great deal of jerking about, grimacing, and laughter "upon demand," laughter "through tears." The dances were performed to the accompaniment of the orchestra; the musicians, dressed in black tuxedos, wore sheets of music instead of shirt fronts. A court violinist played a solo; he depicted "a strongly exaggerated type of overinspired artist suffering from an unhealthy kind of refinement." Out of the trap door a thin stooping man with long hair and an emaciated face appeared, wearing a cape and white tights. As he played, intoxicated by the sound of the violin, the trapdoor rose higher and higher. After he finished playing, he swiftly fell; as Goleizovsky put it, "he is dumped from the sky." "Fantastic women" danced to the music of the violin. They were to be perceived not as reality, but as the materialized sounds of the violin, but this fantasy had a morbid cast. Therefore, the women appeared almost nude: pink tights, a few gold rays around their breasts, and a strip of lightly eddying cloth. In all their movements there was an unnatural affectation. They reached out toward each other, touched one another, and embraced.

Terpsichore and Apollo also appeared at the ball. In this dance, Goleizovsky settled his score with traditional classical ballet. The customary ballet costume—a tutu for the woman and a jacket and tights for the man—was made to appear emphatically banal and tasteless. The ballerina was obscenely naked and adorned with spangles and feathers. Her fleecy-haired cavalier showed little silver wings and exaggeratedly heavy thighs. "The main content of the dance is a lack of content," wrote Goleizovsky in his notes to the script. He wanted to emphasize that such dances to "champagne" music (Goleizovsky's expression) were designed for a stupid, depraved audience.

The fast dance "Folie" (Madness) was performed by two couples with green faces and green hair in lilac and blue-green costumes. The dance was stormy and impetuous, with elements of acrobatics; according to the choreographer's description, it was "something midway between the frenzied dance of wild men and a foxtrot at breakneck tempo." This dance was unexpectedly interrupted by a vision. Surrounded by jailers who had swastikas instead of heads, political prisoners appeared in chains, with yokes around their necks, bleeding. They appeared before the Ruler as a reminder and a warning, and then they disappeared.

After this vision came the culmination of the orgy, the dance of the monks. The monks moved in a line with prayerbooks in their hands. They were dressed in long soutanes. On their heads they wore cowls with narrow slits for their eyes. While the monks were performing a prayerful dance, the entire crowd stood as if for a blessing. But now, from the trapdoor appeared a bacchante (Bank), in long red stockings over flesh-colored tights, silver slippers, and a green cap with little horns. She lay in the middle of the stage. The monks tried to resist temptation, but first one and then another was drawn toward the bacchante. Gradually their clothing fell off. The soutanes rose, baring protruding green tails; the cowls were pushed back, revealing horns butting through next to the tonsures. On their chests, which had sprouted green fur, the crosses still dangled on long chains. Those surrounding them laughingly began to grab the monk-satyrs by the hems of their soutanes. The monks rushed all the more furiously toward the bacchante. Finally, their clothes remained in the hands of the courtiers, and the monks, once and for all transformed into satyrs, began to dance. The entire crowd of courtiers accompanied their dance, the scenery began to move, and the Ruler himself was about to rise from his throne.

At this point, the "Specter of Revolution" arose behind the throne—"tatters of chains, an emaciated face remarkable in its beauty, burning with vengeance." He was portrayed in the form of a dummy (one and a half times human size) whose head turned and whose right hand rose. Everyone froze. The Ruler seized a knife and rushed at the Specter, but he fell and began to roll down the steps of the throne, losing part of his costume on the way. The director intended this to be a device of accusation: "The abominable pile of flesh wallows with a final spasm. All the courtiers, seeing him in such a state, will understand that there is no redemption. Without adornments, their god turned into dust."

It was Goleizovsky's original intention that when the "masses of protest" familiar to the audience from the first scene rushed into the castle, the Specter would appear with them several times on different parts of the stage. For this reason, he suggested having several figures of the Specter, controlled by people sitting inside. During the performance it was different: Goleizovsky put a real leader at the head of the crowd, but not the one from the first scene. Now the rebels were led by a woman (Podgoretskaya). The palace was destroyed—the columns moved together and tipped over, and the bridges of stairs separated. In various areas of the stage, groups of fleeing courtiers and the rebels following them were lit up.

Simultaneously, the scenery for the third scene, "Victory," was formed. It was a cone-like structure, at the top of which Goleizovsky wanted to place a "Specter of Protest" in a purple cloak, with a scythe in its hands. In the course of the work on the ballet it was replaced by a "group of victory" consisting of two men and two women in orange-red clothing with a gigantic banner in their hands. Transparent screens sparkled on their faces and chests. In the sketch, Musatov depicted them with scraps of mica glued onto the paper. This gave the people a fantastic appearance: They were perceived as apparitions from the future or as creatures from another planet. On various levels of the set the "Figures of Protest" were positioned with banners—light scarlet on top and deep purple below. The floor at the foot of the pyramid was strewn with the bodies of the Ruler's wounded servants. Panels of cloth, dropped from above, cut across the stage in various directions. On them, slogans were inscribed: "Labor will rule the world!" "Workers of the world, unite!," and so on. "Slogans flash like lightning, gradually covering the pyramid of Victory," wrote Goleizovsky in the scenario. "The Internationale" resounded.

The program for the anniversary evening was shown on November 5 at a dress rehearsal. After this, The Whirlwind "was withdrawn by the directorate . . . for technical reasons. . . . The first performance has been postponed until November 30," the theater administration announced.[104]

Before The Whirlwind an apotheosis with complex scenery called The Heroic Deed had been shown. To disassemble this set and put up other scenery during the time usually allotted to intermissions was impossible. Moreover, the ballet did not go over well. As Goleizovsky recounted, for the ensemble scenes the second cast, with whom he had barely worked at all, was put on stage. Thus all the carefully regulated groupings, formations, and the dance design, which had been worked out in detail, fell apart: "People wandered around the stage not knowing where to fit in."[105]

After the preview, Goleizovsky submitted the following statement to the director of the Bolshoi Theater: "I request that you withdraw the ballet The Whirlwind in view of its utter lack of organization, due to two ruined, uncompensated rehearsals. In the event of your refusal, I reserve the right to give an explanation to the press, in order to restore my reputation before an audience that has been deceived."[106]

During November and the beginning of December several rehearsals of the ballet took place, but it was not included in the repertory. Nevertheless, reviews appeared in the press in which accusations were leveled at the ballet, many of which were justifiable.

The ballet was conceived as a poster, in which an idea is conveyed in a few expressive images, and emotion is condensed into a symbol. Hence the vortex-like motion of the crowd, the "Specter of Revolution," the monstrous masks of the tyrants and their servants. This scheme was by no means successful in every respect. The initial intention sets up a great deal of window dressing. The revolution is symbolized by a specter, which is depicted by a mechanical figure; in the first and last scene one of the main expressive devices is the written slogans hung onstage. In reworking the scenario in 1927 Goleizovsky deemed it necessary to introduce images of real people leading the uprising. In point of fact, however, they received neither the necessary characterization nor any development. Furthermore, the appearance of the leader of the uprising (actually, two of them: a man in the first scene and a woman in the second) made the very image of the "Specter of Revolution" superfluous. In the ballet two modes of expression were mixed: the allegorical (the "Specter of Revolution," the Ruler dissolving into dust, and so on) and the illustrative (the crowd with their axes and clubs). Along with the theatrical devices of the transformation of the monks into satyrs, along with the jailers with swastikas instead of heads, the choreographer used the everyday gestures of the "orator" in the first scene. Also, the fact that *The Whirlwind* was shown in 1927, right after *The Red Poppy*, affected it adversely.

The Bolshoi Theater was thinking of a ballet in which a people's uprising would be brilliantly presented, a "magnificent finale portraying the collapse of the old world." The theater's plan of preparation for the celebration of the tenth anniversary of the October Revolution states: "The new principles of artistic mime dance applied by Comrade Goleizovsky give one cause to hope that the spectacle will be grand, timely, and heroic."[107] But in *The Whirlwind* the images of the people seemed unconvincing and stilted; it was not without reason that one of the critics wrote that "they were molded out of papier-maché."[108]

Moreover, the forces resisting the revolution were shown as incomparably more interesting. This was the case not only with Goleizovsky. Negative types were easier to translate into theatrical terms. All sorts of "former people,"* black marketeers, hooligans, and riff-raff—all these real-life opponents of the new order reached the vaudeville stage, and then operetta and ballet, as far back as the early 1920s. They appeared in

---

*That is, belonging to classes abolished after the revolution. (Ed.)

Lopukhov's and Deshevov's ballet *The Red Whirlwind* (1924). Prokofiev portrayed them in *Le Pas d'acier* (1927). They survived until the early 1930s, appearing in Shostakovich's ballet *Bolt* (1931).

Although he also focused attention on the negative figures, Goleizovsky chose another route. His revolutionary poster was complicated by motifs of fantasy and eroticism and it had a hint of decadence. His Ruler resembled a poster of Capital, brought to the stage from the lithographs of Viktor Denis and the pages of Demian Bedny. But he was more fantastic. The artist Musatov was attracted by Oriental splendor and gave the Ruler the mysterious inscrutability of a little Chinese god.[109]

The Ruler's surroundings were also depicted through caricature. The scene in the palace was built on a contrast between pathos and buffoonery. In depicting a horrible, absurd world passing into nonexistence, Goleizovsky used the devices of biting grotesque and satirical hyperbole. Dramatic directors operated with similar, hypertrophied methods. For example, Meyerhold did this in political revues, unmasking the "decadent culture of the dying West," or in satirical comedies when he portrayed "former people," the dead phantoms of the past (in his productions of *The Mandate* and *The Inspector General*) by displacing real proportions and hyperbolizing.

"The first scene—protest (the city—the street—the people) must shock; the second scene—the fantastic palace (the despot—the aristocracy—the elect), built as a cartoon of court etiquette and the soft aristocracy—must make one laugh."[110] "This scene is full of refined dances. But I am composing them so that, I think, the audience will laugh," wrote Goleizovsky.[111]

In fact, these scenes occupied a disproportionately large place in *The Whirlwind*. Carefully developing the scene of a monstrous last ball in the last palace, Goleizovsky gave his fantasy free rein. The center of gravity shifted. The reviewer for *Izvestia* wrote: "Most brilliant and interesting, on the general background of a monotonous stage, was the scene 'The Decay of the Bourgeoisie.' The orgiastic, the recherché, and the erotic here completely outweighed the timid attempts at satire, the urge to show in symbolic form the ugly and the disgusting in the way of life of capitalist society."[112] Iving said it even more sharply in *Pravda*: "As a whole, *The Whirlwind* is a strange mixture of boosterism and refined eroticism."[113]

After the final decision was made not to continue staging *The Whirl-*

wind, Goleizovsky's other works were also dropped from the plans of the Bolshoi Theater, particularly *Lola* and *Les Papillons*, with music by Vasilenko. Cut off from further work in the academic ballet theaters and working for the most part in vaudeville (including Moscow and Leningrad music halls), during the late 1920s and early 1930s the choreographer continued to create concert programs for the young dancers of the Bolshoi Theater. In these programs he developed his early discoveries and, through experimentation, sought new resolutions, but many of his most interesting ideas of the 1920s remained unfulfilled.

Leonid Alexeyevich Zhukov

After Gorsky's death there was no choreographer in the Bolshoi Ballet capable of leading the company. Though talented, Goleizovsky was too categorical in his judgment of the old; the Bolshoi Theater was always cautious about him. Even in Gorsky's time the leading posts were occupied by Riabtsev, Tikhomirov, and Zhukov—sometimes together with Gorsky, sometimes singly. Their main concern was traditional repertory, and they were right, as long as the issue was survival with the least possible losses during the period of civil war and destruction. But five years after the revolution, a refreshening of the repertory became urgent, and Leonid Zhukov began staging independent productions.

Zhukov was a dancer for the Bolshoi Theater beginning in 1909. He performed leading roles, especially character or comic ones. As a performer in the Diaghilev's Ballets Russes, Zhukov became acquainted with Fokine's repertory. During the First World War, the dancer put on concert programs and performed in dances he choreographed himself; he worked first in the Alexeyevsky Theater (1916) and then in the Novoslobodsky People's House (1918). Appointed manager of the Bolshoi Ballet in 1922, the following year Zhukov showed two of his works: *Capriccio Espagnol* and *Schéhérazade*, both to the music of Rimsky-Korsakov.

The idea of creating these two ballets had arisen earlier. The names of various choreographers appeared in the minutes of the meetings of the artistic council of the Bolshoi Theater and in the press. In the autumn of 1922 Tairov was named director, Lashchilin choreographer, and Fedorovsky designer. Information about Tairov's work on *Capriccio Espagnol* has not been preserved, but apparently some sort of preparatory plan for the production of *Schéhérazade* did exist. In any event, Tairov invited Pavel Kuznetsov as designer and the latter even succeeded in producing costume sketches (now kept at the Bakhrushin Museum) and a model which was later rejected as not appropriate to the size of the stage at the Bolshoi Theater. Tairov wrote concerning the model: "I consider its form to fully express the idea of the production I have in mind, and to be fully in keeping with my intentions regarding the development and plan of the action."[1] In the beginning of 1923, after Tairov's departure abroad, Zhukov began to choreograph the ballet. At the same time, he was also working on *Capriccio Espagnol*, first as Gorsky's co-choreographer, then independently. *Capriccio Espagnol* was the first to be performed, on May 9, 1923. The conductor Nikolai Golovanov and the designer Fedorovsky worked with Zhukov on this ballet. The authors came to the conclusion that it was impossible to create a story ballet in traditional form to the music of *Capriccio Espagnol*, and their goal became the creation of a "pictorial rhythmic fragment." They announced their impressionistic approach to the production and their intention to start with the music and freely interpret the ethnographic material. The ballet's time of action was the Renaissance. The ballet was to depict "the clash of robust popular spirit with the gloomy fantasy of the Middle Ages, against a background of carnival celebration."[2] Iving's review helps in reconstructing the appearance of this ballet.[3]

The ballet began with the characters coming in front of the proscenium "in dim red-violet light that lends their outlines an odd instability and ominousness." The curtain opened, and the stage blazed with all the colors of southern nature. A yellow as penetrating as summer heat suggested burnt cliffs and sand-covered arenas; red, the color of violent joy, the color of passion and blood, blazed in all hues; next to them was velvet black, as deep as night.

The dances themselves were constructed along the same principle of the opposition of light and dark. The choreographer used sinuous circling formations as the basis for the dances of the villagers. Half-naked mountaineers trampled the earth with powerful muscular legs; peasant women in multi-colored skirts whirled at breakneck speed: "wild leaps, sharp strokes of the hands, untamed turbulence of movement." The dances of the city women and toreadors were austerely linear. Parallel to the footlights lined up rows of women in black, close fitting dresses with high headdresses like the mitres of ancient priestesses and identical dark spitcurls. In their movements there was a triumphant equanimity and a certain gloomy, ominous strength. Their poses changed: "First they kneel on one leg and lean the whole body back, waving a fan, then haughtily move a shoulder forward," but always identically, always "in a uniform turn." The configurations of the dance also changed: "at times they occupy the center of the stage; at times they stop at the steps of the staircase . . . but they are always parallel to the footlights, always on a horizontal." The toreadors were a match for the women. Their dances, distinguished by external harmony, gave rise to a sensation of an internal lack of freedom. The precise, regulated movements revealed people who have totally mastered the art of killing "beautifully."

Capriccio Espagnol was a success. Zhukov was praised both as a choreographer and as a performer—for his appearance in the role of the half-savage shepherd Guido.

The ballet *Schéhérazade* was shown half a year later on December 16, 1923. Golovanov again took an active part in the work, but the designer Fedorovsky gave the production over to his student, Mikhail Sapegin. This was the first theatrical experience for the beginning artist, and it did not bring him fame. Critics were unanimously negative regarding both the mise-en-scène and the choreography.

As in *Capriccio Espagnol*, the authors did not try for historical accuracy in the dance, decor, and costumes. "The style of *Schéhérazade* is Persia, but we modeled it neither after old rugs, nor enamels, nor ancient Persian miniatures, nor did we base it on ethnography and archaeology."[4] Having rejected archaeological naturalism, the choreographer chose the path of stylization, which this time led him into a cliché. In the ballet "a very conventional and not very worthwhile Orientalism" reigned.[5]

The scenario, composed by Zhukov, proved unsuccessful. The authors made a mistake in departing from the rules they themselves had previously proclaimed—not to impose on Rimsky-Korsakov's music a plot that was unnecessarily concrete or complicated by external details. As Sidorov wrote,

The production resembles *The Flying Dutchman*, but with a touch of revolutionary color, when the girl pathetically begs the jailer to hand her the keys and free some slaves along with the "son of the leader of the mountains" (so it seems). Meanwhile, the latter, in quite an elegant pose, is motionless in the middle of the stage. . . . All this "ideology" takes place in a dream and ends with the royal reprisal, after the liberated Zhukov has several times carelessly dragged Reisen along the deck of the ship in erotic ecstasy.[6]

The virtue of the ballet *Capriccio Espagnol* lay in the dances, which showed Spain as Rimsky-Korsakov had heard and portrayed it. One of the basic flaws in *Schéhérazade* was its paucity of dance. Here a great deal of the blame must go to the designer of the ballet, who created a set one could move around on only with the greatest difficulty. The stage represented a tremendous ship, whose deck was tilted in such a manner that the bow was inclined at an angle of approximately 30 degrees. All the action took place on this inclined surface. As one of the reviewers wrote, "One could guarantee that any race horse prancing along such an incline would get a classic case of muscle strain."[7] On the right side of the stage was a gap where the choreographer had to concentrate most of the dancers. Here there was always darkness and commotion. Behind it rose an edifice that suggested a Buddhist temple. The scenery and costumes were opulent: waves of silk, gauze, and velvet, golden decorations, and multi-colored stones. One of the critics even compared Sapegin to Bakst. But the fundamental difference between the artists lay in the fact that Bakst, like no one else, sensed the nature of dance movement, while Sapegin clothed Reisen in a costume of which, in Sidorov's words, "the entire front part turned out to be an immobile thick stone cuirass, completely concealing her movement."[8]

Zhukov's choreographic experiments in many respects repeated Fokine's achievements. This is logical, considering Zhukov's work in Diaghilev's theatrical enterprise. The Moscow choreographer's use of the themes of the Ballets Russes was all the more natural because Diaghilev's productions did not then find their way to the imperial stage. In going the way of Fokine, Zhukov achieved something in *Capriccio Espagnol*. The contrast of the two elements—spontaneity and reason, life-creating and death-bearing—gave birth to conflict. And this conflict was made manifest in dance images.

In presenting *Schéhérazade*, Zhukov made an attempt to "go beyond" Fokine. To Fokine's treatment of Rimsky-Korsakov's poem he opposed his own, claiming "modernity." Hence the motif of the popular uprising and hence also the constructivist stage design; both were a tribute to either politics or fashion. The construction not only did not help the choreographer reveal to the audience the movement of the ensemble on stage in a new way (as Tairov had dreamed, shortly before this),[9] it was not the "basis for the performer's movement"—but it did interfere with perception of the visual image. Therefore Alexei Gvozdev had cause to write about the "utter failure of constructivist principles in the ballet *Schéhérazade*."[10] After *Schéhérazade*, Zhukov planned another ballet to the music of Rimsky-Korsakov, *Antar*, but this ballet was not staged.

Vasily Dmitrievich Tikhomirov

Vasily Tikhomirov was the leading classical dancer in the Bolshoi Theater for over thirty years. Educated first in Moscow and then in St. Petersburg, he knew the traditions of both schools and was familiar with the repertory of both theaters. The Petersburg "mettle" also made itself felt later on: Tikhomirov's object of special concern was always the purity of the classical forms of the dance. Tikhomirov often opposed Gorsky's attempts at breaking academic canons. In objecting to the reworkings Gorsky introduced into the old ballets, he was often right, but he tended to confuse traditionalism with traditions, and in many cases he took narrowly conservative positions.

All of Tikhomirov's major productions were staged in the mid-1920s. *Le Jardin animé*, to the music of Anton Simon, for the charity production of the Assembly of Nobles (1899), several dances from *Le Carnaval* (1913), and *Dances of The Nations* (1914) were all that he created prior to the revolution. Tikhomirov held a number of prominent administrative positions: He was ballet director in 1917, a member of the administration in 1919, and the director of the ballet repertory in 1926. As Gorsky fell ill and began to step aside from the leadership of the company, Tikhomirov's influence increased. In 1923 he introduced changes in *La Bayadère*, reinstating Petipa's "Kingdom of the Shades," which Gorsky had replaced in his production. In 1924 he was involved with the revival of *The Sleeping Beauty*. In 1925, for the hundredth anniversary of the Bolshoi Theater, Tikhomirov staged the second act of the ballet *La Sylphide*.

La Sylphide is the most famous ballet from the repertory of Marie Taglioni. She danced it in Russia in the 1830s, after which the ballet continued to run in Petersburg and Moscow. Petipa revived *La Sylphide* with few changes in 1892, when Tikhomirov was studying in the Petersburg school. In 1922 the ballet, as revised by Vladimir Ponomarev, was an examination performance for the graduating students of the Choreographic School in Petrograd.

Tikhomirov staged only the second act—the scene in the forest where James tries to catch the Sylphide, who flutters among the flowers. He succeeds with the help of a scarf given to him by the witch Madge. But James doesn't know that the evil witch wants revenge on him for an insult he once gave her. The scarf's touch proves fatal: the Sylphide loses her wings and with them her life. The premiere took place on February 2, 1925. The Sylphide was played by Geltser, James by Tikhomirov, and the witch by Alexei Bulgakov. The part of the light-winged sylph, so airy and fragile that any contact with reality was fatal to her, was in no way appropriate to Geltser's talents. Even in her youth, she never considered it proper to take on the role of Giselle. And yet *Giselle*, apart from the fantastic dances of the second act, contains a highly dramatic mad scene that could attract an actress such as Geltser. It is difficult to understand why she suddenly decided to dance *La Sylphide*, that most Romantic of ballets, toward the end of her career.

In staging *La Sylphide*, Tikhomirov sought ways to convey the spirit of the old ballet. The lines of the dance, "simple, calm, and austere," [11] were intended to suggest the prints of ballet scenes from the nineteenth century. The choreographer did not want to introduce into the ballet virtuosic steps that had arisen in later years, when dance technique was rapidly developing and changing.

Making the parts somewhat easier probably served the needs of the leading performers, but merely simplifying the dance proved insufficient to reproduce a Romantic ballet. While it did not have virtuoso spins, turns on pointe, or many other acrobatic steps, the Romantic ballet possessed its own technique, less brilliant but more refined. This was the technique of shades and nuances, gentle transitions, silent flight, and prolonged pauses on half-pointe. Such movements, as well as the special "flying" positions of the arms, imbued the dance with a rare poesy.

The Romantic ballet was primarily spiritual. The dances performed on the stage of the Bolshoi Theater were devoid of this quality. Iving laid the blame on the corps de ballet, which supposedly contradicted the intentions of the choreographer, "destroying the style resurrected from the dust of the ages." [12] Apparently the dancers really could not fathom the spirit of the Romantic ballet, but the choreography itself was in fact far from it. The Leningrad musicologist Evgeny Braudo, who attended the premiere, expressed bewilderment about this performance of *La Sylphide*, "staged for some reason in the bonbon style of the 1880s."[13]

By the style of the 1880s the author of the review meant the customary manner of executing the grand divertissements of the nineteenth century. The virtuosic dancing of this age had its own characteristics, which the academic ballet preserved for the future. Polished on every facet to a diamond sheen, it had a precise, sharp line. Bravura of execution and a bold triumph over technical difficulties were its most important values. Deprived of its effects, such dancing inevitably had to look poor and inexpressive, but this did not lend it poetry. The attempt to impart lyricism to the dance approached sugariness, the "bonbon style."

Briefly put, the production of *La Sylphide* showed that it is possible to convey the style of a different age only by renouncing the customary formulae, reviving those already forgotten, and revealing the as yet unused possibilities of classical dance. This demands not only complete mastery of all the resources of contemporary technique, but also the ability to use them creatively. In *Chopiniana*, Fokine was able to impart the atmosphere of the Romantic ballet, but by no means did he limit himself in the means of expression. The ballerina's quick backward movement on pointe, unimaginable given the dance technique of the 1830s, magnificently expresses the poetry of the Romantic ballet when in Fokine's work it is performed with the accompanying cavalier just barely supporting the ballerina by the wings. That very flight on toe is not seen as a stunt; it helps to create an impression of airiness, of a smooth gliding above the earth. Goleizovsky went the same route when, at the time that Tikhomirov was producing *La Sylphide*, he had already begun to work on the ballet *Teolinda*.

Thanks to the participation of Geltser, whom the audience loved, *La Sylphide* remained in the repertory for some time. This production gave Tikhomirov the opportunity to work subsequently as an independent choreographer.

Many classical ballets still retained in Leningrad which were familiar to Tikhomirov were absent from the repertory of the Bolshoi Theater. For Geltser's sake, he decided to select a ballet built on dramatic clashes and saturated with powerful, "earthy" passions. The ballet *Esmeralda* answered all these demands. Adapted from Victor Hugo's novel *Notre-Dame de Paris* by the choreographer Jules Perrot and with music by

Cesare Pugni, the ballet was performed in Russia from 1848 on. The plot of the ballet was approximately the same as the plot of the opera libretto that Hugo himself wrote (1836). Already in the opera the anti-feudal motifs of the novel were muted. Under the pressure of the censors, the opera and then the ballet acquired a happy ending, and the character of Phoebus was completely changed: A brilliant officer whose thought-lessness is one of the reasons for the death of the gypsy girl turned into her noble defender and savior. In the opera and the ballet Claude Frollo became a man of the world; this also weakened the anti-clerical tendency of the work. Even the central theme of Hugo's novel was absent—the theme of the cathedral as a symbol of the medieval worldview, a huge structure at the foot of which feeble human fates are broken. All the action concentrated on the misfortunes of the heroine.

Even without the social acuity of its primary source, Perrot's ballet was not foreign to Hugo's Romanticism. It retained the novel's play of contrasts. Esmeralda is an idealized Romantic heroine, set off against the demonic villain Claude Frollo. The very character of Quasimodo is a contrast: His monstrous appearance hides a loving soul. The crowd, multicolored and multifarious, is portrayed according to Hugo's traditions.

At the end of the century *Esmeralda* was revived by Petipa in Petersburg (1886). Gradually the features of the ballet spectacles of the day began to creep into the work. The mass ensembles lost their meaning and became "dances for dancing's sake"; many mime scenes were eliminated. But in a number of cases the losses were compensated, even overcompensated. Thus, for example, Petipa put in a new episode at a ball—the dance of Esmeralda who has suddenly discovered that Phoebus, whom she loves, has a fiancée. A street dancer, invited for a fee, must entertain the guests, and Esmeralda dances "through her tears"; she cries and all the same continues to dance, while Gringoire, suspecting nothing, joyfully beats the tambourine.

Tikhomirov undoubtedly had some idea of Petipa's production, which was kept even after the revolution. He had performed in the Moscow version created by Joseph Mendès in 1890, and he used the materials of this production.[14] He was also acquainted with Gorsky's ballet on the same subject, *Gudule's Daughter* (1902). The question of the return of *Esmeralda* to the repertory of the Bolshoi Theater had come up in the early 1920s, but at that time the theater held off from this production "mostly because of the unresolved problem of money." [15] In 1922 it was impossible to find the means for producing a ballet in several acts with complicated scenery. By 1925 the financial position of the Bolshoi Theater had already changed somewhat. It depended on the audience to a greater degree than in the first years of the revolution, when tickets had been distributed through organizations, in part for free, and the theater had lived on state subsidies. Now the policies of the repertory were dictated to a considerable degree by box-office considerations. It was only worth spending money on the production and staging of a ballet if one could hope for good box-office sales.

At first *Esmeralda* provoked some doubts. At the very first meeting where the possibility of staging this ballet was discussed, Yuri Faier, at that time the chief conductor for the Bolshoi Ballet, began to talk about the music: "Along with a number of strengths—danceability, melodiousness, a special lightness and 'comfort' for the creation of various choreographic scenes, this music is not always expressive and is poorly orchestrated; its lightness often turns into a simplification in the outline of the characters," he said, and he advised that Glière rework Pugni's music for the revival. [16]

It was not easy to obtain agreement from the composer to take upon himself such a thankless task. But once he agreed, Glière had a conscientious attitude toward the work at hand. He tried, with the help of more contemporary instrumentation, to give the ballet some unity. Asafiev was in general critical of the results of his work:

> Glière has orchestrated Pugni's ballet richly and amply, sonorously, and at the same time lightly, but on the whole in a quite ordinary way, rejecting subtle devices and without changing the harmonic base. It is pleasant to listen to, although at the same time it is somehow uncomfortable; the colorful "style" of the ballet in places does not at all fit the "two plus two equals four" of the smartly ordinary orchestration. On the one hand, its saccharine beauty is not strong enough to hide the intolerably trivial motifs and the wretched structure of Pugni's music, and on the other hand, the Glière lacquer monotonously coats even those few old-fashioned but pleasant colorations that still glimmered here and there. [17]

Nevertheless, Tikhomirov's new choreographic decision demanded just such a reduction of the music to a common denominator. The choreographer examined the ballet from a position of realism and reality, paying attention to the justification of the plot situations. In editing the music Glière repeated the themes belonging to the characters in appropriate places in order to "emphasize the dramatic moments and give the audience a musical illustration of what was happening on stage."[18] He added to the introduction and expanded the finale of the ballet.

In the reworked plot modern motifs were emphasized. Tikhomirov said that "one of the reasons for staging *Esmeralda* for modern man is that *Esmeralda* particularly brilliantly shows those building the new world what oppression and violence we have left behind."[19] Therefore he deemed it necessary to introduce into the ballet the theme of the cathedral as the expression of the ideas of the Middle Ages.

In Perrot's ballet attention is focused on the individual fates of main characters. In *Gudule's Daughter* Gorsky created a unique chronicle of medieval life in which the cathedral, while not occupying the major place, does in the last act prove to be at the center of attention. It is a silent witness to the evil deeds of Frollo, the meetings of Esmeralda with her mother, and the despair and death of Gudule; it is attacked by the crowd. The concluding scene of the ballet is played out on its highest tower: Quasimodo throws Frollo off as he watches the execution of Esmeralda. Tikhomirov emphasized the theme of the cathedral in every possible way. He created a prologue, for which Glière wrote new music and Mikhail Kurilko made a very impressive set: The cathedral, huge and gloomy, rose over the entire stage. It suppressed everything bright and joyful. In its shadow crimes multiplied. And it is in this very place where the dark genius of Notre-Dame, the archdeacon of Paris, Claude Frollo, lurks motionless among the chimeras baring their teeth. For Tikhomirov, Frollo is a priest, as in Hugo's novel; he is the personification of clerical fanaticism and hypocrisy. The idea that Esmeralda is a victim of the Inquisition is emphasized in the scene of the procession to the execution, when a crowd of churchmen come out of the cathedral and admonish the sinner.

Like Gorsky, Tikhomirov made it his goal to bring out the theme of the people and to emphasize social themes. It is not by chance that on the playbills the ballet was subtitled *Daughter of the People*, perhaps in intentional opposition to Gorsky's ballet, *Gudule's Daughter*. In *Gudule's Daughter* the people, wretched and unfortunate, were indifferent to Esmeralda's fate. At the tragic moment before her execution, only her mad mother defended her. Moreover, Gorsky emphasized that in their misfortune the people could be cruel as well. The tortures Quasimodo was subjected to by the executioner aroused the curiosity of the crowd which gloated over his fate; this episode occupied a large place in the ballet. The reviewers even protested against the length and "gloomy colors" of the scene of "Quasimodo's punishment and the crowd's mockery of him."[20] Tikhomirov said that in *his* ballet "the crowd . . . reacts to even the smallest events. This mob of Paris paupers plays a very active role in the production, which is entirely constructed on the idea . . . of expressing its search for truth, its search for light. . . . This crowd must fill the entire ballet with spirit."[21]

In fact, it turned out somewhat differently. Tikhomirov's characterization of the people was highly inconsistent, because it was put together primarily from scenes that initially had been in completely different ballets. The "Court of Miracles" in many respects suggests Gorsky's production. It is a gathering of wanderers, thieves, and brigands; cripples who throw away their crutches and begin to dance; a "legless" beggar who slithers out of a cart and rises to his feet. Perhaps in Tikhomirov's ballet they were portrayed less naturalistically than in Gorsky's, but nevertheless, in following the old plan, he cast them in the role of Esmeralda's betrayers. Three "kings" of the "Court of Miracles" (they also appeared first in Gorsky's ballet) come to an agreement with Claude Frollo and sell him the gypsy girl. They attack Gringoire, who tries to defend her. This episode was taken from the Perrot-Petipa production (only in that one there was only one "king"—Clopin Trouillefou); this episode was not in Gorsky's version. And the crowd is presented completely differently in the last act. At the doors of the torture chamber the people show their grief and indignation; the women weep. After finding out at the last moment before the execution that Claude Frollo has slandered the gypsy girl, the crowd is ready to tear him to pieces. And, after the clash of Claude Frollo with Phoebus and Quasimodo, when the priests carry the archdeacon's corpse into the church, the people lay siege to the cathedral. Iving describes this scene as follows: "Some begin to hurl stones at the statues of the kings that decorate the parvis. Others try to set the temple afire. The crowd lifts up the unconscious Esmeralda and . . . carries her like a banner."[22]

The character Phoebus is contradictory. As is apparent from the choreographer's scenario, at the ball of Fleur-de-Lys he first behaves in a cowardly manner: "Phoebus turns to Esmeralda, and she rushes toward him—but he coldly orders her to dance."[23] However, at the end of the act, when the mother of Fleur-de-Lys chases the gypsies, Phoebus announces that they are "under his protection, approaches Esmeralda and embraces her, and then they both leave."[24] Nevertheless, in the next scene he again "confesses his love to Esmeralda with the methods of an inveterate rake."[25] In the last scene, Phoebus brings the royal order to free Esmeralda to the foot of the scaffold. And in the finale, leaning against the gallows, he observes the crowd's attack on the cathedral. He watches, apparently, not without sympathy, because Iving concludes the plot description with the following words: "He is a nobleman and he is superfluous in a people's uprising."[26]

Phoebus was played by Tikhomirov and was, as Sergei Gorodetsky wrote, "as handsome as an epic hero."[27] In his interpretation Tikhomirov was obviously leaning toward the traditions of Petipa's ballet—to portray Phoebus as the noble savior of the street dancer. But at certain moments he was attracted by Gorsky who, following Hugo, portrayed Phoebus as frivolous, complacent, and ruthless: in Gorsky's version Phoebus appeared at a balcony with his fiancée at the moment when Esmeralda was being led to the gallows, and at the sight of the condemned girl, who extends her hands to him, he quickly disappeared.

There were members of the press who called upon Tikhomirov to change the conclusion of the ballet so that Esmeralda would be saved from death not through the intervention of Phoebus but by the revolt of the crowd. They also suggested "a more negative shading of Phoebus's character."[28] Undoubtedly, a tragic finale, as in Gorsky's ballet, would have been closer to Hugo's work. But Tikhomirov could not reject such heart-rending scenes as the appearance of the "resurrected" Phoebus at the very moment when the noose is thrown around the neck of the condemned girl; he had to show innocence triumphant and vice punished. The genre of the new ballet verged on the melodrama so popular in the first years after the October Revolution.

Melodrama is democratic in its own way, for it can be grasped by the most unsophisticated viewer. The idea in it is directly manifest, the characterizations are categorical (the author straightforwardly announces his sympathies and antipathies), and the situations allow for the heightened play of passions. Certainly an enthusiasm for melodrama found a reflection in the first attempts of the Soviet ballet theater. Such scenes as the appearance of Odile observing the meeting of Odette and the prince and her madness in the *Swan Lake* of 1920 are melodramatic.

The "accessibility" of melodrama also had its reverse side. The theaters, cautious about social themes, turned to melodrama as a unique surrogate for revolutionary plays. "Political literacy" was served up here in a way entirely acceptable to Philistine tastes. The innocently suffering heroine of the people, or the noble pauper, provoked inevitable sympathy, and the rich man provoked hostility. Meanwhile, the audience was not being shown real life; it was protected from everything that could touch it directly. It was a falsification, and necessarily a "pretty" falsification.

It is not surprising that the attraction of melodrama increased further during the NEP years. Melodramas or the romantic dramas akin to them were produced by the academic theaters, penetrated into the studios, and even onto the popular (people's) club stages, squeezing out the experimental, sometimes awkwardly shaped, modern plays.

The role of Esmeralda in Tikhomirov's ballet generally corresponded to the old version. This conclusion may be drawn from a note in Geltser's own handwriting, which she wrote during the rehearsals. The dancer set down her own mise-en-scène with separate explanations, and sometimes questions. The notebooks that have been preserved describe the first two scenes and the beginning of the last scene of the ballet. Here is Esmeralda's entrance:

Off-stage the tambourines beat out eight bars; she does not enter. Entrance. A gypsy takes her by the hand, pulls at her, and asks if she has earned much money dancing. She says that she was dancing far away and has fetched a lot of money; she takes out a little pouch; and at this point Gringoire falls between her and the gypsy, and she is startled and asks who he is. The gypsy tells her that they wanted to hang him and she repeats . . . to hang him . . . but what is to be done? The gypsy says to her that she must ask the women nearby if one of them will marry him. She goes to the left, asks, and is refused. She says to the gypsy that no one has agreed. She goes to the right, is refused, and again she repeats that no one agrees. Then she goes in a circle, thinking, her hand to her forehead, and says that she will marry him.

Then there is a description of the action up to the end of the first scene: the buffoon-like "wedding" and the general merry-making. The second scene is devoted to Esmeralda's meeting with Phoebus. Egged on by Claude Frollo, Quasimodo tried to kidnap Esmeralda with the help of the gypsies. Phoebus rescues her. Their declaration follows, after which Phoebus gives the gypsy girl a scarf. Then the whole mise-en-scène made famous by Fanny Elssler's performance is reproduced exactly: Esmeralda traces the letters that spell Phoebus on the floor and dances around them, then teaches Gringoire to accompany her on the tambourine. The scene ends dramatically: Frollo appears and pleads for Esmeralda's love, but she runs away.

From the description, it is obvious that Geltser's part subordinated the dance to dramatic performance. The basic action episodes were in mime; sometimes the pantomime was embellished with dancing, but there was little pure dance. Apparently the most significant scene was the famous *pas d'action* by Marius Petipa, which Tikhomirov kept in the third act. Here Geltser's dramatic gifts were evident, while the form remained that of the dance. "Flashes of jealousy are communicated with striking artistic veracity, without turning her head toward Phoebus, but with an internal, pent-up feeling. . . . The dancer's whole body weeps. . . ."[29] In the last scene of the ballet, the procession to the execution, Geltser portrayed the exhausted girl, mutilated by torture, with the utmost realism. In her notebook, she wrote:

Esmeralda comes out the door. She takes two steps, her arms dangling, her knees bent. She wants to hold herself erect but falls, seizing the door. Meanwhile, her head droops and her hand hangs lifelessly. She gets up, gazing straight ahead (her arms also drop, dead weights), as if she wants to take two steps, and she falls, holding onto her leg, entirely limp. Then she lifts her head, but her head can no longer support itself. She moves with her head hanging. Two steps totally drooping. Then she wants to take two ordinary steps and again falls to the floor to the left, grasping her arm. And here she suffers terribly.

Geltser's part was conceived with the idea, as Volynsky wrote, of "having the dance melt in the fire of dramatic talent." [30] Praising Geltser and comparing her with Eleonora Duse and Sarah Bernhardt, the critic explained his idea: "It is not necessary to discuss separately the choreographic part of Geltser's performance of this role. That is only a detail, which one sees but which does not control the impression. The dramatic theme, however, grows into something grandiose." Alexander Tcherepnin wrote: "In the Moscow production, Esmeralda does not dance, she performs. She doesn't dance, but she depicts dance. The dance here is not autonomous, a separate objective per se but only an accompanying feature of the genre that flows from the plot." [31]

The divertissements were intended to compensate for the scarcity of dance in the dramatic episodes. The press noted the success of the dance of the gypsy girls introduced in the first act, for which Glière wrote new music. The greatest innovation was an entire ballet inserted in the third act, at Fleur-de-Lys's ball. The idea of such a "ballet within a ballet" was undoubtedly prompted by Gorsky, in whose *Gudule's Daughter* the ballet *Time* was performed at a ball. In Tikhomirov's production, the performers depicted personages figuring in the tapestry presented to Fleur-de-Lys. These were Diana, in a light blue tunic with a crescent on her head and a bow in her hand, and Venus, in a pink chiton. Fleur-de-Lys herself, clothed in green, represented Flora. Next to her appeared sun-yellow Apollo, Zephyr, Pan, and the Three Graces, whitened so that they seemed to be made of marble, as well as a variety of fauns, nymphs, and bacchantes. This mythological ballet, using purely classical dances, allowed Tikhomirov to sparkle because it was staged precisely as a divertissement from the "grand ballet" of the nineteenth century, and not at all as a dance performance from the early Renaissance. The best performers in the troupe—Podgoretskaya, Valentina Kudriavtseva, Abramova, Ilyushchenko, and Asaf Messerer—appeared here in the variations.

The critics were divided in their assessment of *Esmeralda*. The majority noted the success of the theater, which for the first time in many years had produced a monumental ballet in several acts. Almost all praised Geltser. But the ballet also had its critics. For example, Vladimir Blum, always opposed to the academic theaters, protested against a "daughter of the people . . . in a tutu lined with silver brocade, with the traditional little goat which she coquettishly hands someone (a maid? a confidante?) on the spot."[32] The theater undoubtedly provided grounds for such criticism when, having made realistic pantomime the basic means of expression, it also kept many conventions of the old ballet. This ambivalent *Esmeralda* was uniquely described by Asafiev, to whom the ballet seemed a mixture of old syrup and new sugar, as a result of which "some pleasure is obtained, but with a constant sensation of an admixture in which the sugar interferes with the syrup and vice versa."[33]

The compromises of the ballet were felt within the theater as well. This found expression in a *raeshnik*,* a witty but malicious caricature in verse, written by one of the members of the Bolshoi Theater orchestra, Yakov Korolev. Complaining that "It has no tune and makes no sense, affording little recompense," he ironically depicted a production with "Esmeralda, daughter of the people, and Quasimodo, son of the people, and Notre-Dame's panorama, and a bustle onstage and colors in a rage. . . ." The ultimate conclusion was that "the ballet will net a profit."[34] And here the author of the *raeshnik* proved right. The audience quite eagerly attended the new ballet. *Esmeralda*, first shown on February 7, 1926, ran the greatest number of times (22) and yielded the biggest box office of all the ballet productions of the Bolshoi Theater, although the house did not sell out.[35] At the end of the 1925–26 season, the editorial board of the magazine *Zhizn iskusstva* conducted a poll of the audiences of a number of Moscow theaters. Of the 2,017 people polled, *Esmeralda* attracted the attention of 41 people, of whom 36 liked it and five did not.[36] In the total list of productions, the ballet took twelfth place. But for the Bolshoi Theater, which was at that time in a state of acute financial crisis, even that result was good. Inspired by their success, the authors of *Esmeralda* decided to continue their collaboration.

The Red Poppy

At around the time of the premiere of *Esmeralda*, Glière was working on another ballet at the request of the Bolshoi Theater—*The Daughter of the*

---

*The *raeshnik* was a form of satirical, topical, rhymed verse modeled after, and reminiscent of, the spiels that accompanied the peepshows at eighteenth- and nineteenth-century Russian fairs. The word derives from *raek*, meaning peepshow (which Mussorgsky used as a title for a song). (Ed.)

Port. The book, written by the poet Mikhail Galperin, who then served as literary consultant at the Bolshoi Theater, was given to the composer in late September 1925.[37] At that time Zhukov, the intended choreographer, announced in an interview that the plot of the ballet "embraces the early days of the French Revolution, when the French outlying districts learn about the fall of the Bastille."[38] It is clear from the materials in the archives of the Bolshoi Theater that the premiere was to be in late January 1926 and then was put off until the end of May. In early 1926 the designer Sergei Sokolov presented a number of sketches and the director Valentin Smyshliayev was invited to assist Zhukov. They were to begin production work on February 5, and on the 15th Glière was to present the finished score.

And suddenly at the end of February everything changed. On the 26th a meeting was called by the directorate of the Bolshoi Theater with Tikhomirov, Geltser, Kurilko, Glière, and Faier. At this meeting, the libretto of the ballet *The Daughter of the Port* was rejected: it was found to be "insufficiently dynamic, boring in content, and not ready to be transposed into music."[39] At the same time, the libretto worked out by Kurilko together with Tikhomirov and Geltser for the ballet *The Red Poppy* was presented, and this was found to be "interesting in terms of content and desirable for production in the Bolshoi Theater during the present season." Meanwhile, Glière agreed "to transfer the musical arrangements for the ballet *The Daughter of the Port* to the musical arrangement for *The Red Poppy*." Alexander Shiriayev was invited from Leningrad to replace Zhukov, who was going abroad. Sokolov was replaced as designer with Kurilko. From that day a new ballet—*The Red Poppy*—appeared in the plan of the Bolshoi Theater.

The text of the scenario which Kurilko submitted in February 1926 is not preserved in the archives of the Bolshoi Theater, but apparently it was quite different from the final version. From the announcements about the ballet appearing at various times in the press, it is clear that during the process of work not only the details, but even the treatment of the main characters changed. At first the plot was set forth as follows:

A Soviet ship moors on the shores of China. . . . Dark forces try by means of bribery or deceit to weaken the vigilance of the guards and to rob the steamship or seize it. To this end, the "hetaera" of the port enters; she is known as The Red Poppy. She is an elemental

232

force, a fire-breathing volcano, a thunderstorm, and the idol of the port. And all the hopes of a band of evil-minded pirates to "win over" the captain are pinned on her. In the ballet there is an opium den, a palace of the governor, etc.; the most interesting characters are the father of the hetaera, a worker with no class consciousness, and the Chinese coolies who instinctively sense that the sailors are their friends. The most enthralling moment occurs when the hetaera of the port tries, through bribery and female wiles, to lure the captain into betrayal, but he, firm and unbending, does not give in. The astonishment of the hetaera and her father, who stands nearby, is boundless. This moment is a turning point for The Red Poppy and her father. Class consciousness awakens within them. At the decisive moment The Red Poppy goes over to the side of the Soviet sailor, and her superhuman activity saves the steamship, which safely sails out to sea to the strains of "The Internationale" and the enthusiastic shouts of the coolies.[40]

As is apparent from this note, already at the earliest stage the arrival of a Soviet ship in a Chinese port served as the catalyst for the action. But here, unlike later versions of the scenario, the conflict was built on the threat of the ship's seizure. Kurilko wrote that the idea of showing a Soviet ship was inspired by a notice in the newspaper describing the merchant ship *Lenin*, illegally detained in a Chinese port.[41] In Glière's words, "the idea of the creation of such a ballet (a Soviet captain, a ship, a port, the indignation of the oppressed) was that of the directorate of the theater."[42] In this early version of the libretto, the principal character was that of a "vamp," a temptress, as in quite a few old ballets.

Galperin, the author of the rejected scenario for *The Daughter of the Port*, stuck to the same outline when the directorate suggested that he fill out Kurilko's book so that Glière could continue work with him. Glière rejected this project, but on May 24, 1926, Galperin nevertheless submitted his version of the scenario, entitled "The Red Poppy (The Secret of the Chinese Tavern)."[43]

The action of the ballet takes place in a Chinese port city. The heroine of the ballet is a dancer, but not Chinese—a Frenchwoman, Jeanne. The conflict revolves not around the Soviet ship, but around a diplomatic document: The white colonizers have been trying to get a Chinese Mandarin to sign it, and with this in mind they send him the dancer.

233

The coolies and Chinese revolutionaries, headed by the Russian sailor Krasnov, formerly on the *Potemkin*,* discover the plot. Jeanne, who is infatuated with Krasnov, joins the insurgents. The ballet concludes with the march of the detachments of the people's army, a dance by Jeanne with the red flag, and the appearance at sea of a ship on whose deck is written "Hands off China!" Individual details of the scenario coincide with the future ballet: There is the tavern where they smoke opium, the scene of the "corruption" of the whites, the scene of the coolies unloading the ship. The characteristics of the music of the unloading scene in Galperin's version rather precisely coincide with Glière's (the episode "The Steps of the Coolies"): "The movements of the stevedores are slow and rhythmic, and the music accompanying their measured work is somewhat gloomy and heavy, suggesting some sort of funeral march."[44]

The main action of the ballet was to consist of the conspiracy of the colonizers and the uprising they provoke, and to this was added the story of Jeanne, a melodrama with a touch of the detective story. Kurilko and his co-authors, having rejected adventure motifs (the attempt at seizing the ship) during their work, concentrated their attention on the relationship of Jeanne to the Soviet captain.

The Red Poppy was basically created through the efforts of the same people who had just put together *Esmeralda*. The discussions with Alexander Monakhov and Alexander Chekrygin, in Leningrad, concluded unsuccessfully; Tikhomirov was appointed choreographer for the production. An agreement was also concluded with the director Alexei Dikiy, who agreed to advise the collaborators.[45] Faier worked with Glière. Kurilko had a dual role—that of scenarist and set designer. Soon, however, it became clear that they were a long way from unanimity. "The participation of so many collaborators made the work of composing particularly complex, because each one introduced his own ideas, . . . often totally failing to coordinate them with the plans of his colleagues for development of the plot," recalled Glière.[46] The main problem was that the authors saw the future ballet in different ways.

The second, fantastic act ("The Dream of Tao-Hoa"), about which not a word is said in the early versions of the plot of *The Red Poppy*, was

---

*The battleship *Potemkin*, immortalized by Sergei Eisenstein in his eponymous film, had briefly mutinied against Tsarist authority during the abortive revolution of 1905. (Ed.)

apparently created on Tikhomirov's insistence. "Glière and Tikhomirov spent the summer in Kislovodsk, where the second act of the ballet in fact was written—"The Dream," recalls Kurilko.[47] Faier writes in his memoirs that Tikhomirov considered "acceptable only the second act with the traditional divertissement."[48]

From the papers preserved in Glière's archives it is clear that even in the first scene of this act, an introductory dance episode was thought up as a divertissement along the lines of the ballet spectacles of the nineteenth century. It in no way corresponds to the other totally realistic acts or to the action of the given scene; it is a dance of chess pieces. When the captain is lured into the opium den to be killed, he sits down to play chess. "Two servants come out and open a chessboard." After this follows "The Entrance of the Pieces." They march in—white Chinese chess pieces and then red ones, accompanied by the theme of the song "Dubinushka."[49]

While Tikhomirov and Glière were working in Kislovodsk, Dikiy, who was on tour, received a telegram from the theater administration asking him to create a scenario "at least for the first act." He was also asked to assume responsibility for the general direction of the ballet and was assured that the choreographer would be subordinate to him.[50] And it was Dikiy who introduced corrections into the script, as Glière testifies,[51] and later took on the direction of the ballet as well. As a performer at the premiere, Maria Gorshkova, writes, "The directorial hand of Alexei Denisovich Dikiy was evident."[52]

Could one be surprised that what Tikhomirov invented was not to Dikiy's liking? Although he apparently found a common language with Lashchilin, the choreographer for the first act, as consultant for the entire ballet Dikiy ultimately either had to step aside or insist on his own way. Traces of this struggle are preserved in documents in the Bolshoi Theater archives. In October 1926 Dikiy requested that his name not be put on the playbill; in November he refused to sign the minutes of a meeting whose resolutions he did not agree with; in December, though, he concluded a contract to direct the production, apparently hoping thus to increase his authority. Yet, as Asaf Messerer, one of the performers in the ballet, recalls, after having made "an outline of the first act, in which there proved to be a lot of new things—beginning with the scene of the unloading of the ship and ending with the finale, 'Yablochko,' Dikiy had to refuse to direct the last scenes."[53] Moreover, when in March 1927 the arts council suggested releasing Dikiy from work on *The Red Poppy*, the decision was based on Tikhomirov's statement that the director apparently "up to now in fact has not participated in the staging of the ballet."[54] As a result, the honor of creating *The Red Poppy* for many years was for the most part ascribed to Tikhomirov, who in reality composed only the second act (drafts of the mise-en-scène have been preserved)[55] and Geltser's dances, since during these years the ballerina worked only with him. Lashchilin, who on the playbill was always listed second, was sometimes remembered as the creator of the dances in the first and third acts; it was completely forgotten that the strength of the ballet lies precisely in those acts. An extremely modest person, Lashchilin in fact claimed no credit at all and during the revival of the ballet in late 1949 he simply stepped aside. It is worth noting that in January 1950 Glière gave Tikhomirov a letter of reference to the effect that he worked in close contact with Tikhomirov as the "primary choreographer" and that "the role of V. D. Tikhomirov in the creation of *The Red Poppy* must be considered extremely important."[56] As concerns Dikiy, he ceased to be mentioned at all in connection with *The Red Poppy*.

The differences of opinion between Dikiy and Tikhomirov were not the only factor complicating work on the staging. *The Red Poppy* was born in an atmosphere of bitter quarrels and mistrust. In the theater, there were few who believed there could be a successful re-working of the music and scenario of *The Daughter of the Port* and even fewer who believed in the possibility of creating a revolutionary ballet with the efforts of such inveterate "academics" as Tikhomirov and Geltser. All the authors of the ballet later recalled the difficult conditions in which the work was done.[57] This is also mentioned in the documents of the period. A memorandum devoted to problems of the repertory of the theater after the opening of *The Red Poppy* states: "This production had an uneasy birth. We barely succeeded in scraping together a creative team. . . . The permanent staff resolutely avoided this piece. At one time the choreographers had to invite directors from Leningrad, from the dramatic theater. And pressure, endless pressure. . . . More than once the whole thing fell apart and we lost hope."[58]

The very method of work involved tremendous difficulties for the collaborators. Glière could not keep up with the choreographers. Literally on the run, while the authors were refining the details of the scenario, he was composing the music, often making use of his own old works, putting into *The Red Poppy* not only music from *The Daughter of the Port* but also some from his earlier ballet, *Chrysis*. Kurilko, for his part, could not decide on the sets, which also hindered production.

The history of the "Yablochko" dance is a good indication of this. For a long time, Glière could not compose a dance for the Red sailors in the first act. He wrote a Russian dance tune to the theme of the folksong "Hey, you Vanka, bend and bow"[59] which apparently was not successful. Then the idea arose of using the theme of the *chastushka** "Hey, little apple, where are you rolling to. . . ." It is impossible to determine now exactly who had the honor of inventing this. Faier remembers how after long vacillation he gave Glière this idea. Kurilko maintains that he was the initiator, and it seems to Lashchilin that the idea originated with him. Asaf Messerer's evidence, ascribing the authorship to Dikiy, is also quite logical. He points out that Dikiy was already using the song "Yablochko" in another production: "He really loved that song; in his *The Flea*,** when the ministers see what Lefty has made, they prostrate themselves to its motif and move on all fours around the remarkable mechanical toy."[60] In fact, generally it would be more likely to expect such a daring proposal (as it was then considered) from Dikiy, a man of rich imagination inclined to bold, even mischievous resolutions, than from the other authors of the ballet, who thought primarily in traditional terms.

And really it is not that important who first thought of "Yablochko." The idea was born. It is true that it was not immediately to everyone's taste. The memoirists are united in their description of the composer's first reaction: Glière was insulted to hear such a suggestion. As Messerer says, the orchestra of the Bolshoi Theater also warned that it would not play a "street song." But, as is evident, the rebellion soon quieted down. Glière considered it possible to make use of this advice, in any case. The "Yablochko" motif was at the basis of the sailors' dance, which was probably the most popular number of the ballet; moreover, it became the leitmotif for the Soviet sailors, appearing also in the music of the introduction and in the scene at the opium den.

---

*A *chastushka* is a brief, humorous, often topical folksong. (Ed.)

**Dikiy directed *The Flea*, by Evgeny Zamyatin (based on the story "Lefty" by Nikolai Leskov), at the Second Moscow Art Theater in 1925. (Ed.)

The episode with Glière and his taking offense at "Yablochko" is interesting not just as an anecdote. The idea of using such music on the lyric stage at that time was bound to give rise to doubts. But the point is that *The Red Poppy* absorbed a great deal that at the time was, so to speak, "in the air." In analyzing the ballet, removing layer after layer, we find in each new stratum something of the vivid impressions of these days, some links to current events, to current interests, to the art and mores of the age. The authors of the ballet were able, in each separate instance, to notice and bring out on stage what at the moment was new, relevant, popular, or even simply fashionable.

First of all, a politically compelling topic was selected. It was no accident that the authors firmly rejected the idea of a ballet about the French Revolution and turned toward China. Every day the newspapers reported on the growing Chinese revolutionary movement. In Moscow a society called "Hands off China!" was created; Chinese students were studying in Soviet universities. Many productions of the dramatic and musical theater were devoted to China: *Roar, China!*, by Sergei Tretyakov; *Locusts*, by Émile Fabre; Klabund's *Chang-hai-tang* (The Chalk Circle); *The Yellow Jacket* by Joseph Benrimo and George Hazelton. Even in Vsevolod Ivanov's *Armored Train No. 14-69* one of the heroes was Chinese. In vaudeville, Chinese dances and whole Chinese games were performed. The newspapers published articles about ancient art in China. But selecting the theme was not enough; some twist had to be found to make it serve as a basis for dance action. Here the authors took a well-traveled route and adapted the old forms of the pre-Fokine multi-act ballet to new content.

The Red Poppy was a ballet in three acts. The first act revolved around the embankment of a Chinese port city. A line of coolies was hauling cargo, and there was a bar where the idle public made merry. Malaysian girls danced for the Europeans, fond of things exotic. Another attraction was the dancing of the Chinese woman Tao-Hoa. Li Shan-Fu, an adventurer exploiting her talent, followed her like a shadow. The unloading of a Soviet steamship was in progress. One of the coolies fell under the weight of his load. The overseers tried to raise him with blows. The stevedores became agitated. At this point, the Soviet captain appeared on deck. With an authoritative gesture he commanded that the beating be stopped. Then he ordered his sailors to start work. The Russians and the Chinese quickly finished the unloading. Enchanted, Tao-Hoa strewed the Soviet captain with flowers. One—the red poppy—she put in his hands. Tao-Hoa's behavior aroused the displeasure of Li Shan-Fu, who crudely tore the dancer away. The captain stood up for her. Meanwhile, foreign sailors were gathering on the quay. The dance of the sailors from five parts of the world was crowned by the dance of the sailors from the Soviet steamship.

The first scene of the second act took place in a private house. Fearing the influence of the Russian sailors on the Chinese, who were ready to rebel, the harbor master, Sir Hips, intended to murder the Soviet captain. After welcoming the captain as a guest, the conspirators, headed by Li Shan-Fu, prepared to attack him, but just as they seized their knives, the captain whistled for his sailors. Tao-Hoa witnessed this scene and was deeply disturbed. In order to forget, she smoked opium and fell asleep near the aquarium, looking at the goldfish.

The following two scenes of the second act were devoted to the dreams of Tao-Hoa. The little goldfish, having increased in size, reached gigantic proportions. Out of the gloom emerged the colossal figure of a golden Buddha. The goddesses of ancient legend came to life; a procession of the deity's monstrous guards, warriors with swords, passed by. Tao-Hoa was borne on a litter to the statue of the Buddha. When she reached the foot of the sculpture, bright phoenixes appeared. Together with them she rushed toward the kingdom of dreams. The bright visions crowded out the horrors. Flowers came to life, butterflies and birds fluttered around. Red poppies called Tao-Hoa to the captain, who appeared in a red craft.

In the third act the action shifted to the house of a Chinese banker. A ball was going on, and the guests were dancing the foxtrot, the Boston waltz, and the Charleston; then the artists of the Chinese opera performed. Li Shan-Fu, seeing that the captain liked Tao-Hoa's dancing, decided that she must be the one to bring him the poisoned tea. Exchanging greetings with the captain, Tao-Hoa begged him to take her with him to the Soviet Union. The captain gently refused her request and presented her with a red poppy. The ceremony of tea drinking began. Tao-Hoa took the cup into which Sir Hips had poured the poison but, in giving it to the captain, she spilled the tea. Li Shan-Fu shot at the captain and missed. The guests fled in panic.

This scene led directly into the next one. The Soviet ship was departing, its way lit by the beacon of a lighthouse. Tao-Hoa stood on the embankment, gazing after it. A crowd of armed coolies appeared; a rebellion had started in the city. Taking advantage of the general confusion, Li Shan-Fu shot Tao-Hoa, and she fell. Women and children ran to her as she died. Before her death, Tao-Hoa handed a little Chinese girl the red poppy. The ballet concluded with a triumphant apotheosis.

In the very situations selected by the librettist there was an element of topicality. The opening of the ballet coincided with such events as the raid on the Soviet consulate in Canton, during which the consul and a number of employees perished. On June 7, 1927, the Soviet ambassador P. L. Voikov was killed in Poland. On June 9 there was a meeting in this regard in the Bolshoi Theater.

But the relevant subject was cast in traditional dramatic forms: The action developed in pantomime scenes interrupted by dance divertissements. In the first act this was the performance by the dancers at the port, then the dances of the sailors of various nationalities. In the second there was the grand classical divertissement—the dream. In the third there was the suite of Western dances at the ball in the banker's house and the performance of Chinese opera.

The element of divertissement was reflected in the music of *The Red Poppy*. Most integral proved to be the structure of the first act, where around the two divertissements (the dances in the bar and the dances of the sailors) were grouped musical numbers linked to the theme of the hard labor of the coolies and the indignation growing in their midst. Incomparably more stereotyped was the structure of the two following acts. Here the intervals between divertissements were numbers with abstractly emotional music which allowed for the construction of any pantomime scene "with feelings." It was not by chance that for these episodes the composer used a number of finished works: The scene where Tao-Hoa meditates after the attack on the captain was performed to the Prelude in C minor (Op. 26, no. 2); in the farewell episode in the third act, the action took place to *Romance* (Op. 16, no. 2); Tao-Hoa poured out her sorrow at the departure of the captain to *Chagrin* (Op. 21, no. 3). And, finally, the classical adagio of the second act was a well-known romance for the violin (Op. 3).

The librettists of *The Red Poppy* used many tried-and-true devices of the old ballet. Like Esmeralda and Nikiya, Tao-Hoa was made a dancer to justify her participation in the divertissement. The role of the traditional villain was introduced into the ballet—the adventurer Li Shan-Fu, who oppressed Tao-Hoa, took part in the conspiracy, and finally murdered her. The noble hero opposing him—the captain—was distinguished from the stereotypical positive heroes of the old ballet mostly by his costume. The attempt to identify a ballet character with the Russian national anthem, "The Internationale," raised doubts. The song was heard at his first appearance, was woven into the adagio in the second act, merging with a heart-rending violin romance (Op. 3), and rang out clearly in the apotheosis. This and many other examples of the mixture of revolutionary and artificial balletic motifs gave Alexander Tcherepnin cause to write, "You don't make a statue of a Red Army officer out of whipped cream."[61]

Yet in evaluating *The Red Poppy* now in the context of the developing art of the age, one sees that the authors of the ballet keenly observed the events of life around them. Much in *The Red Poppy* now seems hopelessly dated, but it really began as a quite timely work. The archaic quality of the ballet was itself symptomatic. It was precisely in the late 1920s, when the stormy wave of experimentalism began to subside and a return to a more normative aesthetic began, that it became easier for the adherents of academism to defend their positions. The form of *The Red Poppy* did seem traditional even in comparison with the art of the pre-October period. But the recourse to tradition was not at all accidental and is explained by more than just helplessness. *The Red Poppy* was created under the aegis of Geltser for Geltser. Implacably opposed to the innovations of the choreographers of the younger generation, Geltser and Tikhomirov tried to prove that through the canonical forms of the nineteenth-century ballet spectacle one can depict even revolution in China.

It was no coincidence that they both considered the most important thing in the ballet "The Dream" in the second act staged by Tikhomirov, the very scene criticized by both the partisans and opponents of the production. Geltser said to the representatives of the newspaper *Rabochaya Moskva* that the dream scene "develops the entire internal idea of the play. Here we wanted to show how Tao-Hoa is transformed after her encounter with the Soviet captain."[62] Glière and Kurilko wrote about the same thing even before the production opened. Glière thought of "The Dream" as a symphony where the collision of age-old Chinese culture with new ideas was to be shown. Kurilko intended to express the same idea in the introduction to the ballet, showing first an ancient oak, a gigantic spider web and woman-dragonfly caught in it, then the quay and the approaching ship in the beam of the lighthouse.

Critics like Blum, who criticized the use of the large classical ensemble, were wrong. The idea of showing the experiences of the protagonist not only through dramatic action but also through dance deserved support. *The Red Poppy* was born at the end of a decade of bitter struggle over classical ballet. Some tried to prove that classical ballet had outlived its time. Others just as fiercely defended it, jealously insisting on the inviolability of definite canons once and for all. A third group, the most far-sighted, thought it was necessary to preserve ballet while simultaneously developing it. This was a call to reexamine the attitude toward the ballets of the nineteenth century, which Fokine had rejected, Gorsky had redone, and many others considered hopelessly antiquated. Dance had to recover the seemingly lost right to reflect life in abstract images. Large dance ensembles, where the content was revealed in the juxtaposition and development of choreographic themes, had disappeared from ballet productions since the time of Petipa. Glière, Tikhomirov, and Geltser were determined to revive them.

Tikhomirov and Glière wrote that they would show in "The Dream" how the soul of Tao-Hoa, attracted to new ideas, is freed from the oppression of the age-old traditions and transformed. In reality, however, what they composed repeated all the clichés of the usual divertissements of the old ballets. The choreography of the classical scenes, which was traditional through and through, stereotyped, and in some places banal, ran counter to the attempts of Goleizovsky and Lopukhov, which had demonstrated that classical dance is capable of renewal in response to the demands of the times.

The entire familiar set of dances was included. Tao-Hoa's adagio with four male dancers as phoenixes; the effective variation, based on jumps, of the "Chinese idol"; the groups of flitting butterflies—the female soloists with large white wings, the men in multicolored costumes; the corps de ballet taking tiny mincing steps on toe as the red poppies. The divertissement also included a traditional children's number (dandelions), and ended with the obligatory coda.

Geltser and Glière explained that all the dances had their own hidden meaning. Thus the phoenixes embodied the beautiful, illusory world of old Chinese culture, which only seems eternal ("reborn from the ashes"); in reality it would be replaced by the new one. The phoenixes concealed the path to the new from Tao-Hoa. The butterflies and certain flowers (dandelions and lotuses) were also attracted to the past. They were contrasted to the "revolutionary" red poppies. The phoenixes, flowers, and "celestial spirit" (the idol) were trying to hold Tao-Hoa back. When the phoenixes caught her, the poppies lowered their heads. When she tore herself from captivity and flew toward the ship, the lotuses and dandelions mourned. But this symbolism was extremely naive. There was not much more modern here than in the choral round dances of *Ever-Fresh Flowers*. Even Sergei Gorodetsky, who reacted very favorably to the ballet, wrote, about the second act: "One doesn't want to look at living flowers! In 1927! In Moscow! In the first revolutionary ballet!"[63]

While intending to revive the classic dance in *The Red Poppy*, the choreographer in fact discredited it. All the reviewers amicably criticized the second act. Many directed their criticism at the entire ballet. The luxuriant exoticism that came to the production from the old *féeries* was also very traditional. Certain effects typical of the genre were used in the ballet: the heroine's flight, the appearance of a fantastic ship at the end of the act, and all sorts of transformations in the dream scene. It is true that Kurilko initially intended to modernize this *féerie;* he dreamed of "using films, projected slides, and illuminated costumes," and wanted to lower "huge placards between scenes and write on them the content of the next scene,"[64] that is, to use certain methods of agitprop theater, well-known from Meyerhold's productions. The very idea of transforming *The Daughter of the Port* into *The Red Poppy* probably arose due to the influence of the Meyerhold Theater's production in February 1926 of *Roar, China!* by Tretyakov; but in the process of work on the ballet, it became clear that it required a totally different staging.

Despite a certain external resemblance and even some identical situations (the work of the stevedores at the port, the whites doing the foxtrot, the people's rebellion, and so on), *The Red Poppy* and *Roar, China!* are in essence opposites. The directors of *Roar, China!*, Vasily Fedorov and Meyerhold, were trying to do away with exoticism and firmly rejected any hint of chinoiserie. In *The Red Poppy*, on the other hand, exoticism is emphasized in every possible way. The authors admired "ancient embroidered tapestries, ancient bronzes, vases, wood carvings"; they were enraptured by "the quaint, fanciful effects, the imagination"[65] of the images in Chinese art. They stressed all that a European would find bizarre in the customs, habits, and character of the country. In *Roar, China!* the audience was presented with the "simple bread of Chinese everyday life," which "turned out to be stale, bitter, and meager."[66] *The Red Poppy* was soaked with syrup. Merrymaking, labor, suffering, and death were presented in a confused jumble, and in an affected manner.

The attraction to melodrama as the major form for depicting the psychology of characters in *The Red Poppy* is symptomatic of the fact that the authors of the ballet caught the growing interest of art in a person's inner world. The image of Tao-Hoa was revealed dynamically through the evolution of her character and through the battle of her feelings. Conceived rather primitively and traditionally (the beautiful hetaera tempting the captain), it was gradually transformed and eventually became truthful and touching. To a great extent this was due to the efforts of the performer. In working out the details of the action with the scenarist and in explaining to the composer what music she needed, Geltser achieved the "truth of feeling" she desired. But she also wanted the personal theme —a person acquiring a sense of dignity—to grow into a social theme: A person becomes conscious of the need for freedom for herself and for others. In the ballet all this was given only in hints, naively and sometimes melodramatically. But in working on the character Geltser demanded emphasis on precisely those episodes that helped bring out this theme. Tikhomirov wrote, "Geltser took a very active part in the staging. Her instructions were taken into account in a whole series of scenes (for example, the first meeting of Tao-Hoa with the captain of the Soviet ship, the scene where she begs him to take her to his country, the scene of the attempted poisoning of the captain, and the scene of the behests before death)."[67]

Geltser described how she performed these scenes:

In the first act Tao-Hoa is as if incidental, like a little trinket, an ancient figurine flitting for a moment on the background of a noisy international port. She performs a dance of greeting, filled with coquetry, all based on playing with a fan. The Europeans treat her like a very amusing toy, like a doll. . . . She sees the noble deed of the Soviet captain. . . . This is the first ray in her consciousness. She understands that there is another attitude toward people than the one she has observed up to now. As a sign of welcome she sprinkles flowers over the captain. Her fiancé responds crudely. He wants her to devote all her attention to the regular guests of the restaurant. When the apache seizes her by the throat, the captain intercedes on her behalf, as he would for an abused child.[68]

Glière describes the scene where the captain and Tao-Hoa meet, when he gives her the poppy. The composer thought that "she thinks only of her love," while the captain "tells her that his whole life is the sea and his native land."[69] During work on the ballet Geltser herself made changes in this scene. She emphasized that Tao-Hoa felt not love, but boundless admiration for the captain—admiration not only for him personally but for all that in her mind was associated with his country. The dancer related how this affected the staging of the scene between Tao-Hoa and the captain in the third act, before the tea-drinking ceremony. She gazed with ecstasy at his star, the symbol of a free country. She asked him to tell her about this country. Then, getting down on her knees and folding her hands, she begged him to take her with him. "And he stroked my head and gave me the red poppy. I rose on pointe, then fell and put my head and my whole body in this flower, which completely covered me."[70] After Tao-Hoa's encounter with the captain came the tea-drinking ceremony. Geltser wrote: "She dares not but obey. However, she tries to put off serving. She dances before the captain, flirts with him, and finally, at the decisive moment, when he is ready to drink the poisoned tea, she knocks the cup out of his hands."[71] In the finale of the ballet, "when the heroine was mortally wounded, she was carried to the footlights and placed on an enormous stone. Children surrounded Tao-Hoa. She gave them her legacy: the red poppy she received from the Soviet captain. Very slowly Tao-Hoa stood up, rose on pointe, raised high the flower; there it was, flaming red, symbolizing freedom."[72]

"There was no dance at all here." That was how Geltser characterized the scene where the captain gave her the flower. Indeed, from the descriptions it is clear that all the key episodes that successively revealed the image of Tao-Hoa were in pantomime. This was reaffirmed by Glière, who wrote: "In the Moscow production there was a marked tendency to intensify the mime scenes, while in Leningrad there was a bold stress on modern dance."[73] Her age (in 1927 Geltser was 51), which limited the capabilities of the dancer, naturally forced her to seek other means of expression. The main difficulty here was that a Chinese woman's education would not allow for the free expression of feelings. She hides the struggle that takes place in her soul and all the complex feelings possessing her— pain, fear, humiliation, hope, the gradually growing feeling of protest— under a mask of external calm, politeness, and coquetry. She continually represses spontaneous outbursts of emotion, for this is forbidden.

The mime possibilities of the dancer were limited by complex, masklike make-up and a fixed smile. But the costume and movements emphasized Tao-Hoa's constraints and inhibitions, her physical and spiritual "swaddling." In the photographs, Geltser either kneels or stands with a fan in her hands, in a bright-colored kimono closely fitting her body, in wide trousers hiding her legs. And her elbows are always firmly pressed to her body, her legs close together, her head slightly bent. The dancer holds the fan so that she seems to hide a bit behind it. In all this, there is a suggestion of timidity and lack of freedom. Tao-Hoa acquired freedom of clothing and movement only in "The Dream." There she wore a white semi-transparent blouse with a gold dragon on her chest and matching light, wide trousers. She stands, supported by two cavaliers, in a free arabesque, her arms spread wide. The doll chrysalis changes into a butterfly.

In Tao-Hoa's dances small steps on toe and *batterie* predominate. Iving wrote about the variation in the first act "with many jumps on pointe, as densely sprinkled with *entrechats* as dried figs with seeds,"[74] and about "the dance in the opium den with numerous beats."[75] Much attention was devoted to the graceful play of the wrists and fingers. Geltser carefully learned the technique of handling a fan as the Chinese women do; she took lessons from a Chinese magician in order to learn to use a parasol. In the hands of the dancer the fan and the parasol fluttered as though alive. In their movements one could sometimes read what the laws of education did not allow Tao-Hoa to express directly.

Many artistic devices from drama and vaudeville were used by the authors of *The Red Poppy*. The characterization of the European colonizers was done through the divertissement with Western dances at the ball in the banker's house as well as through the dances at the port bar. The foxtrot, the Charleston, and the Boston waltz gave a direct impression of the 1920s. At that time, they were performed in restaurants and on vaudeville programs, they were taught in dance classes, and they were shown in foreign films and in the Soviet film *Aelita*. The dramatic stage used Western dances and heavily parodied them to discredit the "parasite classes." The dance halls and bars of postwar bourgeois Europe appeared in Meyerhold's *D. E.* and *Lake Liul* (by Alexei Faiko), in Tairov's *The Hairy Ape* (by O'Neill), in the productions of *Proletkult*, the State Jewish Theater (GOSET), and the Operetta Theater. Everywhere that criticism and "unmasking" were needed, the stupefying rhythm of the foxtrot was heard, people moved with a mechanical gait, and mannequin-people with dull, heavily made-up faces shuffled their feet.

But while talented drama directors ended up with a satirical portrayal of the spiritual emptiness of the ruling class, *The Red Poppy* reveled in the Western dances and served them up with full mastery of the art and with all the elegance of first-class performers. Lashchilin announced, not without some pride, that "thirty couples perform a European dance. It is a distillation of all that has been achieved in Europe in the past five years in the realm of dance. . . . I am refracting the achievements of European salon dancing through our great skill in dance."[76] Kurilko's costumes looked magnificent—the black frock coats and white shirt-fronts of the cavaliers, the white uniforms of the English naval officers, and the red dress coats of the Chinese servants. The elegant attire of the women, cleverly sewn with glittery black fringes, was perceived as a clear demonstration of Parisian style.

In the divertissements of the first and second act (the scenes in the restaurant and at the ball), there were European-style vaudevilles (for example "The Dance on a Golden Plate"), as well as Chinese acrobatic dances, which in those years were often included in concert programs. The influence of cabaret dance was also clear in Tao-Hoa's and Li Shan-Fu's adagio in the first act after Tao-Hoa's scene with the captain. Here, juxtaposed with ballet movements, were combinations recalling apache dances, which were widespread in music halls before the revolution and during the twenties: the duet of a brazen, crude man and a frightened woman, totally obedient to him, whom he turns, lifts and flings about.

Despite all the novelty of these dances, it was not the dances that drew the ballet toward Soviet themes. The images of the people, of the masses, proved to be the major discovery. Glière created a collective image of the working people—the Chinese coolies. This was "The Steps of the Coolies" in the first act—gloomy, tense, monotonous music portraying the heavy, joyless work of the stevedores. It is interrupted by the scene in the restaurant, appears a second time (a continuation of work), and after the old man falls and is beaten, it takes on an agitated tone. The same theme in a very changed form, cheerful and radiant, appears in the episode of the joint unloading of the ship. And it is heard again in a new way in "The Dance of the Awakening Coolies," energetic, assertive, and forceful.

However, Glière's precisely outlined plans for the development of the image of the people were not fully implemented in the 1927 production. Both scenes of unloading were staged quite convincingly by Dikiy, but there was nothing specifically balletic in them. And the significance of the dance of the coolies apparently was not understood by the first choreographers. It was interpreted as "a dance of the coolies greeting the captain of the Soviet ship,"[77] and, according to Lopukhov, reduced to "ordinary running about." It is significant that not one of the reviewers of the production mentions this episode. The honor of "discovering" the dance of the coolies belongs to Lopukhov, who staged the first act of *The Red Poppy* in Leningrad in 1929. His dance was based on sharp lunges, sprints, stamping, and energetic gestures, imitating throwing off a yoke and breaking chains, and it had a willful, even martial, style. It was then that a solo dance part appeared, and in time this performer became a separate character; in the postwar versions of *The Red Poppy*, he became one of the protagonists—the leader of the coolies, Ma Li-Chen.

In the first Moscow production, the scene of the people's victory— the final apotheosis—was not a success; "the entire company, the entire school, all the performers and supernumeraries of the Bolshoi Theater, almost 400 people" participated.[78] Many reviewers insisted that the ballet should end with the death of Tao-Hoa. "Who needs this final parade of bustling figures, who are supposed to represent Chinese revolutionaries but who, under shapeless grey overalls like masquerade harlequins, have on fashionable women's stockings or European clothes that peep out, betraying dancers who are clearly hurrying off home and have tossed the harlequin costume over their street clothes? This parade ought to have been eliminated."[79]

On the other hand, a different image, also a mass one and also contemporary—the image of the Soviet sailors—became the major achievement of the Moscow production. The Russian seamen who come to the aid of the tortured Chinese stevedores evoke the sympathy of the audience just by their behavior. They rapidly descend the ladder from the upper deck to the dock, stop the overseers who are beating the coolies, and take over the work. "Bales of goods slip from hand to hand. The coolies throw themselves into the spaces between the sailors. The tempo of work quickens and becomes a frenzied flow of bales jumping from hand to hand. A whistle. The work is finished. The ladder is removed," wrote Glière.[80] The unloading process was theatricalized and resembled acrobatic exercises which the clever, handsome youths executed cheerfully, energetically, and enthusiastically. While this clearly illustrated the idea of workers' international solidarity, it was hardly grounds for speaking of a characterization of the Soviet people that was new to ballet. The grand sailors' dance became this new element.

The formula for the new dance, brisk in an athletic way, youthfully joyful, dashing, and full of vitality, was found on the popular stage in "gymnastic duets" and "youth dances." The numbers were full of bold jumps and swift turns and were performed by Boris Shavrov and Elena Lyukom, Olga Mungalova and Piotr Gusev, and the popular stage dancers Maria Ponna and Alexander Kaverzin. The new type of dance became widespread in drama as well: One only has to recall the acrobatic exercises of the sailors on the sports field in Meyerhold's *D. E.* (1924), in which Gvozdev saw, incidentally, "the prototype of a revolutionary ballet festival."[81] Something similar appeared in other productions as well: The figure of the revolutionary sailor was one of the most popular among Soviet dramatists.

The composer worked up several variations on the lively folksong "Yablochko." The dance opened with a small introduction. At a whistle, the sailors rushed down from the side of the ship on swaying cables. They grouped themselves in a flash, at attention, serious. Again a whistle —"At ease!" All the faces lit up with smiles. To the slow melody of "Yablochko," first the boatswain went around the circle. Clapping wildly, he seemed to wind up the others. Then followed the "promenade" of several seamen in response. The restrained, almost stern coloration of the first variation was somewhat softened in the following ones. At the same time, an energy that at first was hidden became increasingly obvious and the excitement rose. The dance spread, attracting more and more new participants. At times, the theme had an almost lyrical coloration. Then, putting their hands on each other's shoulders, the sailors formed a semicircle and rocked from side to side, as if on the deck of a ship heaved by ocean waves. The teasing, rollicking melody continued to resound and the tempo quickened. The soloists performed in the circle one after another; interrupting each other, they outdid one another in complex squatting positions and every possible trick. One of the solo episodes was comic: a grubby stoker suddenly burst into the shining white ranks; carried away by the merry melody, with a sweeping motion he threw away his canvas mittens and, taking off his soiled jacket, began dancing wildly. Making the rhythm more complex and increasing the tempo and the volume of the orchestra, Glière led the dance to a joyful apotheosis. And Lashchilin was able to convey in the dancing the same constantly growing, unrestrained sweeping image. The joyous intensity of the dance was such that it was no longer perceived as one of the numbers of the sailors' divertissement; at a certain point it took on the force of a symbol. This dance presaged the mass dance images that became an integral part of the Soviet ballet stage during the 1930s.

The Red Poppy is a ballet full of contradictions; at the same time it is typical of the late 1920s. It provoked bitter arguments and serious articles as well as satires and humorous verses. For many months the reviews flooded in, revealing a surprising lack of agreement. The "academics" praised it with certain reservations, mostly for the dream scene. The "leftists" outdid themselves with witty descriptions of the awkward moments in the ballet, and they poked vicious fun at its authors: Tikhomirov, "with his pillar-like legs and a bulge beneath his chest, . . . with his little wings and . . . saccharine smiles," and Geltser, who supposedly "performed . . . like a movie actress in a bad film."[82] The authors, for their part, sought support from audiences of workers. After a meeting with them at workplaces, a "Collective Opinion of Fifty Workers about *The Red Poppy*" appeared, concluding with the words, "Trade Unions, buy your theater tickets for *The Red Poppy*."[83]

And requests for group tickets poured in from all sides. The remaining tickets were literally battled for. Red Poppy perfume and soap, candy and cookies appeared for sale; a café of the same name opened. And the fact that the perfume and candy industries had taken the new ballet into their embrace was symbolic. Not without reason did the "left" intelligentsia consider *The Red Poppy* a concession to the poor taste of the man in the street and criticize it as an attempt to cash in on a revolutionary theme, a manifestation of bourgeois taste decked out in a red toga. The very name of the ballet became a pejorative expression for everything vulgar or cloying in life and in art.

In the late 1920s and early 1930s the bourgeoisie, which had reared its head during the NEP years, had increased its impact on both life and art. The very appearance of the plays *The Bedbug* and *The Bathhouse* testifies to the fact that artists such as Mayakovsky were acutely aware of the threat of the bourgeoisie and reacted furiously to it. In *The Bathhouse*, the ballet is summed up by Ivan Ivanovich: "You were at *The Red Poppy*? Oh, I was at *The Red Poppy*! Amazingly interesting! The flowers flitting about everywhere, the singing, the dancing of all sorts of elves and . . . syphilids."[84] Nikolai Aseyev responded to the numerous advertisements and interviews published in the journal *Programmy gosudarstvennikh akademicheskikh teatrov* (Programs of the State Academic Theaters) with verses in which he predicted that *The Red Poppy* would sprout "shoots of double-dyed vulgarity."[85]

Vsevolod Vishnevsky, striking a blow at the "accommodating reactionary theatrical wing,"[86] took *The Red Poppy* as his main target. The prologue to his play *The Last Decisive Battle* was intended as a parody of the ballet and was also sprinkled with some moments from *Carmen*. Here too there is fraternization between the Russians and the Chinese ("The speaker approaches one Chinese man, takes his hand, and raises his own in a powerful and strong gesture, exclaiming, 'China!' "[87]) and here too there is a young Red officer ("His dagger glistens, he has a pipe between his teeth and a springy walk."[88]). And after the arrest of the smugglers who had come into the restaurant—the triumphant "Yablochko." Then, from the audience, real Red Sailors burst onto the stage and kick out "the sham commander with his lady and the prim little sailors, huddled in a heap: 'Scram, you little playboys!' "[89] Lunacharsky's assessment was much more cautious. However, his evasive reminiscence of *Esmeralda* and *The Red Poppy*, which "have a slight revolutionary touch,"[90] implies that he was not inclined to consider them innovative works.

In the meantime the ballet continued to run with uninterrupted success. In the 1927–28 season it was shown more than sixty times; the hundredth performance took place on December 23, 1928, a year and a half after the premiere. This was an unprecedented event, considering that the total number of ballet performances in a season was usually not more than eighty in the Bolshoi Theater. In addition, *The Red Poppy* was staged in many outlying cities. For a relatively long time the ballet did not appear in Leningrad. As late as 1928 the Leningrad press still called *The Red Poppy* a cheap melodrama and maintained that such a mediocre production would not find a place for itself on the stage of the State Theater for Opera and Ballet. In the meantime, the company had already begun to work on it; the premiere took place in January 1929. The problem of box office returns here too had become quite acute!

Mikhail Kalinin* pointed out the attraction of *The Red Poppy* for the mass viewer. Speaking at the Eighth Congress of the All-Union *Komsomol* in May 1928 he said, "I know that by nine o'clock, the curtain time for *The Red Poppy*, you'll all go. How can this be? Why is this so? You criticized it, wanted to sweep up and throw away everything in the Bolshoi Theater, but you yourselves are going. . . . Everyone is going to see *The Red Poppy*, yet they criticize the Bolshoi Theater everywhere and see nothing positive in it. This is not normal. This is hypocrisy. If people are going to the Bolshoi Theater, then it means that there is something of value there."[91] Kalinin was right. However, the strengths and weaknesses of *The Red Poppy* were evaluated in different ways by different people, both when the ballet was produced for the first time and during later productions. While the 1927 production contained revolutionary elements, it also reflected clearly felt bourgeois tendencies. The "NEP-man"** audience was attracted both by the sugary beauty of the "old ballet" and by the seductive Western social dances brought onstage in the guise of "exposing and unmasking" the attractions of foreign music halls. The proletarian audience was at first a little confused by the magnificent divertissements (the worker-journalists reacted unfavorably); but the authors were able to convince these unsophisticated people that this was in fact the true "height of aesthetics." Gorodetsky was right: "The most dangerous thing is that, with the lack of any established contemporary taste in art, this bonbon can be appealing. . . ."[92] But there was something else

---

*Kalinin was at that time the chairman of the Central Executive Committee of the Soviet government. (Ed.)

**"NEP-man" was a derogatory term used in the twenties for nouveau riche profiteers, the new bourgeoisie that the New Economic Policy created. (Ed.)

beyond this: the enslaved coolies with whom the working-class audience sincerely sympathized; the Soviet captain who appeared to the music of "The Internationale"; the woman who saved him at the cost of her life. And the divertissement of the sailors in the first act, with the rollicking "Yablochko," was truly entertaining.

The pageantry, the theatricality, and the generous use of dance in the ballet also attracted a wide audience. With all its tinsel and superficial prettiness, *The Red Poppy* possessed qualities of "real ballet." It was neither a synthetic production with choreographic elements, nor an allegorical pantomime, nor a stage play done in rhythmic movement, but a ballet rich in dances, in which the superb dancers of the Bolshoi Ballet could display their talents. All these elements also played a role in the fate of the production. *The Red Poppy* was one of the few ballets of the 1920s that was later revived. Although as Soviet art developed new themes the naiveté of the plot of *The Red Poppy* became more and more obvious, and although next to productions that were dramatically unified and created in a consistent style its eclecticism was even less acceptable, for a long time Glière's ballet was still attractive.

In judging *The Red Poppy* now and taking into account the development of Soviet ballet for the following half-century, one can understand both its close ties with its own time and the influence it had on the future. Created at a turning point, the ballet had new qualities destined to become definitive during the 1930s. But there was also much in it that should have served as a warning. *The Red Poppy* proved that classical dance had the right to exist, particularly in the form of extended ensembles, complex choreographic structures, and the very form of the "grand ballet" with divertissements. But the ballet also made it clear that it is impossible to limit dance to a copy of the old, that classical dance had to be enriched.

The Red Poppy also opened the way for modern social themes in the ballet, but, while it noted the correct means for portraying the image of the masses, it also showed naive adaptations (for example, the role of the captain), which subsequently bore bitter fruit.

Because it sought a psychological characterization in Tao-Hoa, *The Red Poppy* presaged the arrival of a new genre —the ballet drama. But the choreographers of the following decades, who in their search for themes turned to Pushkin and Shakespeare, had to overcome its inherent schematism and melodrama. And while genuine artists rejected the pompous splendor and artifice of *The Red Poppy*, those who did not have the gift for "thinking in dance" continued to influence the audience's imagination with the old tried-and-true means.

In spite of the success of *The Red Poppy*, the group that had created it split up. Glière did not write ballets for the next twenty-two years. Tikho-mirov also produced nothing new. Dikiy left the ballet. Only Lashchilin participated in the staging of *The Footballer* in 1930 with Igor Moiseyev. Kurilko worked as a designer in other genres but returned to the ballet only for the revival of *The Red Poppy* in 1949. It is true that he tried to compose another ballet scenario immediately after *The Red Poppy*, also on a theme from contemporary life—the uprising of the Riffs in North Africa and their battle with the French and Spanish. As in *The Red Poppy*, the revolutionary events in *Ab-del-Kerim* were set forth in the form of a melodrama: The daughter of the leader of the uprising, Ab-del-Kerim, falls in love with the leader of one of the mountain tribes, but "she has a rival in Inez, the daughter of the Spanish minister."[93] Kurilko "asked several composers to write music for this ballet," but apparently neither the theme nor its interpretation aroused any interest.

The Red Poppy continued to run at the Bolshoi Theater for many years. It was revived in a new version in 1949; in 1957 the ballet changed its name, becoming *The Red Flower*, and was kept in the repertory until April 1960.

The same tendencies were found in the Leningrad ballet of the 1920s as on the Moscow stage. Here too, old productions were revived and at times made over; here a perhaps even more intensive search for modern content and modern form took place. The difference lay in the fact that in the Moscow Bolshoi Theater there co-existed choreographers with quite different tendencies, for example the innovator Goleizovsky along with the conservative Tikhomirov. Moreover, the activity of the Moscow ballet was not limited to the Bolshoi Theater: Quite a few interesting experiments took place elsewhere. In Leningrad, during the same period, the situation was different. As a result of Fokine's departure in 1918, after five years of other choreographers who showed an inclination toward independent creative activity (Romanov, Balanchivadze, and Petrov), the work of staging ballets in the former Maryinsky Theater was concentrated solely in the hands of Lopukhov. Also, Leningrad did not have as many dance studios and schools as Moscow. The major venue for experiments was still the official stage. Moreover, the studios' initiatives were often tied to the theater. For example, both Balanchivadze and then Lopukhov worked with members of the Young Ballet.

Fedor Lopukhov graduated from the St. Petersburg Theater School in 1905. His artistic career began in the Maryinsky Theater. In 1909 he transferred to the Bolshoi Theater; he spent the 1910–11 season on tour abroad and then returned to St. Petersburg. Early on, Lopukhov was attracted to composition. The choreographer's memoirs, *Sixty Years in the Ballet*, list his first attempts at choreography: beginning in 1906 he staged concert numbers for himself, then, in the prewar years and especially beginning in 1917, he staged a series of dances for his sister Evgenia and her partner, Alexander Orlov. Lopukhov mentions two large productions done on the private stage: *The Dream*, to the music of Nikolai Shcherbachev, and *The Mexican Saloon*, with music by Leonid

Goncharov. He dates them 1916–17.[1] In staging *The Dream*, the choreographer tried to "harmonize with the sounds of the various instruments
of the orchestra and with the course of the theme—the leitmotif, sub-
theme, counterpoint, harmonic changes, etc."[2] Thus the choreographer
was already interested in the problem of the relationship between dance
and music. It is not accidental that in these years he had already begun
to write the book *A Choreographer's Paths*, which devotes considerable
space to this question.

During 1917–19 concerts in the Pavlovsk summer resort hall gave
Lopukhov experience in reviving the classics and in composing new
dances. The choreographer says that even earlier, when he performed
dances in the old ballets, he always tried to examine their structure. On
tours it was necessary to cut or to rework parts of the current repertory,
and sometimes to expand them with fragments in the style of the original. Lopukhov learned to choreograph ballets by imitating the styles of
famous masters. But at the same time, he tried to imagine how he himself would compose the same dance, and sometimes he came up with his
own, different resolution.

By the early 1920s Lopukhov's talents, first as a coach and reconstructor, and then as a choreographer, emerged quite clearly. Boris Romanov's
departure in spring 1920 left the ballet company without an artistic director. At around that time Lopukhov was officially conducting rehearsals
in the theater with the ballet dancers who performed in the operas. The
members of the theater administration, Alexandre Benois, Alexander
Golovine, Boris Asafiev, and Émile Cooper, began to examine his work.
One of their major goals in the first years after the revolution was to save
the legacy of the old ballet.

The Classical Legacy

The repertory of the Leningrad company was distinguished from that of
the Bolshoi by its greater stylistic variety; the ballets it inherited had not
been subjected to the modernization and leveling that Gorsky had carried
out in Moscow. Here the ballets of the nineteenth century—the productions of Marius Petipa and his predecessors—were preserved. Fokine's
works were also kept solidly on stage all during the 1920s.

The Moscow choreographers were not unanimous in their attitude toward the classical legacy. In general, Goleizovsky did not believe it advisable to keep ballets that were outdated in both content and means of expression. Gorsky could not bring himself to reject them quite so categorically; he reworked them, trying to adapt them to his own style and to accommodate changing tastes. Tikhomirov stood for the preservation of everything, keeping it exactly as it had been.

In Leningrad there were also experts on the old ballets who could remember various versions. They could help to revive lost or distorted choreographic fragments and carefully rehearse the productions. Alexander Shiriayev, Vladimir Ponomarev, Alexander Chekrygin, Leonid Leontiev, and Alexander Monakhov saved a great deal from oblivion. But for an artist reconstructing an old production in new conditions, factual knowledge and the ability to copy passively are not enough. The discoveries of the original version as well as the later ones that enriched it had to be kept and at the same time irrelevant accretions had to be thrown out. There had to be an exact sense of what was really hopelessly outdated and should be removed, and what was vital and valuable. A creative approach was demanded that depended primarily on an understanding of the author's intention and presupposed the ability to think critically.

For the first five years after the revolution, classical ballets were shown day after day, in the theater in the winter and on the stages of various parks in the summer. Not only were the scenery and costumes worn out, but also, distortions had been introduced into the choreography. Cutbacks in the company required a reduction of the cast in many dances; one section would be thrown out, another hurriedly inserted. The design was ruined and the choreography rendered meaningless. The old ballets urgently needed to be put back in order. In this regard, the new leadership of the ballet issued the following declaration in October 1922:

> The new management of the ballet has primarily put the most brilliant classical creations of Marius Petipa at the basis of the repertory. In producing them, special efforts are being made to carefully preserve the original choreographic text, which during the past decade unfortunately has been quite distorted with various insertions and restorations "according to the notation."
>
> The goal of the management is to remove from Petipa's ballets everything borrowed and alien that nonetheless has been accepted

not only by the audience but also by "ballet experts" as the genuine creation of Petipa.[3]

The declaration quite precisely defined the line that Lopukhov intended to follow. It also anticipated a future polemic: The reference to restoration according to notation was directed at the former chief director, Nikolai Sergeyev, who had made use of his notes on ballets, which he took with him when he emigrated. Volynsky, who saw in Sergeyev and Nikolai Legat the only choreographers capable of saving the classical ballet repertory, continued to insist at this time that they be invited to do so.[4] "Ballet experts" probably meant Volynsky himself and Yuri Brodersen, a critic who sided with him.

During the first few months of the new season, Lopukhov staged *The Sleeping Beauty* with some changes and made corrections in *Raymonda*, *Harlequinade*, and *The Little Humpbacked Horse*. And at this point arguments flared. Their tone was very accurately expressed in the title of an article by Benois which was published in November 1922—"Piety or Blasphemy." Benois writes that Lopukhov's innovations had stirred up the Petrograd ballet world, which "at every gathering and each encounter" discussed the question of the right of the reconstructor to make changes in the old productions.[5] For his part, Benois opposed treating ballets of the past like "embalmed relics,"[6] while he warned against ignoring the experience of the past; he testified in Lopukhov's favor. Benois's article and Leshkov's article "Staging and Reconstructing Ballets," published in the same issue of *Ezhenedelnik*, help clarify Lopukhov's approach to Petipa's ballets.

According to Benois, Lopukhov's goal was "not so much introducing something new, as the fact that he considered it necessary to return to its former state the old choreography which, under the influence of time, had changed beyond recognition, . . . and had lost even its simple, 'living' sense."[7] He enlivened the ensemble pantomime scenes, for example, the one in which Aurora plays with the spindle: part of the crowd rushes after Aurora, trying to take the spindle away from her. The women knitting in the pantomime scene at the beginning of the first act, the staging of the prologue when Carabosse occupies the king's throne, and many other scenes were all reintroduced.

In some cases, when Lopukhov and the ballet masters could not remember all the details, the choreographer composed the missing parts, trying to imitate Petipa's style. In introducing changes in the dances Lopukhov was quite self-critical and he rejected innovation if he thought it would be detrimental to the general impression. Volynsky, who was extremely critical of Lopukhov, unintentionally convinces us of this. In reviewing Olga Spessivtseva's performance in *The Sleeping Beauty* (late October 1922), Volynsky reports that instead of the new variation composed by Lopukhov which had been used in the previous production, the old one was again being performed.

In November 1923, a year after the beginning of the work on *The Sleeping Beauty*, an announcement appeared in the program: "The Original Version." Lopukhov considered his work done. The choreography had been reconstructed and at the same time music cut out as early as Petipa's time had been restored. Thus a gavotte, passepied, and rigaudon in the hunting scene and a sarabande in the last act appeared, staged and signed by Lopukhov. However, in time it became clear that Petipa had been wiser. Despite their merits, the new dances weighed down a ballet that was already long enough, and later on they were not performed in full. One of the newly staged scenes, however, undoubtedly enriched the ballet. In his article about *The Sleeping Beauty*, published at the start of Lopukhov's work, Asafiev complained that the first part of the symphonic interlude, before the scene of the sleeping kingdom, was not performed at all and that the second part was lost on an audience unaccustomed to music performed independent of dance in a ballet.[8] This idea inspired Lopukhov to compose a new scene: In the depths of the castle covered with spider webs where Carabosse is guarding Aurora, the Lilac Fairy appears as the embodiment of spring and life. Carabosse tries to block her way with her rats and mice, but is forced to retreat. Thus the musical interlude had a scenic interpretation. Now such a resolution has become normal and even seems obligatory. Apparently audience perception has changed since Petipa's time: A demand has arisen for more action and visual devices.

In *Raymonda*, Lopukhov staged his own version of the finale in the second act. According to Benois, Petipa left an obvious "blank" here, which urgently needed to be "filled." To do this, the events that took place after Raymonda's fiancé's victory over Abderâme had to somehow be portrayed to the magnificent music of the apotheosis. In Benois's opinion, Lopukhov did this "superbly, not allowing himself anything that would destroy the conventional style of that ballet."[9]

In restoring the ballets then running in Petrograd in Gorsky's version
—*The Little Humpbacked Horse* and *Don Quixote*—Lopukhov also tried
to keep what was best in them and, where possible, to restore what had
been lost. For example, in his opinion, in *Don Quixote*, "a series of small
details, flashing sparks typical of Gorsky," [10] had been forgotten. Lopukhov tried to reconstruct the choreography well-known in the Moscow
production; in particular he replaced the fandango staged in Petersburg
by Legat with another one in Gorsky's style. In *The Little Humpbacked
Horse*, which was presented in Petrograd in a separate version distinct
from the Moscow one, he reworked the dances, bringing them closer to
the ones he remembered, paying particular attention to Gorsky's "tsar-
maiden" variation. Lopukhov also carefully rehearsed Fokine's ballets—
Une Nuit d'Égypte, *Eros*, and *Le Pavillon d'Armide*—trying to recreate
lost features and nuances.

Thus during two seasons, 1922–23 and 1923–24, almost all of the repertory ballets from the past were put in order. This kind of reconstruction
by the Petrograd experts proved more fruitful than Gorsky's revivals in
Moscow. While in Moscow there was a tendency to depart further and
further from the author's versions, in Leningrad the originals were preserved for the future. Thanks to this activity the Leningrad ballet for
many years became the chief guardian of the ballet legacy.

Of course, here too there were failures. The work Lopukhov did on
The Nutcracker was by no means uncontroversial. The choreographer
parted ways with most scholars in his assessment of the "Waltz of the
Snowflakes" staged by Ivanov. Lopukhov wrote: "The 'Snowflakes' scene
lacks harmony and growth and is incorrectly developed in terms of musical themes. The figures changing after every eight bars cannot be used
throughout the 'Waltz of the Snowflakes.' No attention is paid to the
theme of the chorus singing in the wings." [11] For this reason, in the revival
of *Nutcracker*, the choreographer clearly was freer in his interpretation
than elsewhere. Volynsky did not fail to seize upon this. Immediately
after the premiere, he published an article whose title speaks for itself:
"A Good-for-Nothing Housepainter."* In describing the old waltz step

---

*The reference is to a line in Pushkin's "little tragedy" *Mozart and Salieri*, in which Salieri,
shocked that Mozart would deign to listen to a hack musician, speaks of "a good-for-nothing
housepainter spattering Raphael's Madonna." (Ed.)

by step, he pointed out all the violations committed. It is true, if one is to believe Volynsky, that even prior to Lopukhov's intervention the outline of the dance looked distorted; its figures were devoid of individual characteristics.[12] But in this case Lopukhov followed the path of "correcting" the author's version. Judging by the fate of the production, this path was the wrong one. *The Nutcracker* was revived in February 1923, but by the following season it had already been dropped from the repertory. Considerably later, in 1929, Lopukhov staged his own production, which had nothing in common with the traditional versions; in 1934 Vainonen's production appeared. As a result, Ivanov's "Waltz of the Snowflakes" was forgotten and now this loss can no longer be remedied.

Lopukhov's policy of preserving ballets from the classical legacy, conducted with the support of the ballet administration and such specialists as Benois and Asafiev, won out in the former Maryinsky Theater. Nevertheless, there were also other tendencies. Some proposed that the repertory could be replenished if the Romantic or fairytale plots of old ballets and operas were replaced by modern revolutionary ones. In 1924 Nikolai Vinogradov suggested a new scenario for *The Sleeping Beauty* in which the action of the prologue was moved to five hundred years ago ("the first uprising of the proletariat") and the remaining acts to the future. Instead of the Lilac Fairy there would be an astrologer-philosopher, and instead of Carabosse, his opponent would be a "Universal Duke"; Aurora would be transformed into the "Dawn of World Revolution," and she would be sought for and awakened by the "Leader of the Uprising." The famous panorama of the second act, when in the fairytale, the Lilac Fairy leads Prince Desiré to Aurora, would portray "the city of the commune in the gold of wealth, the silver flame of electric lights, and the red smoke of factories."[13]

No matter how fantastic Vinogradov's project appears now, such reworkings were quite widespread at the time. The theater rejected Vinogradov's proposal, but in another case, when a less famous ballet was under discussion, the board gave in to temptation. In 1925 Leontiev staged the ballet *Candaule*. He added to Petipa's ballet *Le Roi Candaule* content "appropriate to the times" by replacing the palace coup with a popular uprising.

Candaule (renamed by the audience *Scandal*) at that time was the Maryinsky Theater's only departure from the policy they had chosen of preserving the ballets of the past. Lopukhov's later *Nutcracker* (1929) is a case unto itself, where a classical work became the basis for an "eccentric," modernist spectacle. Here the ballet came close to the early experiments of Eisenstein (*The Wise Man*)* and Meyerhold. The appearance of such productions in the early 1920s was justified by the wave of theatrical experiments, but in this case Lopukhov was obviously late in joining them. In one way or another, this production, in which the music was interrupted by the text and dances alternated with colored planes moving along the stage, had nothing in common with the traditional version of Tchaikovsky's ballet and cannot be considered in the context of preserving the classical legacy.

The Firebird

Benois and Asafiev, who supported Lopukhov's policies regarding the old ballets, also helped him in his early independent experiments. In planning a renewal of the ballet repertory after the October Revolution, the leaders of the Maryinsky Theater turned primarily to the ballets of Stravinsky. *The Firebird* and *Petrushka*, produced by Fokine in Paris during the first seasons of the Ballets Russes, did not appear on the Russian stage before the revolution. As early as 1918 these ballets were listed in the theater's plans. At first it was suggested that Fokine produce them, then Romanov. *Petrushka*, as revived by Leontiev, was the first to reach the stage. In late March 1921 the newspaper *Zhizn iskusstva* published a report that "the dancer Lopukhov would make his debut as the choreographer of *The Firebird*."[14]

Lopukhov preferred to create his own choreographic version rather than to revive Fokine's ballet, which he had seen abroad only twice. Moreover, as he confessed, he saw Stravinsky's music somewhat differently than did Fokine. One had to admit that for the Paris production's audience, Russian folklore was something exotic. The fairytale was stylized. While picturesque, the fantastic characters were also somewhat static and one-dimensional. Lopukhov tried to interpret the characters in

---

*Eisenstein's 1923 production for *Proletkult* of Ostrovsky's play *Enough Stupidity in Every Wise Man*, retitled *The Wise Man*, used circus techniques and incorporated film projection. It was the basis for Eisenstein's famous article on his "theory of attractions." (Ed.)

Stravinsky's ballet in his own way. He wanted to add symbolic meaning, seeing in each one either a personified expression of thought or a visual reflection of an historical event.

The choreographer understood the central idea of *The Firebird* to be that of victory over the awful power of Kashchei through the help of reason. Therefore, the Firebird's variations and her adagio with Ivan Tsarevich had to be seen as "the triumph of reason." Kashchei, in Lopukhov's opinion, reflected the popular notion of the Ice Age, encrusted with later impressions from the Mongol-Tatar invasion.[15] This subtext was barely understood by the audience. The printed commentary appended to the program, written in collaboration with Vasily Struve, in which the meaning of the Firebird, the golden apples, the egg in the hollow, and the contrast between the dances of the enchanted princesses and the "Infernal Dance" of Kashchei's kingdom were all explained, did not help. The choreographer's attempt to transform the fairytale "almost into a philosophical treatise"[16] was condemned by all the critics. But something else did make an impression: the uniqueness of the dance ideas and the novelty of the choreographic language.

Lopukhov's production lacked the veneer of Orientalism of Fokine's production. The choreographer wanted to return the characters to their Slavic sources, seeing in the Firebird a kind of "primal bird." The dance steps were selected with the idea of creating a feeling not so much of airiness as of power: strong, assertive leaps, *grands battements*, broad swinging movements.

Mungalova, who danced the Firebird, described her interpretation: "The Firebird is above all a fantastic bird; such birds don't exist. She embodies the sun, goodness, and life, but she is also stern and threatening."[17] The dancer described in considerable detail the variation performed by the Firebird on her first appearance and the adagio that follows with Ivan Tsarevich. In comparing this description with Fokine's version, one notices that Mungalova nowhere writes of the fright of the bird, who is taken unaware by the Tsarevich. Here there are none of the frightened halts, the caution, and the trembling that embellish Fokine's production. On the contrary, her description of the adagio depicts a struggle between two equal beings. In this struggle, the bird's role is an active one. The bird "is surprised by the Tsarevich's fearlessness," she "wants to frighten him," and she "advances toward him with threatening mien, and with

large steps."[18] The bird is powerful, and it costs the Tsarevich considerable effort to subdue her; the bird "tries to trick him and suddenly flaps
her wings so powerfully that the Tsarevich is forced to whirl around, but
he does not let the bird out of his hands."[19] At times the bird uses cunning and feigns defeat in order to slip from his hands and fly off, but the
Tsarevich succeeds in capturing her, binds her wings, and pushes her to
the ground.

Several moments from the adagio are preserved in the drawings of Pavel
Goncharov, the designer for the ballet, which are now in the Leningrad
Theatrical Museum. Lopukhov used acrobatic movements and supports
that were new to the academic stage. There were high lifts with prome-
nades during which the dancer sat on her partner's shoulder or chest. All
sorts of circling, turning movements were used (various forms of *tours*
for the ballerina, including turns with the help of a special revolving stand
set up behind a tree), and lifts during which her partner swiftly spun the
dancer—"he sharply threw her down from his shoulder into his arms,
gave her a half turn in the air, and made her run around him, holding her
by the wing."[20] The critics were especially troubled by one of the figures
of this adagio, which Volynsky, deeply critical of Lopukhov, characterized as follows: "The cavalier turns the dancer upside down and sweeps
her across the floor like a broom."[21] Apparently he was thinking of the
tensest moment of the struggle, which Mungalova also describes: "The
final struggle takes place. The bird flies upward, the Tsarevich catches her
in an arabesque, and sets her on the ground in this position, holding the
raised left leg; he violently pulls the bird toward him, so that she turns.
Immediately he throws her to his chest, and for a second turns together
with her, lowering her head to the ground, then, placing the bird back
on his chest, takes several steps."[22]

Lopukhov built the "Infernal Dance" on echoes of Tatar folklore. Later
he described this dance as follows:

> The entrance of Kashchei's entourage is not a march-procession,
> even a fantastic one, but an entire choreographic action-dance, in
> which Kashchei's retinue appears as an expression of his being and
> his power, and Kashchei's appearance puts an end to the dance.
> All these entrances, extremely difficult in terms of movement and
> rhythm, took place in the form of a musical fugue; this was the first
> part of the "Infernal Dance" which followed it, where his elemental

power is activated. The dance movements of Kashchei's retinue both at the moment of its entrance and in the "Infernal Dance" itself are built on the same movements shown from various angles, in various rhythms and meters. The basis for these dance movements was all types of *pas de basque,* facing to the front, side, and back, both small and large, with jumps. Various forms of the *pas de basque* comprise the basic movements in Tatar folkdances and are enriched by diverse arm movements. I emphasized this in the "Infernal Dance," where the legs of the dancers did the *pas de basque* to a two-beat measure while the arms moved to three beats. There were also various types of runs, all based on the same principle of the *pas de basque.* Of course, the audience might not even have tried to grasp my subtext, but it undoubtedly sensed the power of Kashchei's kingdom, expressed in the "Infernal Dance," as the audience reaction showed.[23]

From this description, one can get an idea of several of Lopukhov's aims during those years. One of the most important was the search for the link between dance movement and music. To this issue he devoted a major part of his book *A Choreographer's Paths*, published in 1925 but written earlier (according to Lopukhov, as early as 1916). Calling this section "Dancing close to the music, to the music, in the music, and dancing the music," the choreographer pointed out the various degrees to which gestures merged with sound—from the simple coincidence of meter to the total unity of dance and music on the basis of a detailed analysis of the score, when movements embody the same idea the music is built on.

Lopukhov tried to formulate basic principles for the correspondence between music and dance. This correspondence had to be not only rhythmic, but also emotional ("the coincidence of the rise of the sound-emotional and the choreographic-emotional"). The curve of the melody should be matched with a curve of the dance line; the coloration of dance movements should correspond to the coloration of the instrumentation. The character of the dance movements ought to be different for music in major or minor keys; the dancing must emphasize changes in tonality. The development of the musical theme demanded a development of the dance theme.

While working on *The Firebird* Lopukhov put in practice several of the ideas he had expounded. It was not coincidental that in his search for themes in the "Infernal Dance" he stubbornly varied the figure of the *pas de basque*. However, here the choreographer's search for the correspondence of sound and movement often had a mechanical result. Afterwards even Lopukhov himself, referring to the disciples of Émile Jaques-Dalcroze, spoke of "rendering the notes with the arms and legs"; seeing as his goal the duplication of the rhythmic and melodic details of the score, the choreographer came to a kind of "danced algebraic equation," in the opinion of Ivan Sollertinsky.[24] This was noted by most of the reviewers of the premiere of *The Firebird*; "The choreographer devoted most of his attention to achieving a strict parallelism between the stage movements and the music. This parallel was sometimes so sharply drawn that the performance suggested rhythmic gymnastics and became monotonous."[25]

Lopukhov's goals were further complicated by the choice of music. In fact, this was the first encounter of the choreographer, brought up on nineteenth-century works, with this composer, who represented the newest tendencies. Lopukhov consulted with Asafiev, who in those years was the most prominent expert on Stravinsky in Russia, and still he did not totally succeed in making the dance language correspond to the musical language. Noting the successful resolution of the lyrical episodes, Gvozdev wrote of the ensemble dances: "The annoyingly repeated gestures (the turning of the hands, for example), the fussy, scattered movements and, primarily, the poverty of the linear formation of the groups —all this proves that the old expressive means of ensemble movement in the stock of the ballet tradition are simply not suited for the interpretation of Stravinsky's scintillating, complicated rhythms and thematic innovations."[26]

The Dance Symphony:
The Magnificence of the Universe

Immediately after *The Firebird* Lopukhov began working on his next production—*The Magnificence of the Universe*. This ballet was performed to the music of Beethoven's Fourth Symphony and its genre was defined as "dance symphony." The ballet *The Magnificence of the Universe* occupies a special place in the history of choreographic theater. It expressed one of the most important tendencies in the development of twentieth-century ballet: the rapprochement of dance with symphonic music to the point of creating ballets that are movement analogues to symphonic work.

The dance symphony was a new genre born at the crossroads of two traditions. One had its source in the "new ballet" of the early twentieth century, which turned toward the staging of symphonic music, and the second was linked to the development of "pure" dance in the "old ballet" of the nineteenth century, primarily as represented by Petipa.

As a result of the symphonization of ballet music (Delibes, Tchaikovsky, Glazunov) during the last quarter of the nineteenth century, the choreographers' attitudes toward music changed as well. Music that served merely as a rhythmic accompaniment was no longer satisfactory; hence the need to stage musical works that were symphonic and instrumental and not intended for the dance. In these works bases were sought for the reform of the ballet production as such. The music of Chopin, Rimsky-Korsakov, Tchaikovsky, and Schumann provided examples of moral depth and abstraction, and contained motifs and images akin to those of Fokine and Gorsky. Built on different laws than those of traditional ballet, this music also helped to liberate dance from the clichés of dance formulae.

With their fondness for dramatizing ballet action, Fokine and Gorsky felt the need for a plot even when using non-program music. The story served as a subtext for the symphonic work, and the stylized dancing reconstituted an image of the country and the age. In such cases, the music was subordinate to the laws of the drama. The music sometimes served as a background as well; then the lack of correspondence between the musical work and the choreographic action was especially obvious. In all these cases, the music was only a springboard from which the choreographer pushed off to fantasize freely. Often the content of the musical work was interpreted arbitrarily, and its form was almost always ignored.

The dance symphony is different in principle from such ballets because it assumes a different interrelationship between music and dance. And here the second tradition comes into play—the tradition of Petipa. The issue here is the use of non-representational dance, for the most part in classical ensembles within large ballet spectacles. In these ensembles, even when it was accompanied by music that seemed tacked onto the ballet (Pugni, Minkus), the dance had its own poetic imagery. The choreographer was able to use the expressive characteristics of this or that movement, juxtaposing similar and contrasting movements and joining moving figures and groups for the creation of an overall image. Naturally, with Tchaikovsky and Glazunov, a higher level of interaction between dance and music was achieved in ballet, a form in itself close to the symphonic. The music gave the dance more depth and significance.

The reformers of the 1910s, rejecting the obsolete rhetoric of the "old ballet," also refused to accept its dance achievements. But the tradition lived on in the works of the classical repertory. For Lopukhov, who was well acquainted with the ballets of Petipa and had worked on restoring them, this tradition was no more remote than the ideas of his older contemporary, Fokine.

The ballet *The Magnificence of the Universe* was the first work in the new genre of the dance symphony. "Liberated and self-contained" dance (Lopukhov), pure dance outside of concrete action, was intended to express thoughts drawn from the symphony and therefore was formally subordinated to its structure as well. Lopukhov's dance symphony has its own peculiarities, based in part on the worldview of the choreographer during the 1920s. The link between Beethoven's music and the choreography was not reduced to an interpretation of the symphony in dance. Lopukhov's idea was more grandiose. Dance united with music was called upon to reveal man's ideas about the world and about complex life processes. Lopukhov's ballet was conceived as a unique "understanding of the world" in dance. The choreographic images of the future ballet were born in the consciousness of the choreographer before he found music appropriate to his intentions. Lopukhov described them in a general way in the book *A Choreographer's Paths*, which preceded the creation of the ballet, and although much changed in the course of the production, his general idea remained the same.

An illustrated brochure was printed for the premiere of the dance symphony *The Magnificence of the Universe*. In the foreword Lopukhov wrote of the "themes of universal significance" that attracted him and of his aspiration to find dance forms for them. They did not fit into the "tight framework of the story ballet" because the point was not individual phenomena but broad generalizations. Not long before, during the civil war, the poets who were trying to express the infinite possibilities of the revolution had depicted it as capable not only of transforming the face of the earth, but even of changing the course of the planets. Lopukhov took a similar path, reflecting on the colossal events taking place on earth, and he addressed his imagination to the cosmic spheres, glorifying the universe, marvelous in its eternal motion, and life, which triumphs over death.

The dance symphony was shown to an audience only once. The program, written by Lopukhov in collaboration with Struve, was pretentious and abstruse. It confused rather than helped the reader analyze the ballet. Nevertheless, until recently Lopukhov's ballet had to be judged for the most part by this program and by other written sources, that is, Lopukhov's ideas about the future dance symphony, set forth in *A Choreographer's Paths* (written prior to the production), and a few reviews, whose authors for the most part did not seriously attempt to understand the choreographer's intentions. The only other sources were Pavel Goncharov's silhouette drawings in the brochure that contains the program.

In recent years several attempts have been made to study this dance symphony seriously. Conversations with Lopukhov and the performers in the production have been conducted, but the most valuable document is the choreographer's notebook, where, along with the music, the dances are transcribed with the help of traditional ballet terminology. Arkady Sokolov's research was included in his dissertation and has been published in part in the anthology *Music and Choreography in Modern Ballet* (1974). Galina Dobrovolskaya's work makes up one chapter of her book, *Fedor Lopukhov* (1976). Each scholar offers a reconstruction of the ballet, an analysis, and an evaluation. It seems that, at the present stage of the study of Lopukhov's legacy, there is reason to rely on the conclusions of these authors.

According to the program, the first part of the ballet (sometimes called "Introduction") included the episodes "The Birth of Light" and "The Birth of the Sun." The slow, significant adagio (the introduction to the symphony) embodied for Lopukhov the magnificence of the world at its birth. Illuminated in light blue, eight youths crossed the proscenium in a chain. They covered their eyes with one hand and with the other seemed to grope their way through the gloom. Fixing their gaze upward, in the distance, eight women moved after them. The combinations of movements and groupings were simple: The dancers sometimes followed one another and sometimes formed couples, and the women ran around their partners. At a sudden swell of sound, when the orchestra rose to a powerful fortissimo for a second before moving on to a more lively, agile theme, came "The Birth of the Sun." After this was the next part of the dance symphony, where the subject was life and death, opposing and interacting with each other. Here one of the compositional motifs was the circle formed by the dancers, which could be understood symbolically as the portrayal of the sun (at this point the lighting changed to yellow), but also as the eternal shift of generations, when life ends with death but death contains new life within itself.

From Goncharov's drawings and the descriptions of the scholars it is clear that one of the most important aspects of the choreography was the replacement of static groups by dynamic ones. At first the men slowly dropped to the floor and became motionless, as if asleep, and the women circled around them. Then, apparently losing their strength, they too dropped down and lay inside the circle, repeating the positions of the men. The men, however, fought off their torpor, rose, and finding strength, the ability to move, and the lightness of a leap, repeated almost exactly the dance of the women. Thus the choreographer revealed the idea contained in the title of this section: "Life in Death and Death in Life"; life (movement) constantly triumphs over death (immobility).

The third part was called "Thermal Energy." This was a dance adagio which used many devices of the traditional classical ballet adagio; it possessed melodiousness, internal harmony, and a firm equilibrium. It was devoid of garish effects and was built on even, flowing movements "without any splashes" (Lopukhov's expression). "They slowly form themselves into images and, as if with velvet tentacles, increasingly grasp one's attention."[27]

The scholars see two fundamental themes in this adagio—one for the women (two soloists) and another for the men. The women began with deep, slow pliés and then led the dance melody, built on a flowing change of positions. In the program this was called "the passive development of the feminine principle." In the men's dance there was a sense of restrained energy, perhaps akin to Spanish dances (this idea comes from Goncharov's drawings, where the dancers' hands are behind their backs and seem to be holding castanets). In the program they were characterized as the "actively pulsating male principle." Both themes were interwoven in the part of the adagio where the men and women danced together. Here, as Dobrovolskaya notes, there are echoes of the famous "Rose Adagio" in

The Sleeping Beauty. The dance was built on combinations in which the women were supported in turn by various partners, moving from one to another. Here, as in *The Sleeping Beauty*, a mood of contemplation and harmony prevailed. Thus the theme stated in the women's dance became the predominant one.[28]

The fourth part was called "The Joy of Existence." Here, without specific concretization but with the use of movements approaching folk dance (for the peasants) or even the grotesque (for the pithecantropes), the choreographer created images of different beings enjoying the blessings of earthly existence. Throughout the peasant dances were motions imitating the swinging of scythes. The section "Games of the Butterflies" was expressed through fluttering, circling steps and skimming runs along the stage. A bird was characterized through flight. At first this was "The First Flight of the Little Bird," where in Goncharov's sketch one sees timidity, uncertainty, and even a certain awkwardness. Then the wing-arms opened wide and carried the bird in free, proud flight ("The Skillful Flight of the Bird").

The fifth part—"Eternal Motion"—was performed by the entire cast of eighteen, illuminated by red spotlights. Their dance, impetuous and joyful, was built on a development and variation on the choreographic theme set forth during the first bars. The scholars correctly see here the connection with traditional forms such as the concluding ensemble coda of nineteenth-century ballets triumphantly crowning the performance. In Lopukhov's dance symphony the group, forming a spiral and embodying "the universe," served as the crowning point.

"The conclusion, built on the notion 'universe,' was to have the magnificent solemnity of the introduction, but was statically performed," wrote Lopukhov.[29] The point is that the music itself lacks "magnificent solemnity." Beethoven's symphony does not conclude, like many others, with a powerful ensemble in which all the instruments merge together in triumphant chords. Almost until the last moment, the noisy "run of sounds" continues. Only at the very end is there a brief slowing down and several successive pauses like meditative, lyrical sighs. During this time, the final group took shape on stage. Two images of it have been preserved: Goncharov's silhouette drawing and the frequently published drawing by Lopukhov, from a working copy of the choreographic score of the ballet.

Eighteen performers formed a chain leading toward the back of the stage and at the same time upward. In the foreground, two women at the end of the chain were lying prone on the floor. A group was "linked" to them: One woman, falling backwards, leaned with her back on that of a kneeling male dancer; another woman, facing him, bent in a deep arabesque. The next couple sat on the floor, and several more sitting or standing figures linked hands in a line with them. A broken line emerged, which seemed to end with two flights: a ballerina on the shoulder of her partner in a "flying" pose, and the final composition, culminating with a woman raised in the air, facing the audience, with two symmetrical kneeling male figures forming a base. As the orchestra concluded the symphony with a loud, joyful exclamation, this light, harmonious spiral rose on the stage.

Lopukhov worked on the dance symphony with the young dancers in the company, for the most part performers with the Young Ballet. Among them were Lidia Ivanova, Alexandra Danilova, Leonid Ivanov (Lavrovsky), Mikhail Mikhailov, Piotr Gusev, Natalia Lisovskaya, Marietta Frangopulo, Vladimir Thomson, Georgi Balanchivadze, and others. Full of enthusiasm, the young people worked during their time off from formal rehearsals. The goals Lopukhov had set were not always understood, but they were attractive. Danilova, who was one of the two soloists in the "Thermal Energy" scene, remembers that in this ballet she encountered unaccustomed rhythmic situations; for example, she had to move her legs to a two-count phrase and her arms to a three-count phrase.[30]

Soon after Lopukhov was appointed artistic director he showed the dance symphony in a rehearsal hall to an invited audience of dancers, critics, musicians, and artists. Asafiev, Gvozdev, Vsevolod Vsevolodsky-Gerngross, Vladimir Dmitriev, Ivan Sollertinsky, and others took part in the discussion. Lopukhov wrote in the notebook containing the dance notation for the symphony: "September 18, 1922. Demonstration of the dance symphony to all the representatives of the arts, and after it a debate, which I consider successful."

For a long time the ballet was not included in the repertory. Only after six months was it shown as a benefit for the ballet dancers, on a single evening after the main production, *Swan Lake*. This proved to be a fatal mistake. The audience at the benefit performance on March 7, 1923, was by no means in a mood for experimental works. Exhausted by the four-act *Swan Lake*, which had been preceded by a formal program (several congratulatory speeches including one by I. V. Exkusovich), the audience read the abstruse text in the little program for *The Magnificence of the Universe* with irritation and irony and did not bother to ponder Lopukhov's intentions. When the curtain went down in the theater, as Nikolai Soliannikov, a dancer in the company, remembers, "Instead of the usual roar of applause there was the silence of the tomb. The audience didn't clap, didn't laugh, didn't whistle—it was silent."[31]

The press responded quickly, harshly criticizing the production. Somehow not one of the critics who had praised the ballet after the rehearsal showing published a review. It is true that at a meeting that took place on April 2 in the Museum of the State Academic Theaters Gvozdev and Anatoly Kankarovich noted "the extraordinary significance of the creation of the dance symphony for the history of choreography; it is a turning point, a shift in the development of the forms of dance art."[32] But these words did not reach the newspapers and magazines. And Volynsky literally breathed poison: "Once a mediocre scribbler, who had shown some talent, dreamed of the magnificence of the universe. After he woke up, he set about turning his nocturnal visions into the images of his favorite ballet. The result was a dance symphony, the likes of which the world has never seen."[33] This is how his article began, and it continued to the end in the same jeering tone.

Yet there was reason to hope that Volynsky might be attracted by the idea of such a ballet. After all, Lopukhov was fighting for "self-sufficient" dance; he wanted to present the classics in all the wealth of their forms, bringing out the internal meaning of each movement. His very intention showed Volynsky's influence. In the program published by Lopukhov there were even quite a few verbal images almost identical to the favorite expressions of the author of *The Book of Exultations*; there are foggy statements such as "our dance art is a hymn to nonbeing, a hymn to the joy of renunciation and of love for heights, from the earth";[34] and there was the opposition of the "passively developing" (for Volynsky, "growing") feminine principle to the "actively pulsating" masculine. However, Volynsky accepted neither what Lopukhov wrote nor what he produced. He had his reasons; the backstage politics in which the venerable critic was involved during those years made themselves felt, pitting him and those close to him against the theater leadership—hence his refusal to accept anything that Lopukhov did. There were artistic motives as well. As regards the written program, Lopukhov's abstruseness was no match for Volynsky's judgments, which—for all their complexity and grandiloquence—were always based on tremendous knowledge and an understanding of the laws of the development of the art. Such an inept adaptation of his thoughts could only irritate Volynsky. And in fact the production itself did not correspond to the ballet theoretician's idea of a ballet with self-contained choreography. Volynsky consistently fought for the preservation of classical dance in its academic forms, objecting to any penetration of what seemed to him extraneous elements. And Volynsky recognized the right to abstraction only through these forms. He celebrated the beauty of the lines of the classical arabesque and protested against its distortion. Lopukhov, however, like all the masters beginning with Fokine, stood for the renewal of the classical language and combined it with other forms of stage movement.

The performance on March 7, 1923, proved to be the only one. The ballet's failure was an even greater blow for Lopukhov because the dance symphony had embodied his program for the future. Few in those years understood how important the idea it stated would be for the development of ballet art. Intelligent dance is capable of making generalizations; it is an independent medium of art that possesses its own arsenal of expressive means. The choreographer has the right to use dance without turning for help to the other arts, just as the composer and painter use their own media. As music is expressive through sounds and painting through pictorial qualities which are not subject to verbal retelling, the dance, too, is expressive even when devoid of any plot and "depicting" nothing in particular. Therefore, the "pure dance" to which the theoreticians and practitioners of ballet in the 1920s reacted so strongly was by no means an empty ornament, "a little flourish," but the result of interpreting life in choreographic form. A choreographic image gives the audience something that cannot be conveyed by any other image—either musical, pictorial, or verbal—because each art possesses its own powers of expression.

Lopukhov had performed a tremendously important act. The time was drawing near when people would begin to question the right of non-illustrative dance to exist and when the salvation of ballet would be seen in its dramatization, or even in the total subordination or replacement of the dance by other arts and in the creation of new synthetic spectacles to replace ballet.[35] But meanwhile, Lopukhov tried to prove that the art of dance per se has content and is capable of abstraction, and that the highest goal of each art is to affect the viewer through its own specific means.

Lopukhov rejected the method chosen by Fokine and Gorsky of finding a subtext for a plot in symphonic music; he also rejected Duncan's notion of trying to transmit the moods the music evoked in her.[36] His goal was to create an image that corresponded to the musical image through the means of instrumental dance. In *A Choreographer's Paths* he writes about the dance of the future, part of which "merges closely with music," about dance and music that "say exactly the same thing," about the "concord between the lines of a dance and the lines of a sound," and about the analogy between major and minor keys in music and the dance system of movements *en dedans* and *en dehors*. All this, in Lopukhov's terminology, is called "dancing the music," as opposed to dancing "close to the music," "to the music," and "in the music."[37] Naturally, such an approach assumes analyzing the musical score, breaking it down into its constituent elements, and then searching for the equivalent movements for each element.

One of Lopukhov's followers, George Balanchine, became a master of symphonic ballet in the West; incidentally, in his youth he performed in *The Magnificence of the Universe*. For him the most important principle was the one that Lopukhov borrowed from Petipa, or, more precisely, that had been a development of Petipa's discoveries in the realm of building expressive choreographic ensembles: dance composition as an analogue to musical composition, beyond literary conjectures, dramatic concretization, and subjective interpretations.

Léonide Massine, who became well known in the 1930s for his ballet symphonies, never saw Lopukhov's ballet, but his experiments in some ways followed the same course. However, Massine came closer to the path of Fokine and Duncan than that of Petipa. If Balanchine studies the music like a professional musician, setting into the language of choreography his perception of the musical ideas, Massine responds to the music like a talented, educated listener. He finds in the music emotions that are consonant with his own lived experiences, and he expresses them through dance, pantomime, groupings, and mise-en-scène.

Probably still other attempts by Western choreographers show an unexpected link with the earliest experiments by Lopukhov. In any case, so it seemed to us when Maurice Béjart's company performed Beethoven's Ninth Symphony, choreographed in the late 1960s. Here there is a common thread not only externally; there are similarities also between plot turns such as "the awakening of humanity" and a resemblance between choreographic devices such as the position of lying on one side with legs pressed to the stomach, from which, as from the "embryonic stage," the dancers strove toward dance-flight. Further analogies come to mind.

All three choreographers tried to extract from the music an idea appropriate to modern times and interpreted it in their own ways, using it as a basis for their own imaginings. Béjart, moreover, considered that he had the right to use any means he liked to express these visions. Lopukhov did not go that far. He even blamed himself later for the free treatment of Beethoven's symphony, seeing it as part of the reason for the ballet's failure.[38] Béjart's experience makes one doubt the fairness of such a self-critical evaluation. Now we are convinced that such a path is also possible and that there is no single path required of everyone. Balanchine, Massine, and Béjart found different things in symphonic music and used it for differing goals, either revealing the spirit and structure of a musical work in dance or making the composer an ally in the struggle of modern ideas.

In some respects Lopukhov anticipated the future, but he remained a solitary figure, misunderstood by his contemporaries. It is difficult to say what path he would have followed later. Probably neither Balanchine's, nor Massine's, nor Béjart's, but rather his own. However, besides *The Magnificence of the Universe*, a ballet that raised questions about the genre of the dance symphony but in no way resolved them, he did not create any other ballet symphonies. The failure of the first ballet immediately put an end to the possibility of further experiments in that direction. The productions Lopukhov contemplated—Beethoven's Fifth Symphony, Tchaikovsky's Fourth and Liszt's *Faust* Symphony—were never staged. For many years, practically until the late 1950s, the very idea of a ballet that lacked concrete dramatic content provoked sharp resistance in the Soviet Union. Only after the ballet *The Leningrad Symphony* was staged in 1961 by Igor Belsky to the music of Shostakovich did that point of view change. Ballets began to appear to symphonic music, concerti, and other forms of instrumental music. Of course, these works are not all of equal value, because much depends on the talent of the choreographer. Only those capable of "thinking in terms of dance," of making dance the bearer of feelings and ideas, have the right to tackle such projects.

The Red Whirlwind

All those who during the 1920s reproached the ballet for backwardness pointed to the absence from the repertory of productions on modern themes. In fact, there were no such ballets for quite a long time. If by modern ballets one means those that depict today's events, then there are not so many even in our time. The critics in the 1920s, indignant at the fact that for the fifth or sixth anniversary of the revolution good ballets about Soviet people had not yet appeared, could not have known that this problem would not be resolved even by the seventieth anniversary of the October Revolution.

Like any other art, ballet must naturally reflect the spiritual world of the people of its age. But in ballet, even more than in any other art, this is not done directly. The modernity of ballet is defined most often not by whether people of our times, heroes of the past, or fantastic beings are included, but by its major ideas, by the degree to which the author has a modern vision of life and a modern evaluation of phenomena. Therefore, ballet fairytales and legends and ballets based on Pushkin and Shakespeare sometimes turn out to be better at showing the modern world than ballets with collective farmers, border guards, and foreign spies. This was the situation in the twenties, too. The ballets created then about modern events and about the revolution proved to be far from the most modern and revolutionary. Addressing Soviet reality and telling of popular uprisings, the choreographers encountered problems so complex that this is where there were most mistakes and least success.

The popularity of a ballet with the audience is by no means the only criterion of its value; a superficial but garish production may have a long run while an experimental work has a poor box-office. Nevertheless, the statistical data for the ballets on modern and revolutionary subjects in the 1920s are extremely indicative. Three Moscow ballets were produced that to a certain degree belong to this category: *Stenka Razin* (1918), shown three times (revived in 1922, it had eleven more performances); *Ever-Fresh Flowers* (1922)—five times; and *The Whirlwind* (1927)—once.

In fact, they did not even become part of the repertory. Only *The Red Poppy* (1927) had a long stage life.

In Petrograd, after Asafiev's and Romanov's *Carmagnole* (1918), a workers' club production about which, unfortunately, no information is available, there were no ballets about the revolution until 1924. In an article timed for the opening of the 1924–25 season, Gvozdev wrote about the goals of the lyric theater and pointed out that "we need to respond to modern times." Further, he stated: "The ballet, preparing for this, is rehearsing a big production, *The Bolsheviks*, which should be a thrilling response to the demands of the times. It is a difficult attempt, and the audience must see this precisely as an attempt and take into account all the difficulties involved."[39]

In its final version this ballet, shown on October 29, 1924, was called *The Red Whirlwind*. A second attempt of the same sort, presented three years later, was Goleizovsky's ballet with a very similar title—*The Whirlwind*. Lopukhov and Goleizovsky chose exactly the same symbolic image —the image of a vortex, a whirlwind, a hurricane passing over the earth, smashing and uprooting everything old. The ballet was choreographed by Lopukhov, according to his own libretto, with music by Vladimir Deshevov (the poem *The Bolsheviks* expanded and reworked for the dance). Deshevov was linked to the TRAM movement (an influential social-political theater group); later he headed the musical section of the Leningrad TRAM and wrote the music for many of its productions. In his libretto, Lopukhov also worked with the forms of the agitprop political club theater, combining naturalistic portrayal with allegory.

The authors called this production "a synthetic poem in two processes with a prologue and an epilogue." Shortly before the premiere, the critic Nikolai Nasilov wrote: "The poem will represent a new form of choreography, not only in terms of its content, as the embodiment of political ideas and their manifestations in dance images, but also in its form, because the poem is a spectacle in which dance, mime, choral singing, and live speech will be united."[40]

The Red Whirlwind opened with a prologue, the theme of which, according to the program, was "a rejection of the cross, the symbol of humility and slavery" and "the aspiration to the star—the symbol of struggle and universal freedom." In the first act (process), an attempt was made to metaphorically present the proletarian revolution as a clash between the forces of revolution and counterrevolution. In related arts, including drama, allegories and symbols were often used to portray the revolution. As indicated above, in the realm of the lyric theater this course seemed correct even to Lunacharsky.

In May 1924 a conference was held at the Theatrical Museum concerning the ideological and artistic goals of the official theaters. Here Lunacharsky expressed his views concerning the abilities of opera and ballet to create a *féerie* or heroic spectacle essential to the masses.[41] There is every reason to think that Lopukhov, as the leader of the opera and ballet theater company, was at this conference and that what Lunacharsky said could only have strengthened his intention to present a dance allegory.

The designer, Leonid Chupiatov, created the painted scenery for the first process—a backdrop depicting a spiral figure in several shades of red, from yellow-orange to deep crimson. The theme of the first process was the battle of revolutionary and counterrevolutionary elements, and as the forces of light took the upper hand, the background also changed; the second spiral had more white surfaces.

The performers in the first process were divided into two groups: the forces of revolution (Elizaveta Gerdt, Viktor Semenov, and forty male and female dancers) and the forces of counterrevolution (Leonid Petrov and twenty students of the ballet school). Chupiatov designed a single dance uniform for them all: a short tunic tightly covering the body like a bathing suit, with strips of cloth on the back, fastened to the arms and legs, which suggested wings as they blew about. All the dancers' wings were dark red; positive and negative characters were distinguished by the color of their tunics—white for the soloists, orange-red for the other representatives of the revolution, and black for the counterrevolution.

The Red Whirlwind was shown almost two years after the dance symphony *The Magnificence of the Universe*. The pretentiousness of the literary program of the dance symphony had in its time provoked a flood of mocking commentaries. Nevertheless, in the first part of *The Red Whirlwind* Lopukhov did something similar. He proposed that in addition to the general symbol of the growing revolutionary surge, the dances would concretely show "the birth of socialism, the dawn and development of the revolution, its struggle with counterrevolution, and the birth and affirmation of communism." Here is how the meaning of the nine numbers comprising this scene was interpreted:

1. The accumulation of the elements of the socialist worldview without nationalist coloration. 2. The accumulated musical energy is transformed into light energy, reflecting the ever-growing complex of socialism. 3. The further transformation of energy from music to light and then into the form of a living organism. 4. A classical choreographic adagio characterizing socialism. 5. The monolith of socialism. 6. The beginnings of the schism. 7. The schism. 8. Revolution and counterrevolution (two themes). 9. The affirmation of the star.[42]

Now Lopukhov's program reads as a curiosity, but also as a document of the age. It reflects the naive, sincere aspiration of the artist, who was very far from understanding social processes, to take part in politics and sociology. The choreographer's intention, of course, could not be implemented in practice. What is important in ballet, however, is not the content of the program, but what happens on stage.

Classical dance served as the chief means of expression. The choreographer used movements selectively, attempting to avoid anything that might look "unmodern" and that might suggest the old "court" ballet. This led to an impoverishment of the lexicon, an imitation of gymnastics, which many at that time used in opposition to "outdated" classicism. All the reviewers wrote that the dancing was simplified, reduced to marching around; the movements suggested Sokol gymnastic exercises, rather than dance, and overall the performance smacked of the rhythmic movements of the Dalcroze school. The photographs attest to this.*

The dancers form a compact group, down on one knee in a row, their profiles to the audience. Their heads are covered with their "wings," which merge with the dark tunics. The light line of legs, bent at the knee, outlines the group with a zigzag. At the same time, several dancers form a three-story composition upstage, standing on each other's shoulders. This is a real "pyramid" like those then staged at all the club dramatizations with athlete performers. A frequent pose had arms and legs flung wide open. A person in a red tunic, with a red band on his head and scraps of calico fastened to his arms and legs, would imitate a five-pointed star: his head, hands, and feet were seen as the five points. The star was

*On Sokol gymnastics, see the note on p. 157.

constantly reproduced in dance designs as well. In the photograph of the final scene of the first process, the entire group of dancers is positioned on the stage in the form of a large star, over which rises a solo ballerina held aloft depicting revolution.

The dances of the revolution, executed by the two leading performers, were based, according to Lopukhov's plan, on the opposition between two principles: the firm and irreconcilable, embodied in an energetic dance by Semenov; and the compromise, whose embodiment was a gentle, "evasive" dance by Gerdt. The imperative principle eventually gains the upper hand. According to the program, the joint dance of the protagonists, their adagio, was intended to characterize socialism. Of course, no one perceived what was depicted on stage as "a variation of opportunism" or as "an adagio of socialism," but merely as ballet dances. The audience saw the usual duet and a "selection of the most ordinary technical figures."[43] Lopukhov's ballet was distinguished from the dances of the traditional ballet by the deliberate paucity of expressive means. Professionals of the highest caliber were putting themselves on a par with amateur productions, and the tremendous wealth of dance forms remained unused. In imposing on the dance functions alien to it—setting forth the content of political slogans—Lopukhov was asking for trouble. In fact, he was criticized; his choreographic compositions were seen as merely illustrative. One of the reviewers wrote: "For some reason the dancers form a circle around Gerdt and Semenov together, that is, evolution and revolution are united. Any sports instructor at a workers' club told to form a pyramid on this theme would have done this in a more politically literate manner—he would have removed evolution from the pyramid, leaving only the revolutionary, virile principle in the midst of the workers."[44]

The second act was treated quite differently. In contrast to the first act, in which a certain abstract idea of revolution was supposed to be expressed, here the intent was to show the participants in the struggle with the greatest possible authenticity. The decor was still symbolic. The red star that had crowned the first process (the dancers formed its outline with their red cape-wings) now appeared as the basic element of the set. It occupied almost the entire backdrop, surrounded by houses and skyscrapers, which the artist had depicted from above, as though from a great height. This decor served as the background for the first episodes of the act that followed the musical introduction. In the program they are listed as follows:

1. Musical Call. 2. The Citizens Awaiting the Revolution. 3. The Revolution. 4. The Entrance of the Plunderers. 5. The Entrance of the Supporters of the Revolution. 6. The Anguish of the Citizens and the Entrance of the Drunken Rabble. 7. The Dance of the Drunken Rabble and Their Arrest. 8. The Entrance of the People Cracking Sunflower Seeds.

Those who feared the revolution appeared on stage: people belonging to classes abolished during the revolution—women with parasols, in dresses with flounces and in hats, respectable gentlemen in long overcoats. Both their costumes and their behavior looked completely realistic. The defenders of the revolution also appeared: sailors, workers, and Red Guards, also shown with down-to-earth realism. And, finally, the dregs of the revolution, its scum: hooligans, plunderers, waifs, and other participants in the dance of the "drunken rabble."

Lopukhov wanted the second scene of this act to be pervaded by the theme of the gradually strengthening ties between city and country. The previous set was replaced by a new one; next to the star and the city buildings stood the large frame of a country cottage, taking up almost a fourth of the backdrop. Against this background eleven scenes were performed, including three described almost identically in the program: "the first contact of the city with the country" (No. 9), "the second contact of the city with the country" (No. 14), and "the third contact of the city with the country" (No. 19). Between them were a colorful "devil's sabbath of the black marketeers" (Nos. 12 and 13), a wild, reckless dance of the riff-raff (Nos. 15 and 16), and pantomime scenes with the mother of a revolutionary (Nos. 10 and 11). The dances were accompanied by a spoken text—shouts and songs. A performer in the production, Leonid Lavrovsky, recalls: "The actors portraying black marketeers appeared on the stage with sacks over their shoulders, approached the footlights, turned to the audience with the words 'Meat! Butter!' and so on, tossed their sacks away, and danced."[45] The choreographer used gymnastic, acrobatic movements. In the dance of the riff-raff, lads dressed in bell-bottomed trousers and open shirts formed a "wheel" and a "bridge" and walked on their hands. Disheveled, lively girls marveled at their agility. Pretending to be frightened, they fell into their partners' arms, spreading their legs wide and revealing blue bloomers sticking out from under their short skirts. The dance was crowned by a rollicking song. In contrast to it rose the song of the Red Army soldiers (No. 17), foreshadowing the "Mayday procession" and "The Oath," (No. 18), the intended culmination of the act.

There was a change of scenery. The star changed its outline: instead of peaceful straight lines it was marked by agitated twists. Bending, it flew as if seized by a whirlwind, on a background of storm clouds and unfurled banners that covered the skyscrapers and huts. The lower edge of the star merged with the flags that people were carrying and the star itself resembled a scarlet banner being torn from their hands. However, the action on stage lacked dynamism. In the photograph there is a large motionless crowd facing the right wings, where a group of people holds a width of cloth with the inscription "Greetings to the *Comintern.*" There are also pioneers with drums, workers in blouses, and peasants in white shirts. Behind them are Red Guards with banners, and upstage, a brass band. Everyone stands with their hands raised identically in greeting and despite the external realism of the costumes and accessories they look unnatural. It was not surprising that the reviewers wrote that the "Mayday procession" proved much less attractive in the theater than in real life. This was also true of the final "union of the peasant with the worker." The "genuine" peasants, feet clumsily shod in bast shoes, scratching themselves with all due natural verisimilitude, lacked artistic truth, just like the posterboard workers.

The major flaw in the second act of *The Red Whirlwind* was the fact that only the negative dramatis personae were characterized in dance. Despite the intentions of Lopukhov as librettist, for Lopukhov as choreographer the central episodes of the act proved to be "the dance of the drunken rabble," "the devil's sabbath with sacks," and the "dance and song of the riff-raff." All these people, who even recently could have been seen in the dark alleys of Petrograd, were in their own way unusual and picturesque. They lived in a world of definite sounds and visual images that were easily theatricalized. The motley rags were picturesque in their own way; the thieves' songs—all those "Alesha-shas" and "Mama-mamas"— gave rise to a special rhythm of movement and suggested a dance theme; the exaggerated manners and the lurching gait transferred easily into a boisterous dance. This was a spectacle of its own, easy to capture and develop by transforming the social types into stage images.

Lopukhov was not alone in sensing the possibilities inherent in such a theme. The colorful way of life of the streets had already been brought to the music-hall stage before it came to the ballet theater; *Tverbul* (Tverskoi Boulevard) by Foregger (1922–23) preceded *The Red Whirlwind*. In many dance revues of those years there were scenes with typical real-life figures: the waif, the lady with her handbag swiped by a street urchin, the street-sweeper, the militia-man, and so on. But the theater, especially the lyric theater, was still getting used to this theme. In the late 1920s the theater truly gave it its due. The first Soviet operettas that appeared shortly after *The Red Whirlwind* (Rudolph Mervolf's *Dunya the Fine Spinner*, 1926, the performance of *Among Three Pine Trees* by the Blue Blouse group,* 1927, and others), also showed the inevitable riff-raff, skid-row bums, down-and-out people, and other similar characters, and made broad use of slang and street songs. Slices of life picked up from the past, still fresh in the memory, also appear in the early operas on modern themes, such as *For Red Petrograd* by Arseny Gladkovsky and Evgeny Prussak (1925), and particularly Deshevov's opera *Ice and Steel* (1930), where one of the central scenes took place in a flea market. Prokofiev's ballet *Le Pas d'Acier*, shown abroad in 1927, also included episodes entitled "the train with black marketeers," "cigarette hawkers," and so on, but here most important was the scene at the factory with the "dances of the machines."

Dealing with positive figures was much more complicated. Such characters as workers, Red Army soldiers, and sailors found their place on the dramatic stage at this time, but only in the theaters of the "left front." In June 1924 the Meyerhold Theater toured in Leningrad. They performed the political revue *Earth Rampant*, in which real motorcycles drove across the stage with a deafening roar and dusty, hoarse soldiers burst in along with them, brandishing real rifles. The premiere of *D. E.* was also presented. Here they chased a football, marched to an accordion, and did

---

*The Blue Blouse was an agitprop theater group that specialized in "living newspapers," multimedia political revues. They published a journal of the same name that gave texts and instructions for amateur groups to follow. The title of their play refers to the Russian folk saying "to lose one's way among three pines," that is, to get lost in broad daylight. (Ed.)

biomechanical exercises. The extreme authenticity of the portrayals was impressive. The use of certain real-life details—in the context of a theatrical performance—became an accepted device. When *The Red Whirlwind* appeared four months later the critics did not fail to reproach Lopukhov with the fact that he had put dressed-up mannequins on stage instead of people. What had been successful in drama did not come off at all in ballet. The choreographer could not find a visual expression for his theme. The illustrative quality contradicted the abstract quality of the dance.

Forty years later Lopukhov called *The Red Whirlwind* his "greatest failure."[46] It is difficult to argue with an evaluation given by the author of a work looking back at it so much later. Yes, *The Red Whirlwind* was a failure; this is borne out both by the rather eloquent responses of the press and by the fate of the ballet, which was shown to an audience only once. Nevertheless, *The Red Whirlwind* is the first ballet about the October Revolution. Lopukhov aspired to conquer heights that when the ballet was in rehearsal (1923–24) had not even been fully mastered by drama, let alone the lyric theater. He aspired to these heights without the possibility of guidance from the experience of his predecessors—he simply didn't have any—very dimly imagining what route he should follow. Literature and the related arts—drama, the music-hall stage—pointed to two possibilities: on the one hand, a metaphorical means for conveying the ideas of the grandeur and power of the proletarian revolution, and on the other, the naturalistic chronicle. To unite these in one work was a mistake to begin with; Lopukhov notes this in his own analysis of his ballet. But the real problem lay elsewhere.

Abstract form and pure illustration equally contradicted the specific nature of ballet. Only the posterboard grotesque, which became the standard method for characterizing enemies of the revolution, revealed new dance possibilities. Gvozdev was right when six months earlier he warned choreographers: "If you rush headlong toward the new slogans of modern art without subjecting them to an organic reworking within ballet itself, as a specific stage genre, then ruin is inevitable."[47] Lopukhov wanted to continue working on *The Red Whirlwind*, in particular to develop "the entrance of the Pioneers in dance."[48] But he was not able to return to the production.

Night on Bald Mountain;
A Tale About the Fox, the Rooster,
The Cat, and the Ram (Renard)

Lopukhov as an artist was an inventor and a pioneer. He was irrepressibly attracted to the new, and for him the new appeared in various guises. Nevertheless, there is a line that can be traced throughout the choreographer's work—the incarnation of Russian folklore on stage.

Even before the war, a dance from the Riazan* region was among the numbers Lopukhov staged for his sister Evgenia and her partner Alexander Orlov. This piece was performed for many years. "The highly artistic Riazan dance of Lopukhova and Orlov" is mentioned in the description of the Mayday celebration of 1920.[49] A publicity notice for the Petrograd dancers' appearance in Moscow observed, "The Riazan dance was truly a triumph and we repeat it three times at every performance."[50]

In the early 1920s theoreticians and practitioners of the theater began to show a special interest in ethnography and were attracted by the traditional theater. On the one hand, ancient theatrical forms were restored, including dance rituals. Beginning in 1923 the Experimental Theater in Petrograd became prominent in this regard. It was headed by Vsevolod Vsevolodsky-Gerngross, who produced, in particular, *A Russian Folk Wedding Ritual*. In 1925 in Moscow the First Scientific Ethnographic Theater presented the "songs and round dances of the Volga Region," "the exorcism dances of the shamans," and so on. On the other hand, during the first years after the revolution, many theater people were possessed by the idea of a new "folk theater" that would grow out of the traditional methods of street theater, with its dynamism, buffoonery, and improvisational techniques. Here the idea was not one of ethnographic verisimilitude but of a selection of the expressive means of folk art, in keeping with the age. Such productions were staged, for instance, by Sergei Radlov in his Theater of Popular Comedy, which was active from 1920 to 1922 in the Iron Hall of the Petrograd People's House. Radlov himself wrote scenarios for "circus comedies," using the methods of the Italian commedia del l'arte; he intended them for actors' improvisations. He also presented classical comedies interpreted with various eccentric tricks.

---

*Riazan, near Moscow, is one of the most ancient Russian cities. (Ed.)

Lopukhov was interested in such experiments. Instead of the clichés of *The Little Humpbacked Horse* he wanted to produce a truly folkloric "skit." He believed that a caustic joke, malicious mockery, and bold laughter could become tools for a new revolutionary art. Moreover, the devices of Russian buffoon (*skomorokh*) humor allowed him to create a performance where "baring the device" would become a rule of the game, where the action performed would be only a staging of the action and the dance an imitation of dancing. Trying to prove the continued value of buffoon play, tricks, and jibes, Lopukhov wrote that it was exactly "right now—given the controversy about principles of theatrical production"—that this was especially necessary.[51] As part of the "controversy about principles" in the 1920s, the author produced several such buffoon productions.

In January 1921 Lopukhov composed the dances for Rimsky-Korsakov's opera *The Snow Maiden*. This was his choreographic debut in his own theater. Asafiev noted the success of the young choreographer. "The ballet dancers' performance of 'buffoon play by the *skomorokhi*' in the third act was a daring innovation in the choreographer Lopukhov's production. This staging is so clever, original, fresh, and musically thoughtful that one can only rejoice and welcome this young talent."[52]

In the same year, the newspaper *Zhizn iskusstva* notified its readers that a new ballet to the music of Mussorgsky's symphonic poem *Night on Bald Mountain* had been included in the repertory.[53] However, this announcement proved premature. The ballet was shown much later—in the spring of 1924 after *The Firebird* and *The Magnificence of the Universe*. In the program the ballet Lopukhov had created was called a "buffoonish, devilish spectacle."

Before the orchestra began to play a noisy band of buffoons with little bells appeared in front of the curtain. A herald appeared with them and summoned the crowd. The performer in this role, the famous mime artist Soliannikov, had considerable experience in the dramatic theater and Lopukhov gave him quite a large spoken part: "Hey, you! Good people! Young valiants, fair maidens, come hither, come hear how Chernobog couples with Ezhi-Baba on Bald Mountain!" Then he crossed to a rock and with a wave of his hand ("Let the show begin!") the performance started.

The ballet included both a calling of a coven and devil worship in the spirit of a black mass (for example, among the performers there is a "censer-bearer"). There was also a devil's sabbath with witches, devils, and skeletons, played by the students of the ballet school. Despite an external resemblance to the composer's program, the images were interpreted completely differently.

Mussorgsky took ancient popular beliefs very seriously as a manifestation of the folk imagination. Here he is similar to Gogol; it is no accident that during the life of the composer the idea already existed of including *Night on Bald Mountain* in the opera *Sorochinsky Fair*.* Mussorgsky wanted to paint a colorful picture of the celebration by the witches and devils on Bald Mountain, a sort of Russian Walpurgisnacht. In order to understand the "mood" of the devil's sabbath, he even turned to documents of the interrogations of people accused of witchcraft.

Lopukhov translated all this to a level of deliberately theatricalized "buffoonery." He wanted to depict the "buffoons mocking the church ritual" of a Christianity violently forced upon ancient Russia. The pagans met in secret and performed a parody in which the main actors were Chernobog and Ezhi-Baba.[54] In the music there is a real unleashing of diabolic forces, a stormy orgy. The composer wrote: "The general character of the music is torrid." Lopukhov's treatment was contrived and in the opinion of Gvozdev "suggests an intellectually cold attitude toward a 'devilish spectacle.'"[55]

This interpretation, however, was in opposition both to the music and to the passion that the first-class character dancers Andrei Lopukhov and Olga Fedorova (in another cast, Valentina Ivanova) brought to the roles of Chernobog and Ezhi-Baba. The appearance of Ezhi-Baba on a two-wheeled cart drawn by four carters was the most effective moment in the ballet. In the very immobility of her figure, covered in close-fitting red tights, there was a suggestion of a flame frozen for an instant and ready to incinerate at any moment. Heading the mad round dance of the witches, both performers were magnificent—they were able to sense and convey the spirit of Mussorgsky's music. Lopukhov created a rich duet for Chernobog and Ezhi-Baba, with varied outlines and newly invented steps; it featured, for example, supports of the male dancer by the ballerina. But most of the group dances, in the reviewers' opinion, lacking

---

*Walt Disney later used Mussorgsky's music in the demonic section of *Fantasia*. (Ed.)

true dynamics ("crowding on the stage, and just that," wrote Gvoz-dev), looked chaotic. Soliannikov complained that Lopukhov ignored the expansive nature of Russian dances and composed dances with "tiny, cramped movements, which sometimes turned into a kind of rhythmic 'patter.' " [56]

The decor also was not really in keeping with Lopukhov's intent: One of the backdrops, drawn by Korovin for some other play, portrayed a thicket and the moon breaking through the clouds. The "buffoon" element really only appeared in the patterned wings. The multicolored costumes by Makari Domrachev were more in line with the choreographer's intentions.

The next time he tried a "buffoon play," Lopukhov enlisted the support of both composer and designer. Right after *Night on Bald Mountain*, he decided to stage *A Tale About the Fox, the Rooster, the Cat, and the Ram (Le Renard)* by Stravinsky, with decor and costumes by Vladimir Dmitriev. However, the production had to be postponed until the score of the ballet (written in 1916–17) was received from abroad. The ballet's premiere took place in France in 1922 (the choreographer was Bronislava Nijinska; the designer was Michel Larionov). Lopukhov's ballet did not reach the stage until 1927. Stravinsky indicated that the text of *Renard* should be sung by four singers who did not participate directly in the action. Located in the orchestra, which Stravinsky recommended be put at the back of the stage, they performed the roles of the four characters of the subtitle.

The first scene begins with loud cries from the rooster, alternately frightening off his enemies and praising himself. The fox appears dressed as a nun and in unctuous tones, like a sanctimonious pilgrim, urges the rooster to repent. Their witty dialogue concludes with the rooster falling into the fox's paws. In response to his sorrowful lamentations, the brave heroes—the cat and the ram—appear and drive off the fox. The rooster, the cat, and the ram begin to dance to facetious singing. They taunt the fox and tease her about her hypocritical ways. In the second scene, the fox again appears before the rooster, but this time in an ingratiating voice she describes the charms of worldly life. Again the greed and imprudence of the rooster lead to misfortune. And again his friends come to his aid. They threaten the fox. Frightened, she conducts a dialogue with her "little eyes," "little legs," and "tail," testing how truly they serve her.

But her tail betrays the fox: "I clung to stumps, bushes, and logs so that wild animals would grab the fox and carry her away." The cat and the ram drag the fox from her lair by the tail and kill her. The defeated enemy becomes a butt for witticisms: Proverbs, clever embellishments on the tale, and mocking bon mots spew forth.

Dancers, clowns, and acrobats had to depict simultaneously what was set forth in the text ("preferably on a trestle stage," Stravinsky indicated). The music and the text provided magnificent material for stage play, suggesting witty, parodic action. There were opportunities for amusing dance-clowning, grotesque dance-fights between characters, and dance-satires, for example, during the parody of the ecclesiastical chants that characterize the fox in the first part. Here everything had to be different from traditional ballet—the direction and the decor, the acting and the dancing. Lopukhov understood this. Together with the designer Dmitriev, the choreographer sought a general principle governing the ballet. Action took place only in the foreground of the stage. The flat shapes of pine trees of various heights and colors served as background. The style of a primitive popular print (*lubok*) in this staging was emphasized by such details as the multi-colored sun, decorated with designs, and an ornate cloud, which the buffoons carried out on poles.

The performers were dressed in Russian blouses, men's longwaisted coats, and leather boots with pleats. They were distinguished by the details of their costumes and accessories: The fox wore a cap in the form of an animal's head and a tail; the ram had a black curly sheepskin coat, curved horns, and a braid down his back; the rooster had a red disheveled wig, a beard, and spurs; the cat had a smooth wig with a part, a headdress like a cat's face, a striped waistcoat, and a tail. In addition to the four main characters, Lopukhov introduced a large number of supporting characters. They included buffoon servants in red caftans, lilac loose-fitting trousers, yellow socks, and bast shoes, a buffoon who portrayed a jagged bough with twigs and leaves onto which the rooster leaped, and so on.

Students from the ballet school performed in the production. Sketches of the costumes for the children playing the fox's little eyes and the fox's tail have been preserved: Huge eyes or a large furry tail were put on over a peasant costume covering the entire upper part of the torso and head, so that below, only the trousers and feet, in bast shoes, were visible. Even the objects mentioned in the text were brought to life: a knife, a window, a stump. Children appeared with little pine trees fastened to their backs; the performers portraying the fox's paws jumped on stilts. Finally, there were also completely incomprehensible characters—"little effigies" and "little subeffigies"—and to top everything off, six speckled hens with little red combs (they were played by the smallest students) who "laid eggs" right on stage.

Stravinsky called *Renard* "a short burlesque for street performances,"[57] and undoubtedly thought that the artists would perform and dance in it differently than they did in the old "classical" ballet. Lopukhov used the huge stage of the Maryinsky Theater and dancers who had been trained within the ballet tradition. Of course he sought new means of kinetic expressiveness, understanding that here the old ones would not do. Lopukhov composed "roosterish" and "feline" movements, so that it would be clear that the buffoons were portraying these animals. In Asafiev's opinion, Lopukhov was able in this way to communicate in stage movement one of the most important features of the music: It was "not a realistic reproduction of animal habits and steps, but a buffoon-like performer's imitation in rhythm and movement, in dance and acrobatics."[58]

"Buffoon-like action" requires graphic, precise, and above all illustrative but not decorative gestures; elastic, dynamic movements; and virtuoso play with objects. In addition to excellent dance technique, the performers had to master at least the basics of circus performing; without this it would have been impossible to portray the buffoons, who were by definition acrobats and clowns. Lopukhov introduced somersaults and insisted that the dancers learn to walk easily on stilts and climb a pole. Gvozdev was hardly right when he wrote: "He did not make his performers train for the sake of the new production, but took from them only what they could give."[59]

Apparently the individual strokes did not succeed in forming a total picture. The dance pantomime with acrobatics and clowning, which was dynamic, mischievous, and still clearly illustrated the music, demanded that attention be focused on the performer. Lopukhov was afraid to leave the dancers alone one-on-one with the audience. Possibly he was afraid of leaving the broad theater stage empty; he filled it with all sorts of supporting characters. Photographs show some individual moments of the action: Here are the characters with animal headdresses and without them, someone on stilts, someone climbing a rope, no less than fifteen youngsters squatting along the backdrop—either an "audience," or buffoon servants. There is also the "sun" and the children dressed as hens, with large white eggs hanging between their legs. In short, the stage is packed with people. Lopukhov did not consider it possible to change the tradition according to which the musicians and the conductor in an operatic theater are in the orchestra pit, but he did not seat the singers in the orchestra; he brought them on stage with the dancers and mimes. In doing this, the director broke the "rules of the game" stipulated quite precisely by the composer.

The critics considered Lopukhov's greatest slip the fact that by extending the functions of the singers he created a second cast of main characters. Along with Konstantin Zuykov (the Fox), Andrei Lopukhov (the Rooster), Boris Komarov (the Cat), and Vasily Vainonen (the Ram), opera artists also performed: Ivan Ershov (in another cast Nikolai Kuklin), Vasily Tikhiy (in another cast Vasily Kalinin), Alexander Fomin, and Nikolai Butiagin. The singers were dressed in the same costumes as the dancers; the only difference was that the latter wore the animal face on the head and the former had it fastened to the waist. Even Asafiev, who was much less critical of the production than the other critics, wrote: "The mistake in this most interesting and undeservedly dismissed production was not in its principles, but in the 'doubling' of singers and actors: Either they should have been sharply separated, as in Stravinsky, or the singers should have been 'whipped into shape' (but this of course is unthinkable)."[60] Soliannikov describes the confusion of the audience before whom "foxes, rams and roosters 'began to duplicate'. . . ."[61] The doubling of characters did not make them more vivid, nor did it add the mischievousness of sheer farce. Gvozdev describes the performers of the fox: "On the stage stood (and I mean stood—nothing more, though we expect movement from the ballet!) a boring-looking character in the style of a *muzhik à la russe*. Next to him hopped his double, a dancer with a mask. Both lacked the sharp flavor and the hint of mockery that so ringingly resound in the musical accompaniment."[62]

Piling up extra characters on the stage also had a negative effect on the music. The orchestra, which was conducted by Alexander Gauk, was somewhat larger than the group Stravinsky had proposed. Nevertheless, it was poorly heard. "The orchestra pit seemed to be some sort of a hole from which only scraps of separate sounds emerged."[63] The critics complained that the singers did not keep time with the musicians, that the stamping and the stilts of all those "little effigies" muffled the chamber-music quality of the ensemble.

The premiere of *Renard* took place on January 2, 1927. After this, the ballet ran only once more, although on February 6 there was a public viewing for journalist-workers. Each time, these performances ended with noisy arguments, almost brawls, in the audience. Eyewitnesses recall that enterprising people organized whistle sales in the theater. The journal *Zhizn iskusstva* wrote: "Whenever Stravinsky's ballet *Renard* is performed, there is an incident. Passions are so inflamed that part of the audience whistles when it ends. The leadership of the theater had to take energetic measures, right up to the detention of the balletomanes who so zealously express their feelings about the production. Several people were arrested and turned over to the police."[64] The notices that appeared after the public viewing also show that most of the audience did not understand the ballet. Several confessed that they viewed the 17-minute production as a confusing prologue to an upcoming ballet and were completely surprised when the whole thing ended.

Of course, the complex modern music of *Renard* is not immediately understood by the unprepared listener. Stravinsky, after all, was creating neither an ethnographic work with direct quotations from folk sources nor a stylization as a farce. After having assimilated a considerable amount of song and dance material, he boldly transformed it into a new type of art. In his own way the choreographer was faced with a similar task. It is most precisely defined by the same words Asafiev used in characterizing Stravinsky's music when he spoke of "recreating the buffoon grotesque in a new context—not in a farce, but in the framework of the highest artistic culture, with the application of flexible modern means of expression."[65]

The critics of the premiere agreed that the abstruseness of the staging interfered with the perception of the music. However, in analyzing the reasons for the failure of *Renard* a half-century later, a modern scholar of Lopukhov's work, Galina Dobrovolskaya, tried to understand the nature of the choreographer's experiment and came to different conclusions. She believes that in dividing each role between a dancer and a singer, Lopukhov gave to each one that which belonged to his art. The singers, given words, took upon themselves the pantomime and acting part of the role, while the ballet dancers worked in the sphere of pure dance and did not try to illustrate the text, since that was not what the choreographer saw as the goal of the dancing. This was a staging device complex enough to approach Stravinsky's music, which Asafiev described as the "*highest* artistic culture" and "*modern* means of expression." However, the experiment was by no means a total success and the critics (particularly Gvozdev and Sollertinsky) who by the late 1920s were preoccupied by the idea of the dramatization of dance did not see the point of this attempt.

Agreeing with Dobrovolskaya's ideas, we see in *Renard* not an unfortunate failure by Lopukhov, but one of the first applications on the ballet stage of the principle of "doubling," at present rather widespread (two Hermans in the ballet *The Queen of Spades*, staged by Nikolai Boyarchikov; two Mayakovskys in Roland Petit's *Allumez les Etoiles!*; five Nijinskys in Maurice Béjart's *Nijinsky, Clown of God*, and so on). But, as was the case with many of the choreographer's early attempts, this discovery was neither understood nor developed. The theater did not take up Gvozdev's call to develop *Renard* "in laboratory fashion, in the studio, eagerly learning through this marvelous material."[66] Lopukhov was not allowed to return to this ballet; *Renard* was shown to an audience only three times.

Pulcinella

Lopukhov's interest in forms of folk theater also found expression in *Pulcinella* (1926), a ballet shown just before *Renard*. The primary source for the production was the Italian commedia del l'arte. Lopukhov first came in contact with commedia del l'arte in 1921 when he staged the dances for *The Servant of Two Masters* at the Grand Dramatic Theater (the premiere was May 20). Benois was the director and designer. His plan for the staging opened up broad possibilities for the choreographer. There were five dance interludes in the production—a Spanish dance, the dance of the peasants, a Turkish dance, the dance of the kitchen boys, a Sicilian dance, and a grand finale. Asafiev selected and orchestrated music by Scarlatti and Rameau. Stefan Mokulsky called these interludes "archretrospective,"[67] which, in any case, testifies to a profound understanding of the material of the period. The collaboration with such a fine stylist and connoisseur of traditional art as Benois undoubtedly taught Lopukhov a great deal. Five years later he used his experience in producing *Pulcinella*, although his own principle of the production was different, not as much of a stylization in the manner of The World of Art.

Commissioned by Diaghilev, Stravinsky had written *Pulcinella* using the music of the eighteenth-century composer Giovanni Battista Pergolesi. The ballet recounted the comic amatory adventures of Pulcinella, taken from an anthology of the same period. The premiere of the ballet took place in Paris in 1920 and was choreographed by Léonide Massine and designed by Pablo Picasso. Lopukhov used only the music; his scenario differed greatly from the original.

In Massine's version, the lively, clever Pulcinella is sought after by all the girls. Rosetta and Prudenza flirt with him, but he prefers Pimpinella. The Dottore and Tartaglia—the fathers of Rosetta and Prudenza—and the lovers of the girls are hostile to Pulcinella. After many mischievous pranks, disguises, and quid pro quos, Pulcinella marries Pimpinella, and at the same time the two other weddings are celebrated.

Lopukhov eliminated both pairs of "noble lovers" and changed the nature of the conflict. His Pulcinella, trying to win Smeraldina's hand, clashed with the wealthy, the famous, and the powerful. Lopukhov's ballet had a definite social orientation: It was permeated by a spirit of anti-bourgeois satire. Lopukhov insisted that Pulcinella was a "worker" and that "working people do not die but are eternally reborn, since life and its progress are affirmed by working people and not by parasites." From this perspective he also composed a new plot, using the principle of Gozzi's *Fiabe*, that is, a mixture of fantasy and realism.[68]

After the dancers presented themselves to the music of the overture, the scene of the "work" of the serving-girl Smeraldina followed. She animatedly poured water from a large garden watering can and flowers sprang up everywhere along her path. The Capitano, Pantalone, the Dottore and Sbirro entered with their servants; then the hero himself appeared. He gaily wooed Smeraldina and wickedly scoffed at his haughty, stupid, and boastful opponents. Their relationship was revealed in Pulcinella's three "tricks," after each of which he was "murdered" and then miraculously resurrected.

During the first trick Pulcinella hid in a "house" which began to rotate so that his pursuers could not enter. When they nevertheless reached the prankster, they tore him to pieces, but each piece immediately turned into a Pulcinella and he thus appeared as five people. During the second trick Pulcinella made a table, at which his enemies were seated, dance. Pulcinella was flattened with huge hammers and wedged into the ground, but from the ground appeared a giant Pulcinella, twice human size. After the third trick he was cut in two, and although his legs continued to dance, Smeraldina, broken-hearted, nevertheless arranged a funeral for Pulcinella. But she sobbed so bitterly that she filled a whole bucket with her tears and Pulcinella revived again. After the three tricks and the three resurrections (between them were two interludes not directly connected with the plot) Smeraldina and Pulcinella danced a love duet (to the music of the gavotte). The musical competition between the trombone and the double-bass was staged by Lopukhov as the dance of Pulcinella and his four doubles. Then from the double-bass appeared four revolting old women who rushed to kiss Pulcinella's four enemies, who fled. Then followed the wedding scene (a minuet). Lopukhov "created a derisively mocking yet mirthful wedding ceremony for Smeraldina and Pulcinella, who laughed and cried as they married—an atheistic wedding ceremony in the spirit of the commedia del l'arte and in the form of a farce."[69] Then Smeraldina brought Pulcinella two "newborn" little girls in a flower basket. The performers said farewell to the audience in the final dance, which united them all—both victors and vanquished. The communal rejoicing was a celebration by comedians who have enjoyed entertaining people in the form of traditional characters—"masks."

Just as Stravinsky created a twentieth-century work based on eighteenth-century music, Lopukhov in turn interpreted Stravinsky according to his own understanding of the modern world. The characters of the Italian comedy and the plots of the harlequinades had long been part of the ballet. But previously, choreographers had borrowed various plot turns and then built upon them a ballet traditional in form (such as *Harlequinade [Les Millions d'Arlequin]* by Petipa). In *Pulcinella* the dance action derived directly from commedia del l'arte. Nothing was allowed to stop the swift course of comedy. Each successive episode represented yet another stage in Pulcinella's struggle with his enemies—yet another trick, another fabricated trap, another of his victories.

Comparing the Paris and Leningrad productions, Alexandre Benois found the former to be more subtle, elegant, and stylistically noteworthy. He thought that Lopukhov had "destroyed the fragile beauty of this paradoxical work by complicating and 'deepening' the subject and transforming the transparent design of Massine's dances by all manner of cunning tricks."[70] But the changes introduced by Lopukhov made the production quite modern. His attraction to a theater of action, dynamic and full of vitality, created a connection between the choreographer and the experimental drama directors of the time, who were also constructing productions according to the rational laws of modern life, which expected clear, definite answers, activity, and impetuous forward movement.

The joyful tone of the production was also in large part due to the designer, Dmitriev. The lightweight white structures against the background of the pale blue backdrop called to mind the production of *Lysistrata* designed by Isaac Rabinovich. But here the three-dimensional construction with rotating towers and an arbor intensified the dynamics of the production. The characters appeared and disappeared on various floors of the construction; the little Pulcinellas in their ridiculous little striped caps leaned out from the windows, settled themselves on the upper balustrade, and sat down in a pack on the arches. The towers circled gaily as though dancing. At the culmination of the performance nothing on stage could remain at rest; both people and things had succumbed to the power of carnival glee.

The characters were dressed in accordance with the traditions of the commedia del l'arte. Comic effect was achieved by a caricatured exaggeration of the details of props, costumes, and make-up: Sbirro's huge wooden sword and his disproportionately long turned-up nose; Pantalone's crooked eyebrows and mustache; the immense, heaving belly of the Dottore, his funny goat-like beard and the gigantic enema-bag he clutched to himself. The masks of the old women were especially complex: on their faces they wore separate mouths with protruding teeth-tusks, and masks with bulging eyes, supported by long eyelashes, were sewn to the wigs. Red and yellow dominated the costumes, and stripes and checks were used a great deal. The figure of the Dottore in his cloak and wide-brimmed hat, Pantalone's cape, and the black gloves of the old women stood out like black spots on the joyful sunny background.

In *Pulcinella* there were echoes of the productions of Tairov, Meyerhold, Vakhtangov's *Turandot*, and Prokofiev's opera *Love for Three*

Oranges, which was staged by Radlov. In looking at new Soviet direct-ing, however, Lopukhov did not copy the devices it discovered; rather, with their help he revived expressive means suitable to a choreographic production. "I created *Pulcinella* as a ballet production," wrote Lopu-khov at the time of the premiere, and he insisted that all the jokes typical of Italian comedy be performed choreographically.[71] Later he refined this idea: "*Pulcinella* required the use of different kinds of masks, and I tried to create these masks in dance, trying to find appropriate movements for each of them."[72]

Each character was given both a specific costume and specific move-ments. From Lopukhov's notes on Dmitriev's sketches it is clear that the pompous, haughty Dottore "walks step by step, shaking his belly," and that Sbirro, thanks to his exaggerated big boots and his manners, those of a true champion of public order, sometimes saluting, sometimes stretching "at ease" ("heels together, toes apart"), acquired an "almost Chaplinesque" gait. Lopukhov's Pantalone "always walks with a mincing gait," now and then feeling for the purse hidden under his cloak. And the Capitano, whose "left leg is much thicker than his right," takes big steps as though he were marching, throwing his "legs out in *grands battements*, although he leans to one side."

The most important part of Lopukhov's production was the rhythm. This affected the action as a whole, the relationship between the indi-vidual scenes, and the individual movements of the actors: Each step cor-responded strictly to the music. In setting forth the principles that guided him in this production, Lopukhov explained that here "there are none of the free movements so often encountered in the old ballets. Everything is strictly measured and carefully studied, even in a simple march."[73] Soliannikov, who played the role of the Capitano, later recalled: "All the action was interwoven and intertwined, as though with slender threads, to the rhythm . . . not a single measure remained free. Each step, each gesture, the smallest movement—everything was immediately fitted into a specific measure."[74]

Lopukhov's demands were hard on the performers, who were used to the pantomime of the old ballets. Even Gvozdev noted this: "The Capitano-Dottore-Pantalone-Sbirro group, the older dancers, should have been 'more tightly pulled together,' for here the performers go out of 'tune' and slightly lose the vividness of their movement; the old un-pleasant clichés immediately pop up, recalling the worn-out methods of portraying comic old men in ballets, tramping about the stage in the various versions of *The Little Humpbacked Horse* and *La Fille du Pharaon*."[75] Gvozdev saw Lopukhov's method of thematically developing the dancing (with each character having his own movement) as an innovative discovery.

The critics considered it remarkable that, after so many experiments and after having tried out so many different forms of dance expression, Lopukhov stayed with classical dance in *Pulcinella*. He gave virtuoso classical dance primarily to the two main characters—Pulcinella and Smeraldina. But Lopukhov applied the traditional technique in his own way. "While borrowing many classical movements from the old choreographic masters, I enriched them with the capricious accoutrements of our time," the choreographer stated.[76]

The critics unanimously recognized the role of Pulcinella as one of the most difficult in the modern repertory. No matter what Pulcinella did— and he did a great deal: played pranks and changed costumes, "became flattened" and "lengthened," died and was resurrected—everything was connected to dance that was both frenzied and attractive, packed with technical tricks. By increasing the difficulties and quickening the tempo, Lopukhov changed the nature of the classical steps and brought them to the level of the grotesque.

At the premiere, the young dancer Boris Komarov appeared unexpectedly in the role of Pulcinella, replacing Leonid Leontiev, who had fallen ill. The reviewers raved about both performers (Leontiev appeared starting with the third performance). The seemingly effortless lightness with which the most puzzling steps were executed became the basic coloration. More subtle nuancing was achieved with the help of mime, which was an important aspect of Leontiev's performance.

In the dances of Smeraldina (Gerdt and Taissia Troyanovskaya) and her friends, for all their complexity, the movements did not diverge from the classical model. "In *Pulcinella* a Smeraldina cannot be created choreographically outside the classical framework," wrote the choreographer.[77] The deviations from the "canons" were not significant. Still, according to Gerdt, it was difficult for the performers to master the transitions between the individual steps and to get used to the strict, bar-by-bar relationship between the movements and the music and to the unaccustomed tempi.

Two interludes were also created as a vehicle for dance: "the unsuccessful supper of the little Pulcinellas" and "the comic Turks." For the entrance of the little Pulcinellas, Lopukhov used a dynamic dance device —running in spirals. The plot of the second interlude (the comic Turks) was perhaps based on one of the dances in *The Servant of Two Masters*. In any event, in Massine's Paris production, there were no Turks—Lopukhov invented them. The dances of Olga Berg, who played one of the comic Turks, were based on extremely complicated movements, primarily turns. All of the critics were particularly astounded by her double *tours en l'air* which as a rule were performed only by men. Lopukhov also introduced purely acrobatic tricks. The male dancers who appeared with Berg amused the audience by performing all sorts of stunts which specifically demanded the ability to stand on one's head; for this, it is clear from the sketch of the costume, special padding was placed in the turban. The introduction of secondary characters—the *zanni*, the little Pulcinellas, the doubles, the ugly old women—permitted the use of buffoon-like elements.

There was good reason to keep *Pulcinella* in the repertory. The ballet was exuberant, clever, and modern in spirit; the audience liked it. It met one of the demands of the age, the need to laugh and joke. Lunacharsky had called for this earlier, when in 1920 he entitled an article published in *Vestnik teatra* "We Will Laugh." He called "the jesters"—that is, the authors and performers of comedies, as well as satirists and humorists— the brothers of the proletariat, its "beloved, jolly, smart, vital, talented, alert, eloquent advisors."[78] Of all the choreographers of the first postrevolutionary decade, Lopukhov alone made use of such folk comedy. Merrymaking took active, life-affirming forms in his ballet. Lunacharsky himself had high praise for *Pulcinella*: "The whole thing is so filled with grace as to suggest a unique children's game, but at the same time, this frankness and playfulness in fact conceals great, self-confident art."[79]

In *Pulcinella* the problem of constructing a ballet was resolved in an innovative way. One of the strengths of the production was the continuous action, the just proportion of its structure. The one-act ballet thus became a transitional step toward the monumental narrative ballets of the early 1930s. *Pulcinella* appeared at a time of heated debate over the relationship between dance and pantomime. As a ballet totally shot through with dancing, it was a very weighty argument for dance as a means of characterization. Moreover, at a time of bitter attacks on classical dance

Lopukhov reaffirmed classical dance, through *Pulcinella*, as the ultimate means of choreographic expression.

Pulcinella's stage life was limited for reasons not related to art. The rights to perform Stravinsky's music belonged to a foreign agency and, according to the contract, after the first ten performances, a new fee had to be paid in hard currency for each additional performance. All ten performances took place with enviable success; nevertheless, the theater was forced to remove the ballet from the repertory.

The Ice Maiden

Petrov's ballet *Solveig*, staged in 1922, had closed in its very first season. However, Asafiev had done a great deal of work on the selection and orchestration of music, and the decor and costumes by Golovine were very successful. Several years later Exkusovich, the director of the official theaters, thought of reviving the idea of a "northern ballet" and approached Lopukhov.

The premiere of Lopukhov's ballet took place on April 27, 1927. This staging of Grieg's music, which in its new version received the title *The Ice Maiden*, proved to be one of the most popular ballets in the repertory and the only one of Lopukhov's works of the 1920s that was performed until almost 1937.

Apparently this was unexpected, even by the choreographer himself; Lopukhov admits that he hesitated for a long time before accepting Exkusovich's proposal. No revelations were to be expected from a ballet such as *The Ice Maiden* to Grieg's music. After *The Magnificence of the Universe*, *The Red Whirlwind*, *Pulcinella*, and *Renard*, where the connection with the newest experiments in art was obvious, a fairytale ballet which was traditional in structure and reminiscent of nineteenth-century ballets-*féeries* looked like a digression. The critics, who a year earlier had fervently supported *Pulcinella*, expressed concern that *The Ice Maiden* might signal a return to the position of the pre-Fokine "old ballet." All the more so since the production kept a great deal from *Solveig*.

The sets of 1922 were used in their entirety, with very little remodeling. Almost all the costumes were also used and relatively few new ones added. Lopukhov made a number of changes in the libretto, and the music was altered accordingly. Work on the additions to the score and the instrumentation was done by Asafiev and Alexander Gauk. The musical introduction to the new version of the music was a *halling** (Op. 71, no. 5). Thus, the national character of the work was immediately made clear. The lively scene opening the production (to the music "Solveig's Song") stressed that this was a world of fantasy—fantasy that also had a national coloration.

In the center of the stage stood a dry, hollow tree, and at its foot a group of children on skis surrounded an old Norwegian man who was telling them a fairytale; in the tree stood the Ice Maiden, in the acrobatic pose of "the ring." This pose immediately served to characterize her. The maiden did not float on a cloud of tulle like an airy sylph, nor did she gaze out from behind a tree trunk like a mischievous dryad. The profile outline of the bent body, which formed a resilient circle with one leg stretched back and the arm thrown back, created a completely different impression. The precise, graphically clear position was as pliant as a snake and coldly passionless.

The action began with the cortège of winter, to the music of the "Gnomes' tune" (no Op., no. 2), performed by characters from Norwegian legends—mountain spirits, trolls, and monsters. In the lead was a remarkable creature—tall and thin, with exaggeratedly long arms and fingers, a hooked nose, and a fantastic mane of streaming, dishevelled curls; the mime actor Vladimir Goss created unusually expressive makeup. Behind him came all sorts of evil forest and mountain spirits with huge heads and frightening physiques—shaggy, twisted, bobbing, hobbling creatures. The complicated masks and props were created by the sculptor Sergei Evseyev. The monsters pulled huge sleighs crowded with moon maidens. After circling the stage, the whole group gathered in the middle. Then the little trolls (small students from the ballet school) with white beards, in red trousers and red caps, began to dance. The trolls held little pine trees in their hands.

The winter procession had a spirit of folklore. The authors admired fairytale Romanticism and showed it slightly humorously. Even the ugliness of the evil spirits was more amusing than ominous. In contrast to Ibsen's trolls ("The Cave of the Mountain King" in *Peer Gynt*) here the monsters were amusing creatures, not spirits of darkness; such an inter-

*A Norwegian folkdance performed by men that displays acrobatic virtuosity. (Ed.)

pretation was doubtless closer to Grieg. Later, when a man came to the snow mountains, he was met by an opponent who was threatening, even cruel, but not the embodiment of dark, base, evil feelings.

When the procession had gone offstage "Solveig's Song" was heard again. From the far wings Asak (Gusev) appeared on skis. On reaching the middle of the stage he stopped and looked around, delighted by the beauty of the forest. Then he dropped to one knee; he grew pensive, and then, as though she were the embodiment of his dream, the Maiden (Mungalova) rose unseen from behind him (she was raised through a small trapdoor device). Thus began the adagio to the music "Notturno" (Op. 54, no. 4), which served as the opening for the action. Here the characterization of the Ice Maiden, which had been painted in one stroke in the prologue, was developed.

Lopukhov used the extraordinary talents of Mungalova and Gusev, the striking flexibility of her thin, elastic body, and his strength and agility, to create a fantastic image. Both were famous on the popular stage as performers of athletic dances, in which classical style merged with gymnastics. Mungalova recounts that after they had listened to "Notturno," Lopukhov suggested that she and Gusev try the individual movements he had planned. "Fedor Vasilievich asked me if I could stand on Gusev's shoulder, and if so, then to do an arabesque standing on his shoulder; the descent from his shoulder absolutely had to be a slide."[80] During these preparatory experiments the famous "ring" was also born. As a joke, Gusev tried to stretch the dancer's left leg, which was raised behind her, to her right hand, as he just barely supported her body. Lopukhov immediately grasped how expressive this chance pose was and asked that it be repeated with Mungalova standing on pointe on the right leg. The ring became the leitmotif of the character of the Ice Maiden. The individual elements of this variation, "The Dance of the Ice Maiden," were invented and gradually developed in the same way, for example, the splits after which the ballerina had to roll herself into a ball and then stand up—all in a ¾ count.

In the dances of the first act Lopukhov showed a fusion of these newly invented movements with the older traditional ones. The character of the Maiden developed logically in this sequence. Appearing from the trapdoor behind her partner, the dancer placed one foot on his hand, which rested on his hip, the other on his shoulder, ascended as though on stairs, and rose over him in an arabesque. Her partner stood up. The adagio developed further in a series of varied and complex lifts. From the position of an airy arabesque, the dancer fell from her partner's shoulder into his arms ("the fish dive"). They were momentarily entwined, then she quickly evaded him, seeming to slip from his hands. Here the motif of the "splits" appeared, which Mungalova did magnificently, lightly and naturally stretched out on the floor. In the middle of these fantastically tortuous combinations the ring again appeared as a leitmotif. In the finale of the adagio, Asak raised the Maiden on his extended arms ("the swallow"), carried her along the footlights across the entire stage, then placed her on a branch of the tree. The tree disappeared with the Maiden (it moved offstage on a plank). The youth gazed as though enchanted at the place where the mysterious vision had appeared to him.

Trolls and kobolds—shaggy beings in flowing, torn clothing—galloped out into the forest glade. They moved in high, grotesque jumps, supported by crooked dried branches (like athletes vaulting with poles). They surrounded Asak, galloped around him, teased him, and "scared" him. This short episode led into the next scene, where the magic of the winter kingdom was revealed to the hero.

From the left wings snow youths came onstage, carrying ice maidens on their shoulders in a pose that presented a fantastic transformation of the arabesque: With her left leg each maiden grasped the youth's right shoulder and thus formed a sharp angle, its apex the knee of the ballerina. The arms of the cavalier and his lady also formed a triangle. The union of the triangles created an unusual figure, which was to be associated with snow crystals. Moving in even steps interrupted by *balancés*, the male dancers gradually formed a circle. The snow and moon maidens also joined the procession along with a large group of students from the ballet school portraying snowflakes. To the monotonously resounding music (part of the "Temple Dance" from the opera *Olav Trygvason*, Op. 50), the round dance slowly circled about the stage. Lopukhov took as his basic form the march—the *entrée*—of the old ballet, but the majestic music and the complex interweavings of the dance outline lent a fantastic quality to the scene. This was the procession of winter, triumphant and at the same time lulling one to sleep.

The energetic dance of the trolls and kobolds (Op. 71, no. 3) was in sharp contrast. They appeared in two groups of four from the left wings and proceeded in a "helical" motion, interweaving their legs and raising their knees high. For a few moments they formed two small circles, as though huddling in a conspiracy. Then, to a fast tempo, one group jumped up and squatted down, clapping their hands, while the other rushed around the stage like a whirlwind. The dance concluded with an unexpected pirouette. The wild dance of the trolls and kobolds is similar in character and even in the choice of movements to such productions of Fokine as the "Polovetsian Dances" and also his dances called *"kriksy-araksy"* for the opera *Ruslan and Ludmila*. One cannot speak here of borrowing; Lopukhov used Fokine's methods independently and creatively.

The next episode of the winter suite was the waltz of the Ice Maiden with the snow youths ("Album Leaves," Op. 28, no. 3). The Maiden again appeared in the tree. The youths leaped across the stage and ran to the tree; to the soaring melody, the Maiden collapsed and fell from the top (from a height of approximately six feet) into their arms. In rushing flight, the youths carried the dancer to the center of the stage, tossed her up to a new surge of the music, caught her, and carefully set her on the ground. Immediately they dropped to the floor and the ballerina stood alone, in the center of the prone figures. Here she danced a small variation full of sharp, stabbing movements on pointe. Asak, who had caught the Maiden, also joined the dance, and again she flew up into the tree from his embraces. This same combination (with the jump and the "take-off") was again repeated, along with a repetition of the melody. The lively waltz was interpreted as a scene of the amusements of the Ice Maiden, mistress of the forest, with her subjects, the snow youths, and with Asak.

After the waltz, "The Dance of the Winter Bird" was performed. To the music of "Little Bird" (Op. 43, no. 4), Lopukhov produced an extremely complex man's variation, which continued the tradition of such masterpieces by Petipa as the Bluebird variation in *The Sleeping Beauty*. There were several identical combinations of aerial movement as in the Bluebird (for example, the combination *tombé, pas de bourrée, entrechat-cinq*), but there were new ones as well, purely Lopukhov's inventions. For example, the male dancer did two *tours en l'air* and then landed in a deep *plié* with a *soutenu* turn. The flights and falls were accompanied by arm movements that further emphasized the "bird-like" character of the design. Boris Komarov and Alexei Ermolayev, virtuosi of classical dance, appeared in the role of the Winter Bird.

The last dance of the suite preceding the general coda was called "The Step of the Ice Maiden." For the Maiden's dance Lopukhov introduced a minuet from a piano sonata (Op. 7, part 3) that was not in the previous version. The first and third parts of the variation were built on combinations of sharp *pas de bourrée* on pointe—sparkling and needle-sharp—and wide splits that contrasted with them. In the middle part was a version of a *jeté* leap in which the forward leg bent at the knee and then straightened, which gave the leap "an especially keen, prickly quality."[81] The sharp thrusts of the forward leg with the bent knee, which first appeared in "The Dance of the Winter Bird," appeared in all kinds of versions in the Ice Maiden's variation. This movement motif was repeated not only in the leaps but also in the *parterre* movements of the ballerina, which were somewhat reminiscent of the men's squatting position. The finale was built around the splits, which were also complicated by a sharp forward thrust of the leg. The ballerina bent backward, as if getting ready to leap, and thrust her leg out in front of her, but she unexpectedly landed in the splits, bending and throwing her torso forward.

"The Step of the Ice Maiden" was performed by the ballerina with an "accompanying" ensemble. Like the ballerina, the dancers in the corps were dressed in short, open, white flannel tunics with silver appliqué. Lopukhov thus used the principle traditional to the nineteenth-century ballet of a multiple reflection of the central character within the corps de ballet (Giselle and the Wilis, Odette and the swans, the shades in *La Bayadère*, and so on). Echoing the monologue of the ballerina, the women dancers shifted their poses when the Maiden moved from one dance phrase to another; they emphasized her descents and flights and strengthened her accents. However, in contrast to the corps de ballet of Ivanov's swans, here the dancing had a different, sharp and graphic character. The snow maidens (dancers from the corps de ballet) and the snowflakes (students from the ballet school) were lying in a wide semicircle. Raising one leg to the first sharp "stride" of the ballerina, they slowly lowered it to the fading dance motif in the music. When the leg touched the other leg, on the floor, the arms, which were stretched out on the floor, took up the movement: Their fluid fingering movements suggested the image of snow swirling over the drifts.

The suite concluded with a coda ("Mountain Tune," Op. 19, no. 1), in which all the characters were united in a circling movement. Whirlwinds swept through holding the Winter Bird high in the air; a dancing vortex spun the snow youths, the ice and moon maidens, and the snowflakes. It was as though the winter storm were gathering its last forces to resist the coming of spring.

The second scene opened with the melody "Morning" from the music for the play *Peer Gynt*. The scenery changed; this was the same forest glade, but the branches of the trees were free of snow, the mountain slopes were shot through with soft green, and the garb of the pines had grown brighter. To the music of the "Waltz-Caprice" (Op. 37, no. 2) spring birds gathered. The leading dance motif was a running "flight," alternating with circling. Groups crisscrossed the stage, sometimes merging, sometimes diverging. Flocks rushed toward each other, met, crossed in rows, and rushed off. Sometimes the general flight abruptly changed direction, as though encountering an unexpected obstacle. Stopping for a moment and breaking into pairs, the dancers began to spin on pointe very rapidly, flapping their "wings," but immediately the lines closed up.

From the side an ancient hag (the mime Goss) drove out a live cow. With the hag appeared a girl in a wide linen peasant skirt and blouse. This was Solveig, who was also played by Mungalova. At the back of the stage, on a high platform representing the mountain slope, Asak appeared, seeking the Ice Maiden. Running downstage, Asak noticed Solveig and stopped, struck by her resemblance to the Maiden. Mungalova says she wanted to portray "a dreamy girl, living in castles in the air," who awaited "the arrival of a fairytale prince."[82] Therefore, upon Asak's appearance she tried to leave, but on seeing the youth's sorrow she immediately returned. The culmination of the scene was the duet of Solveig and Asak, danced to the music of the poem "Erotik" (Op. 43, no. 5); it concluded with their leaving the woods. Asak led Solveig to the people.

The second act of *The Ice Maiden* was realistic: it showed the wedding of Asak and Solveig. The music for this scene underwent very few changes in the new version. The act still opened with "Wedding-Day in Troldhaugen" (Op. 65, no. 6) after which followed the procession of guests to the "Triumphant March" (Op. 56, no. 3). Three Norwegian dances (from Op. 35) were performed. Lopukhov also kept the music for the duet of the newlyweds ("Scherzo-Impromptu" from the *Moods* cycle, Op. 73, no. 2). There was only a slight regrouping of the musical numbers. In the first version, the act ended with a funeral march—the procession with Solveig's body. In Lopukhov's version the scene in which the Ice Maiden, the ruler of the snowy mountains, appeared to carry off Solveig could not exist, since these two characters were merged into one. His Solveig did not die, but disappeared during the ritual leaps over the burning barrels, like a cloud dissolving in the sky. Whether this Ice Maiden existed in reality, taking on for a moment the aspect of a mortal girl, or whether she was a dream, a mirage, remained a mystery. Therefore, the act concluded not with the "Funeral March" but with a very short episode of Asak's confusion and despair, suggesting the finale of the third act of *Swan Lake*: The youth rushed off into the mountains after his vanished bride.

In the second act of *The Ice Maiden* Lopukhov unfolded the colorful pageant of a Norwegian wedding. This was a brilliant theatricalization of authentic national dances and games, as far removed from mere uncreative copying (which was apparently the case in *Solveig*) as it was from stylization. Lopukhov's brother Andrei, who danced in this production, recalled, "The character dances in the second act of *The Ice Maiden* are very close to Norwegian folklore, although they were staged purely intuitively and constructed on a theoretical basis. The choreographer somehow succeeded in stumbling upon ethnographic truth. This, by the way, was confirmed by the Norwegians who saw them. . . ."[83]

Lopukhov's *Ice Maiden* developed the tradition of Fokine's *Jota Aragonesa*. In both works a full union with the music was achieved, which already in and of itself required complex dance, richer than the folk original. And in both, the musical and choreographic image was inseparably linked to the decor; Golovine designed both productions. But in the second act of *The Ice Maiden* the realistic element stood out more clearly than in *Jota Aragonesa* because here there was not a dance suite, as in Fokine, but the reproduction of a ritual.

A gala procession opened the action. The newlyweds rode out on horses: Solveig wore a splendid embroidered dress and a crown-like headdress with many ribbons, and Asak wore a velvet waistcoat and a shirt edged with lace. Then came Druzhko (the best man), along with the matchmakers, Asak's old father with a pipe between his teeth, the bride's dressed-up girlfriends, and armed hunters. Children carried armfuls of flowers. The stage gradually filled with people; the guests positioned themselves around the newlyweds, and then the crowd began to sway slowly. The entire stage rocked gently and evenly in time to the exultant melody praising the young people. The children showered the bride and bridegroom with flowers, the hunters raised their guns to the sky, and deafening shots thundered forth.

The triumphant ceremonies gave way to comic dances: The staid old father (Leontiev) stamped about heavily and the two elderly but rejuvenated matchmakers twined around each other, playing and shoving. Druzhko (Andrei Lopukhov) jumped around the stage with a light, rapid step. He wore wide, heavy women's clothing. In the second, calm part of the dance, Druzhko began to circle slowly, and his skirts fell off; when he freed himself from the first one, there was a second underneath it, under the second a third, and so on until the seventh time. Having thrown off the skirts, Druzhko again began a merry dance. A lively little boy danced with an old man as a partner. At first the old man barely played at dancing, clapping and egging the boy on, but gradually he himself joined in the excitement. Young and old danced together, joining hands, and the jester Druzhko also joined the game. Catching the boy at the ankle with his leg, he circled with him, and both hopped gaily on one leg. The newlyweds performed a small, simple, lyrical peasant dance.

It grew dark. The time had come to move on to the next major part of the wedding games—the leaps over the barrels of burning pitch. The girls scattered and then, supported on both sides by the young men, one after another the girls flew over the barrels. The bride's turn came. A leap . . . and Solveig was gone. Only a wisp of steam hovered over the barrel, floating off toward the mountains. The crowd froze. Everyone turned and, as though bewitched, watched the scrap of fog dispersing in the air. Then, pushing away his father, who restrained him, Asak rushed after the cloud as it flew away.

The funeral march ("In Memory of Richard Nordraak") served as the musical prelude to the third act. The curtain opened to reveal the scenery of the first scene of the first act. Snow was slowly falling. The music was full of suffering, anguish, and premonitions ("Borghild's Dream," from *Sigurd Jorsalfar* [Op. 22, no. 1]) and whirlwinds appeared. They rushed along the stage, and the Winter Bird flew by, pulled along by them. The stage filled with the characters of the winter cortège. After their procession, resembling the beginning of the first act, everything fell silent for a moment. Then Asak rushed into the gorge. Now he came not as he had been in the first act, when he had been serenely admiring the beauties of nature; he was frantic and determined to get his Solveig back from the mountains. In order to make the scene more dynamic Asafiev and Lopukhov put here the music of "Temple Dance" (from *Olav Trygvason*, Op. 50), which in the first act of Petrov's *Solveig* served as the dance of the forest spirits. Asak was met by the heralds of the storm, the whirlwinds. Two little whirlwinds (students from the school) crossed the stage, circling and tossing each other. Hanging about Asak's neck, they dragged him into a spin. Asak shook off one of them, but he continued to turn. At the same time, the second one circled around him, giving him no respite, until the youth fell in exhaustion and rolled along the ground.

But his call was not unheeded; the ice maidens appeared before Asak. According to Mungalova, Lopukhov at first thought of staging a grand adagio with the soloists and corps de ballet in variations and group dances, as in the first act. Then he rejected this idea. The dancer criticized this choreography; in her opinion the ballet deteriorated toward the end. But Lopukhov was right in not impeding the rapidly developing action. He limited himself to a single scene, to the music of the "Waltz-Caprice" (Op. 37, no. 1).

The waltz was danced by eleven maiden-doubles, with Mungalova. Asak rushed toward them, hoping to recognize his vanished bride in one of the maidens. But the heroine of the ballet did not have an independent role in the third act; after returning to her friends, she did not separate herself from their group. The movements of "The Step of the Ice Maiden" flitted by and multiplied, altered and yet painfully familiar. Twelve identical maidens did splits; how could he recognize his chosen one among them? Asak gazed into the face of each one, impatiently shoved her away, and one after the other the ice maidens sank to the ground face down, surrounding the youth in a faceless magic circle. The familiar movement of simultaneously raised legs began. Another moment—and the maidens disappeared. The love of a mortal cannot melt an icy heart. The ruler of the mountains indifferently handed Asak over to the vengeance of the whirlwinds.

There were many whirlwinds—large and small, in loose clothing with torn sleeves, with ragged strips floating around their legs and long, streaming hair. The episode of the final struggle was performed to the music of "Peer Gynt's Homecoming" from *Peer Gynt*. The whirlwinds flung Asak up and down and from side to side, tossed him, circled him, and dragged him along the ground. Sometimes he disappeared in the maelstrom, sometimes he emerged from the most unexpected corners of the stage. Thrown onto the rocks, he swung from a great height (a dummy was thrown down from the platform). To the concluding chords of the music, the whirlwinds flung the youth onto the tree where he first saw the Ice Maiden, and he hung head downwards, his legs catching on a high branch. Man had not succeeded in discovering the secret of nature.

The scene of Asak's death was directly followed by the epilogue. Again "Solveig's Song" was heard. In the center of the stage stood a withered tree, on it the Maiden in the ring pose; at the foot of the tree, as in the prologue, peasants were gathered, listening to the old man's fairytale.

Lopukhov reworked the scenario of the ballet. In the initial version, the main character somewhat resembled the Russian Snow Maiden, Andersen's Mermaid, or Taglioni's Sylphide. The forest maiden Solveig, in the guise of a mortal girl, followed the youth to the world and perished there —melted from the kiss of a man, returning again to the kingdom of ice. This was a theme of great, faithful, sacrificial love. The theme was interwoven with another, also very typical of the Romantic ballet—the theme of unfulfilled dreams. The youth, who had fallen in love with Solveig, died as he searched for her.

The changes Lopukhov introduced into the plot of the ballet at first glance seemed insignificant: Instead of two characters (the cruel ruler of the ice kingdom, Oze, and the forest maiden Solveig), he had one character—the Ice Maiden. In fact, the interpretation of the central image had been radically altered and, consequently, the meaning of the ballet was altered as well. In Lopukhov's version the traditional motif of the dissonance between dream and reality, because of its vagueness (what is the dream and what reality?), acquires the bitter taste of an unrevealed secret. The heroines of the Romantic ballet sacrifice themselves for love and perish, leaving a feeling of pity, remorse, even gratitude (*Giselle*) in the soul of the hero. The Ice Maiden is different. In her, good and evil coexist. She is simultaneously victim and destroyer. Her attempt to draw close to her beloved after taking human form is in vain. Upon returning to her native natural element, she becomes unattainable and unrecognizable when the youth seeks her in the circle of her icy friends, and she dooms him to death.

Lopukhov's Ice Maiden is neither the Snow Maiden nor Andersen's Mermaid. Here there are other associations: an enchanted, deceptive world and a mysterious female image—the possessor of "snake-like beauty" who leads him into an "enchanted circle," into "the aimless winter cold" (Alexander Blok, *The Snow Mask*). The traditional theme approaches the ideas of the early twentieth-century Russian poets. This already indicates that *The Ice Maiden* is not a copy of the "old ballet."

However, the images of Symbolist poetry are also changed to the point of being unrecognizable. Mungalova thought that the Ice Maiden "brings man inevitable doom," and that "her dance ought to be ominous, stern, as if a warning." [84] In reality, the dance language, with its inclination toward acrobatics and athletics, and the clear, precise, somewhat passionless style of performance, were modern. It was said of Mungalova as the Ice Maiden that "in her movements there is no delicate beauty; this is acrobatic gymnastics in the best sense of the word." [85] Those who later accused Lopukhov of cultivating motifs of "decadent" art were unfair to him.

Lopukhov called his production "a classical ballet in a 1927 interpretation." [86] This brief formula proved very apt. *The Ice Maiden* really did return to that which had been forgotten or abandoned in the heat of debate. And at the same time, the ballet revealed new possibilities. The choreographer of the 1920s, an artist who possessed an independent creative style, united in *The Ice Maiden* the abstract dance compositions of Petipa with the pictorial qualities of Fokine's ballets, making them a fact of modern art.

The main theme—man and nature—was developed by means of abstract movements, from one classical ensemble to another. Lopukhov did not limit himself to the traditional structure of the *grand pas* of academic ballet. He preferred the suite form. But, like the choreographers of the nineteenth century he introduced movement leitmotifs, used the device of the solo with accompaniment ("The Step of the Ice Maiden"), and developed complex designs for the group dances ("The Gathering of the Birds"), like an interweaving of "voices."

The fairytale scenes of *The Ice Maiden* in their own way reinstated the forms of the "old ballet" rejected by Fokine. But Lopukhov developed these forms by taking into account what Fokine had given ballet. In *The Ice Maiden* the traditions of the beginning of the twentieth century merged with the traditions of Petipa's "old ballet." The ballet was a response to the words Lunacharsky had addressed to the dramatic theater: "Back to Ostrovsky!"* which should have been read as "Forward, with Ostrovsky!" In any event, Lopukhov read them as "Forward, together with Petipa!" This is how he understood his work in reviving old ballets. This is how he created what was new in *The Ice Maiden*, the first new full-length ballet on the Soviet stage.

Sollertinsky wrote of *The Ice Maiden*: "After the usual ballet miniatures, this is a victory."[87] Sollertinsky was right, because during the late 1920s there was a trend toward narrative and monumental forms. "Only a truly integral, full-length ballet can attract enough of an audience," Gvozdev noted. "Hence it is clear that the form of the *grand ballet* must be retained."[88]

In *The Ice Maiden*, classical dance predominated. This was also in keeping with the slogan "Forward, together with Petipa!" Arguments were still going on about classical dance, its right to exist, and the usefulness of replacing it with other forms of movement. Gradually, however, the arguments accumulated on the side of those who defended the classics. The ballets of the classic heritage were successfully revived, and such luminaries of classical dance as Semenova and Ermolayev appeared on stage. *The Ice Maiden* was also a weighty argument.

Lopukhov made use of academic classical dance in all its diversity. The choreographer's incredibly rich imagination helped him to see new elements even in old formulae. At the same time he applied modern methods, in particular acrobatic movements and combinations. Lopukhov created these by mastering the achievements of the related arts of the music-hall stage and the circus. It was not accidental that, in speaking of the vocabulary of the ballet, reviewers recalled Goleizovsky and Foregger, Balanchivadze, and the music-hall dancer Maria Ponna.

In *The Magnificence of the Universe* and in the first part of *The Red Whirlwind* Lopukhov was trying to express abstract thought and to cre-

---

*Alexander Ostrovsky (1823–86), who wrote, among other works, *The Snow Maiden*, was a socially conscious playwright whose contemporary satires, including commentary on the role of women, were widely known. (Ed.)

ate an abstract image through the movements of classical dance. In *The Ice Maiden* the point lay neither in the creation of a previously unknown genre—the dance symphony—nor in portraying political doctrines in dance, but in developing the principles of the nineteenth-century ballet; within the limits of the ordinary narrative work, compositions appeared in which the author's emotion was expressed and his ideas were revealed through dance movements. This too was "Forward, together with Petipa!"

The second act of *The Ice Maiden* was devoted to character dance that again revived the rules of the old ballets. Character dance, too, was here given new form. Fokine had already viewed dance folklore differently from his predecessors. The basis for the nineteenth-century productions had always been classical dance. The brilliant character dances of Saint-Léon and Petipa were most often divertissements. Their range was limited, and, especially toward the end of the century, few new ones appeared. As a rule the direct link with folk art was lost, and only a certain general idea of the most typical movements and style of performing characteristic of one or another group of people remained. Usually even these movements were subordinated to the same principles as the steps of classical dance (extension, turnout, and the five positions); however, they were applied somewhat more freely. Fokine, who sought for each image only the dance language natural to it, constantly turned to folk dances. Nevertheless, the ethnographic exactness of such dances was relative: In Fokine's work, folklore was still subject to stylization. Even the ballet closest to its original source, *Jota Aragonesa*, was a staged, aestheticized version of the Spanish dances Fokine had seen. Lopukhov brought character dance still closer to ethnographically authentic folk ritual dance.

The interest in character, folk, and social dance was a sign of the times. They were a source of an expressiveness, which to many could not be demanded of classical dance with its "purely ornamental arabesques and twirls," as Gvozdev put it.[89] They were widely used in drama not as inserted divertissements, but as clear characterizations, impressive images: the dances in Vakhtangov's *The Dybbuk*, dances in the productions of the Kamerny Theater—not only in comic operettas, but also in O'Neill's drama, *Desire Under the Elms*; dances occupied no small place in almost all of Meyerhold's productions—*The Forest* (by Ostrovsky), *Bubus the Teacher* (by Faiko), *The Mandate* (by Nikolai Erdman), Gogol's classic

The Inspector General, and so on. National dance folklore enjoyed tremendous success on the music-hall stage: from ethnographic evenings to Goleizovsky's Slavic and Spanish suites. Finally, considerable knowledge in the realm of exotic dance forms was gained during the tours of the Japanese traditional Kabuki theater, the Chinese theater, and Negro operetta.*

In staging the second act of *The Ice Maiden,* Lopukhov took as his model the experience of the ethnographic theaters that studied and staged folklore. But Lopukhov's theatrical mind, the habits of stylization in which he had been trained, and finally, the outstanding quality of Golovine's decorative costumes excluded the possibility of a naturalistic portrayal of reality. The Norwegian cycle staged by Lopukhov initiated a completely new approach to national dances. Folklore remained folklore, but it was raised to the level of the theater. In the future it was precisely this tendency that was developed in the Soviet ballet. The character dance was liberated from its external ornamental quality and approached folk dance, which allowed more freedom, sharpness, angularity—that is, errors—from the point of view of the academic canons.

The Ice Maiden was a ballet addressed to the future, in which something new was born from the revived and reworked past. It revived the full-length ballet, bringing the academic grand ballet of the nineteenth century closer to the new forms of the monumental narrative ballet. It reinstated the classical lexicon, while at the same time making it the language of modern art, and it was oriented toward the search for pure abstract dance. And it pointed the way for the theatricalization of folklore that was most promising for future Soviet choreography.

---

*A black American musical revue, *The Chocolate Kiddies* (known in the United States as *The Chocolate Dandies*), toured the USSR in 1926. The Soviet press referred to it as Negro operetta, rather than a revue or musical. (Ed.)

By the end of the first decade after the October Revolution it was already possible to draw several conclusions. The first important conclusion was that Soviet Russia had been able to preserve the heritage of the prerevolutionary art of ballet. Despite the civil war, destruction, and famine, when the companies lacked leading dancers and choreographers, and it was almost impossible to continue studying in the schools, the ballet survived. At that time some predicted its demise, claiming that this delicate plant could develop only in the hothouse atmosphere of the Imperial Theater. Others thought that it was not worth waiting for ballet to perish on its own; it had to be destroyed as an art that was "socially alien," incapable of serving the cause of the people and accordingly destined for demolition along with the old social order. But the question of the future existence of ballet was decided when those governing the arts proclaimed as one of the basic principles of their policy that they intended to save the classical heritage and to make it the legacy of future generations. Considerable efforts on the part of the ballet workers were devoted to this goal, particularly during the first five years after the revolution. But there was another goal as well.

The art of the stage is a living art. Its future existence depends on the degree to which it can respond to the needs of the time and reflect the interests, hopes, and fears of its contemporaries. The question of the content and forms of a new Soviet ballet arose. The new ballet had a difficult birth. Ballet has always been distinguished by a special dedication to tradition. Accusations of backwardness and demands for immediate reform pursued it throughout the 1920s. In the meantime in its own way the ballet responded to the artistic quests of the times, and it had its own innovators and rebels who declared *The Little Humpbacked Horses* and *La Bayadères* anathema. They experimented. Studying the old means of expression, they dissected them, analyzed them, and verified their usefulness. A shattering of the old and quests for the new were going on even in the ballet.

The dance stage was overwhelmed by a wave of innovation, the same wave on whose crest were born many significant events in the Soviet art of the twenties. In its new works, ballet competed with revolutionary posters and resorted to the methods of agitprop theater; it spoke of the revolution in the language of symbols and allegories. Ballet felt the influence of theatrical constructivism. The fragmented stage platform revealed new possibilities for mass groupings. The decor seemed to be included in the action and imbued it with dynamism. The combined movements of people, sets, and props submerged the audience in an atmosphere of either strenuous work or unrestrained exuberance.

At a time when new means of expression were being born in literature, drama, and film, forms of dance theater also appeared that were previously unknown. In the dance symphony, new connections were made between dance movement and music in order to create an abstract image. Buffoon dances appeared; their farcical mischievousness and all sorts of "merry pranks" sometimes turned into a mockery of the decorousness of the old world, old art and, of course, old ballet. Here the early sprouts of Soviet ballet satire broke through.

The modern world penetrated into the ballet. The themes and plots of ballet in the twenties were not always modern, but the intonation, views, and perception of the world were. The dance caught what was new in the life around it—in the architecture of concrete and glass, severe and bright, in the ascetic austerity of life, in the very appearance of people as they looked when facing many hardships. But the spare style of the ballet in those times was not a result of poverty; spiritual qualities were manifest in it. A lofty idea shone through, liberated from the husks of the random, the petty, and the material. In the art of the dance, the rejection of adornment only set off this spirituality. A luxurious decorativeness, a multiplicity of colors, and minute details were perceived as echoes of bourgeois taste, as concessions to the hostile world of NEP-men and the bourgeoisie. Acrobatic, athletic dance gradually penetrated even into ballet productions. Overalls or leotards which freed the body for movement forced out the tutu; its nobility of form was not perceived at the time. The style of performance changed even within the boundaries of purely classical dance, acquiring energy, breadth, strength, at times even a sharpness of form.

Yet the new elements that appeared as a result of experimentation fitted into the academic repertory with difficulty. Almost all the new ballets had such a short stage life that they were completely lost against the background of traditional, sometimes truly antiquated productions. The changes in the ballet were not very noticeable to the public. Although specialists and critics saw these changes, criticism of ballet as being cut off from modern times did not cease. In the late twenties, at the time when Goleizovsky was working in the Bolshoi Theater and Lopukhov was expanding his activities, strange as it may seem, these reproaches were particularly virulent.

There were reasons for this. Yet another problem of the ballet theater was that as a rule its masters were oriented toward the earlier experiments of the dramatic theater and other related arts, and were now using these results in very different circumstances. For example, the methods of poster/agitprop theater were reflected in the ballet *The Red Whirlwind* (1924), in *The Whirlwind* (1927), and even later in the Lopukhov-Shostakovich ballet *Bolt* (1931). "We saw before us the discoveries of the Blue Blouse and TRAM and dreamed of doing something of equal value. . . . We were attracted to the possibility of putting into dance the motifs of political satire, inspired by the ROSTA windows," Lopukhov recalled of *Bolt*.[1] These were good intentions. And who knows what the attitude toward such a ballet might have been if it had appeared not in the early 1930s but a decade earlier. Lopukhov's *The Nutcracker*, an eccentric ballet, had something in common with Eisenstein's *The Wise Man* and Meyerhold's *The Forest*, but it was not staged until 1929. The "buffoon ballets" were born late, ironically stylized with the devices of Radlov's Theater of Popular Comedy (Narodnaya Komediya). The pace of events was so sweeping that a gap of several years already seemed immeasurably great.*

---

*On the Blue Blouse, see note on p. 284, and on *The Wise Man*, the note on p. 262. TRAM was the acronym for Theater of Working Youth, a branch of *Komsomol* (Communist Youth League) created in 1925 as an amateur proletarian agitprop theater group. The ROSTA windows were satirical political posters in shop windows, sponsored by the state telegraph agency during the civil war years; Mayakovsky was a key ROSTA artist/writer. Meyerhold's production of *The

Toward the end of the decade there was a change in the understanding of what constituted modernity in art. If for the creation of contemporary ballets it had earlier been sufficient to reflect the spirit of the times in the most general form through appropriate emotions, affinity of forms, and a closeness of analogies, now what was needed was the portrayal of contemporary reality rather than abstraction. And the role of art in people's lives had changed. In the first years after the October Revolution art was primarily a weapon of revolution: it agitated, summoning people to battle. These goals naturally presupposed something new in expressive means. Hence the need arose for constant laboratory work, for the refined creation of forms, for witty inventiveness. The path of uneasy quests led the majority of artists to new, revolutionary art.

But the very concept of experimentation often excludes general accessibility. Here lay one of the profound internal contradictions of the art of that time. No matter what was argued about in the late 1920s—whether it was a new film (*October*, by Sergei Eisenstein), a new novel (*Envy*, by Yuri Olesha), or an exhibition by young artists—the argument inevitably hinged on the contradiction between an experiment accessible to the few and a form "understood by the millions." This well-known expression is taken from the 1925 resolution of the Central Committee of the Russian Communist Party "Concerning the Policy of the Party in the Realm of Literature."

Gradually it became possible to discern in the chorus of arguing voices concrete definitions of what might be meant by general accessibility and what the millions needed. The art of the first postrevolutionary years leaned toward abstraction, hyperbole, and extreme feelings, situations, and characters. The image could be raised to a symbol, or it could be lowered to the limits of naturalism where it seemed no longer to be art. One thing was definitive; a single feature was emphasized, set apart, and strengthened. There was no time for psychological analysis, for weighing the pros and cons, just as there was no time for meditating about whether the accused was totally guilty and whether the accuser was totally correct. In the late twenties, having returned to peacetime life, people remembered that there are ordinary human feelings in the world and that not

---

Forest, like Eisenstein's *The Wise Man*, was a politically charged reworking and "circusization" of a classic play by Ostrovsky. (Ed.)

only the upheavals of a national or planetary scale are interesting and important; those which take place in the soul of an individual are important as well.

These people had little experience with art. To grow accustomed to music they had to begin by absorbing the masterpieces of past centuries, for without this basis it was impossible to explain the nature of the quests of the modern composers and innovators. A survey of workers in 1928 showed that they preferred reading famous writers of the past. This is why the aspiration toward art with content and art that was easily accessible gave rise to the slogan "Learn from the classics." The interest in "psychologism" and in showing "real people" focused special attention on the works of Leo Tolstoy. In speaking of the new Soviet novel, constant reference was made to the experience of Tolstoy and to the fact that Fadeyev and other writers used his method of psychological analysis as a model. In 1928 the publication of the first collected works of Tolstoy in 90 volumes was begun.

Similar processes were taking place in drama. As early as 1924 Lunacharsky called for "a return to realistic, socio-psychological, socially oriented theater."[2] And already by 1927 in the production of Trenev's *Liubov Yarovaya* at the Maly Theater and in Ivanov's *Armored Train No. 14-69* at the Moscow Art Theater a path had been found toward revolution "through the soul of man."

The ballet innovators searched in their laboratories for new forms to help the ballet revitalize itself for the mass audience. But the mass audience at that time went to the old ballets, those which the experts thought it could in no way "accept." These ballets attracted those inexperienced audiences by their finery, their fairytale quality, and sometimes by their naive melodrama, but primarily because of the skill of the performers. As regards experiments, the audience shied away from them in bewilderment. "Form understood by the millions" resembled neither the philosophizing of the dance symphony nor buffoonish satire. "The most important question is that of the *content* of the ballet production, which is inseparably linked to the question of precisely which *audience* the ballet is aiming at," Gvozdev wrote in 1928.[3]

Experience has shown that the ballet theater itself has interpreted the question of content in different ways. There are two basic ways to resolve this question. One is the development of content that is specifically dance, for instance the second act of *Giselle*, Ivanov's swan scenes, and many of Petipa's ensembles. Here the choreographer thought in dance images, like a composer who thinks in musical images. The second path is the dramatization of the dance—not just an elementary parceling out of all the narrative functions to pantomime, larded with dance divertissements, but the *ballet d'action*. Quite a few examples of exactly this type have been given by the ballet theater of past centuries, let alone the ballets of Fokine and Gorsky.

Both trends were developed during the twenties. In fact, the idea of dramatizing dance attracted Gorsky, Goleizovsky (*Joseph the Beautiful*), and Lopukhov (*Pulcinella*), as well as the choreographers who worked outside the state theaters. But Lopukhov also built action according to the laws of dance expression by staging the first dance symphony in the history of world theater and composing symphonic ensembles within a story ballet (*The Ice Maiden*). The dance symphony *The Magnificence of the Universe* was shown to the public only once. On the other hand, *The Ice Maiden* became part of the repertory. It would seem that the quest in the realm of pure dance would have been pursued. But in fact this tendency was not developed during the next few decades. It was revived only in the late 1950s and found expression in the broad use of symphonic non-dance music on the one hand, and in the trend toward abstract, complex images on the other.

Beginning in the late 1920s the ballet increasingly moved toward dramatization. The further it went, the more stubbornly theoreticians and practitioners identified content with plot. In this regard, choreographic action based on laws of unique dance imagery and in many respects close to musical imagery, fell from favor along with the major expressive means—classical dance. "Classical dance . . . is a *purely formal, purely decorative* dance art," Gvozdev maintained.[4] Sollertinsky also thought so: "To *mean* something, to bear a concrete thought—this can be done only with theatricalization. Otherwise the ballet will be merely an abstract ornament, an arabesque, a whimsical decorative pattern."[5]

Rejecting the substantive possibilities of dance and its direct expressiveness, Sollertinsky pointed to what seemed to him the sole solution: Only the theatricalization and dramatization of dance, only "danced action" could save ballet. For his part, Gvozdev also suggested "increasing attention to the *meaning* of what is happening on stage and avoiding the lack of a subject," "giving the ballet performers *content* in the action and diverting them from purely decorative, abstract, and subject-less experiments."[6] In sum, the leading ballet critics cast doubt on the experiment of the "dance symphony" and even on the incomparably more promising (at that stage of development) achievement of *The Ice Maiden*, which to a great extent anticipated the gains of the 1960s: With the availability of musical and choreographic dramaturgy, here the images were expressed in the abstract forms of classical dance. But the critics pressed for a different type of production.

By the late 1920s the time for impressionist sketches had disappeared. The time for the poster and the allegory, when a single concentrated image expressed the theme, had also passed. At that time, when the leading genre in literature was the psychological novel, when drama and cinema attempted to show real life and people in that real life, the choreographic theater, which in the last analysis faced similar goals, moved toward the dance-drama.

Ballet productions of this type required a review of expressive means. While the expressiveness of classical dance was rejected, its technical basis was still valued in the dance-drama. Classical training gave the dancer a store of various means to portray various characters. Virtuosic leaps, turns, and *batterie*, appropriately colored, could portray energetic, bold, passionate, rebellious characters, such as those who appeared several years later in Vainonen's ballets and then in Chabukiani's. Fluid arabesques and attitudes became a permanent feature of lyric heroines. A great deal of attention was devoted to character dance. It approached folklore sources; its ethnographic authenticity was heightened through conventional theatrical devices. There is a direct line from the Russian ballets of Lopukhov, the second act of *The Ice Maiden*, and the national programs of Goleizovsky to *The Flames of Paris*, *Partisan Days*, *The Heart of the Hills*, *Laurencia*, and other ballets of the 1930s.

Champions of the dance-drama particularly emphasized pantomime, which from time immemorial has been the basic vehicle for the plot. Great hopes were placed on pantomime during the twenties. Gorsky willingly resorted to all sorts of combinations of pantomime and dance, as did Lopukhov in several of his ballets. The studios, taken with the idea of dramatizing dance, especially cultivated it; for example, Nina Gremina's *Drambalet* (Dramatic Ballet) performed on the music-hall stage.

Again, it was not accidental that the critics and ballet theoreticians of those times wrote so much about pantomime. "A narrative pantomime with a new, modern plot—that is the fundamental, chief task of modern ballet," declared Gvozdev.[7] And Sollertinsky stated, "We view expressive dance primarily as narrative pantomime that . . . is not only performed, but danced."[8]

The first decade after the October Revolution, as no other period in the life of Russian ballet, was rich in varied experiments that produced both mistakes and discoveries. In the following years these discoveries were viewed one-sidedly. Attempts at dramatization during the 1930s produced significant productions innovative for their time such as *The Fountain of Bakhchisarai* by Zakharov and *Romeo and Juliet* by Lavrovsky, but other genres proved to be off-limits during this time. Naturally, the exclusive rights of one artistic fashion at the expense of all the others impoverished the ballet.

The point was not just the lack of variety of expressive means or the paucity of dancing for which productions in the thirties and forties were rightly criticized. Our choreographic theater unquestionably acquired more psychological and emotional depth than ever at that time. Structural logic was another achievement; events were developed in a cogent sequence. To reduce all conflicts to the parameters of psychological drama, to the demonstration of individual personal phenomena, however, was to limit the ballet in content as well as ideological power. Ballet temporarily lost the ability to generalize in that language of rich metaphorical imagery that had inspired the best dance compositions of the past and the valuable experiments of the twenties.

By the middle of the twentieth century, a great deal had changed in the life of the country and consequently in art as well, including the ballet. In looking at what is new one repeatedly notices echoes of the aspirations of the twenties. Invisible threads link the experiments of Gorsky, Goleizovsky, and Lopukhov to the ballets of our contemporaries, the choreographers of the third Soviet generation.

■ Notes

Key to Abbreviations

GAORSS LO	State Archives of the October Revolution and of the Building of Socialism of the Leningrad Oblast
GTsTB	State Central Theatrical Library
GTsTM	State Central Theatrical Museum named after A. A. Bakhrushin
MKhAT	Moscow Art Theater of the USSR named after M. Gorky
Muzei GABT	Museum of the State Academic Bolshoi Theater
TsGALI	Central State Archives of Literature and Art
TsNB VTO	Central Research Library of the All-Union Theatrical Society
VTO	All-Union Theatrical Society

1 Background

1 A. Benois, "Khudozhestvennye pisma. Russkie spektakli v Parizhe," *Rech*, 19 June 1909, no. 165.

2 A. Benois, "Khudozhestvennye pisma. Novaia postanovka *Raimondy*," *Rech*, 22 December 1908, no. 315.

3 *Swan Lake* and *Giselle* were revised by Gorsky again after the revolution, and thus will be discussed later.

4 A. Volynsky, "Baletmeisterskii vopros. (B. G. Romanov)," *Birzhevye vedomosti*, 20 February 1915, no. 14682.

5 See Ash (A. Shaikevich), "Peterburgskie katakomby. Posviashchaetsia Borisu Romanovu," *Teatr* (Berlin), no. 14 (1922): 4–5.

6 Andr. L. (André Levinson), "Balety B. G. Romanova," *Rech*, 2 November 1915, no. 302.

7 V. Svetlov, "Pisma o balete," *Teatr i iskusstvo*, 29 January 1917, no. 5, p. 91.

8 Y. Beliaev, "V balete," *Novoe vremia*, 14 November 1916, no. 14618.

9 De-Nei (I. Schneider), "U A. A. Gorskogo, K 25-letiiu artisticheskoi deiatelnosti," *Rampa i zhizn*, 1 June 1914, no. 22, p. 6.

10 V. Bezpalov, *Teatry v dni revoliutsii 1917.* (Leningrad: Academia, 1927), p. 11.

11 TsGALI, f. 648, op. 2, ed. khr. 24, l. 7.

12 See "Teatr v revoliutsionnye dni. Petrograd," *Teatr i iskusstvo*, 12 March 1917, no. 10–11, p. 191.

13 See "Teatr v revoliutsionnye dni. Petrograd," *Teatr i iskusstvo*, 19 March 1917, no. 12, p. 209.

14 A. Pleshcheyev, "O balete," *Vremia*, 19 May 1917, no. 944.

15 See Tamara Karsavina, *Theatre Street* (New York: E. P. Dutton, 1931), p. 322.

16 N. Soliannikov, "Vospominaniia," manuscript, TsNB VTO, p. 283.

17 See "Budushchee Bolshogo teatra," *Vremia*, 3 May 1917, no. 931.

18 "Baletnye dezertiry," *Petrogradskaia gazeta*, 6 September 1917, no. 209.

19 *Rampa i zhizn*, 19 November 1917, no. 44–46, pp. 4–5.

20 "Pervyi spektakl dlia naroda v Mariinskom teatre. *Ruslan i Ludmila*," *Izvestiia khudo-zhestvenno-prosvetitelnogo otdela Mossoveta*, 1 April 1918, no. 2, p. 34.

21 GAORSS LO, f. 4463, op. 1, d. 68, l. 61.

22 K. Ostrozhsky (K. Gogel), *Vechernie ogni*, 13 May 1918, no. 42, p. 4.

23 K. Ost-y (K. Gogel), "Balet. (*Tshchetnaia predostorozhnost i Chopiniana*)," *Vechernie ogni*, 15 April 1918, no. 21, p. 4.

24 A. P. (Pleshcheyev), "O balete, ego demokratizatsii, fokinizatsii i pr.," *Vechernie ogni*, 29 March 1918, no. 8, p. 4.

25 A. Lunacharsky, *Sobranie sochinenii* (Moscow: Khudozhestvennaia literatura, 1967), vol. 7, p. 502.

26 GTsTM, f. 154, no. 168694/800.

27 TsGALI, f. 648, op. 2, ed. khr. 205, l. 105.

28 N. G. "Sudogovorenie posle prigovora. (O Bolshom teatre)," *Teatralnoe obozrenie*, 13–15 December 1921, no. 8, p. 10.

29 See V. I. Lenin, *Collected Works* (Moscow: Progress, 1976), vol. 45, pp. 428–429 and comments on pp. 706–707. Letter no. 579, dated 12 January 1922:

> Comrade Molotov:
> Having learned from Kamenev that the CPC has unanimously adopted Lunacharsky's absolutely improper proposal to preserve the Bolshoi Opera and Ballet, I suggest that the Politburo should resolve:
> 1. To instruct the Presidium of All-Russia CEC to rescind the CPC decision.
> 2. Of the opera and ballet company, to leave only a few dozen actors for Moscow and Petrograd so that their performances (both operatic and choreographic) should pay* by eliminating all large expenses on properties etc.
> 3. Of the thousands of millions saved in this way at least one-half to be allotted to winnowing out illiteracy and for reading rooms. . . .

> *For instance through participation by opera singers and ballet dancers in all kinds of concerts etc.

> See also *Literaturnoe nasledstvo*, vol. 80 (1971), "V. I. Lenin i A. V. Lunacharskii," pp. 312–313, and A. Lunacharsky, *Lenin i literaturovedenie* (Moscow: Sovetskaia literatura, 1934), p. 107.

30 Letters of A. Lunacharsky, letter no. 16, *Novyi mir*, 1965, no. 4, p. 253. In the commentaries to this letter, it is erroneously noted that apparently Lunacharsky calls manuscript material (which has not survived) a "book," and that in 1922 he reported "on the five-year-long work of the Petrograd State Theaters which was published in printed form." In fact, what is meant is doubtless this issue of the *Weekly* (*Ezhenedelnik*). Lunacharsky understood that the figures published there proclaimed the usefulness of the opera and ballet.

31 V. I. Lenin, *Collected Works*, vol. 45, pp. 706–707 (in a footnote to letter no. 579).

32 See *Literaturnoe nasledstvo*, vol. 80, "V. I. Lenin i A. V. Lunacharskii," p. 368.

33 See "Krizis akademicheskikh teatrov," *Izvestiia*, 21 November 1922, no. 263.

34 A. Potemkin, "Akademiia opery i baleta spasena," *Krasnaia gazeta*, evening edition, 25 November 1922, no. 51.

35 TsGALI, f. 648, op. 2, ed. khr. 271, l. 5.

36 "Likvidatsiia voprosa o zakrytii Bolshogo teatra," *Izvestiia*, 3 December 1922, no. 274.

37 A. Abramov, "Eshche ob odnom burzhuaznom nasledstve," *Vestnik teatra*, 5 April 1921, no. 87–88, pp. 3–4.

38 L. Sabaneyev, "Byt li Bolshomu teatru?," *Ekran*, 15–17 November 1921, no. 7, pp. 3–4.

39 V. Dalsky, "Nuzhen li Bolshoi teatre?," *Teatralnoe obozrenie*, 18–20 November 1921, no. 2, p. 9.

40 G. Kryzhitsky, "Vmesto nekrologa," *Muzyka i teatr*, 28 November 1922, no. 10, p. 3.

41 Silvio, "O balete (Otvet Iu. Brodersenu)," *Krasnaia gazeta*, evening edition, 1 November 1922, no. 32.

42 See *Ezhenedelnik petrogradskikh gosudarstvennykh akademicheskikh teatrov*, 3 December 1922, p. 37, no. 12.

43 GTsTM, f. 154, no. 168694/1037 b.

44 *Literaturnoe nasledstvo*, vol. 80, "V. I. Lenin i A. V. Lunacharskii," p. 369.

45 D. Leshkov, "Tribuna o balete," *Ezhenedelnik petrogradskikh gosudarstvennykh akademicheskikh teatrov*, 29 October 1922, no. 7, p. 30.

46 "Tseli i zadachi gosudarstvennogo akademicheskogo baleta," *Ezhenedelnik petrogradskikh gosudarstvennykh akademicheskikh teatrov*, 5 November 1922, no. 8, p. 61.

47 During the years 1917–22 dancers were accepted from the Petrograd school. The new additions accounted for 45% of the company's members in 1922.

48 Before the war, during the 1912–13 season, the Moscow company, numbering 159, gave 56 performances. During the 1919–20 season the same group, reduced to 138, gave 69 performances, and in 1924–25, when the group numbered only 125, there were 105 performances on two stages (the Bolshoi and the Experimental Theater). The same process of gradually reducing the company (from 166 in 1912 to 119 in 1922) and increasing the number of performances took place in Petrograd as well.

2 The First Years

1 *Biriuch petrogradskikh gosudarstvennykh teatrov*, 16–22 December 1918, no. 7, pp. 56–57.

2 See Y. Yuriev, *Zapiski* (Moscow-Leningrad: Iskusstvo, 1963), vol. 2, p. 310.

3 Homo Novus (A. Kugel), "Zametki," *Teatr i iskusstvo*, 15 September 1918, no. 28–31, p. 288.

4 Yuriev, *Zapiski*, vol. 2, p. 294.

5 M. Kuzmin, "Prival komediantov," *Zhizn iskusstva*, 18 December 1918, no. 40.

6 S., "Khoreograficheskii vecher E. A. Smirnovoi i B. G. Romanova," *Novaia petrogradskaia gazeta*, 29 May 1918, no. 107.

7 *Ibid.*

8 E. Gerken, "Kontsert Smirnovoi i Romanova," *Zhizn iskusstva*, 13 June 1919, no. 162.

9 L. Nikulin, "Petrogradtsy," *Teatralnaia gazeta*, 19 May 1918, no. 20.

10 N. Zb. (N. S. Zborovsky). "Gastroli petrogradskogo baleta," *Nashe vremia*, 14 May 1918, no. 93.

11 TsGALI, f. 794, op. 1, ed. khr. 177, l. 10.

12 *Ibid.*, l. 4 ob., 3 ob.

13 B. Romanov, "Zametki tantsovshchika. (Raboty M. I. Petipa vne repetitsionnogo zala)," *Biriuch petrogradskikh gosudarstvennykh teatrov*, 16–22 December 1918, no. 7, pp. 36–37.

14 TsGALI, f. 2658, op. 1, ed. khr. 692, l. 17, 18.

15 Ash (A. Shaikevich), "E. A. Smirnova," *Teatr* (Berlin) no. 15 (1922): 8.

16 D. Leshkov, *Balet (1917–1927)*, TsGALI, f. 794, op. 1, ed. khr. 52, l. 15.

17 Ash (A. Shaikevich), "Peterburgskie katakomby. Posviashchaetsia Borisu Romanovu," *Teatr* (Berlin), no. 14 (1922): 5.

18 A. Blok, "Bolshoi dramaticheskii teatr v budushchem sezone," *Zhizn iskusstva*, 7 May 1919, no. 130.

19 Romantik, "Russkii romanticheskii teatr," *Teatr* (Berlin), no. 15 (1922): 5.

20 "Russkii teatr za granitsei," *Teatr* (Berlin), no. 14 (1922): 13.

21 S. Grigoriev, *The Diaghilev Ballet 1909–1929* (Middlesex: Penguin Books, 1960), p. 203.

22 D-e. "Za rubezhom. Tanets Parizha," *Novyi zritel*, 5 August 1924, no. 30, p. 8.

23 P. Michaut, *Le Ballet contemporain* (Paris: Plon, 1950), p. 157.

24 Igor Glebov (B. Asafiev). "V balete," *Zhizn iskusstva*, 10–12 December 1920, no. 628–630.

25 A. Levinson, "Petrushka," *Zhizn iskusstva*, 26–28 November 1920, no. 616–618.

26 A. Volynsky, "Khoreograficheskie arabeski," *Zhizn iskusstva*, 17 April 1923, no. 15, p. 4.

27 D. P. (Dominic Platach) "Leonid Leontiev i ego iubilei," *Krasnaia gazeta*, evening edition, 16 April 1923, no. 83.

28 A. Volynsky, "Reforma Gosudarstvennogo baleta. Otkrytoe pismo narkomu prosvesh-cheniia A. V. Lunacharskomu," *Zhizn iskusstva*, 29–31 May 1920, no. 464–466. The same ideas are expressed in Volynsky's article "Proekt vozrozhdeniia baleta. (Zapros A. V. Lunacharskogo)," *Zhizn iskusstva*, 19 June 1923, no. 24, pp. 4–7.

29 F. Lopukhov, "Pismo v redaktsiiu," *Zhizn iskusstva*, 13 November 1923, no. 45, p. 27.

30 L. Leontiev, "V zashchitu padaiushchego Gosudarstvennogo baleta," *Zhizn iskusstva*, 26–27 June 1920, no. 488–489.

31 A. Volynsky, " 'Mokryi rafinad' Moi miniatiury," *Zhizn iskusstva*, 10 June 1920, no. 474.

32 Leontiev, "V zashchitu padaiushchego Gosudarstvennogo baleta."

33 Dominic Platach, "Poka ne pozdno," *Zhizn iskusstva*, 30 August 1921, no. 806.

34 D. Leshkov, "Obzor sezona 1918–1919," for *Ezhegodnik gosudarstvennykh petrograd-skikh teatrov*, TsGALI, f. 794, op. 1, ed. khr. 88, l. 10.

35 *Ibid.*

36 A. Volynsky, "Baletmeisterskie potugi," *Zhizn iskusstva*, 9 May 1922, no. 18.

37 N. Legat, "Baletnoe uchilishche pri Akademicheskom teatre," *Zhizn iskusstva*, 27 June 1922, no. 25.

38 *Materialy po istorii russkogo baleta* (LGKhU, 1939), vol. 2, pp. 207–208.

39 A. Volynsky, "Gde byt russkomu baletu?," *Zhizn iskusstva*, 11 December 1923, no. 49, p. 11.

40 See *Russkaia muzykalnaia gazeta*, 28 October 1907, no. 43, pp. 962–964.

41 TsGALI, f. 794, op. 1, ed. khr. 52, l. 20–21.

42 M. Fokine, *Protiv techeniia. Vospominaniia baletmeistera, stsenarii i zamysly baletov, stati, interviu i pisma* (Leningrad: Iskusstvo [Leningrad division], 1981), pp. 260–261.

43 *Sovetskii teatr. Dokumenty i materialy. Russkii teatr 1917–1921* (Moscow-Leningrad: Iskusstvo, 1968), p. 212.

44 N. Strelnikov, "'Mlada, vampuka akademicheskaia,' (Otkrytie byvshego Mariinskogo teatra)," *Zhizn iskusstva*, 9 October 1923, no. 40, p. 15.

45 Beka, "Vecher P. N. Petrova," *Vestnik teatra i iskusstva*, 3 May 1922, no. 25, p. 8.

46 "*Solveig*. (B. V. Asafiev o muzyke baleta)." *Zhizn iskusstva*, 26 September 1922, no. 38.

47 *Ibid.*

48 *Ibid.*

49 Sketch for the fairytale ballet *Solveig* in two acts and three scenes, the work of A. Shaikevich, P. Potemkin, and B. Romanov (GTsTM, f. 70, no. 116709/273). The manuscript is not dated; it can be dated approximately (from the list of proposed performers appended to it) to the second half of the 1920–21 season.

50 D. Leshkov, "Baletnye zametki," *Obozrenie teatrov i sporta*, 6 October 1922, no. 4, p. 6.

51 "*Solveig*. (B. V. Asafiev o muzyke baleta)."

52 B. Asafiev (Igor Glebov), *Russkaia zhivopis. Mysli i dumy.* (Leningrad-Moscow: Iskusstvo, 1966), pp. 100–101.

53 D. P. (Dominic Platach), "Solveig," *Krasnaia gazeta*, evening edition, 27 September 1922, no. 2.

54 A. Volynsky, "Solveig," *Zhizn iskusstva*, 3 October 1922, no. 39.

55 D. P., "Solveig."

56 D. Leshkov, *Balet (1917–1927)*, TsGALI, f. 794, op. 1, ed. khr. 52, I. 12.

57 From Y. Slonimsky's letter of November 1977.

58 E. Kuznetsov, "Anatomiia zritelnogo zala. (V kulisakh teatralnoi kassy)," *Krasnaia gazeta*, evening edition, 21 October 1922, no. 23.

59 O. Mungalova, "Vospominaniia," manuscript, VTO Archives, p. 3.

60 B. Taper, *Balanchine.* (New York: Macmillan, 1960), p. 58.

61 M. Mikhailov, *Zhizn v balete* (Leningrad-Moscow: Iskusstvo, 1966), p. 43.

62 From Y. Slonimsky's letter of November 1977.

63 Taper, p. 66.

64 Y. B. (Y. G. Brodersen), "Zaria baletnogo renessansa," *Zhizn iskusstva*, 26 June 1923, no. 25, p. 13.

65 A. Kankarovich, "Molodoi balet," *Petrogradskaia pravda*, 21 July 1923, no. 162.

66 A. Gvozdev, "Molodoi balet," *Zhizn iskusstva*, 27 May 1924, no. 22, p. 4.

67 *Ibid.*

68 *Ibid.*

69 Mikhailov, *Zhizn v balete*, p. 45.

70 Li (A. A. Tcherepnin), "Gliadia, kak tantsuiut. Leningradskaia akmolodezh," *Zrelishcha*, 1924, no. 73, p. 10.

71 *Zhizn iskusstva*, 12 February 1924, no. 7, p. 30.

72 "Balet," *Teatr*, 18 December 1923, no. 2, p. 15.

73 A. Twysden, *Alexandra Danilova* (London: C. W. Beaumont, 1945), p. 47.

74 N. Strelnikov, "Zolotoi petushok ili Siniaia ptitsa?," *Zhizn iskusstva*, 2 October 1923, no. 39, p. 17.

75 Igor Glebov (B. Asafiev), "Zolotoi petushok," *Teatr*, 29 September 1923, no. 1, p. 16.

76 I. Rabinovich, *"Eugen Neschastnyi* Tollera. Na stsene byvshego Mikhailovskogo teatra," *Zhizn iskusstva,* 25 December 1923, no. 51, p. 9.

77 A separate chapter is devoted to the work of Goleizovsky.

78 A. Deich, "Ovechii istochnik," in *Spektakli i gody* (Moscow: Iskusstvo, 1969), pp. 32–33.

79 S. Lavrov, "Pervyi vecher M. M. Mordkina," *Zrelishcha,* 3–14 January 1923, no. 19, p. 22.

80 *Ibid.*

81 N. Zb. (N. Zborovsky), "Otkrytie baleta v 'Akvariume,'" *Nashe vremia,* 29 May 1918, no. 106.

82 N. Shilling, "Balet," *Teatralnaia gazeta,* 16 June 1918, no. 24.

83 G. Rimsky-Korsakov, "E. M. Adamovich," manuscript, TsNB VTO Archive.

84 A. P. (A. Pleshcheyev), "Balet," *Vremia,* 7 July 1917, no. 984.

85 "Baletnye novosti," *Teatr,* 16–17 January 1919, no. 2145.

86 GTsTM, f. 154, no. 168694/458.

87 "Bolshoi teatr," *Kultura teatra,* 1 February 1921, no. 1, p. 53.

88 TsGALI, f. 648, op. 2, ed. khr. 187, l. 34 ob.

89 From a conversation with Margarita Kandaurova on November 28, 1967.

90 "Bolshoi teatr," *Kultura teatra.*

91 Vik. (V. Iving), "Karnaval," *Izvestiia,* 11 May 1924, no. 106.

3 Alexander Alexeyevich Gorsky

1 "Teatralnye itogi. Nashi besedy. A. A. Gorskii," *Rannee utro,* 21 March 1918, no. 43.

2 TsGALI, f. 2729, op. 1, ed. khr. 43, l. 2.

3 Quoted according to TsGALI, f. 2729, op. 1, ed. khr. 43, l. 1–2, since the text in the newspaper *Rannee utro* has corrections that obscure the meaning.

4 *Ibid.*

5 *Ibid.,* l. 2.

6 E. Geltser, "Iskusstvo pravdy i krasoty," *Sovetskoe iskusstvo,* 11 July 1937, no. 32.

7 TsGALI, f. 1933, op. 1, ed. khr. 21, l. 112 ob.

8 GTsTM, f. 154, no. 168694/335.

9 TsGALI, f. 648, op. 2, ed. khr. 6, l. 6–7.

10 GTsTM, f. 77, ed. khr. 57, no. k.p. 123938/56.

11 TsGALI, f. 794, op. 1, ed. khr. 177, l. 10 ob.

12 GTsTM, f. 77, ed. khr. 53, no. k.p. 123938/69.

13 N. Kolosov (N. Markvardt), "Balet v 'Akvariume,'" *Rampa i zhizn,* 2 June 1918, no. 22, p. 8.

14 N. Zb (N. Zborovsky), "Balet v 'Akvariume,'" *Nashe vremia,* 25 June 1918, no. 122.

15 N. Shilling, "Balet," *Teatralnaia gazeta,* 16 June 1918, no. 24.

16 *Ibid.*

17 "Novyi letnii teatr (sad 'Akvarium')," *Novosti dnia,* 29 May 1918, no. 51.

18 Shilling, "Balet."

19 B. Asafiev, "Teatr russkoi Ispanii," *Teatr,* 9 October 1923, no. 2.

20 V. B. (V. Belsky), "Balet v 'Akvariume,'" *Zhizn,* 3 July 1918, no. 56.

21 N. Z. (N. Zborovsky), "Balet v 'Akvariume'," *Nashe vremia,* 30 June 1918, no. 127.

22 S. Sol., "Letnii balet," *Chetvertyi chas,* 1 July 1918, no. 27.

23 N. Markvardt, "Balet v 'Akvariume'," *Rampa i zhizn*, 10 June 1918, no. 25, p. 3.

24 *Ibid.*

25 GTsTM, f. 77, ed. khr. 49, no. k.p. 123938/57.

26 This production will be discussed in the section devoted to various versions of the ballet *Giselle*.

27 G. Ianov (G. I. Geronsky), "Balet v 'Akvariume,'" *Novaia zhizn*, 12 June 1918, no. 10.

28 From a letter (addressee unknown—E. K. Malinovskaya?) in the spring of 1919, GTsTM, f. 77, ed. khr. 26, no. k.p. 123938/25.

29 *Rampa i zhizn*, 10 October 1918, no. 37–40, p. 12.

30 TsGALI, f. 1933, op. 1, ed. khr. 12, l. 60.

31 Quoted in *Ocherki istorii russkoi sovetskoi dramaturgii* (Moscow-Leningrad: Iskusstvo, 1954), vol. 1, p. 34.

32 "Prazdnik velikogo obnovleniia," *Pravda*, 9 November 1918, no. 242.

33 TsGALI, f. 648, op. 2, ed. khr. 40, l. 77.

34 Y. Slonimsky, "V chest' revoliutsii," *Neva*, 1965, no. 11, pp. 206–208.

35 A. (V. Ashmarin?), "Bolshoi teatr," *Izvestiia*, 12 November 1918, no. 246.

36 Quoted in V. Beliayev, *Aleksandr Konstantinovich Glazunov. Materialy k ego biografii* (Petersburg: Gosudarstvennaia filarmoniia, 1922), vol. 1: *Zhizn*, part 1, pp. 93–94.

37 V. Kerzhentsev, "Posle prazdnika," *Iskusstvo*, November 1918, no. 6(10), p. 3.

38 A. (V. Ashmarin?), "Bolshoi teatr."

39 *Ibid.*

40 See A. Kleiman, "Moskovskie pis'ma; 2. Baletnye paralleli," *Vestnik teatra i iskusstva*, 21 March 1922, no. 20, pp. 4–5.

41 P. Markov, "Pervye gody; iz vospominanii," *Teatr*, 1957, no. 11, p. 67.

42 TsGALI, f. 659, op. 1, ed. khr. 653, l. 5, 22, 6.

43 A. Pleshcheyev, "O balete (Iz razgovora s Gorskim)," *Vremia*, 19 May 1917, no. 944.

44 TsGALI, f. 1933, op. 1, ed. khr. 12, l. 105.

45 TsGALI, f. 1933, op. 1, ed. khr. 24, l. 2.

46 Y. Slonimsky, *P. I. Chaikovskii i baletnyi teatr ego vremeni* (Moscow: Muzgiz, 1956), p. 327.

47 Y. Bakhrushin, *A. A. Gorskii* (Moscow-Leningrad: Iskusstvo, 1946), p. 40.

48 Y. Bakhrushin, "Balety Chaikovskogo i ikh stsenicheskaia istoriia," in *Chaikovskii i teatr; Stat'i materialy* (Moscow-Leningrad: Iskusstvo, 1940), pp. 126–127.

49 Bakhrushin, *A. A. Gorskii*, p. 41.

50 Pleshcheyev, "O balete."

51 El., "Shchelkunshchik," *Izvestiia*, 18 September 1919, no. 207.

52 Geronsky, "Ekskursii gos. baleta. *Shchelkunshchik* v Novom teatre," *Ekran*, 14–20 March 1922, no. 24–25, p. 9.

53 From a conversation with Vera Svetinskaya, 9 May 1966.

54 *Ibid.*

55 Geronsky, "Ekskursii."

56 Muzei MKhAT, Nemirovich-Danchenko archive, no. 2530. Quoted in L. Freidkina, *Dni i gody Vl. I. Nemirovicha-Danchenko* (Moscow: VTO, 1962), p. 346.

57 A. Levinson, "O moskovskom balete," *Apollon, Russkaia khudozhestvennaia letopis*, May 1911, no. 10, p. 161.

58 "V khudozhestvennom teatre," *Vestnik teatra*, 8–9 February 1919, no. 3, p. 4.

59 Notes and comments by V. Nemirovich-Danchenko on rehearsals of the ballet *Swan*

Lake, GTsTM, f. 1, op. 2, ed. khr. 250, no. k.p. 2975732/251 and ed. khr. 251, no. k.p. 295732/252.

60 Bakhrushin, *Balety Chaikovskogo i ikh stsenicheskaia istoriia*, p. 128.

61 Kv.-D., "Letter to the Editor," *Vestnik teatra*, 22 October 1920, no. 71, p. 18.

62 K. Waltz, *Shestdesiat piat let v teatre* (Leningrad: Academia, 1928), p. 108.

63 TsGALI, f. 1933, op. 1, ed. khr. 25, l. 19.

64 *Ibid.*, ed. khr. 21, l. 18.

65 GTsTM, f. 154, no. 168694/692.

66 "V Vysshem khoreograficheskom sovete pri TsK Vserabisa," *Vestnik teatra*, 28 October–2 November 1919, no. 39, p. 11.

67 I. Schneider, *Zapiski starogo moskvicha* (Moscow: Sovetskaia Rossiia, 1970), p. 195.

68 See M. Dyskovsky, "O khudozhestvennom kontrole," *Vestnik teatra*, 28 October–2 November 1919, no. 39, p. 5.

69 TsGALI, f. 1933, op. 1, ed. khr. 21, l. 194.

70 TsGALI, f. 648, op. 2, ed. khr. 97, l. 15–15 ob.

71 P. Lepeshinsky, *Na povorote* (Moscow: Staryi bolshevik, 1935), p. 114.

72 TsGALI, f. 1933, op. 1, ed. khr. 25, l. 28.

73 *Ibid.*, l. 4.

74 TsGALI, f. 1933, op. 1, ed. khr. 30, l. 4.

75 GTsTM, f. 154, no. 168694/644.

76 *Ibid.*

77 TsGALI, f. 1933, op. 1, ed. khr. 25, l. 32.

78 From a conversation with Anastasia Abramova, 15 October 1967.

79 *Sovetskii teatr, Dokumenty i materialy. Russkii sovetskii teatr 1917–1921.* (Moscow-Leningrad: Iskusstvo, 1968), p. 94.

80 From an unpublished review by Yuri Bakhrushin in the author's possession.

81 Bakhrushin, *Balety Chaikovskogo i ikh stsenicheskaia istoriia*, p. 128.

82 GTsTM, f. 77, ed. khr. 49, no. k.p. 123938/57.

83 Bakhrushin, *Balety Chaikovskogo i ikh stsenicheskaia istoriia*, p. 128.

84 Muzei MKhAT, Luzhsky archive. Quoted in L. Freidkina, *Dni i gody Vl. I. Nemirovicha-Danchenko*, p. 349.

85 GTsTM, f. 154, no. 168694/727.

86 GTsTM, f. 154, no. 168694/691.

87 A. Lunacharsky, "Parizhskie pisma," *Teatr i iskusstvo*, 18 May 1914, no. 20, p. 447.

88 G. Rimsky-Korsakov, *E. M. Adamovich*, manuscript, TsNB VTO archive, p. 11.

89 In the personal archive of Elena Adamovich there is a score of the ballet with Glière's signature.

90 TsGALI, f. 2085, op. 1, ed. khr. 1259, l. 4.

91 Rimsky-Korsakov, *E. M. Adamovich*, p. 13.

92 See Domitsy, "Nash balet," *Zritel*, 6 March 1923, no. 1, p. 5.

93 The ballet was performed until October 1909 and was restaged two years later (23 October 1911) without major changes.

94 A. Tcherepnin, "Giselle," *Teatralnaia gazeta*, 6 December 1915, no. 49, p. 8.

95 N. Churikov, "Moskovskii balet. Postanovki 1906 goda," *Vesy*, August 1907, no. 8, p. 102.

96 M. L-o. (M. Likiardopulo), "Moskovskii balet. *Giselle.*" *Studiia*, 29 October 1911, no. 5, p. 17.

97   Evgeny K., "Mysli o balete. *Giselle*," *Rampa i zhizn*, 9 December 1912, no. 50, p. 9.

98   N. N. (N. N. Vashkevich), "Balet," *Rampa*, 1908, no. 7, p. 111.

99   A. Levinson, "Balet. *Giselle*," *Rech*, 4 November 1914, no. 298, p. 5.

100 S. Grigorov. *Baletnoe iskusstvo i S. V. Fedorova 2-ia. Opyt.* (Moscow: 1914), p. 64.

101 S. Mamontov, "V balete," *Russkoe slovo*, 30 April 1913, no. 99.

102 P. Ivanov (Viach. I. Ivanov), "Zametki o balete," *Teatralnyi kurier*, 30 October 1918, no. 38, p. 3.

103 S. Grigorov, *Baletnoe iskusstvo*, p. 65.

104 GTsTM, f. 77, ed. khr. 54, no. k.p. 123938/70.

105 N. Zb. (N. S. Zborovsky), "Balet v 'Akvariume,'" *Nashe vremia*, 25 June 1918, no. 122, p. 4.

106 N. A. M. (Markvardt), "Balet," *Teatralnaia gazeta*, 21 July 1918, no. 26–29.

107 N. Markvardt, "Balet," *Rampa i zhizn*, 29 October 1918, no. 41–42, p. 9.

108 From a letter by Viacheslav Ivanov to Maria Reisen, personal archive of Maria Reisen.

109 P. Ivanov (Viach. I. Ivanov), "Zametki o balete," *Teatralnyi kurier*, 30 October 1918, no. 38, p. 3.

110 N. A. M. (Markvardt), "Balet," *Teatralnaia gazeta*, 21 July 1918, no. 26–29, p. 6.

111 TsGALI, f. 794, op. 1, ed. khr. 177, l. 5.

112 *Ibid.*, l. 7.

113 From a statement by the artist F. Fedorovsky, GTsTM, f. 154, no. 168694/1059.

114 Domitsy, "Nash balet."

115 Archive of Margarita Kandaurova.

116 Domitsky, "Nash balet."

117 N. Arsky (N. Kovarsky). "*Novyi teatr. Giselle*—debiut V. Kudriavtsevoi," *Zrelishcha*, 20–26 February 1923, no. 25, p. 16.

118 V. Iving, "*Giselle i Chopiniana*," *Izvestiia*, 28 March 1934, no. 74.

119 A. Lunacharsky, *Sobranie sochinenii v 8-mi tomakh* (Moscow: Goslitizdat, 1964), vol. 3, p. 249.

120 Muzei GABT, Gorsky archive, otd. II, ed. khr. 9.

121 N. Petrov, "Teatr v Oktiabrskie torzhestva. Bolshoi teatr," *Teatralnyi kurier*, 12–14 November 1918, no. 45, p. 2.

122 GTsTM, f. 77, ed. khr. 197, no. k.p. 168144 and ed. khr. 198, no. k.p. 168146.

123 The text of the play is in TsGALI, f. 1933, op. 1, ed. khr. 42, l. 2–7 ob.

124 *Ibid.*, l. 3.

125 TsGALI, 1933, op. 1, ed. khr. 42, l. 5 ob.

126 TsGALI, 1933, op. 1, ed. khr. 42, l. 6 ob.

127 Director's production plan, Muzei GABT, f. A. A. Gorskogo.

128 S. Kholfina, "Vospominaniia," personal archive of the author.

129 Nik. "Novyi teatr. Zhivye tsvety," *Zrelishcha*, 14–19 November 1922, no. 12, p. 20.

130 "Detskii prazdnik v Novom teatre," *Izvestiia*, 21 November 1922, no. 263.

131 B. "Vechno zhivye tsvety v Novom teatre," *Pravda*, 24 November 1922, no. 266.

132 *Literaturnoe nasledstvo*, vol. 80, "V. I. Lenin i A. V. Lunacharskii," p. 369.

133 GTsTM, f. 77, ed. khr. 54, no. k.p. 123938/70.

134 GTsTM, f. 77, ed. khr. 49, no. k.p. 123938/57.

135 V. Iving, "Bolshoi teatr," *Teatr i muzyku*, 22 May 1923, no. 11(24), p. 822.

Chapter 4 Kasian Yaroslavich Goleizovsky

1 "Intimnyi teatr," *Teatr*, 10–11 July 1916, no. 1874.

2 *Rampa i zhizn*, 19 February 1918, no. 6–7, p. 9.

3 A. P. (Pleshcheyev), "V studii Gosudarstvennogo teatralnogo uchilishcha," *Nashe vremia*, 17 June 1918, no. 116.

4 From a conversation with Liubov Bank on 23 November 1967.

5 "Studiia baleta pri Teatralnom uchilishche," *Velikaia Rossiia*, 18 June 1918, no. 12.

6 S. Bezsonov, "Balet," *Velikaia Rossiia*, 4 July 1918, no. 26.

7 S. Sol., "Molodezh," *Chetvertyi chas*, 5 June 1918, no. 14.

8 V. Belsky, "V studii Teatralnogo uchilishcha," *Zhizn*, 20 June 1918, no. 46.

9 A. V. Lunacharsky, "Taneev i Scriabin," in *V mire muzyki*, Moscow, Sovietskii kompozitor, 1958, p. 142.

10 N. Satz, *Deti prikhodiat v teatr. Stranitsy vospominanii* (Moscow: Iskusstvo, 1961), p. 57.

11 *Ibid.*, pp. 57–58.

12 *Ibid.*, p. 103.

13 *Ibid.*, p. 97.

14 See *Vestnik teatra*, 9–14 December 1918, no. 45, p. 11.

15 N. Satz, *Deti prikhodiat v teatr*, pp. 97, 107.

16 S. Valerin, "Shaluny," *Pravda*, 26 January 1928, no. 22.

17 *Ibid.*

18 A letter from Natalia Satz of 27 June 1919. The personal archive of Kasian Goleizovsky.

19 Goleizovsky's studio changed names several times. After opening in 1917, it was renamed the First Model Studio of the TEO *Narkompros* in May 1919; for some time (1921) it was called The Quest Studio; finally in August 1922 it received the name The Moscow Chamber Ballet.

20 M. Dvinsky, "N. N. Cherepnin o svoem novom balete *Krasnye maski*," *Birzhevye vedomosti*, 6 October 1912, no. 13181, p. 7.

21 A list of numbers and scenes from the ballet *The Masque of the Red Death*, Goleizovsky's archive.

22 GTsTM, f. 77, ed. khr. 26, no. k.p. 123938/25.

23 Muzei MKhAT, Nemirovich-Danchenko archive, no. 971. Quoted from Freidkina, *Dni i gody Vl. I. Nemirovicha-Danchenko*, p. 345.

24 GTsTM, f. 154, no. 168694/463.

25 *Ibid.*, no. 168694/462.

26 Letter to V. E. Meyerhold. Goleizovsky's personal archive.

27 TsGALI, f. 794, op. 1, ed. khr. 177, l. 19 ob.–18 ob.

28 Truvit (A. I. Abramov), "Vpechatleniia," *Zrelishcha*, 13–19 March 1923, no. 28, p. 11.

29 Truvit (A. I. Abramov), "O produktsiiakh Goleizovskogo," *Zrelishcha*, 8 August 1923, no. 48, p. 5.

30 V. I. (V. Iving), "Novye postanovki Goleizovskogo," *Izvestiia*, 3 August 1923, no. 173.

31 Y. Sobolev, "Bessmertie," *Rampa i zhizn*, 23 March 1918, no. 11–12, pp. 7–8.

32 G. Rimsky-Korsakov, *E. M. Adamovich*, manuscript TsNB VTO Archive, p. 14.

33 Stainitsky, "Moskovskii Kamernyi balet," *Krasnaia gazeta*, evening edition, 4 October 1922, no. 8.

34 L. Entelis, "Stavit Goleizovskii," *Sovietskaia muzyka*, 1965, no. 7, p. 78.

35 M. Gorshkova, "Vospominaniia," manuscript, TsNB VTO, p. 189.

36 Goleizovsky wrote verses for this ballet, which we are quoting here.

37 L. Sabaneyev, "Vecher obnazhennogo tela," *Pravda*, 5 September 1922, no. 198.

38 D. Leshkov, "Baletnye zametki," *Obozrenie teatrov i sporta*, 15 October 1922, no. 12, p. 3.

39 V. Iving, "Balet. Vecher Goleizovskogo," *Rampa*, 19–24 February 1924, no. 7 (20), pp. 5–6.

40 Li (A. A. Tcherepnin), "Gliadia, kak tantsuiut . . . Itogi i vidy," *Zrelishcha*, June 1924, no. 89, p. 10.

41 Li (A. A. Tcherepnin), "Gliadia, kak tantsuiut . . . Ekstrennyi vecher Goleizovskogo," *Zrelishcha*, February 1924, no. 74, p. 6.

42 K. Goleizovsky, "Staroe i novoe. Pisma o balete. 2.," *Ekran*, 15–23 May 1922, no. 32, p. 3.

43 K. Goleizovsky, "O groteske, chistom tantse i balete. 2.," *Zrelishcha*, 20–26 February 1923, no. 25, p. 8.

44 K. Goleizovsky, "Nekotorye razmyshleniia," *Zrelishcha*, 27 June–2 July 1923, no. 42, p. 8.

45 The archives of Kasian Goleizovsky.

46 "Beseda c rukovoditelem Kamernogo baleta K. Ia. Goleizovskim," *Antrakt*, 18–25 March 1923, no. 4–5, p. 11.

47 K. Goleizovsky, "O groteske, chistom tantse i balete, 2.," p. 8.

48 M. Schick, "Vecher Goleizovskogo," *Teatralnoe obozrenie*, 27 December 1921, no. 10, p. 8.

49 S. Lavrov, "Klassika Kasiana Goleizovskogo," *Ermitazh*, 22–28 August 1922, no. 15, p. 5.

50 D. P. (Dominic Platach), "Goleizovskii. (V diskussionnom poriadke)," *Krasnaia gazeta*, evening edition, 11 October 1922, no. 14.

51 N. Lvov, "Goleizovskii i Lukin," *Ermitazh*, 23–31 July 1922, no. 11, p. 6.

52 Quoted from F. Lopukhov, *Shestdesiat let v balete* (Moscow: Iskusstvo, 1966), p. 40.

53 K. Goleizovsky, "Staroe i novoe. Pisma o balete. 2."

54 *Ibid.*, p. 4.

55 K. Ia. Goleizovsky, "Razmyshleniia o sudbakh klassicheskoi khoreografii posle l mezhdunarodnogo konkursa artistov baleta v Moskve," 1969, p. 1, The archives of Kasian Goleizovsky.

56 K. Goleizovsky, "Obnazhennoe telo na stsene," *Teatr i studiia*, 1–15 July 1922, no. 1–2, pp. 36–38.

57 A. Lunacharsky, "Borba za nagotu," *Kievskaia mysl*, 23 June 1913, no. 171.

58 P. Markov, "B. Erdman," manuscript, TsNB VTO Archive.

59 A. Sidorov, "Boris Erdman–khudozhnik kostiuma," *Zrelishcha*, 3–8 July 1923, no. 43, p. 5.

60 Stainitsky, "Moskovskii Kamernyi balet," *Krasnaia gazeta*, evening edition, 4 October 1922, no. 8.

61 K. Goleizovsky, "Staroe i novoe. Pisma o balete. 1.," *Ekran*, 4 May 1922, no. 31, p. 3.

62 "*Smerch* v Bolshom teatre. Beseda s Goleizovskim," *Novyi zritel*, 4 October 1927, no. 40, p. 15.

63 TsGALI, f. 648, op. 1, ed. khr. 696, l. 11.

64 M. Yusim, "K. Ia. Goleizovskii," manuscript, p. 50.

65 See A. Messerer, *Tanets. Mysl. Vremia* (Moscow: Iskusstvo, 1979), p. 65.

66 A. Sidorov, "Goleizovskii na akademicheskoi stsene," *Iskusstvo trudiashchimsia*, 17–22 March 1925, no. 16, p. 6.
67 Bir, "Tsennyi opyt v Eksperimentalnom. *Teolinda i Iosif Prekrasnyi*," *Novyi zritel*, 24 March 1925, no. 12, p. 12.
68 Sidorov, "Goleizovskii na akademicheskoi stsene," p. 5.
69 V. Iving, "Teolinda i Prekrasnyi Iosif," *Zhizn iskusstva*, 17 March 1925, no. 11, p. 5.
70 From a conversation with Sergei Chudinov on January 25, 1968.
71 TsGALI, f. 648, op. 1, ed. khr. 696, l. 10.
72 TsGALI, f. 648, op. 1, ed. khr. 696, l. 11.
73 *Ibid.*
74 *Novyi zritel*, 24 March 1925, no. 12, p. 22.
75 V. Iving, "*Teolinda* v Eksperimentalnom," *Programmy gosudarstvennykh akademicheskikh teatrov*, 17–22 November 1925, no. 10, p. 7.
76 A. Messerer, *Tanets. Mysl. Vremia*, p. 63.
77 A. Sidorov, "Goleizovskii na akademicheskoi stsene."
78 A. Lunacharsky, "Printsipy khudozhestvennoi politiki v Rossii," *Novyi mir*, 1966, no. 9, p. 244.
79 TsGALI, f. 648, op. 2, ed. khr. 90, l. 174 ob.
80 *Ibid.*, l. 180.
81 *Sovetskii teatr. Dokumenty i materialy. Russkii sovetskii teatr. 1921–1926* (Leningrad: Iskusstvo, 1975), p. 111.
82 TsGALI, f. 648, op. 2, ed. khr. 90, l. 174.
83 *Ibid.*
84 *Ibid.*, l. 174–174 ob.
85 TsGALI, f. 648, op. 2. ed. khr. 279, l. 136 and 136 ob.
86 TsGALI, f. 648, op. 2, ed. khr. 90, l. 150 ob.
87 V. Blum, "Dvizhenie 'u vody,'" *Novyi zritel*, 8 June 1925, no. 23.
88 K. Goleizovsky, "Po povody 'dvizheniia u vody,'" *Novyi zritel*, 1 September 1925, no. 35, pp. 5–6.
89 TsGALI, f. 648, op. 1, ed. khr. 696, l. 86.
90 A. Lunacharsky, "Novinki Diagilevskogo sezona. Pismo piatoe," *Vechernaia Moskva*, 28 June 1927, no. 143.
91 TsGALI, f. 649, op. 1, ed. khr. 696, l. 10.
92 TsGALI, f. 648, op. 1, ed. khr. 696, l. 34.
93 From a conversation with Liubov Bank on 23 November 1967.
94 This refers to a ballet Goleizovsky planned, *An Unknown Episode from the Life of Don Quixote of La Mancha*, in 2 acts, 8 episodes, to the music of B. Beer.
95 A. Lunacharsky, "K predstoiashchemu sezonu," *Izvestiia*, 8 September 1925, no. 204.
96 K. Goleizovsky, "Smerch," *Sovremennyi teatr*, 18 October 1927, no. 7, p. 106.
97 TsGALI, f. 648, op. 2, ed. khr. 545, l. 32.
98 *Ibid.*
99 M. Dvinsky, "N. N. Cherepnin o svoem novom balete *Krasnye maski*."
100 Lunacharsky, "Novinki Diagilevskogo sezona. Pismo piatoe."
101 "Oformlenie baleta *Smerch*. Beseda s khudozhnikom N. A. Musatovym," *Sovremennyi teatr*, 18 October 1927, no. 7, p. 107.
102 "*Smerch* v Bolshom teatre. Beseda s K. Goleizovskim," *Novyi Zritel*, 4 October 1927, no. 40, p. 15.

103 From this point on Goleizovsky's article in *Sovremennyi teatr*, along with sketches and archive materials, 18 October 1927, no. 7, pp. 106–107 is used in the description of the ballet.

104 TsGALI, f. 648, op. 2, ed. khr. 541, l. 16.

105 From a letter to the author of this book dated 15 May 1967.

106 From the archives of Kasian Goleizovsky.

107 TsGALI, f. 648, op. 2, ed. khr. 541, l. 25.

108 A. Gidoni, "Balet na izlome (K postanovke baleta *Smerch*)," *Sovremennyi teatr*, 27 December 1927, no. 17, p. 265.

109 In the GABT Museum there is a second sketch of the Ruler's costume, in which he is portrayed as a European monarch with a ribbon over his shoulder and a scepter and an orb in his hands. But the authors of the ballet kept the first variant of the sketch. Iving wrote in *Pravda* that the Ruler is presented as a sort of "Oriental despot."

110 "*Smerch* v Bolshom teatre. Beseda s K. Goleizovskim."

111 Kasian Goleizovsky, "*Smerch*," p. 106.

112 Sergei Bugoslavsky, "Akopera v dni X Oktiabria," *Izvestiia*, 11 November 1927, no. 258.

113 Vik (V. Iving), "*Smerch*," *Pravda*, 25 December 1927, no. 296.

5 In the Bolshoi Theater

1 TsGALI, f. 648, op. 2, ed. khr. 271, l. 61.

2 "K postanovke *Ispanskogo kaprichchio* v Bolshom teatre." *Programmy moskovskikh gosudarstvennykh i akademicheskikh teatrov i zrelishchnykh predpriiatii*, 2nd number, 22–28 May 1923, p. 5.

3 V. Iving, "Balet," *Rampa*, December 11–17, 1923, no. 11, p. 13.

4 "*Shekherazada*. (Iz besedy s L. A. Zhukovym. K blizhaishei postanovke v Bolshom teatre)," *Izvestiia*, 20 November 1923, no. 265.

5 A. Sidorov, "O postanovke *Shekherazady* v Ak. Bolshom," *Zrelishcha*, 28 December 1923–7 January 1924, no. 68, p. 8.

6 *Ibid*.

7 Y. Sakhnovsky, "Dve premiery," *Rampa*, 26 December 1923–2 January 1924, no. 13, p. 6.

8 A. Sidorov, "O postanovke *Shekherazady*."

9 A. Tairov, *Zapiski rezhissera* (Moscow: The Kamerny Theater, 1912), pp. 138–139. It is not impossible that the actual idea of creating a constructivist staging of *Schéhérazade* initially belonged to Tairov.

10 A. Gvozdev, "O novom teatre. Vpechatleniia leningradskogo teoretika," *Zrelishcha*, 5–10 February 1924, no. 72, p. 2.

11 Vik (V. Iving), "Silfida," *Izvestiia*, 10 February 1925, no. 33.

12 *Ibid*.

13 E. Braudo, "V. Muzyka v Moskve. Pervoe stoletie Bolshogo teatra," *Pechat i revoliutsiia*, book 3, May 1925, p. 159.

14 In Vasily Tikhomirov's archives are lists of the performers of the dances, enumerations of the costumes and props, and other materials for the production of 1890. TsGALI, f. 2729, op. 1, ed. khr. 132 and ed. khr. 16, l. 12–14.

15 TsGALI, f. 1933, op. 1, ed. khr. 31, l. 42.

16 Y. Faier, "O sebe, o muzyke, o balete" (variant of the manuscript), the personal archives of Yuri Faier.

17 Igor Glebov (B. Asafiev), "Bolshoi Teatr," *Krasnaia gazeta*, evening edition, 23 January 1926, no. 21.

18 R. Glière, "Muzyka *Esmeraldy*," *Programmy gosudarstvennykh akademicheskikh teatrov*, February 2–8, 1926, no. 20, p. 9.

19 N. Kovarsky, "*Esmeralda*," *Programmy gosudarstvennykh akademicheskikh teatrov*, February 2–8 1926, no. 20, p. 8.

20 B. V., "Teatr i muzyka. Novaia *Esmeralda*," *Moskovskie vedomosti*, 25 November 1902, no. 325.

21 Kovarsky, "*Esmeralda*."

22 V. Iving, *Esmeralda* (Moscow: Teakinopechat, 1929), p. 38.

23 TsGALI, f. 2729, op. 1, ed. khr. 16, l. 25.

24 *Ibid.*, l. 28.

25 Iving, *Esmeralda*, p. 29.

26 *Ibid.*, p. 38.

27 Sergei Gorodetsky, "Ak. Bolshoi. *Esmeralda*," *Iskusstvo trudiashchimsia*, 23 February 1926, no. 8, p. 8.

28 N. Kovarsky, "*Esmeralda*," *Novyi zritel*, 23 February 1926, no. 8, p. 10.

29 A. Volynsky, "Vremia Gorskogo i Geltser. Publikatsiia N. Iu. Chernovoi," *Teatr*, 1976, no. 3, p. 50.

30 *Ibid.*, p. 49.

31 A. Tcherepnin, "*Esmeralda* v balete," *Programmy gosudarstvennykh akademicheskikh teatrov*, 16–22 November 1926, no. 60, p. 6.

32 Sadko (V. I. Blum), "Teatralnye zametki. Na *Esmeralda*," *Zhizn iskusstva*, 16 February 1926, no. 7, p. 12.

33 Igor Glebov (B. V. Asafiev), "Bolshoi teatr," *Krasnaia gazeta*, evening edition, 23 January 1926, no. 21.

34 Y. Faier, *O sebe, o muzyke, o balete*, (Moscow: Sovet kompozitor, 1970), pp. 192–193.

35 GTsTM, f. 154, no. 168694/1167.

36 "Issledovatelskaia teatralnaia masterskaia. Zritel moskovskikh teatrov. Anketnyi odnodnevnik po moskovskim teatram," *Zhizn iskusstva*, 13 July 1926, no. 28, p. 13.

37 TsGALI, f. 648, op. 2, ed. khr. 411, l. 39.

38 "Akademicheskie teatry v predstoiashchem sezone," *Novyi zritel*, 22 September 1925, no. 38, p. 15.

39 TsGALI, f. 648, op. 2, ed. khr. 321, l. 1.

40 "Balet *Krasnyi mak* v Bolshom teatre," *Programmy gosudarstvennykh akademicheskikh teatrov*, 2–8 March 1926, no. 24, p. 12.

41 See M. Kurilko, "Kak sozdavalsia balet," *Sovetskii artist*, 11 June 1952, no. 23, p. 2.

42 TsGALI, f. 2085, op. 1, ed. khr. 368, l. 181.

43 TsGALI, f. 648, op. 2, ed. khr. 470, l. 26–33.

44 TsGALI, f. 648, op. 2, ed. khr. 470, l. 27.

45 TsGALI, f. 648, op. 2, ed. khr. 388, l. 22.

46 TsGALI, f. 2085, op. 1, ed. khr. 368, l. 176 ob.

47 M. Kurilko, "Rozhdenie baleta" in *Reingold Moritsovich Glière. Stati, vospominaniia, materialy* (Moscow-Leningrad: Muzyka, 1965), vol. 1, p. 107.

48 Faier, *O sebe, o muzyke, o balete*, p. 196.

49 TsGALI, f. 2085, op. 1, ed. khr. 68, l. 2.

50 TsGALI, f. 2376, op. 1, ed. khr. 210, l. 3,4.

51 TsGALI, f. 2085, op. 1, ed. khr. 368, l. 180 ob.

52 M. Gorshkova, "Vospominaniia," manuscript, TsNB VTO, p. 321.

53 "Rasskazyvaiut mastera (A. Messerer)," *Sovetskaia muzyka*, 1967, no. 10, p. 94.

54 "Khronika. Moskva. Bolshoi teatr," *Zhizn iskusstva*, 14 June 1927, no. 24, p. 22.

55 TsGALI, f. 2729, op. 1, ed. khr. 18.

56 TsGALI, f. 2729, op. 1, ed. khr. 116, l. 1.

57 *Sovetskii artist*, 11 June 1952, no. 23, pp. 2–3.

58 TsGALI, f. 648, op. 2, ed. khr. 339, l. 29, 30.

59 TsGALI, f. 2085, op. 1, ed. khr. 55, l. 7.

60 "Rasskazyvaiut mastera (A. Messerer)."

61 A. Tcherepnin, "Dialektika baleta," *Zhizn iskusstva*, 23 August 1927, no. 34, p. 7.

62 "Disput o *Krasnom make* u rabkorov," *Programmy gosudarstvennykh akademicheskikh teatrov*, 28 June–4 July 1927, no. 26, p. 11.

63 S. Gorodetsky, "Pobeda klassiki," *Programmy gosudarstvennykh akademicheskikh teatrov*, 21–27 June 1927, no. 25, p. 5.

64 "Oformlenie *Krasnogo maka*," *Programmy gosudarstvennykh akademicheskikh teatrov*, 2–8 November 1926, no. 58, p. 8.

65 "*Krasnyi mak* v postanovke Bolshogo teatra," *Programmy gosudarstvennykh akademicheskikh teatrov*, 31 May–6 June 1927, no. 22, p. 8.

66 V. Inber, "*Rychi, Kitai!*," *Novyi zritel*, 9 February 1926, no. 6, p. 4.

67 "*Krasnyi mak*. K postanovke v Bolshom teatre. Beseda s V. D. Tikhomirovym," *Programmy gosudarstvennykh akademicheskikh teatrov*, 31 May–6 June 1927, no. 22, p. 8.

68 "*Krasnyi mak*. K postanovke v Bolshom teatre. Beseda s E. V. Geltser." *Programmy gosudarstvennykh akademicheskikh teatrov*, 7–13 June 1927, no. 23, p. 8.

69 TsGALI, f. 2085, op. 1, ed. khr. 68, l. 42 ob.

70 "Narodnaia artistka E. V. Geltser rasskazyvaet," Muzei GABT (stenogr. 21 December 1961), p. 29.

71 "*Krasnyi mak*. K postanovke v Bolshom teatre. Beseda c E. V. Geltser," p. 9.

72 E. Geltser, "Pervyi balet," *Sovetskaia muzyka*, November 1962, no. 11, p. 151.

73 R. Glière, "*Krasnyi mak* v. Ak. balete. Pered premeroi," *Rabochii i teatr*, 13 January 1929, no. 3, p. 6.

74 V. Iving, "*Krasnyi mak*. K pervomu vystupleniiu V. Kriger," *Sovremenny teatr*, 3 January 1928, no. 1, p. 8.

75 V. Iving, "V balete. K vystupleniiu A. I. Abramovoi v *Krasnom make*," *Sovremenny teatr*, 20 March 1928, no. 12, p. 248.

76 "*Krasnyi mak*. K postanovke v Bolshom teatre. Beseda s L. A. Lashchilinym," *Programmy gosudarstvennykh akademicheskikh teatrov*, 7–13 June 1927, no. 23, p. 9.

77 *Ibid.*

78 *Ibid.*

79 V. Iving, "*Krasnyi mak* v novoi redaktsii," *Izvestiia*, 6 September 1927, no. 203.

80 TsGALI, f. 2085, op. 1, ed. khr. 68, l. 35–35 ob.

81 A. Gvozdev, "Postanovka *D. E.* v Teatre im. Meierholda," *Zhizn iskusstva*, 24 June 1924, no. 26, p. 6.

82 Sadko (V.I. Blum), "*Krasnyi mak* v Bolshom teatre," *Zhizn iskusstva*, 28 June 1927, no. 26, p. 4.

83 "Kollektivnoe mnenie o *Krasnom make* 50 rabochikh," *Programmy gosudarstvennykh akademicheskikh teatrov*, 28 June–4 July 1927, no. 26, p. 3.
84 V. Mayakovsky, *Polnoe Sobranie Sochinenii* (Moscow: Goslitizdat, 1958), vol. 2, p. 310.
85 Nik. Aseyev, "Shto my tam vidim?" *Novyi zritel*, 4 January 1927, no. 1, p. 5.
86 V. Vishnevsky, *Poslednii reshitelnyi* (GlKhL, 1931), p. 3.
87 *Ibid.*, p. 10.
88 *Ibid.*, p. 11.
89 *Ibid.*, pp. 14–15.
90 A. Lunacharsky, "Novinki Diagilevskogo sezona. Pismo piatoe."
91 M. Kalinin, *Izbrannye proizvedeniia*, (Moscow: Goslitizdat, 1960), vol. 2, pp. 235–236.
92 S. Gorodetsky, "Pobeda klassiki."
93 "Novyi balet," *Komy kuda*, 14–20 May 1928, no. 20, p. 15.

6 Fedor Vasilievich Lopukhov

1 Lopukhov's biographer, Galina Dobrovolskaya, dates them 1918.
2 F. Lopukhov, *Shestdesiat let v balete* (Moscow: Iskusstvo, 1966), p. 213.
3 "Petrogradskie teatry v sezon 1922/23 goda," *Ezhenedelnik petrogradskikh gosudarstvennykh akademicheskikh teatrov*, 1 October 1922, no. 3, p. 56.
4 A. Volynsky, "Kareta skoroi pomoshchi," *Zhizn iskusstva*, 26 September 1922, no. 38, p. 3.
5 A. Benois, "Pietet ili koshchunstvo," *Ezhenedelnik petrogradskikh gosudarstvennykh akademicheskikh teatrov*, 26 November 1922, no. 11, p. 31.
6 *Ibid.*
7 *Ibid.*, p. 33.
8 Igor Glebov (B. Asafiev), "Pisma o russkoi opere i balete (3-e), *Spiashchaia krasavitsa*," *Ezhenedelnik petrogradskikh gosudarstvennykh akademicheskikh teatrov*, 15 October 1922, no. 5, p. 35.
9 Benois, "Pietet ili koshchunstvo," pp. 34–35.
10 F. Lopukhov, *Puti baletmeistera* (Berlin: Petropolis, 1925), p. 17.
11 *Ibid.*, p. 32.
12 A. Volynsky, "Maliar negodnyi," *Zhizn iskusstva*, 20 February 1923, no. 7, p. 4.
13 *Sovetskii teatr. Dokumenty i materialy. Russkii sovetskii teatr, 1921–1926*, pp. 295–296.
14 See "Khronika. Ak.-teatry," *Zhizn iskusstva*, 30 March–1 April 1921, no. 706–708.
15 Lopukhov, *Shestdesiat let v balete*, pp. 239, 238.
16 D. Leshkov, "*Zhar-Ptitsa*," *Zhizn iskusstva*, 18 October 1921, no. 813.
17 Mungalova, "Vospominaniia," p. 8.
18 *Ibid.*, p. 9.
19 *Ibid.*
20 *Ibid.*, p. 10.
21 A. Volynsky, "Balety Stravinskogo," *Zhizn iskusstva*, 26 December 1922, no. 51, p. 2.
22 Mungalova, "Vospominaniia," p. 10.
23 Lopukhov, *Shestdesiat let v balete*, pp. 239–240.
24 I. Sollertinsky, "Fedor Lopukhov. Teatralnye portrety," *Zhizn iskusstva*, 28 February 1928, no. 9, p. 4.
25 "Petrogradskie vesti," *Ekran*, 5–6 November 1921, no. 4, p. 4.

26 A. Gvozdev, "Impressionism i balet," *Zhizn iskusstva*, 25 March 1924, no. 13, p. 7.

27 Lopukhov, *Puti baletmeistera*, pp. 50–51.

28 See G. Dobrovolskaya, *Fedor Lopukhov* (Moscow-Leningrad: Iskusstvo, 1976), pp. 103–104.

29 Lopukhov, *Puti baletmeistera*, p. 50.

30 See Twysden, *Alexandra Danilova*, p. 45.

31 N. Soliannikov, "Vospominaniia," p. 309.

32 Copy of the minutes of the meeting. Archives of Yuri Slonimsky, GTsTB.

33 A. Volynsky, "Tantssimfoniia," *Zhizn iskusstva*, 13 March 1923, no. 10, p. 3.

34 *Velichie mirozdaniia, tantssimfoniia Fedora Lopukhova, muz. L. Betkhovena (4-ia simfoniia) s avtosiluetom Pavla Goncharova* (Petersburg: G. P. Lubarsky, 1922), p. 4.

35 See A. Piotrovsky, "My eto peresmotrim," *Zhizn iskusstva*, 29 September 1929, no. 39, p. 4.

36 F. Lopukhov, "Moi otvet," *Zhizn iskusstva*, 21 February 1922, no. 8, p. 3.

37 Lopukhov, *Puti baletmeistera*, pp. 93, 97, 99, 100.

38 See Lopukhov, *Shestdesiat let v balete*, p. 245.

39 A. Gvozdev, "Nakanune novogo baleta," *Krasnaia gazeta*, evening edition, 30 September 1924, no. 222.

40 N. N. (Nasilov), "Revoliutsionnyi balet," *Zhizn iskusstva*, 26 August 1924, no. 35, p. 18.

41 See "Shcheloch ili kislota?" *Ezhenedelnik akademicheskikh teatrov v Leningrade*, 13 May 1924, no. 13, p. 8.

42 "Programma baleta *Krasnyi vikhr*," *Rabochii i teatr*, 3 November 1924, no. 7, p. 22.

43 Y. Brodersen, "Obnovlenie li?" *Rabochii i teatr*, 10 November 1924, no. 8, p. 8.

44 B. Andreyev, (B. Bashinsky), "Ak.-instsenirovka," *Rabochii i teatr*, 10 November 1924, no. 8, p. 7.

45 L. Lavrovsky, "O putiakh razvitiia sovetskogo baleta," in *Muzykalnyi teatr i sovremennost* (Moscow: VTO, 1962), p. 10.

46 Lopukhov, *Shestdesiat let v balete*, p. 255.

47 A. Gvozdev, "Probuzhdenie *Spiashchei krasavitsy*," *Zhizn iskusstva*, 11 March 1924, no. 11, p. 7.

48 "Khronika. Ak.-teatry," *Rabochii i teatr*, 24 November 1924, no. 10, p. 17.

49 "Pervomaiskie zrelishcha," *Zhizn iskusstva*, 4 May 1920, no. 442.

50 "Peterburgskii balet v Moskve," *Zhizn iskusstva*, 9 September 1920, no. 552.

51 F. Lopukhov, "Staro-russkii glum. K postanovke *Baiki* v Ak.-balete," *Rabochii i teatr*, 7 December 1926, no. 49, p. 11.

52 Igor Glebov (B. Asafiev), "*Snegurochka*. (Akademicheskii teatr opery i baleta)," *Zhizn iskusstva*, 12–13 February 1921, no. 675–676.

53 "Khronika. Balet i opera," *Zhizn iskusstva*, 18 October 1921, no. 813.

54 Lopukhov, *Shestdesiat let v balete*, p. 247.

55 A. Gvozdev, "Dve novye postanovki," *Zhizn iskusstva*, 15 April 1924, no. 16, p. 10.

56 Soliannikov, N., "Vospominaniia," p. 311.

57 Stravinsky, Igor, *Khronika moei zhizni* (Leningrad: Muzgiz, 1963), p. 159.

58 Igor Glebov (B. Asafiev), *Kniga o Stravinskom* (Leningrad: Triton, 1929), p. 155.

59 A. Gvozdev, "*Baika* Stravinskogo," *Zhizn iskusstva*, 11 January 1927, no. 2, p. 12.

60 Glebov (Asafiev), *Kniga o Stravinskom*, p. 155.

61 Soliannikov, "Vospominaniia," p. 322.

62 A. Gvozdev, "Nerazberikha pro lisu, petukha i prochuiu tvar," *Krasnaia gazeta*, evening edition, 4 January 1927, no. 3.
63 A. Rimsky-Korsakov, "Nerazberikha pro lisu, petukha i prochuiu tvar," *Krasnaia gazeta*, evening edition, 4 January 1927, no. 3.
64 Evstafy Petushkov, "Svistuny na *Baike*," *Zhizn iskusstva*, 25 January 1927, no. 4, p. 20.
65 Glebov (Asafiev), *Kniga o Stravinskom*, p. 151.
66 Gvozdev, "*Baika* Stravinskogo," p. 13.
67 *Sovetskii teatr. Dokumenty i materialy 1917–1921*, p. 256.
68 From a letter from Fedor Lopukhov to the author, 3 October 1970.
69 F. Lopukhov, "V glub khoreografii," manuscript, personal archive of Lopukhov.
70 Alexandre Benois, *Reminiscences of the Russian Ballet* (London: Putnam, 1947), p. 379.
71 F. Lopukhov, "*Pulcinella*. (K postanovke v teatre opery i baleta)," *Rabochii i teatr*, 11 May 1926, no. 19, p. 9.
72 Lopukhov, *Shestdesiat let v balete*, p. 247.
73 Lopukhov, "*Pulcinella*. (K postanovke v teatre opery i baleta)."
74 Soliannikov, "Vospominaniia," p. 317.
75 A. Gvozdev, "O novom balete," *Zhizn iskusstva*, 9 October 1926, no. 42, p. 7.
76 Lopukhov, "*Pulcinella*. (K postanovke v teatre opery i baleta)."
77 *Ibid.*
78 Lunacharsky, *Sobranie sochinenii v 8-mi tomakh*, vol. 3, p. 78.
79 A. Lunacharsky, "Moe mnenie," *Rabochii i teatr*, 23 November 1926, no. 47, p. 11.
80 Mungalova, "Vospominaniia," pp. 11–12.
81 Lopukhov, *Shestdesiat let v balete*, p. 250.
82 Mungalova, "Vospominaniia," p. 15.
83 A. Lopukhov, "Dvadtsat let kharakternogo tantsovshchika," manuscript, VTO Archives, p. 22.
84 Mungalova, "Vospominaniia," p. 15.
85 Y. Brodersen, "*Ledianaia deva* v Ak.-balete," *Rabochii i teatr*, 1 May 1927, no. 18, p. 9.
86 "*Ledianaia deva. Solveig*." *Rabochii i teatr*, 19 April 1927, no. 16, p. 12.
87 I. Sollertinsky, "*Ledianaia deva*. (Iubileinyi spektakl baletmeistera F. Lopukhova)," *Leningradskaia pravda*, 29 April 1927, no. 96.
88 A. Gvozdev, "O reforme baleta," *Zhizn iskusstva*, 3 January 1928, no. 1, p. 5.
89 A. Gvozdev, "Reforma baleta. Klassicheskii tanets," *Zhizn iskusstva*, 10 January 1928, no. 2, p. 4.

Conclusion

1 Lopukhov, *Shestdesiat let v balete*, pp. 257, 258.
2 Lunacharsky, *Sobranie sochinenii v 8-mi tomakh*, vol. 3, p. 188.
3 Gvozdev, "O reforme baleta."
4 A. Gvozdev, "Reforma baleta. Klassicheskii tanets."
5 I. Sollertinsky, "Za novyi khoreograficheskii teatr," *Zhizn iskusstva*, 17 June 1928, no. 25, p. 4.
6 A. Gvozdev, "O reforme baleta," p. 6.
7 *Ibid.*
8 Sollertinsky, "Za novyi khoreograficheskii teatr."

About the Author

Elizabeth Souritz, a dance historian who lives in Moscow, studied at the Lunacharsky State Institute of Theater Art, has worked at the A. A. Bakhrushin Museum and the Moscow Theater Library, and is presently the head of the Dance Section of the Moscow Institute of the History of the Arts. Among her publications are *All About Ballet* (1966) and "The Beginning of the Path" in *Soviet Ballet Theater* (1976), and, in English, "Soviet Ballet of the 1920s and the Influence of Constructivism," *Soviet Union / Union Soviétique* 7 (1980): 112–37. *Soviet Choreographers in the 1920s* is a translation of her *Khoreograficheskoe iskusstvo dvadtsatykh godov* (Moscow: Iskusstvo, 1979).

Library of Congress Cataloging-in-Publication Data
Surits, E. IA.
[Khoreograficheskoe iskusstvo dvadtsatykh godov. English]
Soviet choreographers in the 1920s / Elizabeth Souritz ; translated from the Russian by Lynn Visson; edited, with additional translation, by Sally Banes.
Translation of: Khoreograficheskoe iskusstvo dvadtsatykh godov.
ISBN 0-8223-0952-1
1. Choreographers—Russian S.F.S.R.—Biography.
2. Ballet—Russian S.F.S.R.—History—20th century.
I. Banes, Sally.   II. Title.   III. Title: Soviet choreographers in the nineteen twenties.
GV1785.A1S7813   1989
792.8'2'0922—dc20
[B]   89-16877 CIP

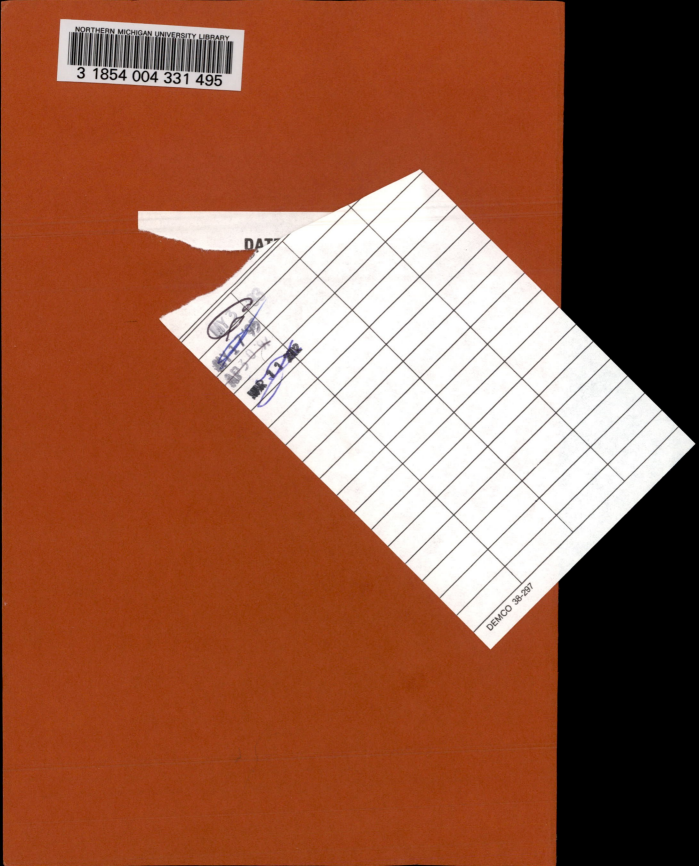

DEMCO 38-297